# ANTISLAVERY
# RECONSIDERED

# ANTISLAVERY
# RECONSIDERED
# New Perspectives
# on the Abolitionists

*Edited by*
LEWIS PERRY
*and*
MICHAEL FELLMAN

LOUISIANA STATE
UNIVERSITY PRESS
*Baton Rouge and London*

Design: Dwight Agner
Typeface: VIP Trump Mediaeval
Composition: Graphic Composition, Inc.
Printing: Thomson-Shore, Inc.
Binding: John H. Dekker & Sons, Inc.

"Am I Not a Woman and a Sister?" by
Blanche Glassman Hersh is adapted from
Chapter 1 of *The Slavery of Sex: Feminist
Abolitionists in Nineteenth-Century America*
(© 1978 by the Board of Trustees of
the University of Illinois), used by permission
of the University of Illinois Press.

LIBRARY OF CONGRESS CATALOGING IN PUBLICATION DATA

Main entry under title:

Antislavery reconsidered.

Includes index.
1. Slavery in the United States—Anti-slavery movements—Addresses, essays, lectures. · 2. Slavery in Great
Britain—Anti-slavery movements—Addresses, essays, lectures. I. Perry, Lewis. II. Fellman, Michael.
E449.A6237      322.4'4'0973      78–10177
ISBN 0–8071–0479–5

# CONTENTS

# INTRODUCTION
## History and the Abolitionists

WHAT IS the place of abolitionism in American history? There are signs that historians in the 1970s are working out new answers to this perennial question. In fact, it is possible that historians' attitudes toward abolitionism, after veering from contempt to celebration in previous decades, may once again be changing direction. The essays in this collection give evidence of a reevaluation—though certainly not of a return to contempt.

A brief sketch of the changing historical reputation of abolitionism may be appropriate at the onset. One point must be stressed: new essays on antislavery movements are ventures into territory that has inspired previous historians to important, often passionate work. The explanation for the changing reputation of abolitionists is not that the facts about them have been greatly disputed; nor is it merely the case that scholars have allowed their judgments to waver in the light of changing public moods. The most important explanation is that interpreting abolitionism inevitably raises questions that go to the heart of what we value in American society and takes us into areas where the beliefs of scholars and general public cannot be held in separation. Linked to racial oppression, sectional conflict, and other subjects central to the historical consciousness of Americans, abolitionism has long captured the interests of a general reading public. As an issue fraught with public implications, abolitionism disturbs the tidy balances professional historians prefer to strike between narrative and analysis, between moral judgment and dispassionate research. Antislavery scholarship instructs us on the experience of some Americans a century ago; it betokens periodic changes in the modern community of professional historians; and it provides signals of the moral ties between that profession and the community as a whole.

The essays in this book respond most directly to the many-sided reassessment of abolitionism that historians carried out in the 1960s. The essays respond as well to negative evaluations from the preceding forty years that scholars in the 1960s sought to overturn. All these waves of revision, moreover, derived basic terms and inquiries from public attitudes toward abolitionism; they usually took it for granted that the movement exercised great influence in its own time. They also joined in according great significance to the inner history of abolitionism—the disputes over matters large and small that fill so many of the records antislavery men and women left behind.

The abolitionists themselves confronted the problem of their place in history. As disruptive interlopers in social and political life, abolitionists were nearly compelled to justify themselves in relation to history. Some turn-of-the-century abolitionists offered the same defense as those accused of religious heresy—God was casting "further light" over the earth and launching a time of innovation. Others pointed back to heroic precedents in the Reformation and the Glorious Revolution. The belief that God was on their side and that his will was made manifest progressively in struggles for religious and political liberty sanctioned their new departure.[1] Similarly, in the 1830s, when abolitionism gained a reputation for uncompromising militance, its champions enlisted the Reformation and the American Revolution to justify the vehemence with which they raised the standard of truth against the obsolete and tyrannical

---

1 See David Brion Davis, *The Problem of Slavery in the Age of Revolution, 1770–1823* (Ithaca: Cornell University Press, 1975), especially the quotation from Benjamin Rush on page 283.

system of bondage. Once again, the moment had arrived when God favored his subjects who cried out for change. In a republic, born of revolution, there was a special place for a disruptive novelty that sought to end the incongruous persistence of slavery.

But this confident rendition of history could not entirely hide an undertow of doubt. Even if God, or a revolutionary heritage, justified a new departure, could it be argued that slavery had, at one time, been consistent with God's plan and earlier states of civilization? Was abolitionism thus based on timeless verities or merely on some current phase of evolution which might prove evanescent? The abolitionist William Goodell, though a believer in Christian missions to the heathen, indignantly denied that the principles supporting antislavery reform related only to modern history. Too many abolitionists, he felt, were attracted to a "lenient" view of history that regarded slavery as having formerly been useful and defensible. He bitterly criticized liberal comrades like Theodore Parker for any ambiguity regarding the morally transient and expedient in past human experience.[2] Behind this theological controversy lurked ancient problems of authority and political presumption—what gave man the right to tamper with the existing disposition of power in society? In worrying over the links between past and future, between the permanent and the transient, abolitionists brushed against crucial questions concerning their own and the nation's social responsibilities. Which of their actions would connote assertions of ageless truths; which would be false presumptions? As for goals, what was owed an enslaved race for its contribution to the development of America? Was antislavery a step in introducing the African into the mainstream of modern American society, or was its message simply one of laissez-faire, let the Negro alone? Before the Civil War abolitionists failed to clarify these implications of their understandings of history, but Reconstruction put them to the test.

Still another historical problem—the significance of conflicts and disagreements among northern reformers—originated in the abolitionists' writings. The most important historical work by an American abolitionist, Goodell's *Slavery and Anti-Slavery* (1855),

2 New York *Principia*, December 3, 1859, p. 1, July 1, 1860, pp. 260–61.

was as heavily concerned with this issue as with African and trans-atlantic history;[3] and newspaper articles and letters by other abolitionists convey the same impression of the abolitionists' almost morbid absorption in their own internal history. Though sometimes tedious to the modern reader, reliving internal history served to heighten solidarity and create a social and historical identity.[4] In addition, it provided a way of evaluating tactics that might broaden the influence of the antislavery minority. With great intensity and a surprising degree of articulateness these reformers anticipated many of the controversies that later would divide left-wing movements in Europe: should they strive for a broad base of support or retain the purity of a vanguard? could reform be enacted via the ballot? were churches antithetical to the ideal society of the future? was pacifism a form of accommodation to the oppressors or an effective means of overcoming them? could reforms be accomplished piecemeal or only through a total overhaul of society? The acuteness with which abolitionists dramatized these questions, in American terms, may have contributed to their appeal to scholars of the 1960s. But the attention they lavished on division in their ranks has not always benefited their historical reputations: sometimes it has been adduced as evidence of the shallowness of their commitment to the needs of black people, South or North. Because of their lavishly recorded inner history, it has always been easy either to dismiss the abolitionists as ranting blunderers or to exaggerate their role as incendiaries.

It is clear, furthermore, that southern reactions gave abolitionists part of their place in history. Powerful men in the South feared the abolitionists' influence on white politicians and—worse, still—black slaves. The continuation of slavery depended on its status as an unquestioned fact of society, so much so that even the stirring up of controversy by a handful of agitators conveyed a kind of horror. Such considerations of their internal security led southerners to call attention to obscure abolitionists in the 1830s, to exaggerate north-

3 William Goodell, *Slavery and Anti-Slavery; A History of the Great Struggle in Both Hemispheres; With a View of the Slavery Question in the United States* (New York: William Goodell, 1855).

4 James B. Stewart, "Garrison Again, and Again, and Again, and Again. . . .," *Reviews in American History*, IV (1976), 539–45.

ern approval of them, and to call for secession thirty years later.[5] After the war, Republican orators in the North depicted abolitionists as exemplars of triumphant northern conscience. Once-despised agitators like William Lloyd Garrison were venerated, and the historical leadership that southern firebrands had once attributed to them was now certified in postbellum northern opinion.

The shakiness of that certification became apparent, however, in the 1880s when Garrison's sons, who were indeed men of influence in their society, assembled a massive biography of their venerable father. These four volumes dredged up the internal history that in the old days consumed so much of the abolitionists' energy. As a result, some northern readers were astonished to learn that antislavery had been faction-ridden and that good old Garrison had been called arrogant, abusive, and heretical. One of Garrison's most earnest critics, the antislavery poet John Greenleaf Whittier, wished that this corner of the past had remained buried. The internal history of the movement had become disturbingly irrelevant to the old heroes' ceremonial importance in post-Reconstruction America.[6]

As it receded in time, abolitionism served more and more as an ideological testing ground for thinking about how individuals could effect change in the American political system. To some, the old abolitionists were emblematic of the disinterestedness of good citizens and thus stood in contrast to labor unions and other clamorous groups who were out for themselves. Causes ranging from civil service reform to the NAACP identified themselves as successors to abolitionism, much in the same way as eighteenth-century men affiliated their antislavery views with sacred legacies from the Old World.[7] To others, abolitionism tested harsher historical realities. Writing three years after the Haymarket riots, James Schouler called Garrison "a bomb-thrower,"[8] an extravagant image to be sure, but

5 See the persuasive analysis of southern responses to antislavery agitation throughout David Potter's *The Impending Crisis, 1848–1861* (New York: Harper & Row, 1976).

6 *Atlantic*, LVII (January, 1886), 120–28; John B. Pickard (ed.), *The Letters of John Greenleaf Whittier* (3 vols., Cambridge: Harvard University Press, 1975), III, 518–19.

7 James M. McPherson, *The Abolitionist Legacy: From Reconstruction to the NAACP* (Princeton: Princeton University Press, 1975), traces these and other post-Reconstruction meanings of abolitionism.

8 Quoted in George Fredrickson (ed.), *William Lloyd Garrison* (Englewood Cliffs, N.J.: Prentice-Hall, 1968), 126. This volume is one of the best surveys of the changing reputation of abolitionism.

one that illustrates the convenience with which abolitionism could be used in wildly divergent ways whenever the limits of agitation emerged as a troublesome issue in American society.

Throughout the first half of this century, historians generally conflated the story of abolitionism with the life of Garrison—and viewed both unfavorably. To historians who regretted the "tragedy" of the Civil War and deplored the "excesses" of Reconstruction, Garrison-style agitation figured as a key instance of an erratic, venomous spirit that led the nation astray. There were exceptions. When Gilbert Hobbs Barnes and Dwight Lowell Dumond assumed the revisionist task of praising the goals and methods of abolitionism, they strove to dissociate the movement from guilt-by-association with Garrison. To him they attributed egotistical bad judgment verging on insanity. But in the churches, in the Midwest, and especially in the inspiring life of Theodore Dwight Weld, they discovered a nobler strand of abolitionism, one whose political effectiveness they saw as incomparably superior. Barnes and Dumond unearthed the past that Whittier wished to leave buried, and restored the focus of antislavery history where Goodell had placed it—on the internal history of abolitionist disagreements. There was some irony in this restoration. Their scholarly purposes were grand: Barnes wished to honor religion as a force in history, and Dumond to accord the Negro a central place in American historical writing. And yet as a result of their work studies of abolitionism concentrated less on these grand themes than on the disputes and personalities of a few reformers, preeminently Weld and Garrison. There is no doubt, however, that the modern era of thorough research on antislavery began with their work.[9]

In the 1960s professional champions rose up to defend Garrison against criticisms leveled by Barnes and Dumond and to absolve the abolitionists as a group of the charges of tactical folly, immoderation, insanity, heresy, and even anarchism that had accumulated

9 Gilbert Hobbs Barnes, The Anti-Slavery Impulse, 1830–1844 (New York: Harcourt, Brace, and World, 1964), reprinted from the 1933 edition with a valuable introduction by William G. McLoughlin; Gilbert Hobbs Barnes and Dwight L. Dumond (eds.), Letters of Theodore Dwight Weld, Angelina Grimké Weld, and Sarah Grimké, 1822–1844 (Gloucester, Mass.: Peter Smith, 1965; 1st pub. 1934); Dwight L. Dumond, Antislavery: The Crusade for Freedom in America (Ann Arbor: University of Michigan Press, 1961).

from the past. Frequently they compared abolitionism with the civil rights movement and with other radical ventures of the 1960s. Scholars wrote about "the new abolitionism" or "the second reconstruction"; and activists of the new era were invited to regard abolitionism much as reformers of the 1830s had treated the Reformation. (Only the maverick social critic Paul Goodman skipped the intermediaries and glimpsed in the student protests of the 1960s a "New Reformation."[10] ) Defenses of the abolitionists varied profoundly: some denied they were immoderate, while others insisted that great evils require immoderation. Some simply denied abolitionists were insane, while others asserted they were unusually happy. In the give-and-take a great deal of original research was accomplished. Some books looked beyond Weld and Garrison and garnered information concerning previously neglected figures; others turned to periods and episodes that had never before been properly investigated.[11] If ever a decade and an historical subject were meant for each other, they were the 1960s and abolitionism.

Some things had not changed. Abolitionists continued, for the most part, to be used as a test case of the limits and possibilities of radicalism in America; and the tactical disputes within abolitionism might still be dragged up or down by fluctuations in contemporary feelings regarding radicals and the political process. In the late 1960s a growing amount of attention was paid to the "racism" of white reformers. As stories about civil rights heroism gave way to tales of name-calling, rock-throwing, and (once again) bomb-planting on campuses, there were some indications that the glorious reappraisal of abolitionism was on the wane.

It was unlikely, however, that antislavery studies could repair to the *status quo ante bellum*. Too much had been learned, too many solid studies had been undertaken—not only about abolitionism but also about slavery and the history of blacks—for there to be any return to a version of history colored by regret over the Civil War.

10 Paul Goodman, *New Reformation: Notes of a Neolithic Conservative* (New York: Random House, 1970).

11 An excellent and highly influential sampler of this work is Martin Duberman (ed.), *The Antislavery Vanguard: New Essays on the Abolitionists* (Princeton: Princeton University Press, 1965). See also Merton L. Dillon, "The Abolitionists: A Decade of Historiography, 1959–1969," *Journal of Southern History*, XXXV (1969), 500–22.

While the evangelical ring of the "new abolitionism" subsided and some of its partisans moved on to new concerns, too many scholars were investigating abolitionism for the subject to drop back to the disreputable state it formerly held in texts and classrooms. By the mid-1970s, in short, not the importance, but the place and reputation of abolitionists in American history was uncertain. They were unlikely either to be attacked as symptoms of a blundering generation or to be hailed as sources of moral inspiration. But they retained their capacity to touch off feelings about contemporary politics, and some of the issues in the American past with which their names were linked had become of livelier concern than ever. Certainly this was true of their links to feminism, and as a new president from Georgia announced the end of a century of sectional conflict, it might hold true of their vision of the South. Antislavery studies were poised at a turning point. Although many scholars were working in the field, perhaps more than ever before, it was difficult to describe a contemporary historical consensus or to predict the direction of future studies.

These considerations were in our minds when we undertook the extensive canvass of working scholars that led to this collection. All the authors are presently engaged in research on abolitionism or related topics. Although no effort was made to secure agreement on any aspect of abolitionism, we hope that by surveying various scholarly approaches the collection may clarify where antislavery studies now stand and in what direction they are, or ought to be, heading.

From reviewing the essays we have received, we conclude that the role assigned to abolitionism in American history is being fundamentally altered. This conclusion can only be a tentative one, for antislavery studies are at a turning point, but there are fewer references to contemporary politics in these pages than would have been true of a similar enterprise in any previous decade. There is a new tendency in antislavery studies to turn to the abolitionists as a means of widening our understanding of the society in which *they* lived.[12]

12 Two thoughtful indicators of the direction of current work are Aileen S. Kraditor, "American Radical Historians on Their Heritage," *Past and Present*, LVI (1972), 136–53, and

We may be observing an adjustment in the public significance of abolitionism that diminishes its utility for measuring the limits and possibilities of radicalism in America. The small-scale conflicts within abolitionism appear to have declined in interest, and there is even less interest in assigning blame for a large-scale war. As these minor and major themes subside, there is a sense in which "abolitionism" may be vanishing from the scholarship of the 1970s: that is, it no longer appears as a discrete entity to be praised or attacked or as a subject in which there is much advantage in specializing to the exclusion of wider social contexts. Abolitionism may have become, for the first time, an *historical* subject, a movement whose appeal derives not from its resemblance (or what in the 1960s was called "relevance") to modern movements, but from what it indicates about fundamental social conflict in a different historical era. As the essays in this volume indicate, today's scholars are likely to look at abolitionists in conjunction with such other segments of their society and culture as the law, the ministry, or ideologies covering economic and political power. They are likely to examine abolitionists in international terms or in relation to comparable movements in the South. Present studies tend to be more precisely defined than those that were typical of other decades, but they are less likely to dwell on the internal history of abolitionism.

What makes abolitionism so interesting in historical studies even after the ringing moral and political echoes of earlier days have died down? It seems clear to us that the lives of abolitionists intersect most of the critical changes from the provincial world of the eighteenth century to the modern era. The abolitionists played a crucial part in defining the responsibilities of citizens in an era when American politics was transformed and given much of its modern, party-oriented character. Similarly, they labored outside denominational circles to redefine the influence of religion on society, and they conducted intense debate over the recast meanings of class, race, and gender in the transformed American system. In addi-

---

Ronald G. Walters, *The Antislavery Appeal: American Abolitionism after 1830* (Baltimore: Johns Hopkins University Press, 1976). The latter work appeared just as this anthology was being sent to press—one more sign that the fascination of abolitionism to historians continues unabated.

tion, the abolitionists tried to reconcile their sense of a special destiny for America with their excitement at participating in transoceanic alliances of conscience. In a period of vast changes in American culture and society, they worked to articulate new and worthy goals. In their personal lives they experienced frequently exciting moments of sharply changing motives. None of these considerations makes them heroes or villains, wise or unwise, but they do illuminate the centrality of the questions antislavery movements raise for historians seeking to comprehend a particularly important era of the American past. It seems likely that forthcoming antislavery scholarship will reach toward the core of fascinating changes in nineteenth-century American life.

# Approaches

# THE BOUNDARIES
# OF ABOLITIONISM

*Ronald G. Walters*

THE MORE that is written about antislavery the more trouble we have finding its boundaries. Thanks to recent scholarship we now can take our choice of viewing abolitionists either as archetypical radicals and reformers or as bearers of the evangelical Protestant tradition; as racial egalitarians or as racists; as sexual egalitarians or as sexists; as members of an international movement, as American idealists, as participants in youthful rebellion, as well-adjusted individuals, and as representatives of social groups caught in major historical processes. Sometimes truth is indeed plural and each of these judgments may well have a measure of validity to it. My discontent is not so much with what historians have done to the abolitionists as with what they have left undone. Despite notable exceptions, they have been more successful at isolating aspects of antislavery than at demonstrating where abolitionism itself belongs in the greater scheme of American politics, society, and culture. By the diversity of their approaches, recent scholars have complicated the tasks of locating the abolitionists in time, in relation to each other, and in relation to nonabolitionists. In order to put the abolitionists back into American history we have to look carefully at some of the boundaries historians have drawn, some they should draw, and some they should not.[1]

It appears easiest to place abolitionism in time. William Lloyd Garrison provided a wonderfully symbolic opening date by beginning publication of the *Liberator* on New Year's Day, 1831. The newness of post-1830 antislavery lay in the insistence of abolitionists like Garrison upon immediate emancipation and in their vision of a biracial America in which blacks would have at least civil equality with whites. Such a stand marked a repudiation of the gradualistic approaches of earlier abolitionists and a rejection of the older colonizationist idea that all freed black people had to be sent out of the United States. Garrison and his peers also broke with their predecessors in the tactics they used. Post-1830 abolitionists were generally more strident, bolder in rhetoric and in deed than most early antislavery men and women had been. Historians, naturally, subdivide the period 1831–1865 into smaller units, but those years do encompass a distinct phase of American antislavery, beginning with the emergence of immediatism and ending with the death of slavery at the hands of the Union army.

We have, then, a neat, logical temporal boundary for antislavery—and yet it has to be pushed outward in both directions or else some of the most interesting questions about abolitionism would never get asked, let alone answered. A bit of this chronological expansion is the legacy of Gilbert Hobbs Barnes, whose *Anti-Slavery Impulse*, first published in 1933, connected antislavery to the Protestant revivalism of the 1820s. But there is no reason to stop with 1820. Even relatively innovative revivalists like Charles G. Finney built upon an earlier evangelical tradition. For that matter, Protestant reform impulses did not end with the Civil War. From the perspective of revivalism, antislavery is simply a major episode in a saga stretching as far back as the early eighteenth century and

1 My use of the word "boundaries" was inspired in part by Frederik Barth (ed.), *Ethnic Groups and Boundaries: The Social Organization of Culture Difference* (Boston: Little, Brown, 1969). I do, however, use the word rather differently from Barth and I take exception to his dismissal of the word "culture" as "nothing but a way to describe human behaviour."

Jonathan Edwards's doctrine of "disinterested benevolence" and as far forward in time as the late nineteenth-century Social Gospel, perhaps down to the present day.

One does not have to place as much weight on religion as Barnes did to believe in the importance of the 1820s. To be sure, evangelical Protestantism fostered an increase in reform activity in that decade and provided many future abolitionists with a background of moral commitment and with experience in agitation. But in quite different ways the 1820s likewise prepared Americans for later conflicts over slavery. Slavery itself refused to die as a political issue, in spite of the relative (and temporary) success of the Missouri Compromise of 1820 in calming controversy over its expansion. Besides poisoning relations between the sections, slavery convulsed the internal politics of some of the newer states, notably Illinois and Indiana, where strong factions sought to establish involuntary servitude in the early 1820s. In even less direct ways the 1820s set the stage for the coming struggle. The decade was particularly important for American economic development, and virtually all changes pointed toward greater divergence between the North and South in material interests, lifestyles, population, and beliefs. At the very least, the moment we begin to look backward past 1831 we have to place antislavery in the contexts of America's peculiar political history and the nation's long-range economic development.

Locating the abolitionists in time also involves seeing where they belong in relation to American reform and radicalism generally. In its oldest and simplest formulation that meant identifying abolitionists with the ideology of the American Revolution. Dwight Lowell Dumond traced abolitionism in "the political treatises of the Revolutionary period; in the legislative acts and court decisions of those states which abolished slavery; in the debates of the Constitutional Convention, and Congresses of the United States both before and after 1789, and the conventions of the new states; and in the climactic public discussion of the Missouri question."[2] Only after doing that in one hundred seventy-four densely packed, double-

2 Dwight Lowell Dumond, *Antislavery: The Crusade for Freedom in America* (Ann Arbor: University of Michigan Press, 1961), 175.

columned pages did he feel prepared to discuss formation of the American Anti-Slavery Society in 1833. Few have been so exhaustive as Dumond, but many have accepted his belief that the real story of antislavery begins with the principles of the Revolution.

To a degree that is true. At times abolitionists adopted the rhetoric of the founding fathers, playing upon the hypocrisy of whites who believed in life, liberty, pursuit of happiness, and rebellion against tyranny—but not for black people. Post-1830 antislavery owed a further debt to the Revolutionary generation for ending slavery in the North, closing the African slave trade, and prohibiting slavery in the Northwest Territory. Had those steps not been taken, slavery surely would have been stronger, less sectional, and less vulnerable than it was by 1831. Yet it is not wholly satisfactory to leave it at that. Abolitionists were themselves ambivalent about the Revolution. Garrisonian nonresistants abhorred the violence that had been used to carry out the principles of the Revolution, and virtually all abolitionists were as willing to chastise the founding fathers for their sins as to praise them for their ideals. In some instances abolitionists were not even terribly conscious of the Revolution's most revolutionary literature: Garrison seems not to have read Tom Paine seriously until the mid-1840s. More to the point, if the Revolution had antislavery implications (as I believe it did), they had to be worked out painfully, haltingly, and unevenly over a half century. To make the Revolutionary era a boundary of antislavery does help put abolitionism within an important strain of secular thought, but nearly every American could be put in the same strain and we are left with the mystery of why only a few became abolitionists and why a new variety of antislavery emerged after 1830.

A number of historians have worried less about connections between post-1830 antislavery and the Revolution than about bringing the story of abolitionism forward in time. The most careful and least controversial of these efforts are James M. McPherson's thoroughly documented studies of former abolitionists' reform activities in the post–Civil War world.[3] Other scholars, writing in the 1960s, at-

3 The most relevant titles by James M. McPherson are *The Struggle for Equality: Abolitionists and the Negro in the Civil War and Reconstruction* (Princeton: Princeton Uni-

tempted to make abolitionism speak more directly to the events of that turbulent decade. In 1965 Howard Zinn declared there was "no point—except for that abstract delight which accompanies historical study—in probing the role of the agitator in the historical process, unless we can learn something from it which is of use today." What we could actually learn was less clear. Zinn's conclusion was that agitation results in "slow dribbles of social progress" and that the civil rights movement of the 1950s and 1960s gave the United States "its only living reminder that it was once a revolutionary nation."[4] Staughton Lynd similarly got lost in his parallels, at times implying that abolitionists were part of a continuous American radical tradition and at other times implying that radicalism in America has been a series of relatively disconnected episodes, each providing present-day agitators with inspiration, comfort, and insight. Zinn and Lynd were not alone in seeking the common ground between antebellum and contemporary radicalism. Aileen Kraditor and Carleton Mabee, for instance, stressed similarities in strategies, tactics, and (to a degree) in goals. Bertram Wyatt-Brown made use of recent psychological studies of morally committed youth to cast light on the psyches and family experiences of abolitionists.[5]

Such scholarship, at its best, expressed a sensitive appreciation of the moral, tactical, and intellectual issues in abolitionism. It also challenged—often indirectly—the practice of presenting 1865 as a sharp dividing line in the history of American radical and reform activity. On some levels the Civil War clearly did mark a new departure for abolitionists: it made their cause respectable, it shook their pacifistic and anarchistic principles, and it ended their thirty-year battle against slavery. Yet as James M. McPherson amply demonstrated, a fair number of abolitionists continued to work for racial

---

versity Press, 1964) and *The Abolitionist Legacy: From Reconstruction to the NAACP* (Princeton: Princeton University Press, 1975).

4 Howard Zinn, "Abolitionists, Freedom-Riders, and the Tactics of Agitation," in Martin Duberman (ed.), *The Antislavery Vanguard: New Essays on the Abolitionists* (Princeton: Princeton University Press, 1965), 446, 451.

5 Staughton Lynd, *Intellectual Origins of American Radicalism* (New York: Random House, 1969); Aileen S. Kraditor, *Means and Ends in American Abolitionism: Garrison and His Critics on Strategy and Tactics, 1834–1850* (New York: Pantheon Books, 1967); Carlton Mabee, *Black Freedom: The Nonviolent Abolitionists from 1830 through the Civil War* (New York: Macmillan, 1970); Bertram Wyatt-Brown, "The New Left and the Abolitionists: Romantic Radicalism in America," *Soundings*, XXXIV (1971), 147–90.

justice long after the fighting stopped.[6] Other writers of the 1960s likewise made it easy to think about continuities from antebellum to postbellum reform merely by presenting abolitionism as a type of agitation existing across time, whether the enemy were slavery, segregation, racism, or something else.

There was a danger to that. Historians in the 1960s overemphasized the parallel between past and present—they gave too much attention to such similarities as civil disobedience, "extreme" language and behavior, and the desire to create a racially egalitarian society. That led to an illusion of connectedness, a false feeling that there must have been a linear progression from the abolitionists to the Freedom Riders and SDS. Yet a characteristic of American radicalism and reform is discontinuity, a failure to sustain movements and institutions across generations. An irony of the post–World War II American Left is that an Indian, Mohandas K. Gandhi, had greater influence on radical nonviolence than our own most prominent nonresistant, William Lloyd Garrison. Antislavery was not a living presence in the 1950s and 1960s; it was rediscovered, largely by academics and not by men and women centrally involved in agitation.

Antislavery was, nevertheless, part of a reform tradition, although one largely unrecognized by historians and abolitionists alike. The tradition was embodied in perceptions of the world rather than in well-defined ideological or institutional continuity. There was a radical potential in its central assumptions, but it was not inherently radical. Its intellectual structure owed much to evangelical Protestantism and to the American Revolution, but it also had origins in seventeenth-century English political thought, natural philosophy, and in the so-called "pseudo-sciences" of the late eighteenth and early nineteenth centuries.

Like many other American reform movements, antislavery achieved its effect by pulling new implications out of words, phrases, and images that were ancient and widely shared. Such was the case when the New England Anti-Slavery Society defined aboli-

6 McPherson, *Abolitionist Legacy*. On the Civil War as a transforming event see George M. Fredrickson, *The Inner Civil War: Northern Intellectuals and the Crisis of the Union* (New York: Harper and Row, 1965).

tionism in 1833. According to the society's *Report*, immediate emancipation meant that "all title of property in the slaves shall instantly cease, because their Creator has never relinquished his claim of ownership, and because none have a right to sell their own bodies or buy those of their own species as cattle." The language was an interesting mixture of Christianity and commerce, and it resonated with what C. B. Macpherson has labeled the "political theory of possessive individualism." The term is Macpherson's own, as is the formal concept behind it. "Possessive individualism" does not represent a consciously articulated body of doctrine but rather what Macpherson calls a set of "social assumptions" underpinning seventeenth-century English political theory and persisting in modern liberal democratic thought. Macpherson has in mind the conviction that freedom means the ability to act independently of others—more specifically, the ability to control one's own property and labor. By that line of reasoning, freedom was a matter of being an autonomous agent in the marketplace, a right denied the slave, as the New England Anti-Slavery Society reminded its readers.[7]

Macpherson simply describes a collection of attitudes that made sense to almost everyone in an emerging capitalistic economy. In itself, possessive individualism did not necessarily lead to antislavery (or to liberal democracy), but it was an instrument of change in the hands of men and women battling against economic or political privilege. During the Revolution it permitted Americans to see taxation without representation as a genuine loss of liberty: the principle of the matter lay in the fact that part of one's property, hence one's freedom, was placed under the arbitrary power of others. Possessive individualism played a similar role in antislavery rhetoric, as when Theodore Dwight Weld declared "SELF-RIGHT is the *foundation* right—*the post in the middle*, to which all other rights are fastened."[8] To take that away was to make a person a slave, no matter

---

7 *Abolitionist*, I (1833), 21; C. B. Macpherson, *The Political Theory of Possessive Individualism: Hobbes to Locke* (Oxford: Oxford University Press, 1962), 263–64, is an excellent summary of Macpherson's argument.

8 [Theodore Dwight Weld], *The Bible Against Slavery* (New York: American Anti-Slavery Society, 1838), 10. Obviously I take exception to Lynd's remark that Paine's *Agrarian Justice* "signified the end of . . . the political theory of possessive individualism." Lynd further believed that Paine began an assault on "unlimited accumulation of property." Yet it was in *Agrarian Justice* that Paine wrote, "I care not how affluent some may be, provided that none be

whether the tyrant was George III or a southern master. Applied to other situations, however, the logic of possessive individualism led to far less radical conclusions. The abolitionists' Jacksonian contemporaries, for instance, used it to justify one kind of capitalism over another when they promoted state banking interests against the "monopoly" of the Bank of the United States.

The very adaptability of possessive individualism helped give truth to Wendell Phillips Garrison's observation in 1893 that "the civil service reformers or Mugwumps come nearer to being lineal descendants of the abolitionists than any other existing manifestation of the national conscience."[9] His father, William Lloyd Garrison, had used the assumptions of possessive individualism to attack the slaveholder for denying the right of human beings to participate freely in the marketplace. The son used the same assumptions to speak for the post–Civil War middle classes who were defending the marketplace from assaults on it by the poor and the wealthy. To a present-day sensibility the liberal reformers, or mugwumps, seem profoundly negative and unpleasant for their racism, elitism, and laissez-faire dogmatism, especially when they are measured against the millenial zeal and egalitarian visions of abolitionists. But abolitionists had likewise thought of liberty as control over one's property (one's self included), and on that point mugwumps, many of them former abolitionists or children of abolitionists, were within a reform tradition, even as they repudiated antebellum calls for equality and for moral action.

The intellectual transition to post-1865 society was made all the easier by yet another aspect of American reform—its long flirtation with science and "pseudo-science" (if there is any meaningful dis-

---

miserable in consequence of it." Like liberal architects of the welfare state, Paine seems to have been willing to concede great wealth to individuals who worked for it, so long as wealth did not bring political privilege for those who had it and starvation and powerlessness for those who did not. Paine was within the tradition of possessive individualism, although on the left edge of it. Tom Paine, "Agrarian Justice," in William M. Van der Weyde (ed.), *The Life and Works of Thomas Paine* (10 vols.; New Rochelle: Thomas Paine National Historical Association, 1925), X, 25; Lynd, *Intellectual Origins*, 75–76. See also Eric Foner, *Tom Paine and Revolutionary America* (New York: Oxford University Press, 1976).

9 Quoted in John G. Sproat, *"The Best Men": Liberal Reformers in the Gilded Age* (New York: Oxford University Press, 1968), 243.

tinction between the two in the early nineteenth century). Few abolitionists went so far as Tom Paine, who spent part of his life as an inventor, but many involved themselves with a variety of medical and biological regimens. Particularly popular was dietary reform—the system promoted by Sylvester Graham—and phrenology, the belief that a person's character was revealed in the shape of his or her skull. Dietary reform, phrenology, and several other antebellum fads promised mankind that moral and physical improvement went together and that both could be achieved by following certain immutable laws. It had become man's duty, Theodore Parker declared in the 1850s, "to unfold and perfect himself, as far as possible, in body and spirit." What transpired in the two decades between Parker's remark and the Gilded Age is quite complex and involves many elements, including spiritualism, another link between the cultures of antebellum and postbellum America.[10] But the point is relatively straightforward: physiological reform and the pseudo-sciences accustomed abolitionists to seeing human progress in terms of laws governing health and reproduction. And that prepared younger abolitionists like Moncure Conway, Wendell Phillips Garrison, and Loring Moody to accept much of Darwinian biology and Social Darwinism. In antebellum America perfectionism had increasingly become a physiological as well as a religious doctrine; in the postbellum world, it was to become even more a matter of biology rather than theology.

There were, to be sure, things former abolitionists and their children found hard to accept in Darwinism, Social Darwinism, and (later) in eugenics. To some the overtones of racism were unconscionable. Many did not like the implication that individual initiative did not count for much in the grand scheme of things, nor did they like to see struggle presented so viciously as it was in the Darwinian jungle—abolitionists had balanced their individualism against a faith in human brotherhood. Yet after 1865 there was an easy translation from the antebellum language of possessive individualism, evangelical Protestantism, and pseudo-science to that of

10 Theodore Parker, "The Three Chief Safeguards of Society," in Samuel B. Stewart (ed.), *Sins and Safeguards of Society* (Boston: American Unitarian Association, n.d.), 53.

Darwinian biology. The millennium, of course, had to be postponed, but progress and evolution took its place after the Civil War, and they were on-going things, guaranteed by natural law. The right of the individual to compete freely became an evolutionary obligation, not just a mandate from God and the marketplace. Darwinian biology continued the process, begun by the antebellum pseudo-sciences, of putting salvation in the flesh and in heaven alike.

Although there were undeniable differences between antebellum and postbellum reformers, the Civil War was not an abrupt break but rather a transition and a parting of the ways. Some antebellum reformers drifted along with their logic and their social position. For them possessive individualism and scientific thought, once weapons against monarchy and slavery, became defenses for the status quo and for a middle class that was both victorious and uneasy in the Gilded Age. Liberal reform was the dead end for that portion of antebellum reform. It took responsibility for progress away from the committed individual and put it on to natural processes; it placed blame for failure on those who failed; and it was irrelevant to the cause of social change in an industrial society. Other former abolitionists and their children, however, continued to fight for social justice. When faced with choosing between their old logic and their old sympathy for the downtrodden, they kept the latter. Unlike the mugwumps, they left an inheritance to mid-twentieth-century reformers, although an ironic one. It was the NAACP, an organization attacked as hopelessly inadequate by the earnest young radicals whom historians in the 1960s saw as the real descendants of the abolitionists.

That is not to say each and every history of American abolitionism ought to begin with seventeenth-century British political theory and continue through late nineteenth-century liberal reform to mid-twentieth-century activism. But the chronological boundaries we choose for antislavery determine the questions we can handle. To stay within the period 1831–1865 means either doing a close exegesis of abolitionism or else dealing with it in relation to other aspects of antebellum culture and society. A longer time span has its disadvantages, but does open up the possibility of placing antislavery in the context of broad, important cultural and social processes.

Doing that, however, requires spotting more subtle things than similarities in tactics and goals between antislavery and later activism. Besides looking to Anglo-American racial attitudes, Protestant traditions, and the ideology of the American Revolution (areas where the most interest has been),[11] a longer perspective on antislavery has to challenge the Civil War as a division in American history, examine the role of natural philosophy, science, and pseudoscience, and face up to the prospect that mugwumps and Social Darwinists may be on a line with abolitionism, just as are the founders of the NAACP and other crusaders for racial justice.

Finding the proper placement in time for antislavery is difficult enough, but there is a second kind of boundary historians feel compelled to draw. It is between groups of abolitionists. The common view is that three main factions emerged in the late 1830s—Garrisonians, evangelicals, and political abolitionists. The Garrisonians remained with the American Anti-Slavery Society in 1840 and usually denounced direct political action. The faction was tinged with various heresies (although not all Garrisonians shared their leader's nonresistance and perfectionism), and by the mid-1840s it took the position that the union between North and South ought to be broken. Unlike the heterodox Garrisonians, the evangelicals were committed to fairly conventional revivalistic Christianity. The majority of them left the American Anti-Slavery Society in 1840 and went into the newly formed American and Foreign Anti-Slavery Society. Their rhetoric and tactics were less inflammatory than those of the Garrisonians and they were far more willing to work through American religious and political institutions. Among the political abolitionists were men like James G. Birney and the founders of the Liberty party, who differed from the evangelicals in little except

11 David Brion Davis, *The Problem of Slavery in Western Culture* (Ithaca: Cornell University Press, 1966); David Brion Davis, *The Problem of Slavery in the Age of Revolution, 1770–1823* (Ithaca: Cornell University Press, 1975); Winthrop D. Jordan, *White Over Black: American Attitudes toward the Negro, 1550–1812* (Chapel Hill: University of North Carolina Press, 1968); Bernard Bailyn, *Ideological Origins of the American Revolution* (Cambridge: Harvard University Press, 1967); Gordon S. Wood, *The Creation of the American Republic, 1776–1787* (Chapel Hill: University of North Carolina Press, 1969). For a complex evaluation of the American Revolution in terms of western political theory see J. G. A. Pocock, *The Machiavellian Moment: Florentine Political Thought and the Atlantic Republican Tradition* (Princeton: Princeton University Press, 1975), 506–52.

their greater involvement in political action. But as time went on the faction also included such ambitious characters as Salmon P. Chase—primarily antislavery politicians who accepted the expedient compromises of the Free Soil and Republican parties.

For the most part historians have accepted the validity of the three-way division of antislavery and have spent their energy debating which faction was right. Gilbert Barnes and Dwight Dumond made an ardent case for the political and evangelical abolitionists, whose "moderation" they felt to be more constructive than Garrisonian extremism. They salvaged the respectability of antislavery by arguing that most abolitionists (unlike that eccentric Garrison) worked within American institutions, paved the way for the Republican party, and generally acted to produce political change in a responsible manner. It was possible to disagree with Barnes and Dumond without having to ask how deep differences actually were between the factions. All one had to do was reverse the value judgment and assert that a "radical" posture, like that of the Garrisonians, is not only morally justified but also has a stronger impact on public consciousness, and therefore a greater political influence than a cautious, moderate approach does. That line of argument has been pursued by several historians, but with most sophistication by Aileen Kraditor. Only a few have raised doubts about whether there really were deep ideological distinctions between factions.[12]

Yet the evidence is ambiguous. The great shattering of antislavery unity in 1840 did come over serious issues. The Garrisonians, Liberty party men, and evangelicals quarreled over the role of women, over whether to engage in direct political action, and over

12 Gilbert Hobbs Barnes, *The Antislavery Impulse, 1830–1844* (New York: American Historical Association, 1933); Dumond, *Antislavery*; Kraditor, *Means and Ends*. Bertram Wyatt-Brown, *Lewis Tappan and the Evangelical War Against Slavery* (Cleveland: Case Western Reserve University Press, 1969), and Lewis Perry, *Radical Abolitionism: Anarchy and the Government of God in Antislavery Thought* (Ithaca: Cornell University Press, 1973) are especially good at challenging the belief that deep ideological differences separated the factions. See also the work of James Brewer Stewart on political and Garrisonian abolitionism, synthesized and expanded in *Holy Warriors: The Abolitionists and American Slavery* (New York: Hill and Wang, 1976). I am using "ideology" in an old and strict sense—that is, as referring to a coherent body of ideas and assumptions. Some scholars include emotional and psychological characteristics in "ideology." To my mind, emotion, culture, and psyche help explain why particular ideologies take hold and assume the shape they do. But I do not regard emotion and psychic structure as ideology.

the posture to take toward American Protestantism. There were also differences in style between groups and still further substantive disagreements in the 1840s and 1850s on such important matters as whether the federal union ought to be broken and whether the Constitution was pro- or antislavery. Still, the factions were not consistently radical or reformist and they were not even homogeneous: each contained people whose beliefs were closest to the dominant ones of the other group. Abolitionists, moreover, got tangled up in nonideological issues. They grew irascible, pushed each other into impossible situations, whispered doubts about each other's fidelity to the cause, and sought personal assurances that could not be given. Put less tactfully, they had personality conflicts which exaggerated their differences over tactics and strategy.

The division of 1840 sounds especially unlike the conventional version of it when we abandon the perspectives of Boston and New York, the home bases of the crucial figures in the schism. Abolitionists in Ohio and several other states did their best to steer an independent course, believing and acting as if the questions dividing their Boston and New York colleagues were not beyond compromise. A number of important abolitionists, including Theodore Dwight Weld, looked upon the events of 1840 as unnecessary and disgusting. William Goodell spoke for them when he prided himself on his "utter refusal to take any part in the foolish quarrel . . . between the abolitionists of the two rival Atlantic cities."[13] If ideology was at stake in 1840, it eluded the notice of Goodell, one of the most perceptive observers of antislavery.

Those historians who like the abolitionists, however, have been especially insistent on drawing sharp divisions between factions. By stressing "real" differences over strategies and goals they have at hand a rationalistic explanation for the unpleasant fact that abolitionists could not get along with each other. Antislavery men and women appear as ideologues and tacticians rather than quarrelsome neurotics (the way hostile scholars once presented them). The issues recent historians have emphasized, moreover, have allowed them to

---

13 Letter to Garrison in the *Liberator*, February 12, 1847. I treat at great length the matters in this paragraph in *The Antislavery Appeal: American Abolitionism after 1830* (Baltimore: Johns Hopkins University Press, 1976), 3–33.

relate each antislavery faction to a faction in the American Left of the 1960s. That, in turn, has permitted them to do precisely what Gilbert Barnes did forty years ago—play favorites. It is a neat technique to work out a critique of the present through analysis of the past, to praise the abolitionists closest to one's own position and attack those most resembling one's enemies. That is partisan history. It also can be very good, and I do not want to deny its legitimacy or the fact that there were real issues separating abolitionists.[14] But at times the way historians group abolitionists shows nothing so much as a natural, human eagerness to read contemporary concerns into history and to praise people we admire.

To conceive of antislavery factions as ideologically defined is also to miss the nonrational elements in abolitionism, including its intense emotional hold. It had a power, an urgency that has never been satisfactorily explained and cannot be in terms of ideas alone. Ideological interpretations further leave out the institutional factors in antislavery schisms. A good case can be made that the American Anti-Slavery Society fell apart in 1840 because it was short of money and because it had already accomplished the one thing only a national society could do: it had sent agents throughout the North to spread the antislavery message and to form state and local societies. By 1840 the strongest of these were quite independent and they had taken over many of the functions of. the parent organization. The American Anti-Slavery Society was not exactly irrelevant in 1840, nor did it entirely collapse of its own weight, but the issues that split it apart were compromised and contained within vital local and state organizations like the Ohio Anti-Slavery Society.[15] Had the American Anti-Slavery Society a crucial role to play in 1840, aboli-

14 McPherson, *Abolitionist Legacy*, has evidence of behavioral and attitudinal differences between factions persisting in the post–Civil War period. Yet the Garrisonians and evangelicals come out relatively close together on most issues, with the political abolitionists generally more "moderate" than either of the other factions. I suspect that is so because the category "political abolitionist" includes people who originally were less engaged in antislavery than were members of the other factions. The closeness of the Garrisonians and evangelicals seems as impressive as the distinctions between them and I find it to be evidence of the general correctness of my point in this section.

15 The Ohio society did split apart two years after the American Anti-Slavery Society's schism, but, I suspect, only because Garrisonians in Boston forced the issue. Even after Ohio Garrisonians withdrew from the state society, the two organizations got along in much more friendly fashion than did the warring factions in the East. Ohio Garrisonians, in fact, elected a Liberty party man to be their president. He accepted, in a show of harmony.

tionists would have made a better effort to save it or to create a viable alternative.

The conventional three-part division of antislavery denies more than the nonrational and institutional features of the movement. It tends to freeze abolitionists at a moment in time and thereby to obscure antislavery as process. We have them as they were in 1840: Garrison the radical, Lewis Tappan and Theodore Dwight Weld the evangelicals, and James G. Birney the political abolitionist. We miss the evolution. If we look at starting points and ending points, however, abolitionists appear more alike than they did in 1840. Garrison, Tappan, Weld, and Birney each came out of the evangelical Protestant tradition; each broke with colonization, and for a time each said much the same thing about slavery and how to end it. Each was more willing than the majority of Americans to concede women a larger role in society, just as each was susceptible to a wide range of pseudo-sciences, fads, and reforms. Eventually each reached a high level of disillusionment with American politics, although each pinned great faith on political change. There were shades of difference along the way: they drew slightly dismilar conclusions from the same assumptions, and some arrived at their destination more quickly than others (part of Garrison's problem in 1840 was in being prematurely heterodox). But antislavery led many men and women down a path that was a lifetime long. People who were seemingly radical in one year voted Republican in another; people who were bitter enemies in 1840 took nearly identical positions later, or else exchanged positions, often still remaining enemies.

Just as there was a dynamic to the lives of individual abolitionists, there was a dynamic to the movement, and factionalization was its dominant characteristic. The major groupings of 1840 went through schisms of their own throughout the 1840s and 1850s. In 1859, after two decades of Garrison's contentious leadership, the American Anti-Slavery Society dwindled to the point where its receipts were $14,239.11, or about one-thirty-fifth of the Bible Society's income in 1854, and a paltry amount for an important reform enterprise. The evangelicals did no better. By the 1850s the American and Foreign Anti-Slavery Society was moribund and Lewis Tappan was experimenting with a variety of tactics. Political abolition-

ists also had their fallings out, especially in 1847 and 1848, when
many of them went óver to the Free Soil movement while others
stayed with more purely antislavery programs. Like the Garrisonians, they continually bickered among themselves, not stopping
until they were either absorbed into the Republican party or else
were encapsulated in hopelessly tiny and inconsequential parties of
their own. To assume that abolitionists divided into three distinct
groups does an injustice to their skill in alienating one another. Continual factionalization, rather than creation of stable organizations,
was the norm for antislavery and it has been the norm for American
radicals and reformers to the present day.

Why that has been the case is not terribly clear, but the only way
to find out is to look at the process of division, rather than at the
divisions themselves. It seems that the answer lies in the psychological and institutional pressures inherent to being a radical or reformer in America. Only self-righteous people have the strength of
conviction to take unpopular stands, and self-righteous people are
unlikely to make the compromises of feeling and principle necessary to keep organizations intact over time. Reform organizations
are vulnerable in another way. There are few means of determining
who should belong and who should not—there are no outside sanctions, no outside authorities to reward the orthodox and punish the
revisionists. Although sometimes committed to broad coalitions,
many reformers and radicals create their own sanctions by formu-
lating strict standards of fidelity to the cause. And that means
interminable quarrels, disagreements, and retreats into smaller,
more restrictive groups, ever in search of the most correct position.
It is a devil's choice: there can be no group without tests of membership, but tests of membership go against the grain of human beings
who trust their own consciences more than they do the will of institutions. Even the Garrisonians, who prided themselves on having
a "broad platform" spacious enough to accommodate all abolitionists, found ways of reading dissenters off of it. They accomplished
that effectively by passing resolutions asserting that all true-hearted
abolitionists should hold such-and-such a belief, and then blandly
declaring that a person could remain a member of the American
Anti-Slavery Society without holding that belief—even though such

persons had serious aspersions cast on their abolitionist convictions.[16] The logic of that position was not exclusively Garrisonian nor was it purely ideological. It was in the situation and it cannot be explored until we see the pattern as one of eternal testing and factionalization rather than as one of fixed boundaries, defined by coherent tactical and ideological issues.

To this point I have not directly criticized the notion that it might be important to study divisions. Yet there does come a time when antislavery has to be treated as a whole. Otherwise there is no way to deal effectively with the crucial matter of why a new form of abolitionism, based on immediate emancipation, emerged suddenly after 1830. If abolitionists really did fall into three distinct groupings with conflicting world-views, then there would be two alternative lines of analysis, neither very fruitful. It would be possible to argue that ideological differences arose after formation of the American Anti-Slavery Society in 1833, which makes for the difficult task of explaining what abolitionists shared before 1833 and why they no longer shared it by 1840. Or it would be possible to try to show that each faction had a different mind-set from the beginning and that something brought them into a fragile coalition from 1833 to 1840. That would require treating each faction's conversion to antislavery separately. More sensible and more consistent with the evidence, it seems to me, is to quit describing abolitionists in terms of three sharply defined positions and ask the commonsensical question of what antislavery men and women had in common and what brought them all to a crusade against an old, well-established institution.

The boundaries between groups of abolitionists, like the chronological boundaries of antislavery, need to be surveyed, challenged, moved around, and, for some purposes, abolished. It is a matter of deciding what we want to know and how best to find it out.

A third kind of boundary—that dividing abolitionists from other antebellum Americans—likewise needs examination. With antislavery, as with almost every other reform, a core of committed individuals devoted their careers to the cause. But a large, blurred

16 Kraditor, *Means and Ends*, makes much of the tolerance of the Garrisonians for dissent in their ranks. But she misses the verbal assaults dissenters had to endure from their colleagues.

periphery of men and women drifted in and out of antislavery or from antislavery to other reforms. We know much less about them, and about the rank and file generally, than about the leaders. There is not even a precise way to distinguish between those who were primarily abolitionists and those whose degree of commitment was less. The term "abolitionist" serves them all, even those who came to the movement after it was relatively respectable and who were driven by political or social ambition as much as by conviction.

That causes trouble for historians when they attempt to say what motivated people to become abolitionists or what it was that made abolitionists different from their nonabolitionist contemporaries. There have been many explanations—evangelical Protestantism, the psychological or generational experiences of reformers, or such sociological factors as status change. A few scholars simply take the abolitionists at face value and characterize them as idealistic men and women, with nothing more needing to be said. Some of these efforts have been insightful, but there are just too many exceptions to every rule—too many evangelical Protestants who did not become abolitionists, too many men and women of rising status who did; too many idealistic Americans who were blind to the evil of slavery, too many from family backgrounds similar to the abolitionists who did not care about emancipation or black people. A certain amount of that is to be expected—social science usually yields probabilities and tendencies, not lockstep cause and effect. The failure of historians to give fully satisfactory explanations of antislavery motivation does not mean that no one should try. It also does not mean that the partial explanations we have are worthless. Some of them, particularly the ones emphasizing evangelical Protestantism, have merit. But the questions remain. Whose motivation are we talking about: the core's or the periphery's? the earliest abolitionists or those who joined late? Do the motives or characteristics we find among abolitionists differ significantly from those of nonabolitionists or antiabolitionists?

The mystery of what was special about abolitionists deepens when we read their propaganda carefully. At its most abstract, their rhetoric expressed concerns common to the day. Their desire to defend individual autonomy against arbitrary power was a moralistic variation on a Jacksonian theme, as was their tendency to place responsibility for success and failure on the individual rather than on government or society. The abolitionist drive to reconcile progress and perfection with virtue and moral order was also prevalent in antebellum American culture. Equally widespread were efforts (like those made by many abolitionists) to balance self-control and spontaneity.[17] Even in imagery and style of argumentation abolitionists mirrored their contemporaries. They appealed for the emotionality of the human heart to prevail over the cold intellect of the head, exactly as popular sentimental authors did. They found their model of social stability in the well-ordered, loving family, precisely as many antebellum Americans did, including some defenders of slavery. Abolitionists turned those and other themes and images into antislavery propaganda, and that was unique to them. The themes and images themselves were common property. If it is difficult to distinguish abolitionists sociologically from a great many northern nonabolitionists, it is equally difficult to distinguish them from other articulate Americans in basic patterns of thought and expression.

It is wrong to expect that abolitionists should have been wildly different from their peers. Aileen Kraditor correctly suggested that reform and radical movements "can profitably be studied as limiting cases of the prescribed consensus" of a period.[18] For reform to have a constituency it must be intelligible, and it can only be if it draws upon conventional symbols and articulates acceptable themes. Anything else would be gibberish. Language (and the culture encoded in it) shapes reform, and reformers are severely circumscribed in the amount they can rework it for their own ends. Reformers must be able to use the language of the day to demonstrate how a particular social situation relates to prevalent hopes or fears. Even then, it takes luck for them to have an impact. Events may help by giving

17 Lewis Perry, " 'We have Had Conversation in the World': The Abolitionists and Spontaneity," *Canadian Review of American Studies*, VI (1975), 3–26.

18 Aileen S. Kraditor, "American Radical Historians on Their Heritage," *Past and Present*, LVI (1972), 144. On pages 141–42 Kraditor remarks that "the study of past reform movements is one of the most useful ways to find out what the prescribed orthodoxy was in a given period and what the mechanisms were for the perpetuation of the ideological hegemony of that period's ruling elite."

urgency and credibility to reform rhetoric, as happened in the 1840s and 1850s when southerners acted in a manner that confirmed antislavery talk of a slave power conspiracy. Very quickly, abolitionist images, symbols, and phrases filtered into the Free Soil and Republican parties, even though most abolitionists remained political outcasts.[19] The power of antislavery propaganda was in its ability to *explain* (sometimes rightly, sometimes wrongly), and explanation is impossible unless reformer and audience operate within a shared structure of assumptions. By saying that, I am not arguing for a revival of consensus history (a relic of the 1950s) with its underplaying of conflict in American life. People can understand each other perfectly and still fight violently. Shared meaning sets the terms of a social debate; it does not stifle the debate or make it less bloody.

I also do not mean to imply that every boundary between abolitionists and nonabolitionists should be erased. So much the better if someone finds startling new sociological, psychological, or ideological differences between antislavery advocates and the mass of Americans—something, after all, did bring men and women to abolitionism. Even with that knowledge, historians would have to show why abolitionists phrased their arguments the way they did, why they chose to talk about slavery in a certain fashion and not in another. That requires searching antislavery rhetoric for its most basic themes and for the social, cultural, and personal meanings they carried. From there we can move outward, across the line defining abolitionism, and see how those themes intersected events, the concerns of other Americans, and larger social and cultural processes. There are places, of course, where the boundaries between abolitionists and nonabolitionists have to be drawn sharply, but we also have to look at where there was no boundary. Otherwise, we will take the abolitionists out of antebellum America and out of history.

Boundaries, we are often reminded, are generally artificial. That is the point of this essay. But no matter how the problem is put, it is

19 David Brion Davis, *The Slave Power Conspiracy and the Paranoid Style* (Baton Rouge: Louisiana State University Press, 1969); Eric Foner, *Free Soil, Free Labor, Free Men: The Ideology of the Republican Party before the Civil War* (New York: Oxford University Press, 1970).

real enough: it is difficult to arrive at satisfactory perspectives on antislavery, despite the vast quantity of scholarship in the past fifteen years. Some of the trouble would vanish if antislavery were restored to the larger world of historical context and historical process. And yet the temptation is to go in the other direction—to describe a small chunk of reality in ever greater detail, not necessarily with greater insight (as happens to most subdivisions of history sooner or later). There is an escape. Anyone concerned about antislavery, or about American reform generally, can be cautious and self-conscious about the boundaries he or she places on abolitionism. We can, moreover, be as sensitive to interaction between a reform movement and its society as we are to what goes on within the movement. The alternative is to lose the vitality of the scholarship of the 1960s and lapse into an elegant antiquarianism. There is the embarrassing danger of saying the same old things about the abolitionists, men and women whose reputation rests on saying new and daring things.

# CONTROVERSIES OVER SLAVERY IN EIGHTEENTH- AND NINETEENTH-CENTURY SCOTLAND *

### C. Duncan Rice

STUDENTS of Scottish history have often emphasized the scale and worth of their country's contributions to various human enterprises. It is actually true that Scotland's involvement in the rise of black slavery, in its maintenance, and in its ultimate overthrow, was out of all proportion to her size. Even after the West India Emancipation Act of 1833, Scottish abolitionist societies were proportionately more active and more radical than other British ones in channeling support to their colleagues in America.[1] These conclusions will help to increase the admiration of Scots for their own past. However, this paper does not attempt to rank Scotland in the moral batting averages for the nations. Its purpose is to help scholars whose interest is in the controversy over slavery in North America, by enabling them to draw analogies from another society. Their thinking may be set upon novel tacks by considering some of the functions which the discussion of slavery took on in eighteenth- and nineteenth-century Scotland.

* This paper is based in part on research made possible by a generous travel grant from the American Philosophical Society.
    1 I have just completed a monograph on their work, entitled *The Scots Abolitionists, 1833–1860.*

It is relatively easy to investigate Scottish antislavery activity. The country is so small that work is more manageable than in the wider field of North America. As a highly literate and rapidly commercializing society, too, Scotland supported a flourishing periodical, almanac, and directory press, which makes it unusually easy to identify the men and women who became concerned over slavery. There are also some parallels, more than superficial, between Scotland's situation and that of the American North.[2] Perhaps it is true that Scottish absorption in religious and benevolent affairs was an expression of frustration at the relative withering of national political life after the union of the parliaments in 1707.[3] In either case, Scotland entered the nineteenth century in a state of acute religious excitement over the so-called Haldane revivals of 1799–1802, which represented a deeply emotive reaction against the formal, intellectualized Presbyterianism which had dominated the country's religion in the heyday of the Enlightenment. This explosion of vital Christianity brought the independents and Baptists into being as real forces in Scottish church history. It also looked forward to the rise of the evangelical party in the established Church of Scotland, which culminated in its division at the Disruption of 1843. The Haldane revivals have real similarities to the Second Great Awakening and its aftermath among American Presbyterians and Congregationalists. Again, Scottish reformers had disproportionately slight power within the British political system, first because of the political ascendancy of the Tory machine of the Dundas family, and in the nineteenth century because of continuing imbalances in provincial representation at Westminster. Even before the West Indian triumph of 1833 turned their attention to the more elusive goal of emancipation in the South, Scots were in a peripheral political posi-

2 For parallels between the American and British antislavery movements, see H. R. Temperley, "The British and American Abolitionists Compared," in M. R. Duberman (ed.), *The Anti-Slavery Vanguard: New Essays on the Abolitionists* (Princeton: Princeton University Press, 1965), 343–61; H. R. Temperley, *British Anti-Slavery, 1833–1870* (London: Longman, 1972); B. Fladeland, *Men and Brothers: Anglo-American Anti-Slavery Cooperation* (Urbana: University of Illinois Press, 1972); C. Bolt, *The Anti-Slavery Movement and Reconstruction, 1833–1877* (London: Oxford University Press, 1969).

3 D. Daiches, *The Paradox of Scottish Culture: The Eighteenth Century Experience* (London: Oxford University Press, 1964), 37ff.

tion not unlike that of American abolitionists weakened by the federal system.

Although Scots could approach slavery with a detachment unthinkable for Americans, they did live in a society that historically had been very heavily committed to it. The importance of Scots in the Chesapeake trade is well known, but they also became busily involved in speculation in South Carolina and Florida.[4] Their flight at the Revolution—they were predominantly Loyalists[5]—only served to intensify Scotland's use of the West India colonies to absorb part of her perennial surplus of poor but highly educated young men. There is no sign that the flow of emigration would have ended if expansion into the virgin lands of Tobago, Demerara, Essequibo, and Berbice had not been checked by the abolition of the slave trade in 1806 and 1807. Like the northern United States, indeed, Scotland retained embarrassing links with slavery in the nineteenth century. The ruin of the West Indies and the Emancipation Act of 1833 affected neither the commitment of Scottish textiles to U.S. cotton, nor of Scottish refining to Cuban and Brazilian sugar.[6] In 1845, when Henry C. Wright criticized Scottish acceptance of southern church funds by quoting the apothegm "Is every Free Church to have a SLAVE-STONE in it?," he was playing on the inchoate fears of a Christian population that was painfully aware that most churches, however indirectly, already did.[7] For Scots as for Americans, the likelihood of complete moral disentanglement was slight, and the anxieties slavery fueled correspondingly great.

In spite of these similarities, most approaches to the study of the

4 H. Hamilton, *An Economic History of Scotland in the Eighteenth Century* (Oxford: Clarendon Press, 1963), 255–71; J. M. Price, "The Rise of Glasgow in the Chesapeake Tobacco Trade, 1707–1775," *William and Mary Quarterly*, XI (1954), 179–99; M. L. Robertson, "Scottish Commerce and the American War of Independence," *Economic History Review*, IX (1956), 123–31.

5 I. C. G. Graham, *Colonists from Scotland: Emigration to North America, 1707–1783* (Ithaca: Cornell University Press, 1956), 150–77; W. Brown, *The King's Friends: The Composition and Motives of the American Loyalist Claimants* (Providence: Brown University Press, 1965), *passim*.

6 R. Campbell, *Scotland Since 1707* (Oxford: Clarendon Press, 1965), 97–111; R. Botsford, "Scotland and the American Civil War" (Ph.D. dissertation, Edinburgh University, 1956), *passim*.

7 H. C. Wright, *The Dissolution of the American Union Demanded by Justice and Humanity, as the Incurable Enemy of Liberty* (Glasgow: David Russell, 1845), 40, quoting the Reverend Dr. John Duncan of the established Church of Scotland.

American controversy over slavery are unhelpful in the Scottish case. The critical discussion of slavery took so many forms, and came from so many quarters, at various points in Scottish history, that it is impossible to fit it all into a unitary pattern. Perhaps Americanists themselves have been too hasty in applying single interpretations to a complex phenomenon that took drastically different forms over a period of a century or more. In either case, most of their hypotheses on the antislavery movement can only be applied to the Scottish problem if they are modified to a point where they become unrecognizable.

The most relevant modern interpretation is the one offered by David Brion Davis in his two *Problem of Slavery* volumes.[8] He contends that the discussion of slavery was frequently a vehicle for arguing out issues which at first sight appear to be unconnected with it. Davis suggests that, at a time of rapid social and intellectual change, slavery became exposed to attack because of the luxuriant series of symbolic meanings it had acquired over the centuries. Slavery lacked the restraints traditional society had reputedly placed on authority. It became a nightmarish extreme of the impersonal hierarchy towards which the modern world was evolving. The self-doubts and anxieties of the very architects of a new industrial society could readily be eased by channeling them into a symbolic aggression against slavery. In Christian terms, too, slavery's long-standing metaphorical connection with sin made it a vehicle for resolving the tensions of evangelical generations whose primary interest was in the wider problems of guilt, accountability, free agency, declension, and personal salvation. The movement against slavery ultimately took on an ideological or institutional momentum of its own, as did the ongoing commitment of its supporters. But very few men and women, when they first took up the issue, were not responding to the tensions from which they suffered in a rapidly shifting social and religious matrix. Davis is the first to resolve the dichotomy between idea and society which has bedeviled work on antislavery and other reform movements. Yet the complexities of an

8 D. B. Davis, *The Problem of Slavery in Western Culture* (Ithaca: Cornell University Press, 1967), *passim*; D. B. Davis, *The Problem of Slavery in the Age of Revolution, 1770–1823* (Ithaca: Cornell University Press, 1975), 86, 227, 249–54, 262–73, 367–73, 377–78, 453ff.

approach which must so often rely on tracing unconscious historical connections are daunting. Davis has drawn us into a through-the-looking-glass world, where it can never be assumed that anything is what it seems to be, or that anyone who talks about slavery does not in fact mean something else.

Those Scots who discussed slavery critically in the eighteenth and nineteenth centuries often did mean something else, or perhaps rather something more, though these secondary levels of meaning were not always the ones to which Davis has pointed. This is not to imply that there is no place, in tracing abolitionist motives, for human pity for the slave. It does not mean that Scottish abolitionists, or any abolitionists, were hypocrites, or that they put the slavery controversy to use for their own selfish ends, though some of them doubtless did some of the time. It is perhaps most helpful to think in terms of the various functions performed by criticism of slavery.[9] Davis has suggested that it served principally to reduce the tensions created by a real revolution in social structure, and to soothe the intense religious anxieties incidental to conversion. In Scotland it had different functions at different times, and different functions for different individuals and different groups of people. Some were the functions outlined in the *Problem of Slavery* volumes, but others were either more specific, or even more general. This paper presents four illustrations of the kind of complexity involved. They are drawn from the scholars of Scotland's secular enlightenment—from some evangelical writers—from the critics of the *Edinburgh Review* group—and from the Scottish churches in the mid-nineteenth century.

The moral philosophers of the Scottish Enlightenment wrote and argued at length on black chattel slavery. Like American scholars, but unlike English ones, they filled a peculiar social position as a professional elite closely allied to the bar and the landed governing class.[10] One of the hallmarks of their work was their interest in

---

9 My use of this concept has been inspired partly by Jonathan Sarna's unpublished work on nineteenth-century missions to the Jews.

10 N. T. Phillipson, "Towards a Definition of the Scottish Enlightenment," in P. Fritz and D. Williams (eds.), *City and Society in the Eighteenth Century* (Toronto: Hakkert, 1973),

the nature of community, and they were fascinated by all social mechanisms different from those of contemporary Britain. Slavery especially intrigued them, and alarmed them, because it represented the negation of that individual autonomy they sought as a balance against the needs of whole societies. Some of their contributions to antislavery ideology, like Hutcheson's theory of benevolence, or Adam Smith's comment on utility in *The Wealth of Nations*, are well known.[11] They also attacked slavery in works on various other aspects of social structure, for instance in the exchange of David Hume and Robert Wallace on the demography of the ancient world, or in George Wallace's treatise on Scots law, which was borrowed by de Jaucourt for the "Slavery" entry in the Encyclopédie.[12] The ethics and expediency of slavery were canvassed repeatedly in the network of convivial and debating clubs which the major Scottish cities supported from the fifties onwards.[13] The treatises of Hume and Robert

125–47; N. T. Phillipson, "Culture and Society in the Eighteenth Century Province: The Case of Edinburgh and the Scottish Enlightenment," in L. Stone (ed.), *The University in Society* (2 vols.; Princeton: Princeton University Press, 1974), II, 407–408; N. T. Phillipson, "Lawyers, Landowners, and the Civic Leadership of Post-Union Scotland," *Judicial Review*, XXI (1976), 97–120.

11 F. Hutcheson, *Inquiry into the Original of our Ideas of Beauty and Virtue* (London: J. Darby, 1726); F. Hutcheson, *System of Moral Philosophy* (2 vols.; London: A. Millar, 1755), II, 202–12; A. Smith, *Inquiry into the Nature and Causes of the Wealth of Nations* (6th ed., reprinted, 2 vols.; London: Bohn's Standard Library, 1887), I, 82–83. On the Scots philosophers in general, see W. Sypher, "Hutcheson and the 'Classical' Theory of Slavery," *Journal of Negro History*, XXIV (1939), 263–80; Davis, *Problem of Slavery in Western Culture*, 374–78, 380, 433–38; C. Duncan Rice, *The Rise and Fall of Black Slavery* (London: Macmillan, 1975), 163–77.

12 D. Hume, "Of the Populousness of Antient Nations," in *Political Discourses* (2nd ed.; Edinburgh: Kincaid and Donaldson, 1752), 161–79; R. Wallace, *A Dissertation on the Numbers of Mankind in Antient Times, in which the Superior Populousness of Antiquity is Maintained* (Edinburgh: Hamilton and Balfour, 1753), 90–91, 168–207; G. Wallace, *A System of the Principles of the Law of Scotland* (Edinburgh: Hamilton and Balfour, 1760), I, 87–96. On George Wallace, see D. B. Davis, "New Side-Lights on Early Anti-Slavery Radicalism," *William and Mary Quarterly*, XXVIII (1971), 585–94, and on the Hume/Wallace controversy, see E. C. Mossner, *The Forgotten Hume: Le Bon David* (New York: Columbia University Press, 1953), 105–33.

13 Minutes and Papers of the Select Society, in Advocates' Mss., Scottish National Library, entries for January 21, February 1, 15, 1757, July 21, 1761; Minute Book of the Belles Lettres Society, *ibid.*, entries for July 6, 1759, January 4, April 25, May 8, 1760, January 22, February 5, 1762; Newtonian Society Minute Book, Ms. Gen. 1424, Edinburgh University Library, entry for September 28, 1761; *History of the Speculative Society of Edinburgh, from its Institution in 1765* (Edinburgh, published for the Society, 1845), Ch. VI, "The Subjects of Debate," topics of April 21, 1772, March 29, 1774, pp. 354, 356. See also pp. 342, 347, 348, 350, 359, 362, 364, 375, 379, 394, 396, 402, 410. On the clubs in general, see Phillipson, "Definition of Scottish Enlightenment," "Culture and Society," and "Lawyers, Landowners, and Civic Leadership"; also D. D. McElroy, *Scotland's Age of Improvement: A Survey of Eighteenth Cen-*

Wallace, for instance, had originally been papers read in such groups. Neither of these men was a professional academic, but the discussions of the clubs influenced and were influenced by the professors who were among their most active members. Their writings on moral philosophy, too, were in most cases the published version of lectures which had been faithfully taken down by generation after generation of Scottish students, complete with their critical content on slavery, and subsequently presented in the grammar schools. Well before the American Revolution, there must have been few Scots educated above the level of basic literacy who were not familiar with the enlightened indictment of slavery.

The most striking thing about this ferment of criticism is that it had no material effect. It left Scotland's institutional connection with colonial slavery untouched. It does not seem to have influenced the behavior of Scottish emigrants, even highly literate ones, however much their mentors had demonstrated that slavery was at odds with the individual autonomy underwritten by natural law. Admittedly learned Scottish criticism focused more often on classical antiquity, or on an abstract conception of the institution, than on the modern British colonies, but it is still extraordinary that it seems so seldom to have been taken literally.

The record of Scottish emigrants in the slave colonies was not a creditable one. As late as 1812, Samuel Taylor Coleridge could note that "of the overseers of the Slave-plantations in the West-Indies three out of four are Scotsmen, and the fourth is generally observed to have very suspicious cheekbones: and on the American Continent the . . . Whippers-in or Neger-Bishops, are either Scotchmen, or (monstro monstrosius!) the Americanized Descendants of Scotchmen."[14] But apart from their activities in the field, their high literacy and disciplined system of patronage gave them a disproportionate share of the posts as clerks, factors, bookkeepers, and

tury *Clubs and Societies* (Pullman, Wash.: Washington State University Press, 1969); J. Strang, *Glasgow and its Clubs* (London: Griffin, 1856); W. R. Humphries, "The First Aberdeen Philosophical Society," *Aberdeen Philosophical Society Transactions*, V (1938), 203–38.

14 K. Coburn (ed.), *The Notebooks of Samuel Taylor Coleridge* (London: Routledge and Kegan Paul, 1973), III, entry no. 4134 [1812].

managers on which the slave system depended. Once overseas, not even the most highly educated shrank from using and profiting from slave labor. One extreme example is James Bruce of Kinnaird, the explorer of Abyssinia, who did not think twice about accepting a white Irish slave as a present from the Bey of Tunis.[15] Archibald Dalzel, the first historian of Dahomey and brother of the first professor of Greek at Edinburgh, slipped easily into becoming a slavetrader and propagandist for the African lobby. Most of the emigrants who took jobs in one part or another of the tropical system simply assumed that social behavior beyond the line was exempted from all normal rules of morality.[16] An early instance of this sense of ethical remoteness is a young Scots lawyer who was living in Barbados in 1736, at the time of Court's conspiracy in Antigua. He hailed it as a reenactment of Catiline's conspiracy, which he hoped might become the subject of a new tragedy entitled *Antigua Preserv'd.*[17] He was unconcerned that the Court plot ended with thirty ringleaders being broken on the wheel, except insofar as this suggested further parallels with the case of Catiline. Both, as he remarked, had had their Fulvia. Late in the century, Captain Marjoribanks, a Scottish abolitionist poet, tried to dismiss all bookkeepers as "low and illiterate (for it is far from requisite that a book-keeper should be able to read) [and] many of them are desperadoes, fraudulent bankrupts, jailbirds, deserters from the troops, runaway seamen, and other vagabonds of all countries and denominations."[18] Yet even he could not deny that a few were "men of *birth,* education, spirit, or sensibility"; and he used the word "sensibility" in the way Henry Mackenzie, the "man of feeling," would have understood it, to denote receptiveness to the sufferings of others. Many of these emigrants to the Caribbean were

15 J. Bruce, *Travels to Discover the Source of the Nile, in the Years 1768, 1769, 1770, 1771, 1772, and 1773* (5 vols.; London: G. J. J. and J. Robinson, 1790), I, xxii.

16 I. A. Akinjogbin, "Archibald Dalzel: Slave Trader and Historian of Dahomey," *Journal of African History,* VII (1966), 67–68; L. K. Waldman, "An Unnoticed Aspect of Archibald Dalzel's The History of Dahomey," *Journal of African History,* VI (1965), 185–92; J. D. Fage (ed.), *The History of Dahomey an Inland Kingdom of Africa . . . by Archibald Dalzel* (1793: reprinted London: Frank Cass, 1967), 5–22.

17 T. Finlay to J. Macfarlane, December 14, 1736, Ms. 6412, f. 71, Pitfirrane Papers, Scottish National Library.

18 J. Marjoribanks, *Slavery: An Essay in Verse* (Edinburgh, 1792), reprinted in *The Mirror of Misery: or, Tyranny Exposed* (New York: Samuel Wood, 1814), 33n.

children of the Enlightenment, but they made no attempt whatsoever to translate its critique of slavery into practice.

This inconsistency would be unimportant, if it did not carry with it the inference that Scottish domestic discussions of slavery were aimed at solving some other problem. It was an inconsistency that was not challenged, or even perceived, until the late seventies. Though the explanation is less a conclusion than a hypothesis, the likely reason for criticism of slavery did not compel these critics of the clubs and colleges to question their own or their country's involvement with the institution. The Scottish philosophers, like their continental colleagues, were absorbed in seeking the point on the line between total liberty (or anarchy) and total subjection (or slavery) most favorable to the maintenance of community and human happiness. The critical discussion of slavery not only enabled them to make a metaphorical denunciation of unbridled authority in general. It also provided them with quasisociological evidence, drawn from field experience with an institution that was an extreme aberration in social structure, to help them deduce the degree of subjection most favorable to the healthy balance of their own society. This was the usual way in which they turned information from other societies and other ages to good scholarly use, and the opposite case was also true. The study of savagery provided complementary evidence on the social effect of what appeared to be total liberty.[19] Archibald Dalzel's *History of Dahomey*, for instance, was not just a proslavery tract: it was an informed comment on the inferences that modern social engineering might draw from the ordering of a savage society. Again, when William Julius Mickle acidly observed that Raynal's admiration for savages implied that "insensibility and happiness proceed in the same gradation, and of consequence the oyster is the happiest of all animals," his real concern was with his own age and his own civilization.[20] Total liberty was as

19 Compare, for instance, H. Home, Lord Kames, *Sketches in the History of Man* (2 vols; Edinburgh: W. Creech, 1774), and D. Doig, *Two Lectures on the Savage State, Addressed to the Late Lord Kames* (London: G. G. J. and J. Robinson, 1792). This problem is more fully explored in R. L. Meek, *Social Science and the Ignoble Savage* (Cambridge: Cambridge University Press, 1976).

20 W. J. Mickle (trans.), *The Lusiad: or the Discovery of India. An Epic Poem, Translated from the Portuguese of Luis de Camoens* (Oxford: Jackson and Lister, 1776), vn.

fascinating to the enlightened mind as total slavery; both seemed distasteful, and both were studied in the present and the past for the same reasons.

It was because criticism of slavery was part of an attempt to solve quite different problems that enlightened Scots could so easily abandon what appear to be antislavery convictions. This is why Henry Mackenzie, in the seventies, published *The Man of Feeling*, the key English text of sentimentality, and *Julia de Roubigné*, a novel with much antislavery content; but could, in 1794, pen a pamphlet demanding the maintenance of the slave trade.[21] It was also why James Boswell, like Archibald Dalzel, could be exposed to all the antislavery arguments of the Enlightenment, but remain convinced, notwithstanding his awe of Dr. Johnson, that even abolition of the trade was visionary.[22] Perhaps, too, it was why Robert Burns, whose favorite book next to the Bible was *The Man of Feeling*, could cheerfully contemplate taking a job as a West Indian overseer until the profits of the Kilmarnock edition made it unnecessary for him to leave Scotland.[23] Even slavery in their own time—hard, tangible institution though it was—was in the first instance criticized by the Scots as a scholarly abstraction. The same lessons could be learned from the structure of West Indian society as, say, from the Spartans' mistreatment of their helots. At least one author, incidentally the brother of the slavetrading historian of Dahomey, found room in his lectures to assess and denounce them both.[24]

The gap between theory and its application only began to close during and after the period of the Scottish counter-Enlightenment. One of the country's contributions to antislavery, and indeed to nineteenth-century reform in general, was the philosophy of common sense, itself a reaction against the skeptical and idealist thought of the Enlightenment proper. Neither its founder Thomas Reid nor its popularizer Dugald Stewart wrote extensively on slav-

21 H. W. Thompson, *A Scottish Man of Feeling* (London: Oxford University Press, 1931), 150–51, 262.

22 Apart from the obvious references in the *Life of Johnson*, see Boswell's splendid poem, *No Abolition of Slavery: Or, the Universal Empire of Love* (London: R. Faulder, 1791).

23 H. Mackenzie, *The Man of Feeling*, ed. B. Vickers (London: Oxford University Press, 1970), vii.

24 A. Dalzel, *Substance of Lectures on the Ancient Greeks* (2 vols.; Edinburgh: A. Constable, posthumously published, 1821), I, 246–51, 269.

ery itself; but their assumption of an intuitively knowable and universally applicable series of moral rules became a fundamental underpinning of evangelical reform, abolitionism included.[25] Even in the eighteenth century, there are hints that common sense was beginning to raise questions about the entirely different canons of ethics applied to society at home and society in the tropical colonies.

In the last quarter of the century, a trickle of Scottish emigrants began to come back from the West Indies seriously doubtful about the morality of slavery. Four of them—Zachary Macaulay, James Ramsay, William Dickson, and James Stephen the Elder—became figures of real importance in the British campaign against the slave trade. Of these, only Macaulay was not closely associated with the teachers of common sense, and even he, before he was sent to Jamaica in disgrace, had found bottle companions of his own age among Glasgow students who were the pupils of Thomas Reid. While Reid was still at King's College in Aberdeen, before his *Inquiry into the Human Mind* brought him a chair at Glasgow, one of his pupils, later a close friend, had been young James Ramsay. The latter attended King's while another of his lifelong friends, James Beattie, was a student at Marischal. Beattie later became the celebrated author of the pseudo–common sense *Essay on Truth*, "the David," as Benjamin Rush put it, "who slew [Voltaire] that giant of infidelity."[26] As a professor at Marischal College, Beattie in his turn became a teacher of James Stephen. In later life, too, he was constantly in touch with his admirer William Dickson, a Barbadian emigrant from Dumfriess-shire who returned to become "the Clarkson of Scotland."[27]

Probably such individual connections are coincidental. We do

25 On the importance of common sense, see S. A. Grave, *The Scottish Philosophy of Common Sense* (Oxford: Clarendon Press, 1960); D. H. Meyer, *The Instructed Conscience: The Shaping of the American National Ethic* (Philadelphia: University of Pennsylvania Press, 1972), 35–42; S. Ahlstrom, "The Scottish Philosophy and American Theology," *Church History*, XXIV (1955), 257–72; D. W. Howe, "American Victorianism as a Culture," *American Quarterly*, XXVII (1975), 524.

26 Rush to J. Kidd, May 13, 1794, in L. Butterfield (ed.), *Letters to Benjamin Rush* (2 vols.; Princeton: Princeton University Press, 1951), II, 748.

27 M. M. Bevington (ed.), *The Memoirs of James Stephen, Written by Himself for the Use of his Children* (London: Hogarth Press, 1954), 179–80; M. Forbes, *Beattie and his Friends* (London: A. Constable, 1904), 266.

not yet have full biographies of these men, and although they doubtless shared the uniformity of ethical expectations that informed the common sense writings they admired, the urgency of their concern over slavery stemmed from their experiences in religious conversion. In that sense they are transitional figures between the generations of the Enlightenment and the first generation of evangelical reform. But insofar as these first few Scots who translated criticism into commitment were influenced by secular teachers, their mentors were those of provincial, counterenlightened Aberdeen. It was natural that they should show little dependence on the skeptical, cosmopolitan world of enlightened Edinburgh, though it had been canvassing a fully developed critique of slavery since the middle of the century. Scotland's secular enlightenment had examined and criticized slavery to solve different problems and meet different needs from those of the early evangelical abolitionists.

For Scottish evangelicals, as for English and American ones, criticism of the institution and the activist commitment to get rid of it were inseparable. By the late eighties, in fact, the whole tenor of Scotland's religious life was changing. The "Ice-Age of Moderatism" had ended.[28] It was no longer the heyday of the clerical princes of the Enlightenment, like Jupiter Carlyle of Inveresk, or the historian Principal William Robertson, whose dalliance with skeptics had so titillated the young Benjamin Rush. As James Beattie once complained, they had been prone to talk "of the eternal concerns of mankind, with a frigidity and languour which a good economist would be ashamed of, in bargaining for half a dozen haddocks."[29] As the century ended, however, by a process that has never been fully explained, the whole balance of intellect in the established Church of Scotland shifted away from the moderate or rationalist party to the evangelical descendants of the old High-flyers or orthodox Calvinists. The academic detachment with which the Enlightenment had discussed problems of social organization, themselves exten-

---

28 G. Yuille, *History of the Baptists in Scotland from Pre-Reformation Times* (Glasgow: Baptist Union, n.d.), 55.

29 Beattie to T. Blacklock, August 1, 1768, in Box I uncatalogued, Acc. 4792, Fettercairn Papers Second Deposit, Scottish National Library.

sions of Beattie's "eternal concerns," became unfashionable. In general it became difficult to discuss the defects of social and religious institutions without feeling a moral imperative to remove them. This was uniquely true of the problem of slavery. An extreme example is the career of Zachary Macaulay, entirely devoted to antislavery after his conversion and return from Jamaica in 1792.[30] By the 1820s, Macaulay was arguing that the French government should punish violators of its legislation against the slave trade with galley slavery or public flogging.[31] That the commitment of an intrinsically humane man could reach an intensity where he wished to substitute one barbarism for another is a measure of the overriding symbolic importance of slavery in the evangelical mind.

One example of slavery's connection with the more fundamental concerns of evangelicals is a pamphlet published in 1796 by Dr. William Innes. Innes began his career in Stirling as a Presbyterian minister, but he was one of many evangelicals who became a Congregationalist in 1800 after being involved in the Haldane revivals. He moved into the Baptist connection soon afterwards. For him slavery was simply one of the many symbols of the way in which "the gratifications obtained from sensible objects" were spreading corruption through society. He was equally appalled by distorted wealth and distorted power. "Gold" had the same resonance for him, the same emotive impact as "slavery," and he found them equally potent as symbols of aberration from a morally ordered society. The only force which could counter them was "the harmonizing principle that supports the universe, the voice of God in the soul of man; it stamps upon the soul *mildness, meekness, humanity.*" Man's natural tendency to benevolence was the divine means of correcting such abuses. He who gave the tendency free rein would win "a compleat victory over all those passions that domineer over unhappy mortals." The good man, anticipating Macaulay, then forgot his own benevolence so far as to observe that slavery "is a crime so monstrous against the human species, that all who practice it, deserve to be

---

30 Viscountess Knutsford, *Life and Letters of Zachary Macaulay* (London: E. Arnold, 1900); C. Booth, *Zachary Macaulay* (London: Longmans, 1934).
31 Macaulay to Sir Charles Stuart, December 26, 1823, Ms. 6228, f. 549, in Stuart de Rothesay Papers, Scottish National Library.

extirpated from the face of the earth."[32] He was only brought to such malevolence by anxiety over the hindrances presented to the building of a meek gospel society, by the multiform types of excessive power and excessive wealth. In this instance, consciously or otherwise, Innes made slavery their symbol. It is not likely that it was of more direct concern to him. Though he became one of Scotland's leading Baptists, he did not appear in the movement for another thirty-five years, when he published a pamphlet on the value of Liberia as a base for African missions.[33]

A second motive for evangelical criticism of slavery, one which was probably much stronger than we will ever be able to prove, flowed from a general concern over Christian free agency. Evangelicals were by no means in agreement about the problem of liberty and necessity, but all were convinced of the dangers of having spiritual free-will circumscribed by earthly agencies. Slavery was the extreme case of interference with the choices, narrow or wide as they might be, which God had left open to moral beings. Attacking slavery thus became a means of arguing for the importance of leaving Christians unimpeded in their free agency under God. Later American literature, too, often argued that the master had presumed to replace the Deity by becoming an arbiter who could deny the slave the free choices which were his means of becoming regenerate and maintaining his progress towards self-improvement. In Scottish sources the theme often remains implicit, but it emerges splendidly in a pamphlet published early in 1833 by James Douglas of Cavers. It would have been out of the question for Douglas to accept the right of any institution to deny individual free agency. He was a Roxburghshire laird of great wealth and deep piety, who had been influenced by the aftermath of the Haldane revivals. It was through his offices that the "Cavers Missioners" planted Congregationalist churches throughout the Borders.[34] Douglas was a prolific writer of

32 [W. Innes], *Important and Interesting Observations on the Abolition of the Slave Trade . . . to Which is Added, a Short Extract and General Idea of the Political Principles of the Celebrated Fenelon Archbishop of Cambray* (Edinburgh: Constable, 1796), 5, 8, 15, 21.

33 W. Innes, *Liberia; or the Early History and Signal Preservation of the American Colony of Free Negroes on the Coast of Africa. Compiled from American Documents* (Edinburgh: Waugh and Innes, 1831).

34 H. Escott, *A History of Scottish Congregationalism* (Glasgow: Scottish Congregational Union, 1960), 334.

devotional, revivalist, and reform materials, and his piece on slavery was not part of a lifetime commitment to abolition. In 1833, however, he seems to have found it the most suitable vehicle for presenting a major point about the relationship between earthly authority and spiritual free agency. In slavery "the great question of liberty and necessity is solved," Douglas wrote. "The freedom of man is at an end, he is actuated not from within, but from without. . . . the cart-whip . . . is the *primum mobile* of them all."[35] For Douglas, the slaveholder's crime was his presumption in taking on the role of God. Slavery had become the symbol of all illegitimate authority obstructing free moral choices under God, without which grace could not be achieved.

Even in the moment of its downfall, slavery retained a specific significance for evangelicals. Perhaps not least because thirty-three, the last two digits of the date when West India legislation was secured, was the age at which Christ died, it was tempting to draw parallels between the atonement and the emancipation. This emerges superbly from a "Jubilee Sermon" written by Dr. Ralph Wardlaw, the most important Scottish Congregationalist of the nineteenth century, and indeed a major figure in the history of his denomination in Britain. On August 1, 1834, Wardlaw preached on Leviticus 25: 8–9—"in the day of atonement shall ye make the trumpet sound throughout the land." His account of the meaning that slavery and freedom held in the evangelical mind was quite explicit. At its simplest, the act of emancipation was itself an atonement, an act of propitiation for national guilt, the guilt of West Indian involvement and the guilt of sinfulness in general: "I am a firm believer . . . in the principle of national guilt . . . this day I seem myself to breathe more easily, as if the heavy sulphurous atmosphere of a gathering storm of divine retribution had been dispelled from over . . . the land of my father's sepulchres." Wardlaw went on to expand on the connection between slavery and sin, emancipation and atonement. All men were disinherited and enchained, "slaves of sin, bondmen of Satan." For humanity at large, the acceptance of the

35 J. Douglas, *Slavery, Sabbath Observance, and Church Reform* (Edinburgh: A. & C. Black, 1833), 3–4.

gospel in Christ made possible by his atonement *was* the jubilee of emancipation. In this forest of evangelical symbols, the eschatalogical importance of liberty for the slaves was that it was conflated with national redemption.

With this groundwork laid, Wardlaw moved to an even more extraordinary level of meaning. For the slaves themselves, earthly emancipation was beginning rather than end, for their true slavery remained intact—"the vast majority of them, alas, are slaves still. They need another emancipation,—the emancipation proclaimed by the Gospel Jubilee . . . while we exult in their temporal freedom, let us not abandon them to a worse and more permanent bondage."[36] Christian missions were essential to begin the real work of liberation. The symbolic use of the concept of slavery had gone through a complete process of inversion in Wardlaw's mind. Temporal bondage had originally been attacked as the symbol of spiritual bondage, but the latter was now to be attacked through missionary efforts for which the emotive fuel was the symbolic force of the former.

These three pamphlets give some impression of the range of Christian concerns which Scottish evangelicals focused on the problem of slavery. There are many more examples, of which the best known is the untitled pamphlet which David Davis suggests tipped the Atlantic movement into its immediatist phase. It was the report of a speech delivered in 1830 by Dr. Andrew Thomson, then the leader of the evangelical party in the established Church of Scotland, and the foremost spokesman of its campaign against the improper use of patronage. At the level of simple social morality, it is clear that Thomson saw both patronage and slaveholding as aberrations, where propertyholding had encroached on areas which were not susceptible to human ownership. The urgency with which he wished to get rid of both, however, was not merely political. Thomson began to demand immediate emancipation because of demonstrable anxiety over individual accountability. Slavery, he thundered, "cannot be persevered in by us, or receive countenance from

---

36 R. Wardlaw, *The Jubilee: a Sermon Preached in West George Street Chapel, Glasgow, on Friday, August 1st, 1834, the Memorable Day of Negro Emancipation in the British Colonies* (Glasgow: A. Fullarton, 1834), 26, 16, 17–18, 34.

us, without involving us in moral guilt."[37] The success of the cause
would be a paradigm for personal as well as national purification.
Once again, the frontal attack on slavery provided a means of releasing the energies and soothing the tensions incidental to evangelical commitment. Men and women who conflated slavery and
sin, and who were beset with anxieties over their own free agency,
accountability, and redemption, could not afford to deplore the Negro's condition and leave him in chains. The Enlightenment's distinction between critique and commitment was, for them, unthinkable.

The moral imperative against slavery was by no means invariably linked with religion. At times what appears to be Christian
fervor was an overlay for wholly secular concerns. This is nowhere
more true than in the writing of the Edinburgh reviewers, a group of
liberal Whig intellectuals, the foundation of whose magazine in
1802 revolutionized British and indeed American critical journalism. A striking example of their attitude is the famous passage by
Henry, Lord Brougham, one of Scotland's most prominent abolitionists and ultimately Lord Chancellor: "Tell me not of rights—
talk not of the property of the planter in his slaves . . . there is a law
above all the enactments of human codes—the same throughout the
world, the same in all times . . . it is the law written on the heart of
man by the finger of his Maker, and by that law, unchangeable and
eternal, while men despise fraud, and loathe rapine, they will reject
with indignation the wild and guilty phantasy, that man can hold
property in man!"[38]

Brougham was as religious as a turnip, and the urgency of his
response to slavery was not spiritual. Like most other social and
political theorists of his generation, he was confident that free labor,
in conditions of open competition, would ultimately oust slavery.
Early in his career, like other critics of the slave trade, he had as-

---

37  A. Thomson, *Substance of the Speech Delivered at the Meeting of the Edinburgh Society for the Abolition of Slavery* (Edinburgh: published by the Society, 1830), 4; D. B. Davis,
"The Emergence of Immediatism in British and American Anti-Slavery Thought," *Mississippi
Valley Historical Review*, XLIX (1962), 209–30. See also J. W. Craven, "Andrew Thomson
(1779–1831): Leader of the Evangelical Revival in Scotland" (Ph.D. dissertation, Edinburgh
University, 1955).
38  *Works of Henry Lord Brougham* (12 vols.; London: R. Griffin, 1857), XI, 216.

sumed that emancipation was politically unattainable, perhaps even politically undesirable in the short term, but that it would in time be achieved by the forces of history.[39] But he conceived the economic world in unitary terms. Any part of the whole which was organized on idiosyncratic principles, however much it was historically doomed, could only work to retard the progress of the rest. Where the Enlightenment had been prepared to admit the need for special social arrangements adapted to the requirements of special local interests, the holistic assumptions of thinkers like Brougham made them acutely anxious about deviations from commonly applicable social and economic principles. This concern is nowhere more evident than among the *Edinburgh Review* group, of whom Brougham was an important member, and by far the most prolific contributor on slavery.[40] From entirely secular premises, Brougham and the other reviewers gradually came to see slavery as the most offensive anomaly of all, the symbolic opposite of every precept of nineteenth-century social engineering.

In this they went beyond their acknowledged mentors, the classical economists. Smith's criticism of slavery, in *The Wealth of Nations*, had only been a gloss, and indeed scholars like Ricardo and Mill, who built on his work, really paid little attention to the problem. At the turn of the century, however, Francis Jeffrey and the young reviewers moved in the same liberal circle as James Anderson of Monkshill, a Scottish agronomist of considerable importance.[41] His magazine, the *Bee*, which was published in Edinburgh from 1790–1794, was an extraordinary potpourri of papers on the science of progress, suffused with faith that the principles of that science could be and should be applied in all ages and all societies.[42] In the

39 *An Inquiry into the Colonial Policy of the European Powers,* (2 vols.; Edinburgh: Balfour, Manners, and Miller, 1803), II, 497–520.

40 On the *Review,* see J. Clive, *Scotch Reviewers: The Edinburgh Review, 1802–1815* (Cambridge, Mass.: Harvard University Press, 1957); J. A. Greig, *Francis Jeffrey of the Edinburgh Review* (Edinburgh: Oliver and Boyd, 1947); C. G. New, *The Life of Henry Brougham to 1830* (Oxford: Clarendon Press, 1961), 21–31, 119–45, 283–304. I have treated this aspect of the *Review* a little more fully in "Enlightenment, Evangelism, and Economics in an Interpretation of the Drive towards British West India Emancipation," in *Annals of the New York Academy of Sciences,* CCXCII (1977), 123–32.

41 E. Fletcher, *Autobiography* (Boston: Roberts Bros., 1876), 82.

42 C. F. Mullett, "A Village Aristotle and the Harmony of Interests: James Anderson (1739–1808) of Monks Hill," *Journal of British Studies,* VIII (1968), 94–118; C. F. Mullett, "The *Bee* (1790–1794); "A Tour of Crotchet Castle," *South Atlantic Quarterly,* LXVI (1967), 70–86.

year of the French Revolution, to the alarm of his subscribers, Anderson had produced a pamphlet carefully outlining slavery's disjunction from the system of incentives behind normative economic behavior. It was only when liberty had given every man command over his own actions that the principle of "self-love" or self-respect could operate freely and constructively for the industry and welfare of society at large.[43] Anderson was a humorless and scatterbrained crackpot, but he was the only Scottish writer whose intolerance of slavery *qua* anomaly led him to anticipate the secularized moral imperative of the reviewers.

The *Edinburgh*, most frequently in the person of Brougham himself, was less exercised over slavery for its own sake, than over its departure from principles of social and economic organization which it considered universally valid and universally binding. It was not just that it feared the power of slavery's evil example, or its tendency to draw capital out of natural channels, or to throw produce on the market at artificial prices. It was not primarily concerned with the cruelty of slavery, though it did not ignore it, and even during the attack on the slave trade it was not critical of "that sentimental sonorous philanthropy by which the cause of humanity has been so often exposed to ridicule."[44] The strongest case against slavery was that its sytem of incentives, its conception of property, and its denial of economic free agency were at odds with a metropolitan image of labor relations which it was now thought imperative to apply universally.

The *Review*'s attitude hardened during the thirty years between its foundation and the Emancipation Act. It was uncomprehending of West Indian agruments that tropical agriculture could not be carried on in the same way as other economic enterprises. It soon began to demand that the planters be forced to accelerate the inevitable transition away from slavery, and their own ultimate downfall, by the various "ameliorating measures." The magazine's central assumption, which did have partial coloring in fact, was that only the obstinacy of the slaveholders prevented them from rising to a higher

43 J. Anderson, *Observations on Slavery; Particularly with a View to its Effects on the British Colonies, in the West-Indies* (Manchester: J. Harrop, 1789), 5–7 and *passim*.
44 *Edinburgh Review*, IV (July, 1804), 477.

prosperity by applying the system of labor incentives that governed economic life at home. It was a short step to call upon government to demolish the whole anomalous structure from the center. Yet the *Edinburgh*'s last article before the emancipation took great care to explain that such losses as the planters' might suffer were a fair outcome of their failure to adopt and observe the same values as other subjects of the empire. Forcibly removing the slaves from their power through emancipation was a last resort, after every more gentle device had been tried to bring them into conformity.[45] The reviewers anticipated the mind-set of Victorian Britain in assuming, not only that the principles of social and economic organization were immutable and universally applicable, but that it was a matter of duty to ensure that they *were* applied universally. Slavery, as a glaring deviation from these principles, could no longer be tolerated. If it had merely been cruel, or unjust, or at odds with the Golden Rule, it might well have been let alone.

In mid-Victorian Scotland, the discussion of slavery took on new forms. Though it was still used as a vehicle for working out deeper religious and social concerns, antislavery controversy took on a greater importance than ever before as a means of expressing denominational rivalries. The slave became an unwitting pawn in sectarian tensions with historical roots deeper than those of abolitionism. Slavery's morality and the need for eradicating it were no longer at issue. After the safe passage of the Apprenticeship Act in 1838, slavery outside the empire was probably a less forceful symbol of evangelical anxieties, but it remained threatening to deeply religious men and women accustomed to thinking in cosmic terms. It was generally agreed that it was still the duty of good men and women to work for abolition throughout the world, especially in the United States. Unfortunately, Britons were no more able than their American colleagues to agree as to the means of carrying on the campaign. After 1841, they split along lines directly reflecting the divisions in the movement across the Atlantic. The principal split was between the radical old organization, or Garrisonian party,

45 *Ibid.*, XLV (December, 1826), 174–89, XLVI (October, 1827), 490–97; LV (January, 1832), 144–82, especially 169–71.

which was heavily represented in Scotland, Ireland, and the English provinces, and the more conservative new group represented principally by the London-based British and Foreign Anti-Slavery Society.[46] The movement's fragmentation went right down to the smallest local societies. The reaction of the Scots was to start using these antislavery feuds as a means of promoting rivalries that had nothing to do with what was happening in America.

It was nothing new for the slavery issue to surface in controversies between rival ideological, political, or economic groups. As early as 1791, Burns's radical friend James Maxwell of Paisley had used the Negro to float an execrable poem on "cursed Aristocracy." Sixty years later, a highlander who had been forced to emigrate to Canada with his people, was able to use the Duchess of Sutherland's friendship with Harriet Beecher Stowe as a means of denouncing the evictions of tenants by her husband and other landowners in the Clearances.[47] In Britain as a whole, slavery was intriguing to all political persuasions. For reformers, it was a distressing flaw in a republican society which might otherwise be held up for emulation. For conservatives, it confirmed their darkest suspicions about republics and made it clear that "democrats may be tyrants, that an aristocracy of caste is more oppressive than an aristocracy of station."[48]

Slavery was also a ready weapon for use in religious infighting. James Beattie, the evangelical, common-sense philosopher, greedily seized the chance to discredit his moderate and skeptical enemies by attacking David Hume's throwaway footnote on black inferiority.[49] Fifty years later, an anonymous clergymen of the established

46 Temperley, British Anti-Slavery, 208–20.
47 On the Prolongation of the Slave Trade (Paisley: Broadsheet, 1791); D. McLeod, Gloomy Memories in the Highlands of Scotland: Versus Mrs. Stowe's Sunny Memories in (England) a Foreign Land: or a Faithful Picture of the Highlands of Scotland (Toronto: Thompson & Co., 1857). See also G. A. Shepperson, "Harriet Beecher Stowe and Scotland," Scottish Historical Review, XXXII (1953), 40–46; F. J. Klingberg, "Harriet Beecher Stowe and Social Reform in England," American Historical Review, XLIII (1938), 542–54.
48 N. W. Senior, American Slavery: a Reprint of an Article on "Uncle Tom's Cabin," of which a Portion was Inserted in the 206th Number of the "Edinburgh Review" (London: Longman, Brown, 1856), 38–39.
49 An Essay on the Nature and Immutability of Truth, in Opposition to Sophistry and Scepticism (2nd ed.; Edinburgh: Kincaid and Bell, 1771), 507–12; D. Hume, "Of National Characters," Essays Moral, Political, and Literary (1754 ed.; London: World's Classics, 1903), 205n. Cf. Hume, "Of the Populousness of Antient Nations," 161–79.

Church of Scotland, then under fierce attack from seceders opposed to religious establishments and therefore fond of pointing to American examples, reprinted Barnes's *Picture of Slavery in the United States* to illustrate the dangers of religious dissent. The toleration of slavery, the Scottish introduction announced firmly, was just another of "the brutal deeds of American republicanism and Voluntaryism."[50] After the movement divided in 1841, however, the Scots went beyond using the simple dichotomy between being for or against slavery. They now assumed total agreement over the need to help the cause in America, but they continued to express the bitter feuds of their chaotic church life through this whole new series of disagreements—not disagreements over the right or wrong of slavery, but over the tactical means by which it should be attacked, and the American allies through whom British support should properly be channeled.

The most striking example of this sort is the furious controversy over the Free Church of Scotland, which broke out soon after the so-called Disruption of 1843.[51] In that year the Free Kirk broke away from the Old or established Kirk of Scotland, ostensibly over the problem of patronage. In its efforts to gather money to replace the stipends and church buildings it had left in the grip of the Erastians, the new group accepted substantial sums from the American South. Though the Free Church was the descendant of the evangelical wing of the Church of Scotland, and none of its ministers was in any sense proslavery, this flew directly in the face of the normal antislavery assumption that there should be no pastoral connection with slaveholders and/or their sympathizers. Three radical American abolitionists—Henry C. Wright, Frederick Douglass, and William Lloyd Garrison himself—therefore descended on Scotland to bring the Free Church back to its duty.

The American visitors could hardly have attracted more unlikely

---

50 *Picture of Slavery in the United States of America: being a Practical Illustration of Voluntaryism and Republicanism* (Glasgow: University Press, 1835), 5.

51 G. A. Shepperson, "Frederick Douglass and Scotland," *Journal of Negro History*, XXXVIII (1953), 307–21; G. A. Shepperson, "Thomas Chalmers, the Free Church of Scotland, and the South," *Journal of Southern History*, XVII (1951), 517–37; G. A. Shepperson, "The Free Church of Scotland and American Slavery," *Scottish Historical Review*, XXX (1951), 126–43; C. Duncan Rice, "The Scottish Factor in the Fight Against American Slavery" (Ph.D. dissertation, Edinburgh University, 1969), 243–61.

allies. At least Garrison and Wright were known for heterodox
views, but this did not prevent members of the deeply conservative
Old Kirk from joining with them in attacking their archenemy the
Free Church. One establishment minister concluded to his satisfac-
tion that the whole incident was of a piece with the conduct of a
denomination that had striven to "rob servant girls of the hard-won
money that ought to have gone for ribbons and gum-flowers, and
washerwomen of their savings-banks accumulations."[52] Even this
could not match the glee with which the Americans were supported
by ministers from the old voluntary or secession churches, which
had been engaged in continual controversy with the leaders of the
Free Church before their own departure from the establishment in
1843.[53] In turn, Free Church leaders were only too glad to turn the
controversy back on their voluntary and established enemies, who
had exposed their flanks by their mutual alliance with one another
and with Americans known to be infidels and Sabbath-breakers. No
voluntary could give a reputable reason for their sudden alliance
with a church which "you denigrate as enslaved, and bondaged, and
erastianised." Once again, the Free Church conviction was that this
kind of behavior was only to be expected from its enemies. It even
pointed to their provincialism. One of them, it was noted, had gotten his degree "from a log-college in the Western States." Should he
therefore, by analogy with the Free Church money, "send back the
degree?"[54] Neither the degree nor the money was ever sent back,
but the controversy is an extraordinary example of the way in which

52 *Fifeshire Journal* [*of 7th and 14th May, 1846*]. *Send Back the Money* (Dundee: Broadsheet, 1846).
53 Minutes for November 18, 1844, Glasgow Emancipation Society Minute Books,
Mitchell Library, Glasgow, Vol. III; *Glasgow Argus*, November 21, 1844; *Scottish Guardian*,
November 22, 1844; *Witness*, November 27, 1844; G. Gilfillan, *The Debasing and De-
moralising Influence of Slavery on All and on Everything Connected with it. A Lecture* (Edinburgh: Free Church Anti-Slavery Society, 1847); G. Jeffrey, *The Pro-Slavery Character of the
American Churches, and the Sin of Holding Christian Communion with them* (Edinburgh:
Free Church Anti-Slavery Society, 1847).
54 *Northern Warder*, February 12, 1846; *The Free Church and Slavery ... a Series of
Papers from the Dundee Courier* (Dundee: Dundee Courier, 1846); *Relation of the Free Church
to the American Churches: Speeches Delivered at the Free Synod of Angus and Mearns* (Dundee: Dundee Courier, 1846); J. Macnaughton, *The Free Church and American Slavery: Slan-
ders against the Free Church Met and Answered* (Paisley: Alex Gardner, 1846), 8; A. Cameron,
*The Free Church and her Accusers in the Matter of American Slavery* (Edinburgh: John
Johnstone, 1846), 31.

disagreements over antislavery tactics could be conflated with other tensions.

It is unlikely that the disputants in the Free Church affair were "using" slavery on behalf of their interest groups in a conscious or sinister way. Deviation from correct principles on slavery readily became part of a wider series of accusations, even if these correct principles were subconsciously and subtly chosen to provide opposites of the ones adhered to by rivals. The disagreement over slavery could certainly furnish quarreling groups with justification in the eyes of neutrals, but it probably had a more important role in providing psychological reassurance, a kind of self-persuasion that loyalties chosen were in fact the correct ones. What appears as the use of slavery as a stick to beat rivals disliked for other social, political, or religious reasons must often have been a simpler reaction. In a society totally agreed that slavery was an enormity, there was much comfort in the reaffirmation that suspect views on slavery were just what one might have expected from a scoundrel like opponent X. It would have been just as encouraging to reflect that he drank, or beat his wife, or patronized whorehouses, but in evangelical circles it was seldom possible to do so, at least in public.

If there is a generalization about those Scots who criticized slavery, it is that they often meant something more when they did so. This is not to imply that they were insincere when they expressed compassion for the poor slave. On the contrary, the importance of the wider concerns which focused their attention on slavery is that they opened the way to a real perception of its misery and injustice. It is not raising "the ghost of Couplands past"[55] to suggest that once the facts about slavery were known, pity alone brought recruits to the cause of abolition. But different men and women reached the point of considering these facts and acting upon them by different ways, for slavery had a different significance for different people, and a different significance at different times and in different places. It is

55 James Walvin of the University of York, speaking from the floor at the May, 1976, New York Academy of Sciences Conference on Comparative Slave Systems. Walvin was referring to Sir Reginald Coupland, the great imperial historian from Oxford, whose Whig/evangelical interpretation of the British antislavery movement is now in rather worse odor than it deserves.

not wholly fair to separate Scottish critics of slavery into these four illustrative groups, for in real life their perceptions overlapped. Doubtless, for instance, the leaders of the Free Church were still driven by some of the anxieties of the early nineteenth century. The common-sense philosophers and the reviewers, again, certainly retained the fascination of the Enlightenment for slave societies as sociological laboratories. But the general point remains. Slavery in history has been all things to all men. This conclusion may be less a generalization than an antigeneralization, but it is as applicable to the study of abolitionists in North America or England as in Scotland.

# Religion

# ABOLITION AS A
# SACRED VOCATION

*Donald M. Scott*

A NEW KIND of antislavery activism emerged in the 1830s: immediate abolition which, in David Donald's words, was "so different in tone, method, and membership from its predecessors and its successor."[1] What distinguished the immediatists of the thirties was the single-minded fervor of their advocacy and the radicalism of their position. Insisting that slavery was sin and that immediate emancipation was the starting point of any genuine antislavery program, they pushed abolition at every opportunity and demanded total compliance with their immediatist posture. There have been, of course, numerous attempts to analyze this abolitionism. In 1933, Gilbert Barnes stressed the involvement of many abolitionists in the fervent revivalism of the 1820s, and many later historians have explored the connections between evangelicalism and abolitionism. Some historians have tried to explain immediate abolition by attempting to discover common characteristics of class, status, and affiliation among the abolitionists, while still others have used a variety of psychosocial models to assess their motivation. In this essay, however, I approach the immediatism of the 1830s from a

1 David Donald, "Toward a Reconsideration of Abolitionists," in Donald (ed.), *Lincoln Reconsidered: Essays on the Civil War Era* (New York: Random House, 1956), 21–22.

51

somewhat different angle of vision, as a form of commitment, an act of adherence to a set of ideas which then shaped the adherent's identity and behavior.[2] From this perspective, immediatism can best be understood as a form of vocation: the immediate abolitionists of the 1830s considered emancipation their essential life-work and derived their basic self-definition and esteem from this role.

Abolitionist commitment thus involved a conscious decision to enlist oneself in the campaign to rid the nation of slavery. What was the nature of this decision, what experiences and institutions shaped it, under what circumstances and through what processes was the abolitionist commitment forged and what was its character? This essay addresses these questions by examining the emergence during the 1830s of one particular group of activists. Much of the abolitionist cadre of the thirties had a confessional relationship to evangelicalism. They had previously experienced conversion and had been inducted into a structure of Christian duty when they committed themselves to immediatism and made it the focal point of their Christian devotion and service. Moreover, a substantial portion of the abolition activists and leaders had experienced a call to the gospel ministry and were either ministers or were in the midst of preparing themselves for it when they were converted to immediatist doctrine. It is upon this group that I focus my attention and I have drawn my portrait of the formation of abolitionist commitment from the ministry which derived from eighteenth-century New England and which, under the Plan of Union of 1801, used Congregational and Presbyterian forms to extend its sway far beyond New England.

Not all abolitionists were evangelicals, nor was there a single path to immediatism. Evangelical laymen like the Tappens and James Birney became abolitionists without any earlier involvement

2 The character of abolitionist commitment is discussed in Sylvan Tomkins, "The Psychology of Commitment: The Constructive Role of Violence and Suffering for the Individual and His Society," in Martin Duberman (ed.), *The Antislavery Vanguard: New Essays on the Abolitionists* (Princeton: Princeton University Press, 1965), 270–98; Martin Duberman, "The Northern Response to Slavery," in Duberman (ed.), *The Antislavery Vanguard,* 295–316; and Gerald Sorin, *The New York Abolitionists: A Case Study of Political Radicalism* (Westport, Conn.: Greenwood Press, 1971). Michael Walzer, "Puritanism as a Revolutionary Ideology," *History and Theory,* V (1964), 59–90, contains a suggestive analysis of the relationship between religious experience and the formation of radical political commitments.

with the ministry, and female abolitionists, many of whom were evangelicals, did not emerge from clerical traditions. Activists were also recruited from those who had never been converted, and some came to anti-slavery out of roles as reformers, publicists, and educators—roles which, in some instances, they appear to have adopted partly out of an inability to have a conversion experience.[3] Thus, in its particular dimensions the notion of abolition as a sacred vocation developed herein describes only immediatists of the New England strain. But I hope that the broader notion of abolitionism as a form of vocational commitment fusing a sense of role with forms of self-definition and esteem might be applicable to other groups of abolitionists as well.

The origins of evangelical abolitionist commitment lay in the particular character of the spiritual episodes that had driven the immediatist cadre toward the ministry in the first place. Conversion was the experience that established a sense of Christian personhood by bringing one into harmony with the ultimate order of existence.[4] One became a *real* Christian not by subscribing to a set of formal doctrines or by enrolling as a member of a congregation, but by *experiencing* a change of person as, through a gift of grace, one came to inhabit a different plane of being in which love and reconciliation to God rather than alienation and self-love became the core of personality. The cadence with which a communicant went through the steps of conversion varied, but from 1790 through the early 1820s those within the New England strain experienced conversion as a

3 Some of the lay figures were similarly caught up in situations that centered around a sense of the conflict between the "world" and spiritual commitment. Moreover, it was in the 1820s that evangelicalism was developing a particular sense of female spiritual vocation. Although the connections between abolitionism and the development of a woman's suffrage movement have been explored, the connections between evangelical experience and doctrine and female abolitionism deserve greater attention. See Kathryn Kish Sklar, *Catharine Beecher: A Study in American Domesticity* (New Haven: Yale University Press, 1973) for a suggestive study between evangelicalism and female vocation.

4 The best sources for the conversion process are personal documents such as diaries, memoirs, and journals and the literature attempting to describe the various ideas and states of feeling that signified any particular stage in the process. William Mathews, *American Diaries: An Annotated Bibliography of American Diaries prior to 1861* (Berkeley: University of California Press, 1945) lists published diaries and autobiographies and memoirs which include selections of letters and journals. In addition the numerous didactic biographies and memoirs of prominent and pious laypersons and ministers are a good source for religious experiences. Evangelical journals such as *Connecticut Evangelical Magazine, Christian Spectator, Spirit of the Pilgrims*, and *Evangelist* contain numerous accounts of conversion.

more or less gradual process that extended back before and well after the actual episode in which grace had been received. The infusion of grace—a real event in time—planted a seed in carefully prepared soil. But this seed then had to be nurtured through a "growth in grace" that was marked by "clear and consistent piety" and witnessed in solid Christian deportment. By the mid-1820s, however, many evangelical youths were having conversion experiences of a rather different order. Though they certainly had been subjected to a firm regimen of evangelical nurture and many may have had bouts of spiritual anxiety before, they *experienced* conversion not as a gradual process but as an abrupt, cataclysmic, and deeply transforming event. Conversion for them was less the careful construction of a mature Christian personality than a concrete experience of "rebirth" in which they felt themselves to have in fact died to sin and been born again into righteousness, to have broken utterly with their sinful past.[5]

The intensity and totality of this sense of transformation reflected the combined force of the spiritual and secular anxieties that encumbered the coming of age for this particular generation. The twenties converts were perhaps the first generation to be fully reared within the new evangelicalism of the early nineteenth century. At least one, if not both, of their parents and most of the significant elders in their lives were professing and active Christians who considered furnishing children with a solid Christian character the highest parental duty. This was not simply a matter of inculcating the appropriate moral precepts: conversion was the ultimate parental goal. In fact, conversion was essentially an experience of youth, the most important ritual attending the passage into adulthood. Preparation for the event began at an early age, but as children approached youth—that period in the life cycle that combined what we separate into adolescence and young adulthood—their elders used all the means at their disposal to push them toward conversion. Youth was the time of life when conversion was expected to happen

---

5 The term "rebirth" does not appear to have been used to talk of the revivals of the first two decades of the nineteenth century in New England. It is used more often to speak of Methodist and frontier revivals or later revivals. Finney's notion (approximated by Nathaniel Taylor) of sinners bound to make themselves a "new heart" comes close to it, and the revivals of the late twenties and early thirties in New England came close to the Methodist experience.

if it were going to take place at all, and elders thus worked to ensure that it would happen before adulthood arrived and the opportunity had passed. Moreover, pastors and parents bore down on youths of this generation with particular intensity because various economic, demographic, and cultural pressures were forcing youths to make their lives away from family farm and home community. Coming of age increasingly involved departing from parental vision and control before one was ready to or had settled into the vocational and marital statuses that had traditionally been associated with maturity and adulthood. This prospect of youths leaving parental control without having become genuine Christians filled elders with terror. Thus did churches gather their youth into special study, inquiry, and mutual improvement societies and cascade them with lectures, sermons, and advice manuals, all of which were designed to press the basic ideas of sin, repentance, and salvation upon them. Everyday events, the personal traumas and anxieties of youthful life, and local tragedies were all held up to them as matters freighted with the warning that they should look to their souls before it was too late, that only the bosom of the Lord could keep them safe from temptation, the ravages of sin, and the terrors of death.[6]

Coming of age created secular anxieties as well. On an unprecedented scale, the generation maturing after 1815 was a dislocated generation, forced to strike out on its own, making its way as it went with few if any familial resources to begin with or fall back upon, with few clearcut institutions to channel it and with few unambiguous cues to follow.[7] For them, coming of age had become an unavoidable process of continuing self-construction which at times amounted to a kind of vagabondage, moving from place to place and pursuit to pursuit, trying, in the words of one particularly battered

6 See Joseph Kett, "Growing up in Rural New England," in Tamara Harevan (ed.), *Anonymous Americans* (New York: Prentice Hall, 1972), and Joseph Kett, "Adolescence and Youth in Nineteenth Century America," *Journal of Interdisciplinary History*, II (1971), 283–98 for discussion of youth and conversion.

7 David F. Allmendinger, Jr., *Paupers and Scholars: The Transformation of Student Life in Nineteenth Century New England* (New York: St. Martin's Press, 1975), contains a superb study of these conditions and this process. Though not particularly concerned with the ministry, it is in effect a study of the population from which much of the ministry was drawn. John Gillis, *Youth and History* (New York: Academic Press, 1974), while not specifically about the United States is nonetheless a useful study for the process of coming of age.

young man, to "get a hold" on life. The initiative in the process, moreover, increasingly fell to young men themselves. How to begin, where to go, what to do, and how to proceed once they had struck out on their own were all matters over which parents could exert little control.

But if theirs was a condition of unprecedented freedom with a myriad of apparent choices and opportunities, theirs was also a formless and fluid world which levied a heavy tax of anxiety and uncertainty and seemed to demand will, persistence, and extraordinary degrees of self-control if it were to be mastered or survived. The language young men fell back upon to describe their lives reveals something of the character of the world as they confronted it. They refer to life as a scramble, a treacherous maze, a whirlwind; and they speak of hopes dashed and expectations disappointed and of the obstacles and treachery they continually confront. Preoccupations with mental and physical health, notations of melancholy, dyspepsia and depression, and fears of madness parade across the pages of their letters, diaries, and journals, and all bear painful witness to the psychic burdens they carried. A letter John Todd (born in 1800) wrote his fiancée at the age of 26 just after he had negotiated the shoals of youth provides a revealing example of how many among this generation experienced coming of age: "My father fell under a heavy blow of providence . . . and I was born an orphan, shelterless, penniless. I was about six years old when I knelt over my father's grave and vowed, even then, to rise above my circumstances. I soon determined to have a liberal education. My friends opposed, obstacles were thrown in my way, everything opposed. I rose above all; I went to college half-fitted; I was sick much of the time owing to too severe application and anxiety. I pressed on, rose above all, and now stand where I can see my way clear."[8]

Evangelical youths of the 1820s and 1830s thus found themselves caught in a psychological whipsaw. As they consulted their own wishes and relied upon their own judgment to work out life goals and improvise strategies to meet them, they came to feel, as John Todd did, that they stood alone with only their own will to

---

8 John Todd (ed.), *John Todd: The Story of His Life, Told Mainly by Himself* (New York: Harpers, 1876).

enable them to survive and succeed. Unlike many of their seventeenth- and eighteenth-century counterparts, they could no longer take their worldly portion as a given, ordered by God's providence, defined by parental resources, and maintained by their own virtue and hard work. With few institutions to protect or guide them, like John Todd who vowed to "rise above all" (and whose address at his Yale commencement was entitled "The Influence of a High Standard of Attainment"), they gave free rein to self-assertion and projected dreams of fame and success as they constructed myths of self-help and the sure reward of virtue and hard work to sustain them. Thus was theirs a life of acute self-preoccupation which fostered if it did not demand a sense of self-esteem and autonomy. (It was a situation to which Ralph Waldo Emerson's doctrine of self-reliance also spoke with considerable resonance.) But at the same time, their religion subjected this sense of self to sustained attack. As their pastors tried to drive them toward conversion and the surrender of self, they were obliged to deliberately undermine this confidence in what amounted to a sustained assault on the very self-esteem and autonomy toward which the young were groping. Again and again the youths were told that their concerns with self and dreams of fame and fortune were the signs of their utter depravity and that if they did not immediately repent and seek God's mercy they would suffer eternal damnation.

Evangelical youths might well listen to preaching about divine sovereignty, sin, and the atonement for some time without any deep sense that they themselves were personally implicated in them. Many went through periods of at least tacit rejection of the idea that nothing they did or were could help them earn salvation, and some even found relief in religions like Unitarianism which had devotional styles that built upon autonomy rather than demanding renunciation of self. But for most of those who remained within the fold, sooner or later the evangelical message would strike home. The immediate circumstances of vulnerability to the message varied— the crises of departure and vocational decision, familial conflict, the death of a peer, a particularly acute sense of disappointment, loneliness, or isolation. But whatever the particular weakness in their resistance to evangelical exhortation, the spiritual process that broke through it was much the same: the doctrines of sin and salvation took on deep personal meaning as the young came to feel that their pastors' descriptions of sin and the torment of life outside God's embrace was a direct portrayal of them. Guilt and self-loathing overwhelmed them as they became convinced that they were slaves to their drives for self-gratification and that their whole lives had been given over to a welter of forbidden desires. Release, in the form of a profound sense of deliverance and change, came with the realization that with Christ's atonement God would grant salvation if only they would truly repent and surrender themselves wholly to him. They felt themselves to have entered a whole new mode of being; feelings of joy and love for a God who would grant such miserable specimens salvation in spite of their sin replaced their anxiety and self-hate.

The intensity of the sense of deliverance undoubtedly reflected the power of the anxieties preceding conversion. But the sense of rebirth itself was equally a function of the kind of revivals in which the conversions took place.[9] What characterized the revivals that converted much of the abolitionist cadre was the way in which they generated and orchestrated collective emotion. They began suddenly, burned intensely for several weeks, and then faded out almost as quickly as they had begun. These revivals centered around protracted meetings which would go on almost continuously for anywhere from four to twenty days. These meetings deployed prayer, exhortation, song, confession, and testimony to mold a mixed assemblage of anxious penitents, newly saved Christians, and established church members into a fervent community of feeling. In sermon and exhortation preachers addressed the anxious, sometimes even calling upon sinners by name, as they tried to make them realize their peril. Penitents especially wrought with a sense of sin came forward to anxious benches to be preached at and prayed over until they cast off sin and surrendered to God. There they would

9 For the revivals of the twenties and thirties see Perry Miller, *The Life of the Mind in America* (New York: Harcourt Brace, 1965); Whitney Cross, *The Burned-Over District: The Social and Intellectual History of Enthusiastic Religion in Western New York, 1800–1850* (New York: Harper and Row, 1965); William G. McLaughlin, *Modern Revivalism: Charles Grandison Finney to Billy Graham* (New York: Ronald Press, 1959); Bernard Weisberger, *They Gathered at the River: The Story of the Great Revivalists and their Impact upon Religion in America* (Boston: Little, Brown, 1958); and Donald M. Scott, "Watchmen on the Walls of Zion" (Ph.D. dissertation, University of Wisconsin, 1968).

confess their awful wickedness in open and tearful agony while those around them beseeched God to give them grace. When conversion finally came, the newly saved would go off with a Christian and pray together in praise of God. Soon they would return to the protracted meeting as they themselves took on the mantle of evangelist, exhorting and praying for those still unsaved. Thus did the new revivals of the 1820s gather agony, beseeching, ecstasy, and zeal into a single emotional force with which to assault the unconverted. In the terms of Charles Grandison Finney, they so intensified the "heat" or "temperature" of the communicants that they "broke down" all resistance to the gospel message.[10]

These revivals, then, were rituals of rebirth in ways that earlier New England revivals had not been. Converts coming out of them after having gone into them with the bundle of anxieties described experienced a dramatic sense that they had surrendered their whole sinful self and made themselves a totally new being. In its force and dramaturgy, the revival both intensified and objectified the sense of total change, as the communicant went from the terrible bondage of sin and self to the joy of righteousness in a matter of hours or days. The revival heightened the penitent's identity as a depraved sinner almost beyond endurance and then assailed it as sinner and evangelist, assisted by the emotionality of the greater audience, wrestled for the sinner's soul until he finally shed his sinful being, an act symbolized by his movement first to the anxious bench and then to the prayer of the saved. Finally, immediate action sealed the sense of the totality of the change as the convert, transported by the fervor of deliverance, returned to urge those still enslaved in sin to repent and surrender to God. Within the revival itself communicants moved into a mode of feeling and acting diametrically opposed to the sin and anxiety of their previous life, experiencing a reconciliation with God in which they felt themselves become a fully dedicated servant of his will. In addition they were drawn into full participation in a community of love, for the revival, while a conquest of sin, centered

---

10 Contemporary accounts can be found in Charles G. Finney, *Lectures on Revivals of Religion*, William G. McLaughlin, ed. (Cambridge, Mass: Harvard University Press, 1960); Charles G. Finney, *A Memoir of Charles Grandison Finney* (New York: A. S. Barnes and Co., 1876); "Report of the Suffolk South Association," *The Spirit of the Pilgrims* (1833), VI, 195–97.

around the active expression of evangelical love and concern. Beginning as the objects of concern of the revival, the convert ended up in a posture of intense solicitude for those who remained the victims of sin.

Among certain converts this experience of rebirth fostered an equally intense sense of spiritual calling. It was not new, of course, for a convert to develop a sense that he had been called to the ministry. A "call" had ordinarily grown out of a feeling that one's piety was such that it could best be expressed by a specific vocational commitment to the ministry, and one's realization of this constituted the call. Recognizing and accepting the call was the first step toward the ministry, but a young man did not think of himself as having entered upon his sacred office until he had finished formal preparation and was at least licensed if not ordained. For those who experienced it, however, spiritual rebirth fostered a more immediate sense of calling. They saw their whole lives as changed, feeling that they had to drop what they were doing or had planned to do and dedicate themselves fully to God's service. Even before entering a specific clerical office, they felt that this life of active consecration and service had begun *now*. And they acted upon this sense immediately in the very revivals that had converted them, leading prayers, counseling the anxious, and exhorting their unconverted friends. Some went on forthwith to assist in other revivals. As Theodore Weld, referring to his own conversion by Finney in 1826, put it, conversion "put an end to my studying. I was with him in his meetings, speaking and laboring all that summer."[11]

The intensity and dynamism of their piety was informed by an equally expansive sense of their spiritual office. The New England ministry had long been endowed with special responsibilities for moral and social order. Until the early decades of the nineteenth century, this guardianship was construed in largely localistic terms; although a unique kind of public office, the sacred office had been above all a local one, and with the exception of a few professorships all clergymen served as town pastors. Order was thought to reside in

11 Theodore Weld in Lyman Beecher, *The Autobiography of Lyman Beecher*, Barbara Cross, ed. (Cambridge, Mass: Harvard University Press, 1962), II, 232–35.

stable and orderly communities, and the town minister acted as the ideological, institutional, and symbolic center that held a town together as a community. Pastors were ordained to town pulpits which they were expected to serve for their entire professional life, and almost three-quarters of all the settled pastors in eighteenth-century New England spent their whole career in just one pulpit. By the second decade of the nineteenth century, however, the locus of clerical guardianship and professional definition had begun to shift from the local communion to a new level of translocal institutions. The evangelical ministry underwent a fundamental transformation as Second Great Awakening churchmen devised a vast network of new institutions—benevolent associations, clerical journals and devotional weeklies, colleges and seminaries—in their effort to "evangelize the nation."[12]

This structure spawned a large number and variety of nonpastoral posts, all of which were highly esteemed for the importance of their service to evangelicalism as a whole. By 1830, dozens of new editorships, professorships, secretaryships, and agencies in the national benevolent societies had been set up, not to mention the foreign and home missionary posts. The new professorships gained particular prestige. Indeed, men like Samuel Miller, Herman Humphrey, Lyman Beecher, and even Charles Grandison Finney, who had enjoyed influence and renown as giants of the cloth outside college and seminary, often crowned their careers by taking on the presidency of a college or seminary. In addition, missions and agencies began to attract many of the most talented, zealous, and esteemed young ministers. Such missionary efforts gained enormous attention in the burgeoning evangelical press, which celebrated the zeal and self-denying piety of the home and foreign missionary as the perfect embodiment of Christian piety and ministerial spirituality.[13] Even

12 A starting point for the ministry is Sidney Mead, "The Rise of the Evangelical Conception of the Ministry in America," in H. Richard Niebuhr and Daniel Williams (eds.), *The Ministry in Historical Perspective* (New York: Harpers, 1956), 207–49. The best analysis of the clerical office in colonial New England is David Hall, *The Faithful Shepherd* (Chapel Hill: University of North Carolina Press, 1973).

13 *Panoplist* and *Connecticut Evangelical Magazine* are filled with reports on missionary work.

the local parish was emplaced in the broader evangelical cause. Most clergymen still settled into pulpits, but a minister had become far more than simply a local preacher. In his 1814 ordination sermon Lyman Beecher exhorted the young minister not to confine his "eye, heart, and ear to the narrow limits of an association. . . . The state, the nation, the world demand your prayers, and charities and enterprise."[14] Increasingly, many churchmen weighed a pastorate according to whether it was a station of greater or lesser usefulness to evangelicalism as a whole. In fact, the clerical leadership itself had taken the lead in rupturing the ordination bonds that the eighteenth century had valued so highly, arguing that the claims of the larger cause justified disrupting the local communion and moving Elias Cornelius from his Salem, Massachusetts, pulpit to the general-secretaryship of the American Education Society, Moses Stuart from his New Haven pulpit to Andover Theological Seminary, and Lyman Beecher from Litchfield, Connecticut, to Boston.[15]

This new ministerial structure, then, had fostered a very different conception of the ministerial office. No longer was a clergyman an "ambassador of God" called for life to minister to a single, particular congregation. Whatever his particular post, he was now much more likely to perceive himself as an agent of organized evangelicalism. No longer did a minister construe himself as one belonging to a town because of his office; he functioned consciously as a dutiful occupant of a particular post which he would surrender if service to the larger cause demanded it. Moreover, the clergy conceived of this cause in ever more expansive terms. The new structure embodied a comprehensive social vision that traced social order to the creation of a pious national community rather than to maintaining orderly towns. And by the late twenties the rhetoric describing the evangelical cause had begun to take on a millennial cast, as a number of evangelicals, inspired by the extraordinary success of their efforts and by the fervent new revivals which seemed to

14 Lyman Beecher, "The Building of Waste-Places," *Works* (Boston: John P. Jewett, Co., 1853), II, 147.
15 This transformation is given detailed treatment in Donald M. Scott, *From Office to Profession: the New England Evangelical Ministry, 1750–1850* (Philadelphia: University of Pennsylvania Press, 1978).

be sweeping the country, began to convince themselves that their era stood on the brink of the millennium. As Lyman Beecher, the preeminent leader and architect of the new evangelicalism put it, "It was the opinion of Edwards that the millennium would commence in America. When I first encountered this opinion I thought it chimerical; but all provident developments since and all existing signs of the times lend corroboration to it."[16]

Young men entering the ministry in the 1820s and early 1830s were the first to receive their ministerial socialization fully within this new structure. Many had been converted in the fervent revivals that had fanned the sense of millennial expectancy. Moreover, they no longer received their clerical education by reading divinity for a few months or a year with a practicing parish minister, but received it in a theological seminary. First instituted in New England with the founding of Andover Seminary in 1808, the seminary was a significant departure from earlier forms. Representing both a formalization and standardization of clerical training and a dramatically increased emphasis upon purely "professional" training, the seminary institutionalized a three-year curriculum as the norm. Of greatest significance, however, was the overall environment it established. First, it involved a considerable transformation of scale. In the "schools of the prophets" or eighteenth-century Harvard and Yale, not more than a half-dozen candidates were present at any one time. By 1820, Andover gathered well over 100 students and teachers together each year. In addition, these ministerial candidates were collected in a separate, exclusively ministerial institution where they could concentrate on preparing themselves free of the distractions of broader secular institutions and communities. Finally, in the seminary, candidates for the sacred office were not only given a systematic curriculum, they were also cascaded with lectures and sermons that stressed the vast importance of the evangelical cause and the nature of the various campaigns to effect a moral reformation among the American people and bring them under evangelical dominion.

16 Lyman Beecher, *A Plea for the West* (Cincinnati: Truman and Smith, 1835), 10. See Ernest Tuveson, *Redeemer Nation: The Idea of America's Millennial Role* (Chicago: University of Chicago Press, 1968).

Many seminarians devoted spare time to work with the benevolent associations (which were often headquartered in the seminaries) and frequently served as agents for them during vacation periods.[17]

The ministerial recruits from the new revivals, then, not only possessed a demanding and intense form of inner piety, they were also imbued with a demanding sense of spiritual office. To the older generation, the millennial rhetoric provided a vocabulary which could encompass the evangelical system they had constructed and the unparalleled success they seemed to be having. The fervent ministerial recruits from the new revivals, however, took their definition of their essential spiritual task from this sense of millennial expectancy. They felt that God had called them to usher in the millennium, and this notion of their agency dominated their subsequent sense of their essential office, even though its specific dimensions were not always very easy to fathom.

On the surface, it was the ardor of their piety and the breadth of their evangelical vision that seemed to distinguish these young men. At the core of their dedication, however, was a rather different style of vocational piety, one characterized by a demanding inner spiritual discipline and an equally compelling need for continuing moral activism. Rebirth had broken their bondage to sin, but continuing triumph over it could only come if their striving toward perfect holiness, a frame free of sin and filled with evangelical desire to redeem the world, was unrelenting. Religious conversion is frequently accompanied by a transcendent disregard of the world. For the recruits from the revivals, however, rebirth led not to disregard of the world but to implacable hostility to the world as it was sinfully constituted. As Christians born to righteousness they were as obliged to combat the sinful world as they were to rid themselves of all remnants of sin. Rebirth thus in no way diminished their sense of the reality of sin. Instead it created intense hatred of it as the hor-

---

17 See Natalie Naylor, "Raising a Learned Ministry: The American Education Society, 1815–1860" (Ph.D. dissertation, Columbia University, 1971); Leonard Wood, *A History of Andover Theological Seminary* (Boston: John P. Jewett, 1885); Joseph Vaill, "Theological Education in Connecticut Seventy Years Ago, as Connected with Dr. Charles Backus' Divinity School," *Congregational Quarterly*, XIV (1864), 137–42; Mary Gambrell, *Ministerial Education in Colonial New England* (New York: Columbia University Press, 1911).

rendous bondage from which they had been delivered and against which they had been called to wage unrelenting war.[18] It was in such activism that they both realized and intensified their identity as re-born Christians and agents of God's ultimate millennial purpose. As one evangelical put it, it was not "till we rise to a higher sphere, *the sphere of doing*" that we can "rise to the knowledge of God," for it was only in doing that "we give life to our speculations, and sub-stance to our creed, and meaning to our professions."[19] If they ever allowed themselves to relent in their continual war against sin and for the millennium, they would find themselves once again bereft of a sense of reconciliation and closeness to God.

Such was the spiritual and vocational context out of which evangelical commitment to abolitionism was forged. Immediatism found its most fertile ground among young evangelicals who were caught up in the grip of this new and dynamic form of sacred voca-tion, but who had not yet translated it into a form that matched either the intensity of their inner consecration or the scope of the task to which they had dedicated themselves. They possessed a sense of calling that united a drive for perfect personal holiness with insistent moralism. This spirituality, in turn, was attached to a no-tion of the sacred office that extended well beyond specific tasks and positions to embrace the ultimate millennial cause. In effect, these evangelicals were caught up in an open-ended spiritual and voca-tional spiral: their piety demanded expression in concrete moral ac-tivism, pursuit of which fostered a need for greater holiness which itself then needed more satisfactory channels of expression. Existing institutional forms, moreover, proved inadequate to contain or ex-press either the form or the intensity of their vocational sense. It is not surprising that very few of the evangelicals who became aboli-tionist activists in the 1830s had worked out a settled ministerial identity or position at the time of their adherence to abolitionism. A

18 A particularly good source for the inner vocational sense is Gilbert H. Barnes and Dwight L. Dumond (eds.), *The Letters of Theodore Dwight Weld, Angelina Grimké Weld and Sarah Grimké, 1822–1844* (Gloucester, Mass: Peter Smith, 1965), and Dwight L. Dumond, *The Letters of James G. Birney* (Gloucester, Mass: Peter Smith, 1965).

19 Beriah Green, *The Divine Significance of Work: A Valedictory Address at Oneida In-stitute* (Whitesboro, N.Y.: Oneida Institute, 1842), 12.

large portion became abolitionists while they were still ministerial
candidates, agents in one of the enterprises, or young preachers
serving as home missionaries rather than as regular, "stated" pastors. Moreover, men like Beriah Green, Amos Phelps, and Elizur
Wright, who had been ordained before turning to abolitionism, had
not firmly settled upon the pastorate as the vehicle for their sense of
divine service, but had moved to nonpastoral posts when they were
converted to immediatism.[20]

Although these were the conditions from which evangelical abolitionism emerged, the commitment itself was formed around a
specific idea, namely the notion that slavery was sin, an idea that
grew directly from standard evangelical images of sin. Sin was a
"temper of mind," a disposition of heart and will in "obstinate dissent and enmity against God." Churchmen had traditionally considered pride the essential attribute of a sinful frame of mind, but by
the early years of the nineteenth century they had come to see
selfishness, a constant craving for self-gratification, as the fundamental temper of sin. Whatever the particular sin might be, they
depicted it as an appetite or craving that eventually became an all-
consuming lust leading to temporal and eternal destruction. This
vision of the "nature and consequences of sin" found its fullest
expression in the idea of intemperance, which by the 1820s was considered the most heinous example of sin as self-gratification. Intemperance, indeed, gave sin a horrifying tangibility, providing churchmen with a way to depict graphically the course of sin from the
initial desire through the final ruin. Whatever the course of a particular descent into hell, somewhere along the line the sinner usually fell into intemperance, and began to turn his energies to satis-
fying a thirst that quickly took control of him and led inexorably
to the commission of the most horrendous crimes. Indeed, the tab-
leaux depicting intemperance invariably had a final scene in which
the opposition between selfishness and benevolence was played
out in stark terms: the drunkard not only destroyed himself, but

20 See John Meyers, "The Agency System of the Anti-Slavery Movement and its Antece-
dents in Other Benevolent and Reform Societies" (Ph.D. dissertation, University of Michigan,
1961).

sacrificed the health and well-being of wife and children (usually murdering one of them in a drunken rage) toward whom he was by nature and religion to exercise the greatest benevolence. The portrait of intemperance as sin went further, furnishing evangelicals with metaphors for describing the world of nineteenth-century America. They used intemperance to depict how the pervasive materialism of American culture enslaved the soul. Indeed, evangelicals invariably pictured intemperance as an intrinsic element of economic life: the strain of competition and the pursuit of gain was either sustained by drink (the excitement of commerce and speculation needing the artificial "stimulus" of alcohol), or drink furnished evening refuge from the marketplace, and, finally, the only solace for ruin or disappointment.[21]

The attack on slavery appropriated and expanded these images of the nature of sin and the world. Slavery, even more than intemperance, exemplified self-gratification—beyond sacrificing the needs of others, it appropriated the whole human being and turned the slave into an object whose whole purpose was to serve the desires of the master. As Beriah Green, one of the earliest evangelical abolitionists, put it, "His wife, his children, himself, soul and body, another man, under protection of bloody laws, seizes as his property and turns them to such account as his pampered appetites and inflamed passions demand."[22] The most vivid result of slavery (to which abolitionists turned again and again) was a system of lust, of unleashed, illicit sexuality. Slavery made the female slave the helpless victim of the master's insatiable sexual desires, since under slavery, one early abolitionist wrote, "the marriage relation, the source of all others, is out of the question. And in its stead is introduced a system of Universal Concubinage."[23]

21 See, for example, Edward Hitchcock, "On Intemperance in Eating," *The American National Preacher*, VII, 337–52, 369–80; Sylvester Graham, *A Lecture to Young Men on Chastity* (Boston: George W. Lights, 1831); Joel Hawes, *Lectures Addressed to the Young Men of New Haven and Hartford* (New Haven: Cooke and Company, 1828); and Lyman Beecher, *Six Sermons on the Nature, Occasions, Evils, Signs and Remedy of Intemperance* (New York: The American Tract Society, 1828).

22 Beriah Green, *The Divine Significance of Work*, 8.

23 Samuel Crothers, *An Address to the Churches on the Subject of Slavery* (Georgetown, Ohio: n.p., 1831), 10.

This portrait of slavery as sin exemplified the general existence and operation of sin in American society. If their conception of intemperance had reflected the evangelicals' sense of the nature of the world and how it encased the individual in sin, slavery provided a more systematic and inclusive image of the sinfulness in American society. Slavery was not simply a state of being and behavior, it was also an institution whose tentacles spread throughout society and implicated everyone, North and South alike. As an economic system, of course, slavery was the opposite of the free-labor system. In this vision, however, slavery in its essence did not differ from the broader American life, but seemed to take to its logical end point that lust for gain and the willingness to sacrifice all to selfish ends that dominated American life. This point was made most vividly in abolitionist portraits of the slave trade. There the slave was dehumanized into a commodity, solely a source of profit for the trader, whose relation to the slave was totally commercial and exploitative, utterly unalloyed with feelings of responsibility or benevolence. Slavery thus captured and objectified the deepest evangelical sense, not only of the nature of sin as lust, but of American society as totally encrusted in sin, as wholly opposite in its structure and modes to the disinterested benevolence of the divine order.[24]

Such unalloyed sinfulness was a powerful and resonant image, one to which young evangelicals laboring under a demanding and expansive sense of spiritual vocation were particularly susceptible. If slavery were the ultimate embodiment of lust and self-gratification, then the "downtrodden, helpless, hopeless" slave would be the ultimate object of genuine benevolent concern.[25] Indeed, as one young evangelical, James Thome, put it, "I know of no subject

24 See, for example, Samuel Crothers, *Strictures on African Slavery* (Rossville, Ohio: n.p., 1833); James T. Dickinson, *Sermon Preached in the Second Congregational Church, Norwich, Connecticut* (Norwich, Conn: M. R. Young, 1834); Bèriah Green, *Four Sermons Preached in the Chapel of Western Reserve College* (Cleveland: Cleveland Herald, 1833); Theodore Weld, *American Slavery as it is: The Testimony of a Thousand Witnesses* (New York: American Anti-Slavery Society, 1839); Amos Phelps, *Lectures on Slavery and its Remedy* (Boston: New England Anti-Slavery Society, 1834). Essential for slavery and conceptions of sin are David Brion Davis, *The Problem of Slavery in Western Culture* (Ithaca: Cornell University Press, 1966), and David Brion Davis, *The Problem of Slavery in the Age of Revolution, 1770–1823* (Ithaca: Cornell University Press, 1975).

25 Green, *Four Sermons*, 41–42.

which takes such strong hold of a man as does abolition. It seizes the conscience with an authoritarian grasp, it runs across the path of the guilty, goads him, haunts him and rings in his ears the cry of blood. It builds up a wall to heaven before and around him! It goes with the eye of God and searches his heart with a scrutiny too strict to be eluded. It writes 'thou are the one' upon the heart of every oppressor."[26]

More central, however, than the fact of the discovery of the claims of the slave on evangelical energies and affections was the nature of the recognition of the sin of slavery. In a very specific sense, the evangelical abolitionists of the early thirties were converts. Immediate abolition was at heart a theological conception uniting the image of the sin of slavery with the basic evangelical doctrine of Christian duty toward sin. Moreover, the final step in the making of an evangelical abolitionist was an explicit spiritual experience that fastened the commitment to abolitionism as firmly as his initial conversion had fixed his commitment to God and the gospel ministry. The insight that slavery was sin hit the evangelical abolitionist with a force comparable to that with which a sense of his own depravity had originally struck. The truth of the doctrine of immediate abolition was accepted in the same way in which a convert was said to have a "saving knowledge" of Christ and similarly became the foundation of Christian identity and action.

The conversion to immediatism came in several ways. Some were brought to it by a charismatic figure with whom they had an intimate spiritual relationship. Those in the grip of the millennial spiritual discipline were especially dependent upon and susceptible to the influence of spiritual peers. Institutional decorum and established rituals had played a relatively minor role in shaping their spirituality. Their model of a religious community was less the ordinary church than the new revival in which intensity of piety rather than designated position conferred spiritual authority. Moreover, a particular form of spiritual friendship was an essential part of

26 James A. Thome, *Speech of James A. Thome of Kentucky delivered at the Annual Meeting of the American Anti-Slavery Society, May 6, 1834* (Boston: New England Anti-Slavery Society, 1834), 7.

their religious experience, serving both confessional and vocational functions. They prayed and worshiped together, chastized each other for spiritual failings, discussed the obligations of their common consecration, and spurred each other to greater fidelity to the divine cause.

Frequently, a young man looked for spiritual guidance to those he considered more advanced in piety and dedication. A letter from J. L. Tracy to Theodore Weld in 1831 exemplifies this kind of spiritual relationship. Weld wrote Tracy suggesting that he had let his trust in God wane and Tracy replied, assuring Weld that his "kind admonition will not be lost on me," and confessing that "I never expect to find another such friend in this world and I trust I shall so act so much the part of a disciple of Jesus as not to forfeit what I have already received, your own confidence and friendship."[27] Many of the initial leaders of immediatism came to their abolitionism through this kind of relationship. A spiritual exemplar would cascade his "friend" with antislavery tracts and personal letters devoted to the subject and would bombard him with direct personal counsel and prayer sessions until the friend recognized the awful truth of slavery and committed himself to its eradication. Theodore Weld, far and away the most effective apostle of abolitionism, was brought to it by the English emancipationist Charles Stuart, an older man who had long been Weld's confessor, confidant, and closest friend, and by Beriah Green and Elizur Wright. Weld, in turn, converted James Birney and H. B. Stanton, among many others.[28]

27  Barnes and Dumond (eds.), Weld-Grimké Letters, I, 56.
28  The character and importance of these bonds can be seen in the correspondence between the Oneida seminarians in ibid., 26–38, 52–54, 78–94, 106–109, 112–14, 178–204; and in Dumond, Letters of James Birney. Accounts of the conversion of Weld are in G. H. Barnes, The Anti-Slavery Impulse, 1830–1844 (New York: Harcourt, Brace, and World, 1964), and in Benjamin Thomas, Theodore Weld: Crusader for Freedom (New Brunswick: Rutgers University Press, 1950). Good accounts of Weld's effectiveness as an apostle of abolitionism are contained in John L. Meyers, "The Major Effort of National Anti-Slavery Agents in New York, 1836–37," New York History, XLVI (1965), 162–86, and John L. Meyers, "The Origins of the 'Seventy': To Arouse the North Against Slavery," Mid-America, XLVIII (1966), 29–46. A superb study of female bonding in this period suggestive of the bonds the abolitionists established is Carroll Smith-Rosenberg, "The Female World of Love and Ritual: Relations between Women in Nineteenth Century America," Signs: Journal of Women in Culture and Society, I (1975), 1–31.

More systematically organized and collective efforts also converted ardent young evangelicals to the abolitionist cause. These conclaves occurred in the early thirties in many of the colleges and seminaries where Yankee evangelical influence was especially strong. The prototype of the more collective ritual for converting people to immediatism, however, was the famed "Lane debates," the eighteen-day series of meetings that Weld directed at Lane Theological Seminary in Cincinnati, Ohio, in March, 1834. The debates were wildly successful: they converted almost the entire student body to abolitionism and provided the model for the attempt of the next few years to convert the whole evangelical community to abolitionism. The term "debates" is a misnomer. What happened at Lane in March, 1834, was really a revival. The sessions were orchestrated as a protracted meeting, designed to establish conviction about slavery in the same way that a revival established conviction of sin, by cascading the emotions until Truth was felt with such intensity that it became the ground for all subsequent spiritual action. The mechanism for the actual conversion to immediatism, moreover, was "sympathy." The meetings were organized to evoke "an excitement of sympathy" that so deeply involved the students in the plight of the slave and a heartfelt comprehension of the horrible sin of slavery that they would *feel* the utter necessity for immediate emancipation.

The sessions devoted an immense amount of time to prayer; prayers opened and closed each session, and punctuated each exhortation and confession. Everyone was implored to turn his private prayers to the subject. In no sense were these prayers *pro forma*. Based on the "prayer of faith" used in revivals, they were meant to cleanse the group's spirit and prepare it for the reception of Truth. Testimony and confession similarly punctuated the sessions as speakers—especially those like William Allen, a southerner who even stood to inherit slaves, and James Bradley, a former slave and the one black student in the seminary, who had firsthand knowledge of slavery—tried to engender feeling for the horrors of it in others. The orchestration of the whole process was very deliberate and very effective. The lectures, confessions, and exhortation combined to arouse the deepest sympathy for the slave victims as well as deep loathing for the sin itself, and to foster an inescapable inner necessity to act. In Weld's words, "light was elicited, principles fixed and action followed."[29] Moreover, just as recruits from the new revivals felt themselves compelled to translate their consecration into immediate action, the Lane students began to put their newly discerned principles into practice. They formed an antislavery society, set up Bible schools and various benevolent agencies among the free blacks of Cincinnati, and enrolled themselves as agents of abolition, traveling around trying to convert the larger evangelical community. When the school trustees tried to ban the antislavery society, the students withdrew from the seminary, condemning it as unChristian and unfit to equip them as true ministers of the gospel.[30]

Whether it happened individually through personal charismatic influence or in a more collective ritual, the conversion to abolition elevated one to a new spiritual and vocational plateau. Immediatism was less a program of what to do about slavery than, in evangelical terms, a "disposition," a state of being in which the heart and will were set irrevocably against slavery. In the heartfelt reception of the truth about slavery, immediate abolition followed psychological and doctrinal necessity in the same way that hatred of sin followed a saving knowledge of Christ. Indeed, for the abolitionist, the conversion to immediatism bound one's whole sense of identity and esteem as a Christian and an agent of God to antislavery activism, making immediatism the sign of whether or not a person was a saved Christian. Slavery and the slave thus provided a unified focus for the two basic emotions around which the sense of Christian being and vocation revolved—the deeply felt hatred of sin and the equally fervent evangelical love for the victim of sin. Abolitionism

29 *Statement of the Reasons which Induced the Students of Lane Seminary to Dissolve their Connection with that Institution* (Cincinnati: n.p., 1834), 4.

30 For the Lane episodes see Robert Fletcher, *A History of Oberlin College* (Oberlin: Oberlin College, 1943) I, 150–65; Barnes, *Anti-Slavery Impulse*, 64–73; Scott, "Watchmen on the Walls of Zion," 329–89. Contemporary accounts are contained in H. B. Stanton, "Letter," and Huntington Lyman, "Letter," both in *New York Evangelist*, March, 10, 1834; Augustus Wattles, "Letter," *Emancipator*, April 22, 1834; Barnes and Dumond (eds.), *Weld-Grimké Letters*, I, 137–40.

thus was not simply another in a sequence of evangelical causes. For the immediatist converts abolition became the essential embodiment of their sense of sacred vocation. As the objectification of the sin of the world, slavery became the foe to be conquered in the millennial battle to which they had consecrated themselves.[31]

The conception of abolition as a sacred vocation helps illuminate the immediatists' intemperate style and their radical stance toward existing ministerial and evangelical institutions. Abolition in a very precise way was a form of evangelicalism and they were its evangelists. Their mode of persuasion was identical in tone, structure, and epistemology to the address that any evangelical preacher worth his salt would use to break down a sinner's resistance to Truth. Slavery was sin and as sin had to be relinquished and fought against, just as in a revival a sinner had to repent immediately and turn his energies against sin. Indeed, for the abolitionist activist to insist on anything else was unthinkable. Gerrit Smith put it very explicitly when he challenged Lyman Beecher's refusal to adopt immediatism while still avowing that slavery was evil. "Now if I were standing by," Smith wrote, "whilst you were laboring to bring a fellow sinner to repentance, and, instead of countenancing your solemn and urgent exhortation, you should relieve his pressed conscience by telling him, not yet, you would not be likely to number me amongst the advocates of the doctrines of Bible Repentance."[32] The immediatists similarly refused to compromise their stance when opponents insisted that their denunciation of Christian slaveholders as vile sinners and their charge that Christians who did not accept immediatism had leagued themselves with the devil undermined Christian progress by retarding revivals, dividing churches, and destroying benevolent enterprises. The abolitionist stance was

31 See David Brion Davis, "The Emergence of Immediatism in British and American Anti-Slavery Thought," *Mississippi Valley Historical Review*, XLIX (1962), 209–30; Anne C. Loveland, "Evangelicalism and 'Immediate Emancipation' in American Anti-Slavery Thought," *Journal of Southern History*, XXXII (1962), 172–88. As a "disposition" in this sense, immediatism could go in a number of specific tactical directions. See Aileen S. Kraditor, *Means and Ends in American Abolitionism: Garrison and His Critics on Strategy and Tactics, 1834–1850* (New York: Random House, 1967).
32 Gerrit L. Smith to Lyman Beecher, *Philanthropist*, I, September 23, 1836.

essentially an ante- (rather than anti-) institutional one. The doctrine that slavery was sin and hence had to be condemned and renounced was the antecedent principle against which they judged any idea, action, or institution. Thus they could not mute their rhetoric or agitation out of loyalty to existing ministerial or evangelical institutions. In effect, they now inhabited a different ministry, one which might be ideological and abstract but which was nonetheless as clear in its imperatives as the most carefully prescribed ministerial routine.

# WIDENING THE CIRCLE
## The Black Church and the Abolitionist Crusade, 1830–1860

*Carol V. R. George*

ACCORDING TO a friend's report, the Reverend Noah C. W. Cannon, a black Methodist itinerant preacher and aspiring author, had just finished his service one Sunday evening in 1830 at a rural charge near Denton, Maryland, when he became involved in a potentially life-threatening situation. As the friend recalled, shortly after returning to his stopping place to spend the night, Cannon was confronted by a group of men who arrested him, alleging his resemblance to a man accused of murdering several women and children. The local magistrate subsequently released him, after acknowledging that Cannon's features in no way conformed to the description of the suspect, and the preacher left town the following morning. But it was not long before he realized that several men were still pursuing him; he rode his horse into a swamp and lay down along the side of the road until they passed. "He began to pray that the Lord would send rain to drive his pursuers in the house." The rain came; Cannon cautiously moved around the house to which his would-be captors had retired, and, successfully eluding the dogs sent out to track him, mounted his horse and bolted across a stream to safety, the current carrying the dogs away. The minister rested that night at the home of friends in Georgetown, Delaware, before assuming his next preaching assignment in Washington. In the meantime, his pursuers had returned to Cannon's host in Maryland, where they broke into a trunk he had left behind, hoping its contents would "throw some light on the movements they supposed were going on among the colored people." They found only papers and Masonic books.

While Cannon went on to have a useful, and in some respects unique, career in the ministry of the African Methodist Episcopal church—writing books and traveling on various circuits that took him to virtually all the free states and into Canada—for the next three decades he and other AME itinerants steered cautiously around that rural Maryland district.[1]

Some twenty years later, in October, 1851, another black Methodist minister, Jarmain Wesley Loguen, was also threatened with arrest. Loguen, himself a self-proclaimed fugitive slave, purportedly participated in the "Jerry rescue" in Syracuse, New York, when another runaway, Jerry McHenry, was boldly seized by antislavery men from local arresting officers, in violation of the Fugitive Slave Law. Faced with the prospect of not only arrest but a return to slavery, Loguen nevertheless spoke to a crowd that collected at Syracuse City Hall. The clergyman had made no secret of his status as a fugitive; indeed, it had become part of his public image as antislavery lecturer and personal host to hundreds of runaways. Loguen told the gathering that autumn evening that he fully intended to violate the Fugitive Slave Law, saying, "The time has come to change the tones of submission into tones of defiance—and to tell Mr. Fillmore and Mr. Webster, if they propose to execute this measure upon us, to send on their blood-hounds." Noting that friends had urged him either to purchase his own freedom or to allow them to do so, he rejected the principle behind their attractive and generous offer. "I owe my freedom to the God who made me," he said, "and who stirred me to claim it against all other beings in God's universe. I

---

1 Alexander W. Wayman, *My Recollections of African Methodist Episcopal Ministers, or Forty Years' Experience in the African Methodist Episcopal Church* (Philadelphia: AME Book Rooms, 1881), 7–11; Daniel A. Payne, *History of the African Methodist Episcopal Church* (Nashville: AME Sunday School Union, 1891), 253–55. Like all memoirs, Wayman's account needs to be read critically. Both Wayman and Payne were nineteenth-century AME bishops, the latter serving also as a very conscientious church historian.

will not, nor will I consent, that anybody else shall countenance the claims of a vulgar despot to my soul and body." Denouncing the hated measure, Loguen concluded, "Whatever may be your decision, my ground is taken. . . . I don't respect this law—I don't fear it—I won't obey it! It outlaws me, and I outlaw it, and the men who attempt to enforce it on me."[2] Loguen did accept the judicious counsel of friends who advised him to seek a temporary haven in Canada until the passions aroused by the Jerry rescue cooled down. But he returned the following year and resumed his activities as a preacher, antislavery lecturer, land agent, and conductor on the underground railroad. In 1864 he was elected a bishop of the African Methodist Episcopal Zion church, a post he filled until his death in 1872.

Their dramas played out some twenty years apart in time, what do Cannon and Loguen have in common besides their experiences with oppression and their Methodist affiliation? Their personal dissimilarities are a matter of record: Cannon, erratic and eccentric, spent most of his career virtually unnoticed in the itinerant field; while Loguen, methodical and comparatively more settled, achieved national recognition as an antislavery activist. Yet they and other black ministers apparently shared certain assumptions about the role of the black church in the quasi-free society of the antebellum North.

The purpose of this essay is twofold: first, by drawing on the careers of some forty black clergymen in the period between 1830 and 1860,[3] to suggest the need for a new appreciation of the mul-

2 Jarmain Wesley Loguen, *The Reverend J. W. Loguen, as a Slave and as a Freeman* (reprint; New York: Negro Universities Press, 1968), 391–93. More biography than autobiography, Loguen's life story nevertheless conforms to what is known about his stand and his activities.

3 Information on the forty clergymen whose careers are relevant to this study is uneven in quantity—generous for those whom I have referred to as a clerical "talented tenth," limited for those who served in small parishes or the itineracy. It is also important to remember that during the thirty-year period being examined, 1830–1860, men frequently changed jobs and roles, resulting in some cases in a change of status. Henry McNeal Turner, for example, who was a young clergyman in 1860, was elected an AME bishop in 1880.

The categories which follow are drawn impressionistically, and are intended for reference. Theodore Hershberg's quantified study of free blacks in Philadelphia is useful, and might well be adapted for other cities.

BLACK CLERICAL ROLES, 1830–1860
*Group I—The "Talented Tenth"*
   Amos Beman (Cong.; Conn.), Samuel Cornish (Pres.; N.Y., N.J.), Alexander Crummell (Epis.; R.I., Pa., N.Y., D.C.), Henry Highland Garnet (Pres.; N.Y.), James Gloucester (Pres.; N.Y.),

tidimensional quality of black clerical leadership, mindful that the
parochial role of the clergy was as much a response to the interests
of their constituent communities as their public, political activities,
and helped foster a kind of parochial abolitionism; and second, to
consider the various ways the black church and its ministers contributed to the abolitionist and civil rights movement, and the
heightening of black self-awareness. The two objectives are interre-
lated.

One must begin by shaping a broader, more inclusive working
definition of leadership, stripped of the cultural accretions, elitist
overtones, and white expectations that have long been associated
with it. In a recent study of black abolitionism, Jane and William
Pease have noted that a leadership gap separated those black spokesmen at the top of the movement from those they were supposed
to serve, an observation echoing that of some contemporary critics
of the black church in the nineteenth century.[4] While it may be true

---

James T. Holly (Epis.; Conn.), Jarmain Wesley Loguen (AMEZ; N.Y.), Daniel A. Payne (AME;
Md., Pa.), J. W. C. Pennington (Cong.; N.Y.), Charles Ray (Cong.; N.Y.), Christopher Rush
(AMEZ; N.Y.), Samuel Ringgold Ward (Cong.; N.Y.), Peter Williams (Epis.; N.Y.), Theodore
Wright (Pres.; N.Y.)

*Group II—Denominational or Regional Ministries*
Morris Brown (AME; Pa.), Daniel Coker (AME; Md.–West Africa), William Douglass (Epis.;
Pa.), Hosea Easton (Cong.; Mass.), George Hogarth (AME; N.Y.), J. Sella Martin (Bapt.; Mass.),
Nathaniel Paul (Bapt.; N.Y.), Thomas Paul (Bapt.; Mass.; N.Y.), John Peterson (Epis.; N.Y.),
William Paul Quinn (AME; Pa.), Henry McNeal Turner (AME; Ga.), Alexander Wayman
(AME; Ohio), Lewis Woodson (AME; Pa.)

*Group III—Essentially Local Ministries*
Philip Brodie (AME; Ohio), Noah Cannon (AME; Pa., itineracy), John Cornish (AME; Pa.),
Isaiah DeGrasse (Epis.; N.Y.), Clayton Durham (AME; Pa.), Moses Freeman (AME; Ohio),
James King (AME; Ohio), J. W. Lewis (Bapt.; R.I.), William Levington (Epis.; Md.), Daniel
Peterson (AME; N.Y., Liberia), Elymas Rogers (Pres.; N.J.), Samuel Snowden (Mass.), Edward
Waters (AME; Md., Pa.)
NOTE: Denominational abbreviations: Congregationalist (Cong.); Presbyterian, (Pres.); Epis-
copalian (Epis.); African Methodist Episcopal Zion (AMEZ); African Methodist Episcopal
(AME), and Baptist (Bapt.).

4 Jane H. Pease and William H. Pease, *They Who Would Be Free* (New York: Atheneum,
1974), 186–93. The Peases conclude, "Whether assessed by its goals or its organizational effi-
ciency, black abolitionism was a failure." (page 297). The existence of a leadership gap, they
suggest, was one of the reasons for the failure; too many black leaders were guilty of "num-
beroneishness." Their study surveys the full spectrum of black abolitionism, although clergymen figure largely in it, as they did in the movement itself. Their work supplements Benjamin
Quarles's fine study, *Black Abolitionists* (New York: Oxford University Press, 1969), and the
numerous autobiographical and/or biographical accounts of members of the clerical "talented
tenth." A helpful new contribution is Joel Schor, *Henry Highland Garnet: A Voice of Black
Radicalism in the Nineteenth Century* (Westport, Conn.: Greenwood Press, 1977).

that a competency gap distanced the members of the clerical elite at the top of the social pyramid from the mass of common laborers and black servants below, the structure was composed of several levels of leadership. Leadership was more dispersed than a narrow definition of the term would allow. Not confined to a few notables selected and patronized by white (and other black) antislavery activists, it was as likely to be found among men in small parishes and on the itinerant circuit who, despite their less favorable circumstances, were able to stoke the fires of antislavery sentiment by suggesting new options to the black folks who heard them from day to day. The church was as close to a grass roots movement as the free black community could sustain at that stage in its development, and Cannon was one model of a grass roots leader. There were, in fact, a variety of clerical styles, three of which are outlined in the discussion that follows.

A redefinition of black clerical leadership requires a new perception of the efforts of those who advanced the objectives of the antislavery movement in significant but generally unheralded ways. Thus, a reassessment of what qualified as legitimate abolitionist activity also is clearly in order, a major revisionist effort only hinted at here. While members of the clerical elite traveled, wrote books, and addressed antislavery audiences, as noted in the press, their less distinguished brothers built Sunday schools, raised money, and joined or sponsored local groups responsive to community needs, all efforts which had the effect of heightening the racial consciousness and collective identity of black people. Measurable sociopolitical progress alone is an inadequate gauge for evaluating the effectiveness of the church; its enduring contributions lie primarily in other areas.

The particular mission of most black churchmen was to improve the quality of life for black people. While long-range goals were often blurred, many of these clergymen were engaged in the short-run with activities that would promote self-respect, self-worth, and control over one's life. Some did this by supporting moral improvement, others by focusing on local and denominational growth, and still others by promoting political involvement. They were aided in these endeavors by the fact that the church could draw from a well of shared history and common experiences to fill a collective need for liberation. Furthermore, if one agrees with James Cone's contention that the fundamental theme of black biblical exegesis has been liberation,[5] then one can speak as well of the development of a committed community of interest, albeit in an embryonic sense. The church gave black people a chance to exercise institutional control and an opportunity to gain self-respect. One result was that by 1860, although material circumstances for free blacks had deteriorated, church members were able to point to progress of a different kind; they witnessed a new sense of personal and racial pride, and a developing ability to exert autonomous control over an important area of their lives.

When organized immediatist abolitionism appeared on the public scene in 1830, the black church was simultaneously entering a new, more secure and outward-turning phase in its development, a congruence that increased the likelihood of interaction between the two efforts. Although the centrality of the church and the role of the clergyman in the black community had long been accepted, the corporate existence of the institution in America dated only from 1773, when the first formally organized black church appeared. In the years immediately following, churchmen were of necessity preoccupied with challenges to institutional legitimacy and autonomy; by 1830, however, having weathered the attacks of critics and demonstrated the viability of black religious separatism in the free states (though it was still suppressed in southern and border states), clergymen had acquired sufficient confidence and experience to move beyond concern with mere survival to matters of program. That black clerical leaders and white abolitionists would borrow ideas and personnel from each other seemed inevitable; many of their goals appeared similar, and both groups were testing their approaches in a society unreceptive, when not openly hostile, to them.

Participation in antislavery activities was one of the factors that helped produce a black clerical elite. A much larger group of ministers served in middle-class or historically notable black parishes, and a still greater number worked in small congregations and on the

5 James Cone, *Liberation: A Black Theology of Liberation* (New York: J. B. Lippincott, 1970), 23ff.

itinerant circuit. But those relatively few men who were prominent in abolitionist circles received maximum exposure and hence national and international stature. A selection process—responsive to indications of personal talent as well as external pressures—helped catapult these men into the limelight, creating a nineteenth-century equivalent of what W. E. B. DuBois termed in the twentieth century a "talented tenth," that is, a small minority of gifted and educated people whose efforts would hopefully contribute to the elevation of the race. Thanks to the efforts of recent historians and biographers, we are coming to know more about these prominent black abolitionists, and can trace their tortuous paths through Garrisonianism and, for most, into the Liberty party. Yet it is misleading to regard this elite as representative of black clerical abolition; most black clergymen were engaged on more mundane levels, attracting minimal attention outside their communities. As a consequence, we know little about the ministries of these historically obscure figures, and even less about their role in the intellectual filtering process by which ideas were transmitted from the top down and received from the bottom up.

The black clergymen who publicly participated in the antislavery crusade were privileged in ways not directly related to their involvement with the movement. Although many of them were former slaves or fugitives, they were gifted with personal qualities that may have placed them further along on what William and Jane Pease have described as the "continuum of freedom." According to the Peases, "Where individuals found themselves on the continuum of freedom and how they understood its meaning was, in short, the most important single fact shaping the black crusade (for abolition and civil rights) in the antebellum North."[6] Where a black clergyman found himself on the continuum of freedom depended, of course, on a host of variables, some of which were beyond his control—talent, skill, education, luck, appearance, location. Higher social status might be achieved, or it might be conferred.

If a competency gap separated members of this clerical talented tenth from the mass of poor black workers, it generally did not cor-

6 Pease and Pease, *They Who Would be Free*, 286.

respond to their relationship with their immediate constituencies, where members, some of them advantaged themselves, supported the political activism of their ministers. In the vanguard of antislavery activity, the ranks of this clerical elite included Congregationalists Amos Beman, J. W. C. Pennington, Charles Ray, and Samuel Ringgold Ward; Episcopalians Alexander Crummell, James T. Holly, and Peter Williams; Presbyterians Samuel Cornish, Henry Highland Garnet, James Gloucester, and Theodore Wright; African Methodist Episcopal Zionists J. W. Loguen and Christopher Rush; and the African Methodist Daniel A. Payne. Out of this group of fourteen, only three belonged to independent black denominations; the majority served in traditionally white religious societies. They interacted regularly with white abolitionists, and while they respected the tolerance displayed by upper-middle-class whites, they were not misled by what passed for white altruism. Most would have agreed that white patronage had somehow facilitated selective black mobility, while simultaneously rejecting the notion that white standards were the only measure of black "leadership."

The prominence these men enjoyed set them apart from not only the disadvantaged laity but from their less renowned colleagues as well: there were, however, two harsh realities that served to remind all of them of their shared history and existential situation. One was the continuing pressure of discrimination, and the other was the lack of economic security.

While the passage of the Fugitive Slave Law posed a collective threat to the security of all free blacks, it was the daily acts of intolerance and discrimination that most deeply affected those victimized by them. Itinerant preachers and missionaries feared for their very lives; prominent ministers and settled pastors in socially prestigious curés suffered less dramatic but perhaps equally demoralizing forms of injustice. Peter Williams was forced by his bishop to resign from the board of the American Antislavery Society, and in 1834 his church was sacked by mobs; Alexander Crummell, Isaiah DeGrasse, J. W. C. Pennington, and Amos Beman were denied admission to educational institutions; Theodore Wright was harassed at Princeton Seminary by a group of rowdies; Henry Highland Garnet, Crummell, and Pennington were ejected from public conveyances; Samuel Cornish was refused tea at an inn.[7] William Douglass, rector of the prominent parish of St. Thomas Episcopal Church in Philadelphia, where the carpets were thick and the organ music first-rate, reportedly had "no more seat in the Episcopal Convention of that State than if he were a dog."[8] The list of abuses is long, and then incomplete. For while clergymen who were public figures could call attention to acts of injustice, local preachers like Noah Cannon had to fight their battles unaided and unnoticed.

Economic insecurity was as much a part of the fabric of life for black clergymen as was discrimination. It acted as a great leveler, reducing the possibilities for individual success, at least in an economic sense, to insignificance.

The inability of most clergymen to achieve economic security from their parish work alone did have the advantage, not always perceived by them as such, of keeping them close to the secular world where the members of their congregations earned their daily bread. The clerical talented tenth, whose visibility extended beyond the parish limits, were frequently able to supplement their earnings with vocationally related tasks, such as teaching, writing, and antislavery lecturing, but such income was unpredictable and debt was common.

It was an economic strain for black people to support a church and its program; the ubiquitous financial crunch was as much a part of black church life as family life. Church membership in the free black community was proportionately smaller than it was in the white, although the census of 1850 indicated that the ratio of clergy to laity was roughly comparable in both communities.[9] Nonmembers might develop informal associations with particular churches,

7 Cornish described the incident in *The Emancipator*, August 17, 1837; it is quoted in Roi Ottley and William J. Weatherby, *The Negro in New York: An Informal Social History* (New York: Oceana Press, 1967), 42. Ottley and Weatherby contend that there was a group of white toughs in New York City, called the Blackbirders, who made it a practice of harassing free blacks for the purpose of capturing them as fugitives and selling them as slaves to traders.

8 Samuel Ringgold Ward, *Autobiography of a Fugitive Negro* (reprint; New York: Arno Press, 1968), 283. Ward also cites the indignities suffered by other free black men of stature. The circumstances that led to the founding of St. Thomas Church are discussed in Carol V. R. George, *Segregated Sabbaths* (New York: Oxford University Press, 1973), 63.

9 Report of the Superintendent of the Census, *The Seventh Census* (Washington: Armstrong, 1853), 29, 30.

and even contribute to their support, but generally the burden of devising ways to meet expenses fell to a faithful remnant. And their personal resources were meager. In New York City, for example, the largest class of free black workers in 1850 was made up of servants whose cash income was negligible.[10] For purposes of comparison, it is useful to note that white employees engaged in working with cotton goods in the state in that year earned a monthly income of $18.32, representing an annual income double that received by traveling AME preachers.[11] Allowing for a handful of notable exceptions, black churches were financially poorer than white churches of comparable size, because their members earned less and endowments were nonexistent. Few congregations could maintain the salary of a clergyman of the stature of Henry Highland Garnet, who in 1857 earned $500, including $200 from the American Missionary Association for serving as a city missionary.[12] A comfortable church like St. Philip's Episcopal in New York City, which even in the nineteenth century had an endowment growing out of property grants from wealthy, white Trinity parish, was unique; in most black churches the budget was too tight to be stretched to make ends meet. The result was that black ministers had to devise ingeni-

10 J. D. B. DeBow (comp.), *Statistical View of the United States, Compendium of the 7th Census* (Washington: Nicholson, 1854), 80, 81. DeBow's figures for those jobs in New York City requiring education that were filled by blacks is as follows: clerks, 7; doctors, 9; druggists, 3; lawyers, 4; merchants, 3; printers, 4; student, 1; teachers, 8; ministers, 21.

11 *The Seventh Census, 1850.* The figures for those working in "Cotton Goods" in the state were: $18.32, males; $9.68, females. The New York African Society for Mutual Relief, a black benevolent organization founded in 1810, would have confirmed the existence of a much larger group of black professionals and businessmen in New York City. See John J. Zuille (comp.), *Historical Sketch of the New York African Society for Mutual Relief* (New York: n.p., 1897), available on microfilm. See also Edgar J. McManus, *Black Bondage in the North* (Syracuse: Syracuse University Press, 1973).

12 Quarles, *Black Abolitionists,* 80; Schor, *Henry Highland Garnet,* 29, 144, 210. Clerical compensation is difficult to calculate, in part because supplementary income is rarely recorded. J. T. Holly, the rector of St. Luke's Episcopal Church, New Haven, was supposed to receive $150 per year, but in three years' time (between 1857 and 1860), the salary fell in arrears by $139.25. In 1839, Amos Beman, a Congregationalist minister, was scheduled to receive the handsome salary of $400; he managed to raise most of it among his members, but finally had to call on white aid. See Robert Austin Warner, *New Haven Negroes* (New Haven: Yale University Press, 1940), 78–94. The large and prestigious AME church in Cincinnati in 1858 listed an annual stipend for its minister of $437, although the budget for the entire denomination in 1846, with 69 ministers, was only $7,231.03. See Benjamin W. Arnett (ed.), *Proceedings of the Semi-Centenary Celebration of the African Methodist Episcopal Church of Cincinnati* (Cincinnati: Watkin, 1874), 25; and Henry McNeal Turner, *The Genius and Theory of Methodist Polity, or The Machinery of Methodism* (Philadelphia: AME Church Publication Department, 1885), 241.

ous ways to cover their expenses, including resorting to white patronage.

The financial strain was even greater for those clergymen who did not share the prominence of the talented tenth. If the members of the talented tenth formed a clerical elite, visible, active on the antislavery circuit, comparatively more privileged than their colleagues, another and larger category of ministers was made up of those who served in what might be termed middle-class (or historically notable) parishes. As concerned about abolitionism and civil rights as their more distinguished brothers, they tended to be not as well educated nor as well positioned socially as the others, and consequently had fewer resources to draw upon. Their tenuous financial circumstances forced them to look for additional income in farming, teaching, shopkeeping, barbering, smithing, or any number of other skilled tasks. Economic considerations also had the effect of limiting the amount of time they could give to the abolitionist campaign; Samuel Ringgold Ward, himself prominent in antislavery circles, noted, "The anti-slavery cause does not, cannot, find bread and education for one's children." [13] Not that ministers in this second group did not assume leadership positions, but rather the nature of their circumstances was such that they were limited to participation in local, regional, and denominational activities. The Reverend Lewis Woodson, for example, recently referred to as the "father of black nationalism," was an AME minister in Pittsburgh and a prominent figure at the 1841 meeting of the Pennsylvania State Convention of Colored Freemen, who supplemented his income by working as a barber. [14]

But the vast majority of antebellum black ministers belonged neither to the talented tenth nor to what might be conveniently termed the clerical middle class. The members of this third and largest group passed their careers in ministries to the local community or in traveling circuit. Primarily preachers, in their own eyes

13 Ward, *Autobiography of a Fugitive Negro*, 117.
14 Schor, in *Henry Highland Garnet*, 154, refers to Floyd J. Miller's study, "The Father of Black Nationalism," *Civil War History*, XVII (December, 1971), 310–19. See also *Proceedings of the State Convention of the Colored Freemen of Pennsylvania* (Pittsburgh: Matthew Grant, 1841), 16. There were seven Methodist clergymen along with Woodson (who served as secretary) who answered the roll at the convention.

and those of others, they were compelled to seek secular employment to meet personal and family economic burdens. Unsophisti-
cated by the standards of antislavery audiences, and isolated from
that reformist milieu, they worked at tasks similar to those of their
parishioners. A random sample of preachers who fit into this category indicates that most were African Methodists, either AME or
AMEZ; in the period before the Civil War the total number of black
men ordained to the Episcopal priesthood, for example, amounted to
only seventeen, while in 1856 there were that number of AME
preachers on the New York circuit alone.[15] Typically, ministers in
this category received the "call" to preach in late adolescence or
early adulthood, moved about regularly after ordination, and were
minimally literate in the conventional sense. They left few records
or printed sermons, and emerge from history only in the minutes of
denominational conventions, where their presence and parochial activities are noted along with their rare statements to the delegates.
There was no leadership gap in the field; a favorite expression
among African Methodists was "like priests, like people."[16] In fact,
where a leadership gap did exist, it tended to operate in a negative
way, with members of the congregation readily filling any power
vacuum they perceived. The paradoxical result was that the African
Methodists' inability to implement clerical authority in the field
encouraged the growth of lay leadership, with members vying for
control of budgetary matters, ministerial selection, and program direction. But even a professionally ineffective local preacher provided
both a role model and a symbolic center for the congregation.

While most northern church-going blacks in the period before
the Civil War were Methodists by persuasion or adoption, a glance at
the religious affiliation of members of the clerical elite reveals that
Methodists were underrepresented in the circle of antislavery activists. The denomination did not contribute leadership to the formal organizations of the abolitionist movement in proportion to its
members. There were, of course, notable exceptions, such as Christopher Rush, Richard Allen, J. W. Loguen, and Daniel A. Payne. But

15 George F. Bragg, *History of the Afro-American Group of the Episcopal Church* (Baltimore: Church Advocate Press, 1922), 15; Payne, *History of the AME Church*, 416.
16 Payne, *History of the AME Church*, 179.

one generally looks in vain to find the names of black Methodists among those who traveled the established antislavery route, or who held high office in abolitionist organizations. This limited involvement may be related to the original decision Methodist clergymen made to join with a racially separated religious body, as well as to their generally straitened circumstances. It is also true that parochial concerns began to demand more attention from ministers and bishops than had been the case when the groups were small and members were few. But perhaps when evaluating black Methodist involvement, or lack thereof, we need to refocus our frame of reference. Instead of asking why so few black Methodist clergymen held prominent positions in abolitionist organizations, one might well ask what defined a particular activity as authentically abolitionist or pro–civil rights. Or one may ask, why white antislavery activists failed to join with local black clergymen to advance the civil rights of a particular congregation, as in Noah Cannon's situation. If abolitionist activity were redefined along these lines, black Methodists and others would occupy more conspicuous places in accounts of the reform crusade. Furthermore, such a redefinition would encourage a new appreciation for the effectiveness of the church as a grass roots movement, along with a willingness to acknowledge the efforts of less distinguished members of the clergy whose form of parochial abolitionism appeared as important to the members of their congregations as the political activism of their more prominent colleagues.

If a new, more inclusive understanding of civil rights activity incorporated the following efforts—strengthening a black witness in American life, promoting black institutional growth in churches and schools, and counseling racial cooperation and aid to fugitives—then the work of black bishops William Paul Quinn and Daniel A. Payne, for example, would qualify. Payne, the better known of the two primarily because of his writings as a church historian, was vitally interested in educational development, while Quinn, elected an AME bishop in 1844, was more concerned with expansion and membership growth. Quinn successfully extended AME influence into Ohio and the western territories; Payne, with somewhat less immediate success, waged what was at times an un-

popular, single-handed campaign for AME educational development
for clergy—as in his founding of Wilberforce University—and for
young children and adults as well. Although denominational needs
took precedence, neither man neglected the larger issues confronting free blacks. In his episcopal address to the AME conference in
1851, Bishop Quinn charged his listeners to honor their commitment to preach despite the difficulties created by "prejudice and persecution." Advising cooperation, he said, "We should work together.
Nine times out of ten when we look into the face of a white man we
see our enemy. A great many like to see us in the kitchen, but few in
the parlor. Our hope is in God's blessing on our own wise, strong,
and well-directed efforts."[17] Similarly, Bishop Payne urged the judicious exercise of power in church governmental affairs by noting,
"[T]he American republic oppresses and enslaves every man who
has a drop of African blood in his veins, and hunts the panting fugitive like a wild beast. . . . It is a fact as disgraceful as it is painful that
no despot in Asia, Europe, or Africa is as cruel and relentless in the
persecution of its victims as the American republic."[18] In consequence of that fact, Payne urged denominational reconciliation and
understanding. Both men, like many of the clergy in the field, offered informed leadership to the members in their care, whose needs
were allegedly at the heart of reform efforts to improve civil rights. It
may also appear that by describing their episcopacies in this way,
Payne and Quinn agreed with the board members of the New York
Committee of Vigilance who expressed a preference for "practical
abolitionists."[19] But their printed sermons suggest that their practical programs emerged out of theological-philosophical presupposi-
tions.

Their theology, like that of most of their colleagues, was nineteenth-century evangelical Protestantism, heavily weighted in the
direction of a humanized, liberating Christology. But they took special pains to balance the claims of the sacred and the secular, a

17  *Ibid.*, 256–57.
18  *Bishop Payne's First Annual Address to the Philadelphia Conference of the AME
Church* (Philadelphia: Sherman, 1853), 17. This address is also found in Charles Killian (ed.),
*Bishop Payne's Sermons and Addresses, 1853–1891* (reprint; New York: Arno Press, 1972).
19  New York Committee of Vigilance, *First Annual Report, 1837.* Theodore Wright and
Samuel Cornish were among those who signed the report.

reflection, in part, of the duality of Protestantism itself. More than that, it was the result of seeing God acting in history on behalf of oppressed peoples. Bishop Benjamin Arnett was presumably describing the collective mind of the AME church when he said, "Our organization, like others, had its general and special purposes. The general purpose was to assist in bringing the world to the foot of the cross of Christ; and the special was to assist in relieving the African race from physical, mental, and moral bondage."[20] Christ presumably brought relief, release, and liberation, but there was plenty of room for human agency, and that was the special purpose of the AME church. Theoretically, this high mission not only made every church a unit in a relatively broadly based civil rights organization, but also harmonized with an important aspect of the abolitionist crusade insofar as reformers were concerned about the physical, mental, and moral bondage of blacks. In practice, however, the church often fell short of its special mission.

It is not being unduly defensive of the AME church to observe that institutional change develops at a snail's pace, the result of the cautious, protective inclinations of those in decision-making positions. In the antebellum period, black Methodism was a neophyte organization, its members, according to Bishop Payne, largely untutored, underemployed, and regularly subjected to intimidation.[21] While Presbyterians and Congregationalists could flex their spiritual muscles on the slavery issue, guardedly confident that state legislatures would not close their doors, African Methodists enjoyed no such assurance. When a majority report on slavery, denying membership to those who held slaves, was presented to the 1856 AME general convention, it was labeled radical and hotly debated. Not that AME delegates seriously believed that there were many, if any, slaveholders in their midst, but rather that the statement would be regarded as a symbol of the church's political stance. A milder, compromise report was finally passed, essentially because partici-

---

20 Arnett, *Proceedings of the Semi-Centenary Celebration*, 12.

21 *Bishop Payne's First Annual Address*, 11, 12. The same year that Payne gave his address (1853), the Pennsylvania Society for Promoting the Abolition of Slavery reported that Bethel Church had the largest black Sunday school, with 524 students, followed by St. Thomas with 183. See Benjamin C. Bacon (comp.), *Statistics of the Colored People of Philadelphia* (Philadelphia: T. Ellwood Chapman, 1856), 10, 11.

pants were persuaded that adoption of the stronger statement would result in the closing of struggling southern black churches and encourage the arrest or intimidation of itinerants in border states. To pass the more radical report simply as a witness was useless, said one delegate, because "Every colored man is an abolitionist, and slaveholders know it."[22]

Black churches witnessed to their antislavery sympathies in other, less overtly political ways. Settled pastors promoted Sunday schools and tried in addition to maintain day and evening schools. Most congregations had women's auxiliaries; in the AME church they were known as Dorcas societies and reportedly served as "an auxiliary of the Vigilance Committee, and as such gathered the necessary clothing and food for the passing runaway." Harboring fugitives qualified anyone willing to take the risk as a practical abolitionist, and the degree to which one publicized such activity enhanced its value as a political act. J. W. Loguen's reception of runaways was as generally known as his stand against the Fugitive Slave Law; he claimed that 1,500 fugitives had passed through his door at 293 East Genesee Street in Syracuse.[23]

Some individual AME churches had a better opportunity than others to implement their mission to relieve the physical and spiritual bondage of Africans. Perhaps a brief sketch of the development of one AME parish can serve to illustrate some of the general problems that pastors and parishioners confronted as they tried to shape a viable black institution. Allen Temple, Cincinnati, is admittedly not typical of AME congregational development. Founded in 1823, it had a tradition which contributed to its enduring prestige and size. Its early history was also determined in part by its geographical location at the very edge of free soil. But its local problems did reflect some common struggles.

The AME church first planted its branch of Zion in Ohio in 1823, and the circuit was served by a series of itinerant preachers. Before

22 Payne, *History of the AME Church*, 337–45. Quarles, *Black Abolitionists*, 56, quotes a black editor in 1849: "The mind does not take its complexion from the skin. To be a colored man is not necessarily to be an abolitionist."

23 Ottley and Weatherby, *The Negro in New York*, 85; Loguen, *The Reverend J. W. Loguen*, 444; J. W. Loguen to Gerrit Smith, July 14, 1855, Ms., Syracuse University Library.

that time, black Methodists had to worship in white congregations, and according to AME Bishop Arnett, were denied the freedom of emotional expression granted to whites. On a particular Sunday in Cincinnati, says Arnett, a black man, overcome by the evangelical fervor of the white preacher and straining against the urge to leap or shout—practices specifically denied blacks—stuffed a handkerchief in his mouth. He burst a blood vessel and had to be carried out.[24] That event catalyzed black support for a separate church, and after some jockeying with white authorities, the black Methodists were given permission to meet separately. Still officially associated with the white denomination, the black congregation objected to being supplied by a white preacher, and asked to have a man of their own choosing. James King, a slave in Lexington, Kentucky, who was allowed to hire his time, was permitted to fill their pulpit for several years, traveling regularly between Ohio and Kentucky, until an antislavery judge forged freedom papers for him. Settled in Ohio, King was responsible for leading the exodus of black Methodists out of the white denomination and into the African Methodist Episcopal church. Further discriminatory behavior by whites precipitated the second move. Father King, as he came to be known, was insulted when, in the company of another local black preacher, Philip Brodie, he attended a Methodist camp meeting and was told to wait to take communion until all the whites had been served. The two men reportedly said that they did not believe in two saviors, one for whites and one for blacks. When news reached them in 1823 of the success of the AME church in Baltimore, they determined to change their allegiance to African Methodism.

According to the church's chronicler, Bishop Arnett, the society soon acquired a number of labels; it was known variously as the "antislavery church," the "black abolitionists," and "King's niggers." The church aided fugitives, became a station on the underground railroad, and in the mid-1830s invited Lane Seminary students to come and teach in their Sunday and day schools. Arnett contended that there were many "appeals to Jehovah to come in his own way

24 Arnett, *Proceedings of the Semi-Centenary Celebration,* 14.

and deliver his people from worse than Egyptian bondage. Thus the fire of liberty continued to burn and the ministers fanned the coals and raised the fire to flames."[25]

Arnett's flowery prose aside, his basic outline can be taken seriously as it fits a pattern common to other black churches. Refusal to accept white discrimination, coupled with a desire for free religious expression and an avowedly antislavery stance describe a significant part of the story of autonomous black religious institutional development.

There is also a demonstration of growth and maturation in Arnett's account. Once the initial fight over separate identity was resolved, the campaign moved to higher ground. Seemingly parochial concerns, over the budget and the Sunday school, had wider ramifications for the cause of antislavery and civil rights. Struggles between clergy and laity over matters of property and finances, Arnett believed, taught black people "knowledge of business and power of control over men." In the South, it "stimulated the hope of the people," by giving them glimpses of freedom and black mobility.[26]

By the 1850s, a separatist undertone pervaded the message of most black churches, which is not surprising given the increasingly oppressive racial climate of opinion. Separation corresponded to renewed interest in emigration, which was then being argued by some supporters as a way of acknowledging race pride and collective identity. Notable clerics like Henry Highland Garnet and Daniel Payne became converts to emigration, and both men became officers in the African Civilization Society, an organization intended for the "civilization and Christianization of Africa," which quickly became embroiled in the politics of the antislavery movement since it was perceived as an offshoot of the American Colonization Society.[27]

25 *Ibid.*, 19–20.
26 *Ibid.*, 100–101. Arnett's experience, as pastor of what became known as Allen AME Temple in Cincinnati, a large and important parish, may have influenced his perspective somewhat. In 1861, Alexander Crummell had the impression that Cincinnati had more wealthy blacks than any other city in the country. Crummell, *Charitable Institutions in Colored Churches* (Washington: n.p., 1892).
27 Payne, *History of the AME Church*, 170, 171. Useful information on the African Civilization Society is available in Schor, *Henry Highland Garnet*. The society, formed in 1858, and dominated by Garnet and also Martin Delany, grew out of the heat of emigrationist ferment in the fifties. See *Constitution of the African Civilization Society*, and *Board of Directors*, on microfilm, Schomberg Collection, New York Public Library.

Both the new appeal for emigration, based on racial integrity, and the churchmen's continued insistence on the need for self-respect, sprang from a common source.

Despite the pervasiveness of discrimination, the church, according to its supporters, did achieve some success in developing in its members a renewed sense of dignity, hope, and self-worth. Arnett addressed the issue when he said, "Here, then, is a key to explain the success of this [AME] church: Self-Respect. Its founders respected themselves, and they demanded respect from others. If the whites would not respect them, they could at least respect themselves." In 1859, J. W. C. Pennington found cause for optimism: "The race has been preserved mainly by the desperate hope for a better time coming. Their night has been long and their darkness dense. But their day has been slowly dawning, till, even now, while we speak, the sunbeams appear." Less poetically, M. H. Freeman noted that the essential goals for free blacks were "self-appreciation" and a "higher manhood." These spokesmen were addressing a widely held racist perception of blacks, which the Reverend Hosea Easton identified as the assumption that the slave was a mindless amoral "machine," and the freeman was something less than human. William Douglass commented that the slave system "blots out the moral image traced by God and says 'it is a thing.'"[28] For free blacks, self-respect and civil rights were two sides of the same coin, payment against the debt of "thing-ness."

Black churches not only preached self-respect, they gave people practical experience in acquiring it by opening up opportunities to exercise authority and gain new skills. An elderly parishioner of Arnett's in Cincinnati recalled in 1874 that "the great question proposed for solution fifty years ago was, can colored men conduct successfully a religious organization?" Citing the half-century of growth and achievement of the AME church, he concluded, "If these

---

28 Arnett, *Proceedings of the Semi-Centenary Celebration,* 99; J. W. C. Pennington, "The Self-Redeeming Power of the Colored Races of the World," *Anglo-African Magazine,* I (October, 1859), 314; M. H. Freeman, "The Educational Wants of the Free Colored People," *Anglo-African Magazine,* I (April, 1859), 119; Hosea Easton, *A Treatise on the Intellectual Character and Civil and Political Condition of the Colored People of the United States* (Boston: Isaac Knapp, 1837), 51; William Douglass, "The Forebearance and Retributive Justice of God," *Sermons* (reprint; Freeport, N.Y.: Books for Libraries Press, 1971).

are not a full and complete refutation of the position assumed by our opposers, and a clear vindication of the correctness of our views, nothing can be." But the Episcopal minister James T. Holly demurred from such a view, suggesting instead that only by emigrating to Haiti could blacks hope "to inflame the latent embers of self-respect." The young African Methodist clergyman Henry McNeal Turner saw things differently. Attempting to convince a southern black youth to join the AME church in the 1850s, Turner said, "We have our own bishops, and we, as a race, have a chance to be somebody, and if we are ever going to be a people, now is the time." This sense of growing self-confidence is also evident in Howard Bell's assessment of emigrationist sentiment, and can apply to the church. In Bell's opinion, "Had conservative leaders of Negro thought been further removed from their own problems, they might have been able to see more clearly the growing faith of the colored man in himself which was, to some extent as least, responsible for the demand for emigration and Negro nationalism. Perhaps this new faith which [Martin] Delany and [J. M.] Whitfield were preaching, was understood better outside of abolitionist circles, than within." [29]

The question of whether all, some, or only a few black churches were outposts of the abolitionist and reform crusade cannot be answered without reevaluating what should be considered valid, useful contributions to the movement. Certainly our vision needs to extend beyond the efforts of the clerical talented tenth. Black churches varied in the extent to which they provided moral, physical, and intellectual training grounds for their members. Some, like Allen Temple, were busy stations on the underground railroad; others, like the congregations of Lewis Woodson and Henry Highland Garnet, supported the political activism of their ministers. Most offered regular and heavy doses of moral reform. All black churches provided ideological supports not found in the dominant

29 Arnett, *Proceedings of the Semi-Centenary Celebration*, 31; James T. Holly, "A Vindication of the Capacity of the Negro Race for Self-Government and Civilized Progress," in Howard Brotz (ed.), *Negro Social and Political Thought, 1850–1920* (New York: Basic Books, 1966), 142 (Holly's "Vindication" appeared in 1857); Robert Anderson, *The Life of the Reverend Robert Anderson* (Atlanta: Foote and Davies, 1900), 46; Howard H. Bell, *The Negro Convention Movement, 1830–1861* (reprint; New York: Arno Press, 1969).

white society. Whether that made all of them agents of the abolitionist and civil rights campaign depends on how widely we draw
the circle describing such activity. The church, like abolitionism,
helped foster the development of self-respect and black consciousness.

# Politics

# THE JACKSONIANS
# AND SLAVERY

*Leonard L. Richards*

PERHAPS John Quincy Adams was right, after all. He never accepted the popular notion that his defeat at the hands of Andrew Jackson in 1828 marked the "triumph of democracy." That was merely political hogwash put forth by the Jacksonians. In his eyes, Jackson's presidential victory was a triumph for southern slavemasters.

Until recently, twentieth-century historians paid no heed to the acerbic loser. Giving him low marks as an analyst, political historians simply dismissed Adams's observations as those of a cantankerous old man, while singing the praises of Jacksonian Democracy. Indeed, for many years the only serious debate was over the origin of the democratic upsurge. In one book, the typical democrats were simply farming folk and restless pioneers; in another, the urban masses; in another, expectant capitalists; and in still another, a motley assortment of all three.[1] The slavery question seldom entered the discussion.

---

1 See, for example, Frederick Jackson Turner, *Rise of the New West, 1819–1829* (New York: Harper and Brothers, 1906); Charles and Mary Beard, *The Rise of American Civilization* (2 vols.; New York: Macmillan Co., 1927), I, Chap. 12; Arthur Schlesinger, Jr., *The Age of Jackson* (Boston: Little, Brown and Co., 1945); Richard Hofstadter, *The American Political Tradition* (New York: Alfred A. Knopf, Inc., 1948); Chap. 3; Lee Benson, *The Concept of Jacksonian Democracy* (Princeton, N.J.: Princeton University Press, 1961); Robert V. Remini, *The Election of Andrew Jackson* (Philadelphia: J. B. Lippincott Co., 1963).

At the same time, oddly enough, antislavery scholars turned out a spate of books indicating that the slavery question took on a new urgency during the Jacksonian years. Many dated the new upsurge with the appearance of Garrison's *Liberator* in 1831. Others placed more emphasis on Nat Turner's slave uprising, which later in the same year sent a chill of terror through the white South. Some pointed to 1833, when Parliament abolished slavery in the British West Indies and American abolitionists organized for a national crusade. Still others emphasized 1835, when northern abolitionists bombarded the South with antislavery pamphlets, creating a furor from Charleston to New Orleans, and causing citizens in Mount Meigs, Alabama, and in East Feliciana, Louisiana, to post $50,000 each for the delivery of Arthur Tappan, president of the American Anti-Slavery Society, dead or alive.[2]

No one doubted for a moment that major politicians responded to these developments. Yet, since most politicians were obviously hostile to organized antislavery, students of the antislavery movement generally ignored them. Typically, researchers spent thousands of man-hours trying to understand the differences between major abolitionists such as Theodore Dwight Weld and William Lloyd Garrison, and only a minute or two on the major politicians. Did Whigs and Anti-Masons differ from Democrats on the slavery controversy? Where precisely did Senator Buncombe stand? Such questions, in effect, were left to political historians, who in turn were far too busy determining how many workingmen supported Andrew Jackson, or how many rich men voted Whig, to provide any answers.

Now, perhaps, the tide is turning. In a now famous article, which first appeared in 1966 and has been reprinted many times, Richard H. Brown contended that Martin Van Buren and others fashioned the Jacksonian coalition to protect slavery. After watching James

2 See, for example, Gilbert Hobbes Barnes, *The Anti-Slavery Impulse, 1830–1844* (Washington, D.C.: American Historical Association, 1933); Dwight L. Dumond, *Antislavery* (Ann Arbor: University of Michigan Press, 1961); Louis Filler, *The Crusade Against Slavery* (New York: Harper and Brothers, 1960); John L. Thomas, *The Liberator* (Boston: Little, Brown and Co., 1963); Russel B. Nye, *Fettered Freedom* (East Lansing, Mich.: Michigan State University Press, 1963); W. Sherman Savage, *The Controversy over the Distribution of Abolition Literature* (n.p., 1938); Bertram Wyatt-Brown, "The Abolitionists' Postal Campaign of 1835," *Journal of Negro History*, L (October, 1965), 227–38.

Tallmadge, Rufus King, and other northern congressmen lambaste slavery and the three-fifths rule during the Missouri crisis, Van Buren and his colleagues concluded that the collapse of Jeffersonian Republicanism might lead to antislavery political parties. To offset this, according to Brown, they constructed a party that would fight the old battles of Jefferson's heyday once again, quiet the slavery issue, and protect the South's dominant position within the Union.[3] Antislavery scholars, in turn, have found bits of evidence that lend some credence to Brown's hotly disputed thesis. It was the Jacksonians, they argue, who took the lead in trying to stamp out abolitionism.

As yet, no one has gathered and analyzed enough evidence to prove or disprove Adams's contention about the triumph of the Democrats. Brown and others have provided little more than a few telling quotes and interesting leads. And Brown, as his critics insist, may have overstated his case.[4] Still, while the picture as a whole is incomplete, blurry, and perhaps distorted, a few lines seem sharp.

It is now clear that Adams had a better case than historians of Jacksonian Democracy generally have acknowledged. Too often, in trying to link Jackson's smashing victory with the "triumph of democracy," they simply repeated self-serving quotes and colorful anecdotes. One book after another, for example, told about the rollicking partisans who romped through the executive mansion on inauguration day, muddying rugs, smashing china, and jumping enthusiastically to get a glimpse of Old Hickory. This thundering herd, so the story went, represented a new democratic force in Washington politics. "It was a proud day for the *people*," exclaimed the Jacksonian propagandist Amos Kendall. "General Jackson is *their own* president." Such remarks were repeated endlessly, often as gospel.

Historians should have known better. Even Adams spotted a basic fact in the election returns that historians long ignored. Sour and uncharitable, he read the returns as a defeat for democracy and a victory for the South. He was hardly an unbiased observer, of course, but neither were the Jacksonians. And, like the Jacksonians,

3 Richard H. Brown, "The Missouri Crisis, Slavery, and the Politics of Jacksonianism," *South Atlantic Quarterly*, LXV (Winter, 1966), 55–72.

4 See, for example, John M. McFaul, "Expediency vs. Morality: Jacksonian Politics and Slavery," *Journal of American History*, LXII (June, 1975), 24–39.

he failed to give the opposition their due. Jackson had been trounced in New England, which was Adams's home ground, but Old Hickory had done well in other northern states, and overall had won 50.3 percent of the northern vote.

Still, there is no doubt that the magnitude of Jackson's victory was due to the South. He carried most southern states by whopping majorities, and won 72.6 percent of the southern vote. And, thanks to the mechanics of the three-fifths clause and the electoral college, his 200,000 southern supporters provided him with far more help, man for man, than some 400,000 northerners: 105 electoral votes as compared with 73. Hence, unless one is willing to say that the slaveholding states were much more democratic than the free states, or that Virginia was less aristocratic than states like Ohio and Vermont, then the old thesis of triumphant democracy must be laid aside.

Jackson's popularity in the South, of course, hardly proves that the Jacksonians were the prosouthern, proslavery party. His southern landslide obviously had much to do with his being a favorite son, the South's foremost Indian fighter, the hero of the Battle of New Orleans, as well as a rich Tennessee slaveholder. Certainly once Old Hickory was off the ticket, many prominent slaveholders deserted the Democratic fold, refusing to support his hand-picked successor, Martin Van Buren of New York. Indeed, the wily New Yorker was lucky to break even in states where Jackson encountered little more than token opposition, or no opposition at all. In 1832, against Henry Clay, Jackson won the major slaveholding states by a margin of nearly three to one; in the same states, four years later, Van Buren polled 173,000 votes to his opponents' 174,000.

But Van Buren ran against local favorites, an obvious handicap, and did better than any other northern candidate has ever done under such circumstances. Shall we conclude that Van Buren, compared with Jackson, did poorly in the South—and thus by implication score a point against Brown's thesis? Or shall we say that Van Buren, as a northerner running against home-grown heroes, did remarkably well in the South—indeed, far better than could be expected—and thus perhaps add credence to the claim that the Van Burenites were "northern men with southern principles"?

However we put it, there was clearly a darker side to Jacksonian Democracy, which for years liberal historians ignored, placing Jackson high in the galaxy of liberal heroes, and ranking him as one of the nation's five or six truly "great" presidents. Arthur Schlesinger, Jr., in his celebrated *Age of Jackson*, even managed to write 530 pages on Jackson and the American liberal tradition without discussing Jackson's Indian policy.[5] But times have changed. Recent studies of racial injustice have undermined the reputations of Jefferson, Jackson, and other heroes of the liberal past. In Jefferson's case, liberals can still rise to his defense, pointing for example to the Northwest Ordinance of 1787, which barred slavery from the Ohio Valley. In Jackson's case, little can be said.[6] It was virtually impossible to find a black man, noted an English visitor in 1835, who was not "an anti-Jackson man."[7]

We always knew, of course, that both Jefferson and Jackson were slaveholding presidents. In times past, however, we were told repeatedly that Jefferson was an extremely kind master who was somehow sucked into the vicious slaveholding system despite his good intentions, and that he suffered from anguish and guilt all his life. Not much was ever said about Jackson's conscience, whether he suffered from guilt and anguish, but he was said to be fond of his house servants. We knew about his temper tantrums, his vindictiveness, his violent acts, but somehow we concluded that those outbursts were directed against the rich and the powerful—bankers and political enemies, Indian warriors and British soldiers—and not against some hapless slave who happened to cross him. Indeed, after reading Schlesinger and other Jacksonian enthusiasts, it seemed that in fact Old Hickory's temper was a well-controlled tactic tuned to good causes, rather than a genuine character flaw.

Then in the 1960s disconcerting evidence began trickling in. Not much could be said when Jefferson was shown to be a racist, since everyone else was shown to be a racist too. And not much could be

5 Schlesinger, *Age of Jackson*, first appeared in 1945.
6 For Jefferson's defense, see William W. Freehling, "The Founding Fathers and Slavery," *American Historical Review*, LXXVII (February, 1972), 81–93. For Jackson, see F. P. Prucha, "Andrew Jackson's Indian Policy: A Reassessment," *Journal of American History*, LVI (December, 1969), 527–39.
7 Edward S. Abdy, *Journal of a Residence and Tour in the United States of North America, from April, 1833, to October, 1834* (3 vols., London: John Murray, 1835).

said when a few historians insisted that Jefferson lusted after his mulatto slave, Sally Hemings, who also happened to be his late wife's half-sister. The Sally Hemings story was old hat, and the evidence was somewhat shaky. But a short article by William Cohen on Jefferson's treatment of his slaves shook the liberal faith. Poor James Hubbard! He disliked being a slave on Jefferson's farm, and ran away repeatedly. Once when Hubbard was recaptured, Jefferson noted: "I had him severely flogged in the presence of his old companions." The words leapt out from the page, and so did the evidence that Jefferson bought and sold slaves regularly, and even broke up slave families when it was to his financial advantage.[8] True, Jefferson was no Simon Legree, but he hardly qualified for sainthood.

Less attention has been focused on Jackson's private life, yet old and damning evidence has been rediscovered. Apparently Jackson was like most big planters in his concern about the health and well-being of his slaves. But Jackson also conspicuously exercised his property rights, buying and selling slaves regularly, and even wagering them on horse races. And at times he was undoubtedly a hard master; in 1804, for example, he advertised for a runaway slave, promising a fifty dollar reward "and ten dollars extra for every hundred lashes any person will give to the amount of three hundred."[9]

The "ten dollars extra for every hundred lashes," however, has not hurt Old Hickory's reputation nearly as much as the contention that Negro-haters naturally gravitated to the Jacksonian party. It too is an old supposition, dating back to Jackson's presidency. Like an old piece of furniture, it was discarded years ago, only to be later rediscovered, refinished, and updated. Thanks to recent research, it seems sturdier now than ever before.

Jackson's opponents, it is clear, were anything but tolerant. In a society in which politicians of all stripes abused blacks, there is no doubt that many Whigs stoned abolitionists, demolished black churches, and razed black districts. One of the most outrageous

8 William Cohen, "Thomas Jefferson and the Problem of Slavery," *Journal of American History*, LVI (December, 1969), 503–26.

9 Chase C. Mooney, *Slavery in Tennessee* (Bloomington: Indiana University Press, 1957), 52, 91; Michael Paul Rogin, *Fathers and Children: Andrew Jackson and the Subjugation of the American Indian* (New York: Alfred A. Knopf, Inc., 1975), 57; James C. Curtis, *Andrew Jackson and the Search for Vindication* (Boston: Little, Brown and Co., 1976), 135–37.

race-baiters in the North, James Watson Webb of the New York *Courier and Enquirer*, was a Whig. But the Whigs were never united on the race question, and a few Whig leaders clearly sympathized with the plight of the dark-skinned. Many more hated the Irish and the Catholic church far more than they hated blacks. And oftentimes, many of them were simply too busy denouncing the Pope, Bishop John Hughes, and "scheming Jesuits" to be "nigger-knocking."

The Jacksonians, by contrast, were generally of one mind. Historians have unearthed a few who sympathized with blacks or worried much about Catholics, but generally speaking the party of Jackson was the party of the Catholic immigrant, and Democrats marched shoulder to shoulder on the race question. Quite a few of them, in earlier days, had led racist drives that stripped blacks of the vote in Connecticut, New Jersey, and New York between 1818 and 1821. In Pennsylvania, Democrats led the crusade that disfranchised black voters in 1838. Subsequently, whenever the question of Negro suffrage arose in the free states, Democrats were vehemently against it, while often half of the Whig leaders and perhaps a third of the Whig voters supported it. Year in and year out, when it came to race baiting, no one exceeded the followers of Old Hickory, who spewed forth a constant stream of venom against the dark-skinned. Thus, while free blacks had little reason to be grateful to the Whigs, they had few doubts about which party hated them most.[10]

Even though the Democrats outdid the Whigs in capitalizing on white racism and in tormenting blacks, that hardly proves that Old Hickory and his followers took the lead in favoring slaveholding interests. Both parties, it could be argued, supported slavery. Northern politicians, Whigs and Democrats alike, may have felt a bit inconsistent celebrating human freedom on the Fourth of July and then sup-

10 James T. Adams, "Disfranchisement of Negroes in New England," *American Historical Review*, XXX (December, 1925), 543–47; Dixon Ryan Fox, "The Negro Vote in Old New York," *Political Science Quarterly*, XXXII (June, 1917), 252–75; Marion T. Wright, "Negro Suffrage in New Jersey, 1776–1875," *Journal of Negro History*, XXXII (April, 1948), 168–224; Edward R. Turner, *The Negro in Pennsylvania* (Washington, D.C.: American Historical Association, 1911); John L. Stanley, "Majority Tyranny in Tocqueville's America: The Failure of Negro Suffrage in 1846," *Political Science Quarterly*, LXXXIV (September, 1969), 412–35; Phyllis T. Field, "Republicans and Black Suffrage in New York State: The Grass Roots Response," *Civil War History*, XXI (June, 1975), 136–47; Ronald P. Formisano, "The Edge of Caste: Colored Suffrage in Michigan, 1827–1861," *Michigan History*, LVI (Spring, 1972), 19–41.

porting a slavemaster for president on election day—but they did it nevertheless.

And men of both parties desperately wanted to keep slavery out of the political spotlight. Knowing that slavery could easily shatter their national organizations—not to mention the Union itself—they preferred to fight over banks, tariffs, and roads. In adopting this stance, of course, they effectively supported slavery. Keeping slavery out of the political limelight was by far the most effective way of protecting slavery and the South's position within the Union.

But did both parties act the same or did one do more than the other to keep slavery out of the political arena? Political historians, by and large, have ducked the question by pretending that slavery was largely a dead issue between 1821 and 1845. Politicians, so the story goes, stumbled upon the explosive slavery question in 1819 during the Missouri crisis, then virtually forgot about it for twenty-five years while they fought over banks and tariffs, and then rediscovered it at the time of Texas and the Mexican War. That bit of received wisdom will not stand scrutiny.

First of all, the arguments against slavery were obviously well established before the Missouri debates. There is no evidence whatsoever that James Tallmadge, Rufus King, and others were fumbling about in 1819, looking for words. They hardly needed a Garrison or a Weld to supply them with arguments, to teach them that slavery was evil or that the three-fifths rule benefited the South at the expense of the North. Indeed, they clearly had all the basic arguments at their fingertips when the debate began. They went right for the jugular, hammered away for hours on end, and said virtually everything that was ever to be said on the slavery question.

Once the Missouri donnybrook was over, moreover, there was no way that politicians could rest easy about slavery or forget the arguments against it. Antislavery clearly had momentum throughout the Western world, and the old institution of slavery was rapidly giving way. By 1804 all northern states had either freed their slaves or adopted a program of gradual emancipation. In Haiti black revolutionaries abolished slavery in 1804. Argentina and Colombia adopted gradual emancipation in 1813 and 1814; Chile abolished slavery in 1823; Central America in 1824; Mexico in 1829; Bolivia in 1831. England began using its naval power to suppress the Atlantic slave trade in 1820, and in 1833 British abolitionists finally succeeded in getting Parliament to abolish slavery in the British West Indies. By the time of Jackson's presidency, in short, the American South was beginning to stand out like a sore thumb, and the United States was being taunted throughout the Western world for claiming to be "the land of liberty" when one-sixth of its people were still in chains.

In retrospect, only two major obstacles stood in the way of antislavery agitation. One was the communications network, which was both primitive and costly. Antislavery agitation was still hard and heavy work. Until canals, railways, the telegraph, and a steam-powered printing press made travel and communications cheap and almost instantaneous, it was incredibly difficult to draw people with similar opinions or parallel interests into cooperative activities. Even in the East, there were still dozens of isolated communities— like the Berkshires in Massachusetts—that had nothing to do with the rest of their states.[11] Poor and costly communications, in effect, governed: it worked against national unity, and also against sectionalism; it worked against all attempts—and particularly those of the poor—to build well-coordinated pressure groups. Only those with money or know-how could be heard.

The American Anti-Slavery Society overcame this obstacle in the 1830s. With few friends, thousands of enemies in the North as well as in the South, and only a shoestring budget, abolitionists managed not only to be heard, but also to "frighten millions out of their senses." They convinced thousands that the average planter was a brute who lusted after black women, mutilated his slaves, and sold his own mulatto children "down river." They reworked the southern image so well that "Christian women of the North" immediately thought of the slave trade and the whip whenever they heard the word "South." Their success in spreading their message—and in upsetting thousands—was largely due to their expertise as communicators.

Trained mainly in evangelistic work and seasoned in temperance and other reform movements, abolitionists took full advantage of

11 See, for example, Richard D. Birdsall, *Berkshire County: A Cultural History* (New Haven: Yale University Press, 1959), Chap. VII.

every advance in communications. Like Methodist circuit riders, Weld and other antislavery preachers moved from community to community, organizing scores of men, women, and children into antislavery societies—thus increasing the antislavery network from 47 societies in 1833 to over 1,000 by late 1836. Like Charles Grandison Finney and other evangelists, antislavery organizers relied heavily on church women, who technically had no political voice but who industriously gathered thousands of signatures for massive petitions to Congress calling for the abolition of slavery in the nation's capital. To present these petitions, abolitionists shrewdly chose as their primary spokesman John Quincy Adams, who after his presidency became a congressman, and who commanded more attention than anyone else in Congress.

In the meantime, when the introduction of steam-power presses and other technological innovations suddenly cut the cost of printing in half, Arthur Tappan and his New York associates moved quickly. In 1835 they increased their publications by nine times, and tried to flood the country with tracts, newspapers, kerchiefs, medals, emblems, and even blue chocolate wrappers bearing the antislavery message. By late July the tracts and newspapers reached southern ports. The South exploded, and overnight organized antislavery became the hottest issue of the day.

That brings us to the second major obstacle, politicians who were determined that antislavery would never get into the political spotlight. Now, politicians stepped in to keep antislavery out of the political spotlight. Most determined, naturally, were the great planter-politicians. Throughout the South, Whigs and Democrats alike raised a hue and cry, claiming that antislavery agitation would lead to slave insurrections, disunion, civil war. They demanded that their northern brethren silence Garrison, Tappan, and other "incendiaries." Hotspurs went further, insisting that abolitionists be jailed as criminals, or better yet sent south for trial. Few northern leaders were willing to go that far,[12] although many cheered on mobs that

12 For the problem that northern leaders faced in trying to placate the South, compare Thomas M. Owen, "An Alabama Protest against Abolitionism in 1835," *Gulf States Historical Magazine*, II (July, 1903), 26–34, and Charles Z. Lincoln, *State of New York: Messages from the Governors* (11 vols.; Albany: State Printers, 1909), III, 594–604, with the correspondence between prominent New York politicians in November–December, 1835, in the Martin Van Buren Papers, Library of Congress, and in the William L. Marcy Papers, Library of Congress.

terrorized abolitionists, sacked newspaper offices, and destroyed antislavery presses. Overall, northern Democrats were more responsive than northern Whigs, and the party of Jackson and Van Buren included most of the hard-liners.

Jackson, like politicians generally and southern politicians in particular, came down hard against abolitionists. In his annual message of December, 1835, he denounced them as "incendiaries," called for "severe penalties" to suppress their "unconstitutional and wicked" activities, and praised those northerners who mobbed antislavery lectures, broke up antislavery meetings, and destroyed antislavery presses. He recommended that postmasters publish the names of everyone who subscribed to antislavery papers "for there are few so hardened in villainy, as to withstand the frowns of all good men." He called for legislation to stop Arthur Tappan and his associates from sending "incendiary" literature through the mail into the South.[13]

Such legislation failed to pass the Senate, but it was merely a legal nicety. The Jackson administration had already stacked the deck against Tappan and his associates. As soon as the pamphlet controversy developed, Postmaster General Amos Kendall, with Jackson's blessing, encouraged postmasters to violate federal law by excluding antislavery materials from the mails. They did so gladly. Indeed, anticipating Kendall's support, the postmaster of New York City had already made it his policy to stop abolitionist literature at its point of origin.[14] That alone killed the pamphlet campaign. Though unlawful, this policy remained in effect until the Civil War.

Jackson's congressional followers, in turn, took the lead in excluding antislavery from the political arena. When Congress convened in December, 1835, southerners were screaming for Tappan's head and insinuating that all northerners, including Van Buren, were soft on abolitionism. Tempers got even worse when southerners discovered that Congress had been deluged with antislavery petitions

13 James D. Richardson (ed.), *Messages and Papers of the Presidents, 1787–1897* (Washington, D.C.: Government Printing Office, 1896), III, 175.
14 Samuel L. Gouverneur to Amos Kendall, August 7, 10, 18, 1835; Gouverneur to Alfred Huger, August 8, 1835; Kendall to Gouverneur, August 16, 22, 1835, all in the Samuel L. Gouverneur Papers, New York Public Library. For Jackson's view of the matter, see Kendall to Jackson, August 7, 1835, and Jackson to Kendall, August 9, 1835, both in Andrew Jackson Papers, Library of Congress.

calling for abolition in the District of Columbia. To placate the South and to quiet the slavery controversy, northern Democrats in 1835 supplied the needed votes to pass the first of many "gag rules." Part of a package presented by Henry Laurens Pinckney, a former South Carolina nullifier, the "gag" prohibited the House of Representatives from printing, discussing, or even mentioning the contents of antislavery petitions. Such petitions were to be "laid on the table" with "no further action whatever." The main purpose of the gag, according to its sponsor, was "to arrest discussion of the subject of slavery within these walls." [15]

That it undoubtedly did. The gag came when the American Anti-Slavery Society was at its peak. The society outwardly seemed to be rich and powerful, growing and dynamic, worth paying attention to. Its methods were the same as those of the British abolitionists, the very methods that purportedly had forced a reluctant Parliament to abolish slavery in the British West Indies. In 1837–1838, the society bombarded Congress with over 130,000 petitions (each with hundreds of signatures) calling for the abolition of slavery in the nation's capital, along with another 32,000 petitions for repeal of the gag rule, 22,000 against the admission of any new slave state, 21,000 for legislation barring slavery from western territories, and 23,000 for the abolition of the interstate slave trade. The House received none of these petitions. What if it had? What if a dozen or so of these petitions, each signed by "fifteen hundred women" as one horrified Virginian put it, had reached the floor of Congress? My guess is that the tumult and shouting would have made the Bank War seem like a teapot tempest.

As it was, the Speaker of the House had his hands full keeping John Quincy Adams and a small band of northern Whigs from violating the gag and presenting the forbidden petitions. Indeed, Adams's tactics kept the House in continuous uproar: one Alabamian became so angry that he wanted to horsewhip the former president; a South Carolinian roared that the old man ought to be criminally indicted by the District of Columbia for inciting slaves to rebellion; and the House eventually tried "the madman from Mas-

15  At this session, debate over slavery and abolition consumed by far the greatest amount of time. See *Register of Debates*, 24th Cong., 1st Sess., *passim*.

sachusetts" for censure. Meanwhile, thousands of northerners who were temperamentally too conservative to become abolitionists identified with Adams in his battle for "the sacred right of petition." But even though the gag proved troublesome and cost the South friends, most southern congressmen thought it was a small price to pay to keep "Arthur Tappan and the infuriate demoniacs associated with him" out of the political arena. And thus, over the violent objections of Adams and others, the gag was renewed at each session of the House until 1844.

But where *precisely* did the parties stand? How many northern Democrats sided with the South and how many northern Whigs stood by "the madman from Massachusetts"? To sharpen the picture let us focus upon the various responses to Pinckney's resolutions.

The South Carolinian presented three resolutions, all of which were pro-South, yet regarded as "compromises" by southern hotspurs. At first glance, only two seem to have dealt with questions in dispute. Just weeks before Pinckney took the floor, the Washington *Globe*, a Van Buren paper, had claimed that the right of petition was an "unlimited natural right," and that Congress had just as much authority over slavery in the District of Columbia as, say, the South Carolina legislature had over slavery in South Carolina.[16] Two of Pinckney's resolutions, in effect, called upon the editors of the *Globe* and all like-minded folk to recant. Northern politicians were to agree not only to the gag rule, but also to the proposition that Congress should *not* interfere "in any way" with slavery in the District of Columbia.

Eighty percent of the northern Democrats went along with the South, as compared with less than 10 percent of the northern Whigs. Here is a breakdown of the vote:[17]

|  | For the "gag" | Against |
|---|---|---|
| Northern Democrats | 59 | 15 |
| Northern Whigs | 1 | 46 |

|  | For "no interference" | Against |
|---|---|---|
| Northern Democrats | 68 | 7 |
| Northern Whigs | 4 | 38 |

16 Washington *Globe*, December 31, 1835, January 1, 1836.
17 Computed from *House Journal*, 24th Cong., 1st Sess., 881, 884. I used several sources

The striking difference in the vote, moreover, can be completely ac-
counted for by party affiliation. Primary personal characteristics, as
far as I can tell, made little difference. Take, for example, upbringing.
For years historians have maintained that the "New England conscience" played a determining role in the antislavery movement.
Yet, once party is kept constant, Yankee upbringing does not make
much difference, as the following table shows:

|  | Percent for "gag" | |
|  | Northern Democrats | Northern Whigs |
| Yankees (52 total) | 77 | 0 |
| Others (69 total) | 81 | 5 |

Such voting behavior was typical. Historians have sometimes argued that northern Democrats "sold out" in 1836 because Van Buren
was running for president, and he desperately needed southern support.[18] While this too might be true, they continued to vote with the
South, roll call after roll call, for the next twenty-five years. Similarly, the eminent Gilbert Hobbes Barnes misled a generation of historians by arguing that the Whig vote changed from year to year,
depending on whether the Whigs were a minority trying to make
trouble for the Democratic majority, or a majority trying to legislate
Whig programs. In fact, at no time did northern Whigs support the
gag, while at each session of Congress until 1844 northern Democrats supplied the crucial votes to renew the gag. And this behavior,
it is now clear, was part of a general pattern. After tabulating and
analyzing all roll call votes in the House from 1836 to 1860, historian Thomas B. Alexander recently found that the two parties were
remarkably "consistent" and "persistent" in the way they responded
to the slavery question. Beginning in 1836, writes Alexander, the
Whigs divided sectionally and never achieved any unity on the issue
of slavery, while northern Democrats stood with their southern
colleagues and thus the Jacksonians always "clung together on the
essentially Southern side."[19]

---

in determining party affiliation, but mainly *Biographical Directory of the American Congress,
1774–1971* (Washington, D.C.: Government Printing Office, 1971).

18  See, for example, McFaul, "Expediency and Morality," 24–39.

19  Barnes, *Antislavery Impulse*, Chap. XI–XVIII; Thomas B. Alexander, *Sectional Stress
and Party Strength* (Nashville: Vanderbilt University Press, 1967), *passim.*

There were times, of course, when northern Democrats did vote against the South, but even on such occasions they were outdone by northern Whigs. Take, for example, the famous Wilmot Proviso which was added as a rider to one bill after another during the Mexican War. Since David Wilmot was a Pennsylvania Democrat, one might think that proportionately more Democrats than Whigs voted to bar slavery from the territory taken from Mexico, but this was not so. Here is how northerners voted in February, 1847:[20]

|  | For Wilmot Proviso | Against |
|---|---|---|
| Northern Democrats | 58 | 16 |
| Northern Whigs | 54 | 1 |

And here is how they stood two weeks later:

|  | For | Against |
|---|---|---|
| Northern Democrats | 47 | 22 |
| Northern Whigs | 49 | 0 |

Week after week, year after year, more Whigs than Democrats took a stand contrary to the South's.

Yet we still cannot assume that northern Whigs sympathized with the abolitionists. Most Whigs saw themselves as defenders of northern rights, or as defenders of the Constitution, rather than as defenders of the likes of Garrison, Weld, or Tappan. Indeed, most northern Whigs branded abolitionists as "crackpots," "fanatics," "amalgamationists," and "incendiaries." As far as I can determine, men like Daniel Webster and William Henry Harrison never had a kind word for the abolitionists, and even Adams preferred to keep his distance. However, not *all* northern Whigs were just defending northern rights, just standing up for the Constitution, as Adams's biographers claim he was.[21] Some were hostile toward the South, yearning to make trouble for the great planter-politicians whom they deeply resented, secretly hoping to destroy them.

Perhaps the response to Pinckney's other resolution provides some evidence of antisouthern Whig feeling. At first glance, the resolution had nothing to do with anything in dispute. It simply re-

---

20 All figures here computed from *Congressional Globe*, 29th Cong., 2nd Sess., 425, 573.

21 See, for example, Samuel Flagg Bemis, *John Quincy Adams and the Union* (New York: Alfred A. Knopf, Inc., 1956), Chap. XVII.

peated a maxim that politicians, North and South, had always agreed on: that Congress had no constitutional power to interfere with slavery in the slaveholding states. Lincoln would support it even on the eve of the Civil War. Yet in 1836 Adams and eight other northern Whigs not only voted against this resolution, but also made it clear that Congress, under certain conditions, had the right to interfere with slavery in the South.[22]

Indeed, shortly after the vote, Adams lectured southern representatives on the war powers of Congress. He was sharp, caustic, even though the crucial vote on Pinckney's gag had yet to come. Southerners ought to know better, he said. As "slaveholding exterminators of Indians," as warmongers hungering for Mexican Texas, they ought to fully understand the war powers of Congress. "From the instant that our slaveholding states become the theater of war, civil, servile, or foreign . . . the war powers of Congress extend to interference with the institution of slavery in every way by which it can be interfered with!"[23]

What are we to make of this tongue-lashing? Adams often was given to invective, and he excoriated Boston Brahmins as well as southern slavemasters, Daniel Webster and Harrison Gray Otis as well as Andrew Jackson and John C. Calhoun. But to picture the old curmudgeon as simply an ardent defender of northern rights and the Constitution, a document which he likened to a "menstruous rag," is a bit far-fetched. There was more to his passion than that. Among other things, Adams blamed the "Sable Genius of the South" for ruining his political career, for standing in the way of everything he held dear.[24] He wanted his pound of flesh in return.

Adams and most of his cohorts, moreover, were not typical Whigs of the Webster-Clay school. They followed different drummers: one or two sympathized with the abolitionists; several were active in one of the other great moral crusades of the age; most were former Anti-Masons, and all but one represented districts in which

22 *House Journal*, 24th Cong., 1st Sess., 876. See also *Register of Debates*, 24th Cong., 1st Sess., 4027ff (May 25, 1836).
23 *Register of Debates*, 24th Cong. 1st Sess., 4046ff (May 25, 1836).
24 See, for example, his letter to Rev. Charles W. Upham, February 2, 1837, as quoted in Henry Adams, *The Degradation of the Democratic Dogma*, introduction by Brooks Adams (New York: Harper and Row, 1969), 24–25.

antimasonry had run rampant. Like Adams, they had castigated both Andrew Jackson and Henry Clay, along with other prominent Masons, for being members of a "vile conspiracy" which supposedly had subverted the rule of law, corrupted local and state governments, to the point that Masons could literally get away with murder. Especially suspicious of Jackson, who had scorned antimasonry, they never doubted for a moment that Old Hickory and his followers were up to no good. Like Adams, they quickly perceived a new evil, a monstrous Slave Power, which threatened to fasten fetters upon the entire nation. Unlike their fellow Whigs, they fought the "Slave Power" on every issue, not only over all three of the Pinckney resolutions, but consistently for years to come.[25]

This battle was exacerbated not only by the prolonged controversy over antislavery petitions and the gag rule, but also by two other developments. On the one hand, Jacksonian expansionism constantly reinforced the suspicions of Adams, his fellow Anti-Masons, and other northern Whigs. On the other hand, the decision by the Jacksonians to require a two-thirds majority in nominating presidential candidates strengthened the South's position within the Democratic party.

At first, only a few radical abolitionists and inveterate Jackson-haters claimed that Jackson's land policy was part of a slave power conspiracy. But by the 1840s, this disquieting murmur grew into a mighty roar as thousands upon thousands of northerners became convinced that an avaricious slave power dictated the nation's expansionist impulse. In practice, Jacksonian land hunger always seemed to benefit the plantation South far more than the free Northwest. It was largely happenstance, according to most historians; but it happened enough to convince suspicious northerners that it was not merely accident.

Jackson's Indian policy, for example, did far more for the South than for any other part of the country. When Old Hickory took office, most northern tribes had already been stripped of their potency, while the southern tribes were not only still formidable but also in possession of some of the richest land in the South. After

---

25 This paragraph is based on career-line studies of the congressmen.

barely winning congressional support for Indian removal in 1830, the Jackson administration pursued a vigorous policy to get this land. The Indian removal bill gave the president power to initiate land exchanges with various tribes. Force, fraud, bribery, and murder—all were used to get the desired treaties. Then troops were used to drive the tribes off their native lands and across the Mississippi. Indian removal led to one atrocity after another, and several Indian wars, which cost the nation thousands of lives and millions of dollars. In return, Jackson's policy opened up to white occupancy 25 million acres in the South, including pockets in western North Carolina and southern Tennessee, huge tracts in northwestern Georgia and eastern Alabama, and the northern two-thirds of Mississippi. Northern gains, by comparison, were less dramatic.

Jackson and his followers also led the demand for northern Mexico. When several Mexican states revolted in 1835 against General Santa Anna, the Jacksonians enthusiastically supported Sam Houston and his Texas rebels. In defiance of existing neutrality agreements, the Jackson administration allowed the Texans to enlist recruits and raise money and supplies in the United States. And, on the pretext of protecting the United States against Indians, Old Hickory ordered a large detachment of soldiers under General E. P. Gaines to the Texas border—and then, after Santa Anna's defeat, into Texas itself, where they remained until December, 1836. Mexican authorities concluded that United States troops were there to safeguard the results of the rebellion. They protested vigorously to Washington—only to be treated like vermin. There was never any doubt that Jackson dearly wanted Texas.

According to Adams, it was no mere coincidence that the annexation of Texas would also benefit the South. The Texas revolution, said Adams, was a criminal act set off by slavemasters and land speculators. The whole affair was a wicked conspiracy plotted by Jackson and southern slavemasters, and aided by Van Buren and northern "doughfaces," to steal free soil from Mexico in order to bring in a covey of slave states so that the slave power would always dominate the Union. Rather than fighting for freedom, the Texans rebelled because Mexico had abolished slavery! They were fighting to keep their slaves in chains! Sam Houston did not just happen to migrate to Texas; he was sent by Jackson as part of a conspiracy![26] Not too many northerners, it was true, accepted such reasoning, but enough did to assure Old Hickory that Texas might touch off the whole explosive issue of slavery, at a time when he was trying to engineer Van Buren's election. After his hand-picked successor was safely elected, Jackson officially recognized Texan independence, but neither Jackson nor Van Buren dared to push for annexation.

Their caution, of course, not only kept slavery out of the political arena, but also dampened the hopes of the annexationists in their party. It took a president without a party, John Tyler of Virginia, to bring slavery to the fore. Denounced publicly as a traitor to the Whig party, Tyler pushed for the annexation of Texas in the early 1840s, hoping that the Texas issue would enable him to run for president in 1844 as the candidate of a new pro-Texas third party, or better yet as the Democratic nominee. Secretly, a treaty of annexation was made with Texas. When the treaty was sent to the Senate in April, 1844, Secretary of State John C. Calhoun sent along a copy of a dispatch he had written to the British minister, Richard Pakenham, denouncing England for trying to interfere with slavery in Texas, singing the praises of slavery, and justifying annexation as a defense measure in behalf of slavery. Calhoun's dispatch not only raised the cry of "Slave Power Conspiracy" to a fever pitch, but also shocked congressmen who had no sympathy at all with the antislavery movement. Still, when it came to vote, Democrats proved once again that they were zealous expansionists. As always, southern and western Democrats pushed for annexation while Whigs—North and South—were in opposition.

Ardent expansionists, however, had a problem in 1844. In the wake of Calhoun's Pakenham letter, Van Buren came out against the annexation of Texas, and he had more than enough delegates pledged to him to win the Democratic nomination on the first ballot—if only a simple majority was needed for nomination. Fortunately for the expansionists, they could argue that a two-thirds majority was needed, if the party followed the 1832 rule. Back then, in

---

26 *Register of Debates*, 24th Cong., 1st Sess., 4046ff. See also John Quincy Adams to Benjamin Lundy, May 12, 20, 1836, and Adams to Charles Francis Adams, May 24, 1836, all in the Adams Papers (microfilm).

choosing the vice-presidential nominee, the party had adopted the two-thirds rule so that areas in which the party had no strength—namely, New England—would not be decisive in the balloting. With the help of disillusioned Van Buren delegates, pro-Texas strategists convinced the convention in 1844 to adopt the two-thirds rule. It succeeded in blocking Van Buren's nomination and, after a long deadlock, in making James K. Polk of Tennessee, a zealous expansionist, the party's nominee.

Not only did Polk push the country into war with Mexico, thus making the expansion of slavery the centerpiece of American politics, but the two-thirds rule quickly became a permanent weapon of the South in controlling the choice of presidential nominees. Once established, it was impossible to dislodge, lasting until 1936. Like the gag, it was a terrible nuisance, plaguing Democratic conventions with long deadlocks. But it was also a mighty weapon: northern Democrats had to pay heed to their southern brethren, even though the North far surpassed the South in population; presidential hopefuls had to satisfy the South, prove that they were indeed "northern men with southern principles," or suffer the fate of Van Buren.[27]

Adams died in 1848. He was still in Congress, hoping to fire off another blast at "Mr. Polk's War," when he collapsed at his desk. By then, the die was cast, and only northern Democrats like Lewis Cass, Franklin Pierce, and James Buchanan had any chance of winning southern approval and hence their party's nomination. By then, Adams was absolutely certain that the South had the Democratic party in its pocket. He was also certain that historians would bear him out. They did for many years, and perhaps they will again . . . someday.

27 James S. Chase, *Emergence of the Presidential Nominating Convention, 1789–1832* (Urbana, Ill.: University of Illinois Press, 1973); Charles G. Sellers, *James K. Polk, Continentalist, 1843–1846* (Princeton, N.J.: Princeton University Press, 1966), Chap. II and III; David M. Potter, *The South and the Concurrent Majority* (Baton Rouge: Louisiana State University Press, 1972).

# THE FORGOTTEN REFORMERS
## A Profile of Third Party Abolitionists in Antebellum New York

*Alan M. Kraut*

RECENT EFFORTS of cliometricians to explore the character and social composition of antebellum political parties suggest that the same concepts and methods might be used to study the efforts of those reformers who sought to battle slavery through the political system.[1] Many political abolitionists sought to bore from within either the Democratic or the Whig party during the 1830s and 1840s. Others, however, rejected the major parties as irretrievably dominated by the "slave power" and sought refuge in third parties.

The Liberty party, a third party dedicated exclusively to slavery's abolition, has received sparse attention from historians. The party was organized on April 1, 1840, at Albany, New York. Prominent abolitionists such as Myron Holley, Gerrit Smith, Joshua Leavitt, and William Goodell were instrumental in its founding. Well aware that slavery was an institution under state, not federal, jurisdiction,

1 Lee Benson, *The Concept of Jacksonian Democracy: New York as a Test Case* (Princeton: Princeton University Press, 1961); Michael Fitzgibbon Holt, *Forging a Majority: The Formation of the Republican Party in Pittsburgh, 1848–1860* (New Haven: Yale University Press, 1969); Ronald P. Formisano, *The Birth of Mass Political Parties, Michigan, 1827–1861* (Princeton: Princeton University Press, 1971). A recent article that provides an excellent review of the literature is Ronald P. Formisano, "Toward a Reorientation of Jacksonian Politics: A Review of the Literature, 1959–1975," *Journal of American History,* LXIII (1976), 42–65.

these Liberty men demanded immediate abolition, but drafted a platform that settled for "the absolute and unqualified divorce of the General Government from Slavery." To that end they pressed for the elimination of slavery from the District of Columbia and the territories, and the termination of the slave trade.[2] These measures remained the foundation of the Liberty party program until internal controversy over strategy and tactics factionalized the third party and caused its dissolution several months before the presidential election of 1848.

Few voters supported the Liberty program at the ballot box during the party's brief existence. In the presidential election of 1844, the Liberty men managed to capture the balance of power in the key electoral state of New York, but it was a Pyrrhic victory that succeeded only in defeating Whig candidate Henry Clay and in providing the margin of victory to a more ardent foe of abolitionism, Democrat James K. Polk. Though 1844 was the Liberty party's peak year at the polls, abolitionist presidential candidate James G. Birney received a popular vote of only 62,197 votes nationally, a mere 2.3 percent of the total.[3]

The failure of the third party to be successful at the polls, or even to survive for a substantial period as a gadfly in the political system, has permitted historians to justify neglect of the Liberty party by derogating its significance in the moral struggle. Forty years ago, Gilbert Barnes described the third party as the "most pathetic residue of antislavery organization," while more recently Aileen Kraditor characterized the Liberty party as an organization that was "conceived in frustration and self-delusion, acted out a farce, and died by betrayal."[4] These grim assessments fail to credit the Liberty party with being the first effort by reformers to attempt moral

2 The first actual Liberty party platform appeared in 1844. See "Liberty Platform of 1844," reprinted in Kirk N. Porter (comp.), *National Party Platforms* (New York: MacMillan, 1924), 7–15. There had been no national Liberty party platform in 1840, but an editorial by Joshua Leavitt in the *New York Emancipator*, July 15, 1841, defined the province of third party abolitionists.

3 Svend Petersen, *A Statistical History of the American Presidential Elections* (New York: Frederick Ungar Publishing Co., 1963), 27.

4 Gilbert Hobbs Barnes, *The Anti-Slavery Impulse, 1830–1844* (New York: Harcourt, Brace and World, 1933), 176; Aileen Kraditor, "The Liberty and Free Soil Parties," in Arthur M. Schlesinger, Jr. (ed.), *History of the U.S. Political Parties* (New York: Chelsea House Publishers, 1973), I, 741.

change, embodied in a third party, through the political system. The Liberty party also provided the first organized introduction of the slavery issue into the partisan political arena at the local, state, and national levels.

The limited amount of research done on the Liberty party since Theodore Clarke Smith's study in 1897 has provided historians with little new basis for revising these appraisals. With few exceptions historians have settled for periodic reshufflings of the quotations of third party "verbalizers, the lecturers, journalists, and pamphleteers—and the activists or organizers." Even Richard Sewell's comprehensive narrative, though sympathetic to the Liberty party, is not methodologically innovative.[5]

Two previous studies produced by David Donald and Gerald Sorin, respectively, have attempted a fresh approach to abolitionism, though not to the Liberty men in particular.[6] Donald and Sorin each hoped to shed new light on antislavery reform with collective portraits of prominent abolitionists. Both historians agreed that abolitionist leaders were most often born in New England, or they were of Yankee parentage, and they were Protestant in religion. The reformers' piety was frequently sparked by the revivalism of the 1820s and 1830s. Both historians found the abolitionists in their respective samples to be well-educated, moderately prosperous, and often employed in a learned profession (doctor, lawyer, minister). Donald

5 David Brion Davis, "Introduction," in David Brion Davis (ed.), *Ante-Bellum Reform* (New York: Harper and Row, 1967), 10; Richard H. Sewell, *Ballots for Freedom: Antislavery Politics in the United States, 1837–1860* (New York: Oxford University Press, 1976). Until the publication of Sewell's volume the only published book on the Liberty party was Theodore Clarke Smith, *The Liberty and Free Soil Parties in the Northwest* (New York: Longman's Green and Company, 1897). Other articles include: Julian R. Bretz, "The Economic Background of the Liberty Party," *American Historical Review*, XXIV (1929), 250–64; R. L. Morrow, "The Liberty Party in Vermont," *New England Quarterly*, II (1929), 234–48; Joseph G. Rayback, "The Liberty Party Leaders of Ohio: Exponents of Antislavery Coalition," *Ohio State Archeological and Historical Quarterly*, LVII (1942), 165–78; Hugh H. Davis, "The Failure of Political Abolitionism," *Connecticut Review*, VI (1973), 76–86; John L. Hammond, "Revival Religion and Antislavery Politics," *American Sociological Review*, XXXIX (1974), 175–86. Unpublished doctoral dissertations on the Liberty party include: Margaret Louise Plunkett, "A History of the Liberty Party with Emphasis Upon Its Activities in the Northeastern States" (Cornell University, 1930); John R. Hendricks, "The Liberty Party in New York State, 1838–1848" (Fordham University, 1959); Alan M. Kraut, "The Liberty Men of New York: Political Abolitionism in New York State, 1840–1848" (Cornell University, 1975).

6 David Donald, "Toward a Reconsideration of the Abolitionists," in David Donald (ed.), *Lincoln Reconsidered* (New York: Random House, 1956), 19–36; Gerald Sorin, *The New York Abolitionists, a Case of Political Radicalism* (Westport, Conn.: Greenwood Press, 1971).

concluded that the abolitionists he examined were part of a declining rural elite, often involved in farming, but rarely engaged in manufacturing or commerce. Sorin, on the other hand, described his sample to be an urban-based group of sincerely idealistic reformers, many of whom were involved in New York's expanding economy of manufacture and trade.

Though a number of individuals included in each study were prominent Liberty men, neither historian limited his work to third party reformers. In neither study were Liberty men distinguished by the authors from those who were not. Also, both studies were based on samples drawn by the historians themselves, rather than on lists compiled by the reformers. These qualities make Donald's and Sorin's studies of little value in understanding Liberty party reformers.

More useful and provocative is an impressionistic portrait of Liberty party rank and file voters developed by Lee Benson in his study of the 1844 election in the state of New York. According to Benson, most Liberty voters lived in "small, moderately prosperous Yankee farming communities." They tended to have "considerable standing in their communities and much better than average education." Benson also postulated that most third party men shared a common set of "radical religious beliefs" involving righteous secular activity as the key to spiritual salvation and that they were ex-Whigs, politically. Whigs believed that the state had the right to take a positive, activist stance for the "material and moral well-being of society." [7] Benson speculated that the Liberty men, coming from an activist religious tradition, desired a political party that could help make the world holy. The shift to the abolition party seemed natural, he wrote, to those who sought higher moral ground on the subject of slavery than the Whig party had reached by the 1840s. Benson hoped that others would test his hypotheses. Despite his call in 1961 for systematic reexamination of the Liberty party or those who supported it at the state level, there have been no such studies published.

New concepts of the political party developed by contemporary political researchers and already used by cliometricians in several

7 Benson, *Concept of Jacksonian Democracy*, 210, 212.

studies of antebellum politics suggest a revised conceptual framework with which to approach the Liberty party. Political parties in America have been traditionally defined as competing organizations that "put forward candidates for office, advocate particular courses of government action, and if their candidates win, create enough of a sense of joint responsibility for the direction of government." However, political parties have increasingly become accepted by historians as reference groups through which voters "define themselves." Politics, then, "acts as a sounding board for identities, values, fears, and aspirations." And each political party's character is respectively shaped by the character of those groups whose concerns that party embodies.[8] These conceptualizations suggest that much may be learned about a party by examining the social composition of its constituency.

The lack of adequate evidence has proven a persistent obstacle to the study of the Liberty party's social composition. There is no official list of third party voters, and aggregate analysis at the township level has proven difficult. Because a low percentage of voters cast third party ballots even in towns where third party candidates "ran well," generalizations drawn on the demographic structure of a whole town or ward are of dubious value in describing the small proportion of the town's population that voted Liberty.

The discovery of new data makes it possible to examine the Liberty party's rank and file. The new material consists of two poll lists from 1841 and 1845, and other fragments of data on the Liberty electorate in the town of Smithfield in western New York, and a statewide list of subscribers to a New York Liberty party newspaper. An analysis of the social characteristics of the individuals on these lists provides a profile, however incomplete, of the Liberty party's social composition in western New York. This profile of third party voters furnishes a basis for speculation about the character of the Liberty

8 V. O. Key, Jr., *Southern Politics in State and Nation* (New York: Random House, 1949), 298–311; Frank J. Sorauf, *Political Parties in the American System* (Boston: Little, Brown and Company, 1964); Richard Hofstadter, *The Paranoid Style in American Politics and Other Essays* (New York: Random House, 1967), ix; Murray Edelman, *The Symbolic Uses of Politics* (Urbana: University of Illinois Press, 1964), 166–67; Robert K. Lane, *Political Life, Why and How People Get Involved in Politics* (Glencoe: Free Press, 1959), 299–300; Philip E. Converse, "The Nature of Belief Systems in Mass Politics," in David Apter (ed.), *Ideology and Discontent* (Glencoe: Free Press, 1964), 206–61.

party and the values, fears, and aspirations of those who cast ballots for it.

It is important to note the difference between poll lists and poll books. Before the Civil War, a form of *vive voce* voting was practiced in several states. In those states all votes were cast by voice or by a ticket handed to the election officials at the polls and then read. The election officials announced audibly the vote of each person as an election clerk recorded the voter's name by precinct and the name of the candidate for whom he voted. This information was then recorded in a poll book and became part of the official record. Poll lists, in contrast, were neither the result of *vive voce* voting, nor were they part of a civil division's official election records. Poll lists were informal lists of voters in each town or ward and how those voters cast their ballots. Poll lists were often compiled by party leaders for campaign purposes. Both poll list and poll book research permits historians to investigate the social composition of a party by examining the demographic characteristics of individual voters.[9]

The poll lists located among the papers of Liberty spokesman Gerrit Smith include the names of 182 individuals, 54.2 percent of the eligible voters living in Smithfield during the 1840s.[10] It is not known who compiled these lists or how they were compiled, or for what purpose. They were handwritten, but the script is not the

9 Poll books have been found in Virginia, Maryland, Rhode Island, Illinois, and Missouri, but not in New York. A poll list for Lansing, Michigan, was used by Formisano in *Birth of Mass Political Parties*, 318–23. An example of recent poll book research is Paul McAllister and John M. Rozett, "Voting Behavior in the Late Jacksonian Period: The Conceptual and Methodological Significance of Poll Book Research" (paper presented at the Sixth Conference on Socio-Political History, Brockport, 1973).

10 The first list, "Voters of the Liberty Ticket in Smithfield, November 1.2.3. 1841" includes the names of 49 Liberty voters and 12 voters who were expected to vote Liberty, but did not vote at all in that year's election for state senator. A second list, "Voters of DIST NO 1, NOV ELECTION," includes 89 Smithfield individuals who voted in the 1845 election for state senator. Forty-nine voters were designated "Antislavery Voters"; 32 were considered "Pro-slavery"; 2 were "Voters for the first time for the Liberty Party"; 4 were "Those who have heretofore voted for the Liberty Party but did not vote at the last (1845) election"; and it was "Doubtful" how two individuals on the list cast their ballots. A third document, a "Town Canvass for the Spring of 1844 for the Smithfield town election of March 1844" was also found. It includes, by office, the candidates of the Liberty party and the party of "Rum and Slavery," i.e., the Democratic party, the vote each candidate received, and the majority by which the Democratic candidate won. The Whig candidates are not included on the list. The names of 18 Liberty men and 18 nonabolitionists were taken from the canvass and added to the other names in the Smithfield sample. All three lists were located in the Gerrit Smith Miller Collection at Syracuse University.

careless scrawl of Gerrit Smith. Nor is there any reference made to these lists in any of Smith's correspondence. One can only guess whether Smith commissioned a Liberty party secretary or one of his own clerks to keep a record of those who could be counted upon and those who could not.

Eighty-eight voters, 48 percent of the poll list sample and one-fourth of Smithfield's eligible voters, can be described with available demographic data. Fifty-five of those individuals were Liberty men and thirty-three were not. Because the poll lists do not distinguish Whigs and Democrats, all voters who did not cast Liberty ballots will hereafter be referred to as "nonabolitionists."

An additional list was also found, in Smith's handwriting, which cites the names of subscribers to an unnamed Liberty newspaper.[11] Because the list is dated December 12, 1849, well over a year after the original Liberty party had been formally dissolved, it most likely refers to one of the newspapers that continued to support Gerrit Smith and his faction, the National Liberty party, that survived after the original Liberty party's formal dissolution in 1848 (perhaps the *Liberty Press* of Utica, New York). The list includes the names of 191 subscribers cited by village and county of residence. Data were recovered for 94 individuals, all but 4 of whom were residents of western New York towns, as were the Smithfield voters.

The individuals on all lists were examined with regard to a set of six social characteristics: age, race, occupation, wealth, religion, and ethnocultural background (including nativity). These characteristics were chosen for analysis in studying the Liberty party's rank and file voters because students of contemporary political behavior have determined them important to the formation of an individual's political orientation.[12] However, because neither the Smithfield sample nor the newspaper subscriber sample has been scientifically drawn, no claim of statistical significance or precision can be made. Bold generalizations on the social composition of the entire Liberty party

11 "The following are the names of the subscribers who have paid subscriptions to the Liberty Party Paper . . . ," December 12, 1849. This list is located in the Gerrit Smith Miller Collection.

12 Angus Campbell, Philip E. Converse, Warren E. Miller, Donald E. Stokes, *The American Voter* (New York: Wiley, 1960). See also, Lane, *Political Life*.

based on such fragmentary data would be dubious. Nevertheless, an "ensemble" of impressionistic and empirical evidence does suggest a portrait of the western New York Liberty man.[13]

During the 1840s, Smithfield's reputation as the hub of antislavery reform in western New York was out of all proportion to its size and appearance. Organized in 1807 on a tract of land purchased from the Oneida Indians, the town appeared typical of the small, thriving farming communities that dotted western New York's landscape during the antebellum period. Over thirty years after its formation, Smithfield was still the smallest town in Madison County with a total area of only 582 square miles and just 4 percent of the county's population (1,629 of a total 40,987 individuals).[14] The Liberty party received much of its electoral support from voters in the towns of New York, but the small town of Smithfield was by far the party's banner town. Smithfield voters gave Liberty candidates an average of 36.8 percent of their vote in the elections between 1840 and 1847.[15]

The town had been a Democratic stronghold throughout the 1830s and that pattern persisted in the election of 1840. Fifty-four percent of Smithfield's voters cast ballots for incumbent Martin Van Buren that year, even as the Whigs were carrying the rest of Madison County for William Henry Harrison. In the next two elections, the Democrats sustained slight declines in the percentage of the vote they had received in 1840, but still managed to hold the town because the Whigs suffered even sharper losses. The trend continued until 1843. In that year's election for state senators, the Whig vote declined only slightly (4.5 percent) from 1842, but the Democratic percentage of the vote plummeted, declining almost 14 percent. Between 1843 and 1847, the

13 The term "ensemble" was used to describe the synthesis of all available empirical and impressionistic, individual, and aggregate data on voters in a single town by Ronald P. Formisano to describe his case study of Lansing, Michigan. Formisano, *Birth of Mass Political Parties*, 318–23.

14 Population data for 1845 cited in *Census of the State of New York for 1855* (Albany: C. Van Benthuysen, 1857), xxiii; Hamilton Child (ed.), *Gazetteer and Business Directory of Madison County, N.Y. for 1868–69* (Syracuse: Hamilton Child at *Syracuse Journal* Office, 1868).

15 New Yorkers contributed almost 40 percent of the national Liberty vote in the presidential election of 1840 (2,790 of a total 7,053 votes), and 25 percent of the national total in 1844 (15,814 votes of a total 62,097). Petersen, *Statistical History*, 24–26. For analysis of the New York Liberty party vote at the township level, see Kraut, "Liberty Men of New York," 157–208.

Liberty party carried the town of Smithfield in every election for statewide office (see Tables 1 and 2).[16]

TABLE 1

Madison County and Smithfield in the Presidential Election of 1840
(percentages are in parentheses)

|  | Whig (Harrison) | | Democratic (Birney) | | Liberty (Van Buren) | |
|---|---|---|---|---|---|---|
|  | No. | % | No. | % | No. | % |
| Madison County | 4,114 | 47.7 | 4,266 | 49.6 | 240 | 2.8 |
| Town of Smithfield | 185 | 54.1 | 123 | 36.0 | 34 | 9.9 |

TABLE 2

Election Results in Smithfield, 1840–1847

| Whigs | Office | Democrats | | Whigs | | Liberty | |
|---|---|---|---|---|---|---|---|
|  |  | No. | % | No. | % | No. | % |
| 1840 | President | 185 | 54.1 | 123 | 36.0 | 34 | 9.9 |
| 1841 | State Senator | 132 | 53.2 | 70 | 28.2 | 46 | 18.6 |
| 1842 | Governor | 168 | 51.8 | 61 | 18.8 | 95 | 29.3 |
| 1843 | State Senator | 128 | 38.1 | 48 | 14.3 | 160 | 47.6 |
| 1844 | President | 111 | 30.9 | 74 | 20.6 | 174 | 48.5 |
| 1845 | State Senator | 73 | 25.8 | 47 | 16.6 | 163 | 57.6 |
| 1846 | Governor | 107 | 39.1 | 56 | 20.4 | 111 | 40.5 |
| 1847 | Lt. Governor | 58 | 31.4 | 49 | 26.5' | 78 | 42.2 |

Data are not available on the previous political affiliations of Smithfield Liberty voters. One can only speculate in the absence of such data, but it appears that in Smithfield the Liberty party may have drawn on the support of former Democrats as well as of former Whigs.

When variables other than previous political affiliation were examined, Liberty voters and their nonabolitionist adversaries ap-

16 The electoral data for Smithfield and Madison County for 1840, 1842, and 1844 were available in Edwin Williams (ed.), *New York Annual Register* (New York: Turner and Hayden, 1830–1845). Data for 1846 was available in O. L. Holley (ed.), *New York State Register* (Albany: C. Van Benthuysen and Co., 1846). All other electoral data were obtained from county canvasses reprinted in local newspapers such as *Madison Observer*, *Madison County Whig*, *Madison Democrat*, and the *Chittenango Herald*.

TABLE 3
Liberty and Nonabolitionist Voters
Distributed by Value of Real Estate Owned

| Value of Real | Liberty | | Nonabolitionist | |
|---|---|---|---|---|
| Estate ($) | No. | % | No. | % |
| 0–100 | — | — | — | — |
| 101–250 | 5 | 12.5 | — | — |
| 251–500 | 3 | 7.5 | — | — |
| 501–750 | 4 | 10.0 | 6 | 24.0 |
| 751–1,000 | 5 | 12.5 | 2 | 8.0 |
| 1,001–2,500 | 9 | 22.5 | 4 | 16.0 |
| 2,501–5,000 | 10 | 25.0 | 9 | 36.0 |
| 5,001–7,500 | 1 | 2.5 | 1 | 4.0 |
| 7,501–10,000 | 2 | 5.0 | 1 | 4.0 |
| 10,001–15,000 | — | — | — | — |
| 15,001–and over | 1 | 2.5 | 2 | 8.0 |
| Missing | 15 | | 8 | |
| Base | 40 | | 25 | |

peared to be similar in race, age, and economic wealth. All voters in the Smithfield sample were Caucasian and the majority of both Liberty men (67.3 percent) and nonabolitionists (66.7 percent) were between the ages of twenty-one and fifty years of age. Similar age distributions of Liberty men, nonabolitionists, and the general population suggest that age is a negligible factor in distinguishing the social characteristics of third party voters from those of their opponents.[17]

Economically, Smithfield was a rural, agricultural community, only marginally involved in western New York's growing commercial economy that was concentrated north of Smithfield in the port cities of the Erie Canal. Eighty percent of Smithfield's work force was employed in agriculture during the 1840s in spite of soil that

17 All data on age, value of real estate owned, occupation, and place of birth were recovered from the *Population Schedules of the Sixth Federal Census of the United States: 1840* (microfilm). The age of sample members was calculated for 1845, when they were deciding whether or not to vote for the Liberty party. Fuller discussion in Kraut, "Liberty Men of New York," 307–61.

was a "sandy and gravelly loam." [18] In such a community the value of the real estate that men owned was an important indicator of their relative wealth. Here again, there was a negligible difference between Liberty men and nonabolitionists. Almost half (19, or 47.5 percent) of the Liberty men and the majority of nonabolitionists (13, or 52.0 percent) for whom economic data could be recovered owned real estate valued between one thousand and five thousand dollars. In the lowest and highest categories of wealth as measured by the value of real estate owned, the differences between Liberty men and nonabolitionists are minimal (see Table 3).

The most marked difference between the social characteristics of Liberty and nonabolitionist Smithfield voters appears to be in their occupations. While two-thirds of the nonabolitionists in this agricultural community were farmers (66.7 percent), fewer than half (39.6 percent) of the Liberty voters earned their livings tilling the soil. Over 50 percent of the Liberty men in the sample worked at nonfarming occupations in Smithfield as compared with only 30 percent of the nonabolitionists in the sample (see Table 4).

TABLE 4
Liberty and Nonabolitionist Voters Distributed by Occupation

| Occupation | Liberty | | Proslavery | |
|---|---|---|---|---|
| | No. | % | No. | % |
| Farmer | 21 | 39.6 | 22 | 66.7 |
| Other | 30 | 56.6 | 10 | 30.3 |
| "None" | 2 | 3.8 | 1 | 3.0 |
| Missing | 2 | | 0 | |
| Base | 53 | | 33 | |

Most of those Liberty men not engaged in agriculture were either artisans or local merchants, or else they were involved in the learned professions. However, over one-fourth of those Liberty men *not* involved in agriculture were cited on the state census rolls as "laborers." Not a single nonabolitionist was so listed (see Table 5).

Without benefit of letters or memoirs, it is difficult to know pre-

18 Child, *Gazetteer*, 50.

TABLE 5
Liberty and Nonabolitionist Voters Not in Agriculture
Distributed by Occupation

| Occupation | Liberty No. | % | Nonabolitionist No. | % |
|---|---|---|---|---|
| Laborer | 8 | 26.7 | 1 | 10.0 |
| Artisans | 12 | 40.0 | 7 | 70.0 |
| blacksmith | 4 | | 1 | |
| shoemaker | 3 | | | |
| distiller of oils | 1 | | | |
| harnessmaker | | | 1 | |
| carpenter | 1 | | 2 | |
| wagonmaker | | | 2 | |
| hatter | | | 1 | |
| "manufacturer" | 1 | | | |
| miller | 1 | | | |
| cabinetmaker | 1 | | | |
| Merchant | 5 | 16.7 | | |
| "merchant" | 2 | | | |
| grocer | 1 | | | |
| butcher | 1 | | | |
| shoe merchant | 1 | | | |
| Clerk | 1 | 3.3 | | |
| Learned Professions | 4 | 13.3 | 2 | 20.2 |
| lawyer | 1 | | 1 | |
| doctor | 1 | | 1 | |
| minister | 2 | | | |
| Base | 30 | | 10 | |

cisely what was meant by the designation "laborer." It may be that these individuals did occasional agricultural labor, or they may have been manual laborers in the community who did not till the soil at all. During this period there was a so-called "journeymen's migration" of craftsmen, who came to western New York from the eastern counties of the state and from New England in search of a job, rather than cheap land to farm. A study of Vermont migrants notes that "many young Vermonters had served a regular apprenticeship or had picked up a hit-or-miss knowledge that fitted them to earn a living at carpentry, blacksmithing, printing, surveying, and the like; and that it was these men who were in the best position to try their luck in a half-dozen different communities before they finally settled in any place that they could call their home."[19] These journeymen who did not own shops of their own may well be the laborers cited in the census.

During the 1830s, abolitionists had defined the social group from which they drew most of their support as the "bone and muscle of society." Farmers were occasionally included under this rubric, but primarily the term referred to the "honest, hard-handed, clear-headed free laborers and mechanics of the north." Slavery, on the other hand, found its champions in the North among two other groups. Some antiabolitionists were of society's "tail," the street rabble that attacked every moral principle of Christian society, but many others were from society's "head." These "gentlemen of property and standing"—merchants, bankers, lawyers, politicians, and clergymen—were the "aristocracy of the North." They feared the social chaos that abolition brought to their communities and the potential loss of status to themselves.[20]

The occupational data available for Smithfield suggest that the majority of both Liberty men and nonabolitionists were of society's "bone and muscle," but the Liberty electorate appears to have had a greater percentage of the town's "laborers and mechanics" in its ranks than did the opposition parties.

Liberty voters and nonabolitionists in Smithfield also differed in their places of birth, though the differences were less marked than the occupational distinctions. Eighty percent of all Smithfield townsmen and the majority of both Liberty men and non-abolitionists were born in New York State. But a substantially higher percentage of Liberty men than nonabolitionists were born out of state. Most of these out-of-staters were New England born, primarily from Massachusetts, Vermont, and Connecticut. While only 15 percent of Smithfield's entire population was born in New

19 Lewis D. Stilwell, "Migration from Vermont (1776–1860)," *Proceedings of the Vermont Historical Society*, V (1937), 244.

20 "Hints on Anti-Abolition Mobs," *Anti-Slavery Record*, II (July, 1836), 73–82; William Goodell, *Slavery and Anti-Slavery* (New York: William Harned, 1852), 400–407; Leonard L. Richards, *Gentlemen of Property and Standing, Anti-Abolition Mobs in Jacksonian America* (New York: Oxford University Press, 1970), 166–67.

England, almost one-third of the Liberty sample were native New Englanders (see Tables 6 and 7).[21]

These first generation New Englanders residing in Smithfield were part of the "late or filling-in migration" that concluded the so-called "Yankee Diaspora," an internal migration that had already brought thousands of Yankees to western New York since the 1790s.[22] Men whose parents and grandparents had made the journey

TABLE 6
Liberty and Nonabolitionist Voters Distributed by Place of Birth

| Place of Birth | Liberty No. | % | Nonabolitionist No. | % |
|---|---|---|---|---|
| New York | 30 | 56.6 | 25 | 75.8 |
| New England | 17 | 32.1 | 7 | 21.2 |
| Other States | 1 | 1.9 | — | |
| Other Countries | 5 | 9.4 | 1 | 3.0 |
| Missing | 2 | | — | |
| Base | 53 | | 33 | |

TABLE 7
New England Born and Nonabolitionist Voters Distributed by State

| State | Liberty No. | % | Nonabolitionist No. | % |
|---|---|---|---|---|
| Massachusetts | 4 | 23.5 | — | |
| Vermont | 4 | 23.5 | — | |
| Connecticut | 4 | 23.5 | 5 | 71.4 |
| Maine | 2 | 11.8 | 1 | 14.3 |
| Rhode Island | 1 | 5.9 | — | |
| New Hampshire | 2 | 11.8 | 1 | 14.3 |
| Base | 17 | | 7 | |

21 The remaining 5 percent of Smithfield's population included individuals from other states and five men born in Great Britain or her possessions (three from England, one from Ireland, and one from Scotland). Only twenty-two blacks, 1.3 percent of the population, resided in Smithfield. As none of these individuals was taxed, they could not vote.

22 Dixon Ryan Fox, *Yankees and Yorkers* (New York: New York University Press, 1940), 194.

could be found in all three political parties in Smithfield, but a higher proportion of first generation Yankees in the town gravitated to the Liberty party than voted for its adversaries.

Some of these native Yankees "filling-in" the populations of Smithfield also appear to have been "journeymen" migrants. Of the twenty-four native Yankees in the Smithfield sample for whom occupational data could be recovered, fourteen of the seventeen Liberty voters (82.4 percent) as compared with one of the seven non-abolitionists (14.3 percent) were involved in "bone and muscle" occupations other than farming.

Smithfield's longest-term residents, according to the sample, were more often Liberty men than nonabolitionists. The small town's leading citizen was Gerrit Smith, who resided in the family mansion in the tiny village of Peterboro in Smithfield. The mansion became Smith's headquarters for diverse reform activities. A wealthy philanthropist, Gerrit Smith dedicated much of his life and fortune to the abolition of black slavery, and it was largely Smith's vigorous activity in behalf of the slave that earned Smithfield and the rest of Madison County the reputation of being a "cauldron" of abolitionist propaganda.[23]

Scions of the community such as Smith and Rennselaer Northrup were active in the third party. Each had resided in Smithfield for more than forty years by 1845. However, there was also a slightly higher percentage of Liberty men than nonabolitionists among the town's more recent arrivals (see Table 8). Forty percent of the Liberty men in Smithfield had resided in the town less than a decade, while 33 percent of the nonabolitionists had arrived in the period 1835–1845.[24] Six New Englanders were among those who had resided in Smithfield for fewer than ten years and five of them were Liberty men. In Smithfield, then, the third party was vigorously supported by a number of community elders, but the third party's ranks also

23 *Madison Observer*, November 29, 1843. The most thorough biography of Smith is still Ralph Volney Harlow, *Gerrit Smith, Philanthropist and Reformer* (New York: Henry Holt and Company, 1939).

24 All data on length of residence included in this study were obtained from the manuscript rolls of the *New York State Census, 1855*, located at the county clerk's office, Wampsville, Madison County. The length of residence prior to 1845 was determined by subtraction.

TABLE 8
Distribution of Liberty Men and Nonabolitionists
by Length of Residence in Smithfield Prior to 1845

| Length of Residence (in years) | Liberty | | Proslavery | |
|---|---|---|---|---|
| | No. | % | No. | % |
| 1—5 | 6 | 17.2 | 4 | 22.2 |
| 6—10 | 8 | 22.9 | 2 | 11.1 |
| 11—15 | 3 | 8.6 | 2 | 11.1 |
| 16—25 | 4 | 11.4 | 2 | 11.1 |
| 26—35 | 5 | 14.3 | 6 | 33.3 |
| 36 and over | 9 | 25.7 | 2 | 11.1 |
| Base | 35 | | 18 | |

contained a substantial proportion of new arrivals, some of them part of the last trickle of Yankee migrants headed west.

The newcomers to Smithfield arrived in a community that had been touched by the spirit of moral reform years before the founding of the Liberty party. By 1840, the town had already been the site of numerous reform meetings and conventions. It was also the home of the nation's first temperance hotel, where no "intoxicating liquors" were served and where a traveler might be assured that his rest would be disturbed by neither "dancing parties," nor the antics of "ungoverned and idle boys." [25]

Church membership lists are not extant, but aggregate data and impressionistic sources suggest that the town's aura of morality was religiously inspired. The town's sectarian life was dominated by the Presbyterians and Baptists, each denomination claiming a membership of 30 and an average weekly church attendance of 200, respectively. Both denominations built permanent edifices in the town and these were the only church structures in Smithfield until the 1840s; the few members of the Methodist Episcopal Church held meetings in the school house and later in the Presbyterian Church.[26]

In 1847, Gerrit Smith financed a third church structure in

25 Card advertising Peterboro Hotel, June, 1845, located in Gerrit Smith Miller Collection.
26 *New York State Census, 1855*, 446, 464; L. M. Hammond, *History of Madison County, State of New York* (Syracuse: Truair, Smith and Co., 1872), 728.

Smithfield to house the Church of Peterboro, a nondenominational Christian church in the village of Peterboro. Smith established the church in 1843 as a religious vehicle for abolitionism and other moral reforms at a time when most ministers refused to have such public issues as black slavery debated from the pulpit on the Sabbath. Church membership rolls for the Church of Peterboro are not intact, but it "drew from the sectarian organizations many numbers," according to at least one county history.[27] Whatever the "numbers," the controversy stirred by the founding of a church dedicated to moral reform only fueled the flames of moral activity in Smithfield.

In addition to those religious and moral influences unique to Smithfield, the town was also visited frequently by itinerant evangelists. These traveling preachers were participating in the religious revivals or "Second Great Awakening" that swept across New England and western New York during the 1820s and 1830s. Notices in local newspapers suggest that Charles G. Finney and other renowned evangelists pitched their tents in Smithfield regularly and held major revivals there in 1820, 1821, and 1831.[28] Occasionally they were also invited to deliver a sermon from the pulpit of local churches. The evangelists claimed the conversion of many souls, and although it is difficult to determine the significance of such conversion experiences on an individual's behavior patterns, they certainly contributed to Smithfield's aura of godliness.

Social scientists do not know precisely how demographic variables interact with a town's milieu to produce a given political orientation, or the party preference of an individual living there. It is equally difficult, in the absence of written testimony, to assess the influence of an opinion leader, such as Gerrit Smith, on the political behavior of individual Smithfield voters.[29]

27 Gerrit Smith, *Creed of the Church of Peterboro* (n.p., November 29, 1843); John E. Smith, *Our Country and Its People, Madison County, New York* (Boston: Boston History Company, 1890), 395–96, 610.

28 One evangelist who stopped at Smithfield regularly to hold revival meetings was the Reverend James H. Hotchkin, who wrote *A History of the Purchase and Settlement of Western New York, and the Rise, Progress, and Present State of the Presbyterian Church in that Section* (New York: M. W. Dodd, Brick Church Chapel, 1848); see pp. 135, 139, 142.

29 The role of the opinion leader in shaping political behavior is discussed at length in Paul F. Lazarsfeld, Bernard Berelson, and Hazel Gaudet, *The People's Choice, How The Voter Makes Up His Mind in a Political Campaign* (3rd. ed.; New York: Columbia University Press,

Gerrit Smith was a millionaire landowner, who also invested in New York's growing network of canals and railroads. His economic profile qualifies his inclusion among the state's "gentlemen of property and standing," and one New York census even recorded his occupation as that of "gentleman." [30] Smith's political and social attitudes, however, were completely opposite those of the wealthy who had scorned abolitionists during the 1830s. His profound religious and moral convictions caused him to commit much of his energy and fortune to a wide variety of moral reform movements. It took a personal experience, though, to radicalize Smith's attitude toward abolitionism.

In October, 1835, Gerrit Smith was a moderate on abolitionism when he accepted an invitation to an antislavery convention in Utica, New York. The meeting was dispersed by a mob and Smith invited the delegates to reconvene their meeting the next day at his Peterboro mansion. It became a part of Smithfield's local lore how 104 delegates boarded a canal boat at Utica, traveled the Erie Canal, disembarking at Canastota, and then trekked in the dark of night to Smith's home, four infirm abolitionists riding the distance in a wagon. The experience drove Smith toward a more radical antislavery position than he had previously held.[31] And by the late 1830s, Smith was among those abolitionists urging political action in behalf of the slave, including the formation of the third party that Smith later named the Liberty party.[32]

---

1968), Chap. 5 and 12. See also, Robert E. Lane and David O. Sears, *Public Opinion* (Englewood Cliffs: Prentice-Hall, Inc., 1964), 43–56; Alan D. Monroe, *Public Opinion in America* (New York: Dodd Mead and Company, 1975), 75–76.

30 Harlow, *Gerrit Smith*, 22–45; *New York State Census, 1855.*

31 Harlow, *Gerrit Smith*, 122–24. The tale of the march from Canastota to Peterboro was told to the author by Mrs. Roger Dorance in an interview, July 22, 1974. Her husband is a great-grandson of Dr. John Dorance of Peterboro, a "Pro-Slavery" man, according to the Smithfield poll list of 1845. A letter from Elizur Wright, Jr., to Theodore Weld mentions an inn "on the road from Utica to Peterboro," which indicates some disagreement on how the delegates reached Peterboro. Wright to Weld, November 5, 1835, in Gilbert H. Barnes and Dwight L. Dummond (eds.), *Letters of Theodore Dwight Weld, Angelina Grimké-Weld and Sara Grimké 1822–1844* (reprint; New York: DaCapo Press, 1970), I, 241.

32 In a letter to William Goodell, editor of the Utica *Friend of Man*, on February 8, 1840, Gerrit Smith suggested that the new political arm of the abolitionist movement be named the Liberty party. William Birney, *Sketch of the Life of James G. Birney* (Chicago: National Christian Association, 1884), 29. Birney indicates that during the campaign of 1840 the party was known by different names: Antislavery, Abolition, True Democrat, and Republican, in addition to Liberty.

The Liberty party's success in Smithfield must be attributed, at least in part, to Smith's efforts. However, even under his watchful eye, the town's voters gave the third party a majority of their votes only once in the party's eight-year existence, in 1845. His fellow townsmen may have admired Smith and deferred to his opinion on various matters, but only on a single election day did most of them concur with his opinion of the Liberty party.[33]

Gerrit Smith's influence on voters was subtle, often only by example. In certain cases, however, Smith may have exercised a more direct effect. Caleb Calkins was Smith's personal secretary and is cited as a Liberty voter on the poll lists of 1841 and 1845. A native of Aurora, New York, Calkins was a farmer's son, who had received a high school education and had spent two years at Hamilton College. In 1838, he received a letter from Gerrit Smith requesting him to accept a position as Smith's private secretary. Calkins took the offer and served Smith in that capacity for almost fifty years.[34] Calkins and Smith shared a warm personal relationship over the years and it is quite possible that Smith's activism was a factor in Calkins's decision to vote for the Liberty party.

Smith's relationship with Nehemiah Huntington, in contrast, may have exercised a negative effect in behalf of the Liberty party. Huntington was the first attorney to settle in Peterboro and was a pillar of the community. He had come to the town at the age of thirty-one, in 1807, having graduated from Dartmouth College where he had been a classmate of Daniel Webster's. In 1828, at the age of fifty-two, Huntington decided that his law practice was no longer doing well and he was in need of a position. Gerrit Smith hired Huntington to take charge of Smith's land office. Huntington proved competent and their relationship, though businesslike, was

33 It is clear from the order in which the names are listed in the manuscript census and the testimony of a local historian that several of the Liberty voters in the sample lived in close proximity to Gerrit Smith in the village of Peterboro. The Smith mansion was located at one corner of Peterboro's village green. Liberty men James Barnett and Horace Brown lived two and three houses away from Smith, respectively. William Martindale lived several houses farther on along the commons. George Klinck, a cabinetmaker, and Hiram Hadden, a shoemaker, lived and worked nearby. However, nonabolitionist voters also lived near Smith. Emmon Downer, Moses Howe, and Dr. John Dorance and his son, John, Jr., lived but a short walk from Smith's home.

34 John Smith, *Our Country and Its People*, 393.

cordial. In February, 1843, however, Smith claimed that economic circumstances forced him to fire Huntington and another clerk, Federal Dana.[35] There were hard feelings connected with the incident. Huntington's political affiliations before 1843 are not known, but in the spring of 1844 he was elected justice of the peace as a Democrat and on the 1845 Smithfield poll list Huntington is recognized by the Liberty party as being a nonabolitionist.

Possibly Huntington was a loyal Democrat all along, though it is unlikely that Smith would have entrusted his affairs to one whose principles were suspect on the crucial issue of abolitionism. It may also be that if Huntington abandoned the Liberty party for the Democratic party, his apostasy was unrelated to his bitterness toward Smith. Smith's role in shaping the political behavior of his fellow townsmen remains vague. It is apparent, though, that not even he could dissuade some Smithfield voters from the "vacillating course" that Liberty spokesman William Goodell claimed was characteristic generally of the third party's electorate.[36]

In the absence of a complete set of poll lists, or of an official record of individual voting behavior, it is impossible to know which Liberty voters did "vacillate" in their support of the third party. Nor is it possible to know whether all those individuals whose names appear on Gerrit Smith's list of Liberty party newspaper subscribers actually voted for the third party. The subscriber list includes the names of such known Liberty party supporters as Street Dutton and Henry Bradley, but the party preference of others on the list cannot be verified. Nevertheless, subscribing to the third party's newspaper at a time when only a remnant of the party remained does suggest a strong interest in third party abolitionism and invites a comparison of the subscribers' social characteristics with those of the Smithfield Liberty voters.

There is a marked similarity between the demographic profile of

35 *Ibid.*, 714; Harlow, *Gerrit Smith*, 22, 40; Gerrit Smith to Nehemiah Huntington and Federal Dana, February 23, 1843, in Gerrit Smith Miller Collection.

36 Goodell, *Slavery and Anti-Slavery*, 472. Occasionally this vacillation benefited the Liberty party. Two Democratic town officials in 1844—Hiram Hadden, who was both collector and constable, and Edwin Messinger, the Democratic superintendent of schools—wavered in their alliances. They were elected as Democrats in March, 1844, but they were cited as Liberty voters on the November, 1845 poll list.

the subscribers and that of the Smithfield Liberty voters. In race, age, and wealth, the newspaper subscribers differed little from the Smithfield Liberty voters and nonabolitionists cited on the poll lists. All the subscribers were Caucasian and almost two-thirds (66.0 percent) of them were under fifty years of age. As in the Smithfield sample, the majority of the subscribers (61.1 percent) owned real estate property valued at between one thousand and five thousand dollars.

The majority (61.0 percent) of all subscribers earned their livings in agriculture as did most Smithfield residents. However, in western New York, where over 75 percent of the work force were farmers, a smaller proportion of the subscribers tilled the soil for a living than did the state's working population generally. Almost 40 percent (39.8 percent) of the subscriber sample was involved in nonfarming "bone and muscle" occupations as compared with only 25 percent of the state's work force. As in the Smithfield Liberty party sample, most (75.0 percent) of the nonfarmers in the subscriber sample were artisans or local merchants. However, only one subscriber was cited as a "laborer." The populations of western New York towns besides Smithfield thus appear to have also been visited by "journeymen" not as interested in farming as most of their neighbors (see Table 9).

TABLE 9
Distribution of Liberty Newspaper Subscribers by Occupation

| Occupation | Number | Percent |
|---|---|---|
| Farmer | 56 | 61.5 |
| Other | 35 | 38.5 |
| laborer | 1 | 2.9 |
| manufacturer | 18 | 51.4 |
| merchant | 7 | 20.0 |
| "learned professions" | | 25.7 |
| clergyman | 2 | |
| clerk | 1 | |
| doctor | 4 | |
| dentist | 1 | |
| lawyer | 1 | |
| Missing | 3 | |
| Base | 91 | |

As in the Smithfield sample, most Liberty newspaper subscribers were born in New York (57.4 percent) and most of those born elsewhere were of New England stock (36.2 percent of the subscriber sample) (see Table 10). Only three individuals in the sample (3.2 percent) were born in other states and three in other countries (3.2 percent). Length of residence data were not available for the subscriber sample, so it is impossible to know precisely when Liberty newspaper subscribers settled in western New York.

Of the thirty-four Yankees in the subscriber sample for whom occupational data could be recovered, twenty-three (67.6 percent) were farmers and eleven (32.4 percent) were engaged in other occupations. A majority of New England–born Liberty voters in Smithfield were in nonagricultural occupations, while the majority of New England–born Liberty newspaper subscribers were farmers. Yankee Liberty voters residing in Smithfield, then, more frequently came from nonfarming occupations than did those Yankees who subscribed to the Liberty newspaper and resided in various other western New York towns.

TABLE 10
Distribution of Liberty Newspaper Subscribers by Place of Birth

| Place of Birth | Number | Percent |
| --- | --- | --- |
| New York | 54 | 57.4 |
| New England | 34 | 36.2 |
| Vermont | 6 | |
| Connecticut | 8 | |
| Rhode Island | 5 | |
| Massachusetts | 13 | |
| Maine | — | |
| New Hampshire | 2 | |
| Other States | 3 | 3.2 |
| Other Countries | 3 | 3.2 |
| Base | 94 | |

The collective portrait of the Liberty man that emerges from the poll and subscriber lists only partly confirms Lee Benson's earlier impressionistic portrait of the third party voter in the election of 1844. The Liberty voter of this study resided in a "small moderately prosperous Yankee farming community," but does not appear to have often been an individual of "considerable standing in the community," though some were prominent citizens. Nor does the Liberty voter appear to have possessed a "better than average education."

It is unclear whether most third party voters were former Whigs, as Benson suggests. In Smithfield, it appears that some third party support may have been drawn from Democratic ranks. Benson suggests that former Whigs who had been attracted to the activist posture of that party were inspired by "radical religious beliefs" to vote for a party even more activist than the Whigs on moral issues. All available impressionistic evidence does mention the importance of the evangelists in shaping the positive attitude of western New Yorkers toward reform. Benson's scenario, however, fails to explain adequately why some Whigs responded to revivalism by voting for the Liberty party, while most did not.

The absence of letters and diaries leaves an irreparable gap in any discussion of Liberty party support. Without written testimony there is no evidence to demonstrate the manner in which the social composition of the third party's electorate contributed to the formation of an abolitionist political perspective. Nor is there a way to determine precisely those variables that, more than others, influenced the behavior of third party men. Some speculation, albeit based on limited data, is superior to rank impressionism, however, if only because it may suggest fruitful new sources of evidence and paths of research for others to pursue.

Several years after the formal demise of the Liberty party, William Goodell described the influence of religion on its rank and file: "Whatever our missionary and evangelizing orators intended, whatever they were thinking of, they were God's instruments, for putting into the minds of others 'thoughts that burned' for the emancipation of the enslaved." Goodell suggests that Liberty men were particularly inspired by the revivalists' gospel during the Second Great Awakening. Even non-Liberty men often described those who attended third party meetings and celebrations as especially "somber men," or men more "deeply imbued with religious principles" than most.[37] The evidence, however, is inconclusive that Liberty men were more religious than their neighbors who chose not to vote for the third party.

If not more religious, Liberty men may have been more affected than others by the broader anti-institutionalism of the 1830s and 1840s of which revivalism was a part. Charles G. Finney and other evangelists nurtured a suspicion of various existing institutions by urging their flocks not only to renounce evil, but to "sever all institutional connection with it," as well. This religious genre of anti-institutionalism, known as "come-outerism" to contemporaries, involved abandoning the world's sinful ways and entering a "new relationship" with that world.[38] That relationship included a commitment to creating a better world, a task that could be accomplished through moral reform. Liberty men denounced the Democratic and Whig parties as sinful institutions for sanctioning the federal government's protection of slavery. Many third party voters may have perceived their vote for the Liberty party as a rejection of immoral institutions and as proof positive that they desired to "come out" from sin.

The question remains, however, why some New York townsmen living in an atmosphere rarefied by revivalism came out for the Liberty party, while most did not. A clue may be found in the occupation and nativity of the individuals in the Smithfield and Liberty newspaper subscriber samples. A recent study of the decline of orthodox Calvinism in New England suggests that men's worldly lot often had an impact on their spiritual condition and commitments: "As Yankees became more prosperous and secure, some of their sense of dependence on God evaporated." In eastern New England, many Yankees turned from the rigid Calvinism of their forefathers to Unitarianism. These "optimistic, energetic 'merchant princes' of Boston . . . did not take it kindly when Calvinist clergymen informed them they were miserable sinners. . . . Many of them, having made their own way economically or socially, expected to win their spiritual salvation with equal success." A few Unitarians turned to

37 *Ibid.*, 387–88; *Buffalo Daily Gazette*, July 10, 1844.
38 Lewis Perry, *Radical Abolitionism, Anarchy, and the Government of God in Antislavery Thought* (Ithaca: Cornell University Press, 1973), 92–93.

transcendentalism and denounced southern slavery, but most did not.[39]

Just as socioeconomic changes altered the spiritual commitments of many prosperous New Englanders, similar factors may have affected some less affluent artisans, merchants, and laborers of western New York. Often those members of New York's "bone and muscle" who were Liberty men had recently emigrated from New England. Some historians have found the connection between faith and geographic mobility "unmistakable" and that "come-outers in America have always been go-outers." Evangelical minister James H. Hotchkin, who preached in many western New York towns, including Smithfield, observed that recently arrived settlers were often "thoughtless on the subject of religion, immersed in the concerns of life and regardless of the institutions of the Gospel," but ultimately were responsive to revivalism.[40] Western New York's "bone and muscle," especially those of New England heritage, were less directly dependent on nature and the weather than farmers, and perhaps they were also more in touch with the process of mobility or change. Individuals such as these may have welcomed come-outerism as a departure from the Calvinist orthodoxy still practiced by many western New England farmers and those in western New York. Their support for the Liberty party may have been an indication of a spiritual renewal.

The Liberty party was a protest against the sinful labor system of black slavery and the immoral political parties defending it. As free white men who possessed the right to exchange their labor for goods and services, New York's "bone and muscle" may have been moved by Liberty appeals that linked the interests of the slave to those of all free white workers in the North. Liberty men claimed that slavery's survival was due in large measure to the efforts of a northern "aristocracy" that had on various occasions "mobbed, cheated and gagged" reformers. Only a joint effort by "white laborers of the North and South" could challenge the slave labor system sustained

39 Daniel Walker Howe, "The Decline of Calvinism: An Approach to Its Study," *Comparative Studies in Society and History*, XIV (1972), 317, 322; Perry, *Radical Abolitionism*, 102.

40 William McLoughlin, Jr., quoted in Perry, *Radical Abolitionism*, 92; Hotchkin, *History of Western New York*, 26.

by northern aristocrats. Failure meant not only the continued existence of black slavery, but the possibility that free white workers
might themselves be "reduced . . . to the condition of serfs" by a
"system of class legislation" that northern aristocrats would eventually sponsor.[41]

In 1846, New York Liberty men sought to insert a clause in the
state's proposed new constitution that would end property qualifi-
cations for black voters. Referring to their party as the "Poor Man's
Party," Liberty men asked voters to consider whether the parties
that held the "poor *black* man" in slavery could be true to "the poor
white man" or "faithful to the rights of the white poor!" [42] Such
speculation may have struck a responsive chord in those western
New Yorkers who sought to come out from sin while acting to calm
their fears of social and economic oppression.

New data have made possible an innovative approach to the
study of the Liberty party. Previously unanalyzed lists of Liberty
party advocates—two poll lists and a list of Liberty newspaper subscribers—have permitted the first demographic analysis of some
rank and file third party men. The resulting profile of these individuals is the basis for a fresh hypothesis on the character of the
Liberty party in the antebellum party system. Those historians who
focused on the thought and behavior of the third party's elite found
the Liberty party to be merely an abortive attack on slavery, ill-
conceived and soon abandoned, and therefore barely worthy of mention. This study, however, poses another explanation. The third
party may have been a reference group for voters in the political
system experiencing an important religious transformation that affected their attitude toward a variety of secular institutions. Liberty
party voters sought to change their relationship to a sinful world by
creating a better one. Their own socioeconomic backgrounds caused
them to be especially sensitive to the plight of the black slave. Liberty voters sought to cripple the institution of black slavery through
the use of a new political organization unsullied by those who

41 *Address read at the New York State Liberty Convention held at Port Byron, on Wed-
nesday and Thursday, July 25 and 26, 1845,* pamphlet, Olin Library, Cornell University.
42 "The Poor Man's Party," a circular signed "Your Friend," n.p., dated Peterboro, October
17, 1846.

wished to use the power of government to defend a system of labor that was morally sinful and socially regressive.

Rank and file studies can illuminate the character of antebellum reform movements, though more information is necessary before it is clear which theories of human behavior, if any, are useful in explaining the motivations of individual reformers.[43] This examination of some rank and file Liberty party supporters suggests the need for a new appraisal of abolitionism's social origins and particularly the social roots of the Liberty party's forgotten reformers.

43 Some efforts to apply particular models of human motivation to the abolitionists have been persuasively refuted, i.e., David Donald's tension-reduction model. See Robert Allen Skotheim, "A Note on Historical Method: David Donald's 'Toward a Reconsideration of the Abolitionists,'" *Journal of Southern History*, XXV (1959), 356–65; Sorin, *New York Abolitionists*, 3–25. Martin Duberman and others questioned the value of a psychohistorical approach to abolitionism during the 1960s, but efforts are proceeding to explain reformers' motivation by examining psychological profiles derived from family correspondence. Lewis Perry, "Psychology and the Abolitionists: Reflections on Martin Duberman and the Neoabolitionism of the 1960's," *Reviews in American History*, II (1974), 318–22. Meanwhile, others are seeking the roots of abolitionism in broader social theories of modernization; see Eric Foner, "The Causes of the American Civil War: Recent Interpretation and New Directions," *Civil War History*, XX (1974), 208–209.

*Individuals*

# RICHARD DAVIS WEBB
# AND ANTISLAVERY
# IN IRELAND

*Douglas C. Riach*

POSTMAN, printer, and librarian for the transatlantic Garrisonian movement, the Dublin abolitionist Richard Davis Webb (1805–1872) immersed himself throughout his adult life in American antislavery. With Richard Allen and James Haughton, he was a founding member and leading activist in the Hibernian Anti-Slavery Society (HASS) which, with other groups in Edinburgh, Glasgow, Leeds, and Bristol, constituted the provincial network of British support for William Lloyd Garrison and the American Anti-Slavery Society. The purpose of this essay is to examine the careers of Webb and his Irish colleagues in order to show not only the plethora of possible motives for British involvement in American abolitionism, but also the nature of British reformers' relations with their American counterparts.

Allen and Haughton had been active in the campaign against West Indian slavery, as had Webb's father and brothers.[1] Webb's own

---

1 Studies such as F. J. Klingberg, *The Anti-Slavery Movement in England* (New Haven: Yale Historical Publications, 1926) had suggested that British abolitionism was a triumph of disinterested philanthropy. However, in *Capitalism and Slavery* (New York: Russell & Russell, 1961; first published in 1944), Eric Williams argued that abolitionist motives, whatever their sincerity, were in essence irrelevant, since it was the emergence of industrial capitalism that ultimately decreed the end of plantation slavery in the British colonies. Many of Dr. Williams's assumptions have in turn been challenged and rejected as overly mechanistic in a

emergence as an abolitionist, however, came with the formation of the HASS in September, 1837. The main aim of this society was to secure the overthrow of the West Indian apprenticeship system, which had been set up in 1833 after the abolition of colonial slavery, but which had been denounced by British abolitionists as a form of slavery in disguise. Like other British antislavery grops at this time, however, the HASS refused to confine its interests solely to the situation in the West Indies; it indicated that it would also watch, with "hopeful" sympathy, the activities of the abolitionists in America. When apprenticeship was abolished in 1838, those who had been engaged in the campaign against it saw no reason to repudiate their commitment to stand clear from the sin of slavery, or to dismantle organizational structures. Slavery existed still in many places throughout the world; and what the British abolitionists did was to direct their efforts against slavery in the United States.

This focusing of interest in the American situation reflected the specifically transatlantic perspectives of British nineteenth-century reform. Webb once confessed that he had looked on America as the "glory of the world," as representing the potential if not the actual achievements of regenerate man.[2] Hence the strengthened imperative to remove that blot from a country which in many respects served as a kind of moral exemplar: nonresistance, temperance, opposition to capital punishment, these and other causes were taken up by Webb and his friends in deliberate emulation of American precepts and often with the active encouragement of visiting Americans. Finally, there were strong personal reasons for Webb's interest in America. His sister and uncle settled there, his son Richard visited on three separate occasions, and his daughter Deborah, who was married to the grandson of James Hargreaves, inventor of the spinning jenny, visited once. Webb on several occasions toyed with the idea of emigrating to the United States, and visited once, as did Richard Allen.

Haughton, Allen, and Webb were typical of British abolitionists

series of recent publications; see, for example, Roger Anstey, *The Atlantic Slave Trade and British Abolition 1760–1810* (Atlantic Highlands, N.J.: Humanities Press, 1975), and the review of this by David Brion Davis in *Times Literary Supplement*, October 24, 1975, p. 1263.

2 *National Anti-Slavery Standard*, October 28, 1847, p. 87.

in that all three were, and so considered themselves, members of the middle class. All prospered in their lifetime. Webb frequently complained of the long hours involved as a printer and bookseller, but his house and land purchases indicate a growing prosperity; and at any event, his main interest was America and not business. Haughton, too, was by 1850 able to retire from his business as a grain merchant and to devote himself to the philanthropic affairs which, following his wife's death, succeeded in filling the spiritual emptiness in his life. Richard Allen was a prosperous wholesale draper whose growing wealth enabled him by the mid-1840s to make yearly trips to England and the continent, thus curtailing his contributions to antislavery, and enabling Lucretia Mott to warn him tartly against letting the "deceitfulness of riches . . . choke the Divine word, that it becomes unfruitful."[3] The HASS members were dubbed "antieverythingarians" in the local press. They did not mind: at all events it indicated a measure of public recognition. But the epithet was curiously inappropriate for men with such a positive conception of what sort of society they would like to live in. Haughton in particular aimed at the creation of an Irish society in which social tensions and frictions would disappear through the acknowledgment by all classes of their mutual interest and obligations. Haughton was distressed at the disdain shown by the upper and middle classes towards the activities of the HASS, and in his attempts to bring cohesion to Irish society he came increasingly to rely on the efforts of the "humbler" classes through temperance, education, and an adherence to moral values, as these were indicated by a commitment to secure the abolition of American slavery. The upshot was that the Dublin abolitionists attempted to reach working-class audiences on a scale and with a consistency unmatched elsewhere in the British Isles, perhaps excepting the campaign against the Free Church of Scotland.[4]

Webb, Haughton, and Allen organized a series of regular meetings at the Royal Exchange in Dublin, and at these a range of

---

3 Lucretia Mott to R. D. Webb, September 10, 1847, in Anti-Slavery Letters to Garrison, Boston Public Library.

4 For this campaign, see George Shepperson, "The Free Church and American Slavery," *Scottish Historical Review*, XXX (1951), 126–43; C. Duncan Rice, "The Scottish factor in the fight against American slavery" (Ph.D. dissertation, Edinburgh University, 1969), 273–344.

topics—peace, antislavery, temperance, and British India—were discussed in rotation. The audiences at these meetings were what Webb called the "ragamuffins" of Dublin—the urban working class with whom he and Haughton had first made contact through their associations with the Irish temperance movement and the Dublin Mechanics' Institute. Both men were sensitive to the needs and interests of their listeners. Webb was aware that their interest in American slavery would not be unrelated to a wider interest in America itself, which stemmed partly of course from their view of the country as a possible place to settle. With his deep knowledge of American affairs, Webb was prepared to present a range of information about geography, climate, and employment prospects which must have been of immense aid to the potential emigrant. Visiting American abolitionists normally spoke at the Royal Exchange meetings before addressing the special audiences that were convened in the hope of interesting a more "influential" section of the public in American luminaries. Nathaniel P. Rogers described the Royal Exchange as the "Faneuil Hall of Ireland"; and many visiting American abolitionists to Dublin shared his preference for the ragamuffin audiences.[5]

The Dublin case provides interesting information with respect to the contention that a concern with black slavery reflected a deep anxiety over the ways in which society was structured, ordered, and disciplined in an industrial age.[6] The anxiety was obvious, the manifestations of it less so. Thus Haughton's and Allen's first public contacts with Daniel O'Connell in the 1830s came in response to the Dublin guilds and trade unions: though what all three were objecting to was not guilds or unions as such, but their use of restrictive practices and frequent recourse to violence. Similarly, Webb considered that Chartism as a moral force could in fact be beneficial if it imparted to the working classes a new sense of dignity and worth. And if he never really espoused radical ideas about the restructuring of society, he did recoil from the "absurd deference" shown by most British in their movement in the 1850s. But the per-

5 *Herald of Freedom*, August 12, 1842, p. 99.
6 David Brion Davis, *The Problem of Slavery in the Age of Revolution* (Ithaca: Cornell University Press, 1975), 453–69.

sistence with which men like Haughton outlined proposals to effect some kind of reconciliation in Ireland was indicative of their acute awareness of the sheer prevalence of social discord, suffering, and turmoil in that country. And for this misery American reference points of the most distressing kind sprang immediately to mind. Thus an anguished Frederick Douglass was forced to draw comparisons between Irish peasant cabins and the worst slave quarters; and Webb remarked that an American contemplating the religious strife in Ireland could be forgiven for assuming that the country was inhabited by a "mixed population of Garrison abolitionists and McDuffie slaveholders."[7]

At first sight it seems incredible, given the appalling social conditions in Ireland, that the country could produce any sustained involvement in a cause so geographically distant as American antislavery. Yet these very conditions may, in fact, have propelled Webb into an abolitionist career. The evil of slavery, he insisted, was that it constituted a form of moral anarchy: its fascination lay in its operation as an extreme and unacceptable form of social control. As dissenters, the HASS abolitionists were already excluded from conventional avenues of power, status, and acceptability in Irish society. This, it may be supposed, both prompted an interest in the affairs of another country and heightened, if only through a sense of powerlessness, their feelings about the precarious and unjust nature of the social order in their own.

Webb and Allen were born into Irish Quaker families. As elsewhere, the Society of Friends in Ireland had a distinguished reputation for involvement in philanthropic affairs. Yet individual Irish Quaker families such as the Wrights of Dublin could produce one emigrant offspring who became a planter, slaveholder, and eventually American consul in Cuba, where he bitterly condemned the West Indian emancipation. The recent history of the Society of Friends in Ireland had, in fact, been characterized by schism and disruption, in which both American Friends and American issues had played a notable part.

Visiting American Quakers Job Scott and David Sands had been

7 R. D. Webb to Edmund Quincy, August 16, 1843, in Webb-Quincy Letters, Boston Public Library.

prominent in disputes relating to the introduction of evangelical
tenets among Irish Quakers, many of whom, such as Abraham
Shackleton of County Kildare, objected to what they saw as the
supplanting of notions of the Divine Light by dogmatic theories on
the attainment of salvation. As a result, between 1793 and 1804,
against a background of widespread social turmoil in Ireland, the
Irish Quakers were torn by disputes identical to those which were to
trouble the transatlantic Quaker community for the next fifty years.
This had two results. First, in reaction, Irish Quakers—even more
than their brethren elsewhere in Britain—were determined at all
costs to preserve the unity of the Society of Friends. Secondly, Irish
Friends tended to see Garrison and his supporters in an all too familiar context of disruptions, American in inspiration and involving
disquieting disputations about the fundamental beliefs of the society. They involved themselves in the question of American slavery. For example, they provided aid for the manumission schemes
run by Quakers in North Carolina, and in their yearly epistles to
America expressed a concern for the slaves. But Webb suspected that
their primary sympathy was for the American Friends who had to
live with slavery rather than for those blacks who had to live in it.
He saw the reaction of the Irish Quakers to the antislavery disputes
among Indiana Friends in 1843 as epitomizing a pathetic preoccupation with institutional unity at the total expense of moral truth, and
railed at their manifest refusal to support the HASS. When for the
first time, in the full flood of British outrage at the plight of the
fugitive slave in 1851, the Dublin Friends did show a willingness to
join in an antislavery society with members of other denominations,
Webb responded with a combination of contempt and sheer provocation that mortified even Richard Allen. As far as Webb was concerned, the Irish Quakers, like many others in Britain in the 1850s,
had come manifestly late to antislavery. He doubted their real sincerity, questioned their motivation, and did not think that they
would make any effective contribution to the cause.

For one of Webb's questioning mind—and also possibly for the
Unitarian James Haughton whose Quaker father had been disowned
for opposing the new stress on scriptural authority—there was a
long tradition of intellectual dissent among Irish Quakers. This was

at times described as skeptical, deistic, and rationalistic by its deni-
grators. There are, for example, remarkable parallels between Abraham Shackleton and Webb.[8] Both men refused to accept the Bible as
an infallible guide, and both were ardent abolitionists. Both were
educated at the same school, Ballitore, where Webb acquired his first
taste for literary society. And, finally, both men eventually left the
Society of Friends, after a long and most rigorous examination of
their beliefs. This very process of examination may have provided a
further reason for Webb's career as an abolitionist, since for those
personally embroiled in crises of religious conversion or commitment, slavery was a compelling symbol. Arguably this would apply
more strictly to Richard Allen, who as a young man underwent
periods of agonizing spiritual despair, than to Webb, for whom the
quest for intellectual understanding contained an undoubted exhilaration. Yet it was in many ways a long and lonely transition,
from the young man whom Lucretia Mott had joshed in 1840 for the
relative orthodoxy of his religious ideas, to the man who on his
deathbed was reading Thomas Paine and whose doubts about the
hereafter were worrying even Garrison. Webb was also perturbed at
the effect of his religious views on his family, and the fact that his
son Alfred in particular was most distressed at the discrepancies between his father's and Quaker teaching. There was, as Webb saw it, a
circular process in operation: serious reflection on social evils inevitably led a person into the antislavery camp; exposure to abolitionist thinking fueled the compulsion to explore ideas; and hence
his inclination to champion the cause of those American abolitionists whose ideas were also branded as heretical.

It was largely Webb's family circle who made up the Dublin
group attending the World Anti-Slavery Convention in London in
1840: they included Webb himself, his wife Hannah, his brothers
James, Henry, and Thomas, his cousin Anne Allen with her husband
Richard, and finally his sister-in-law Maria Waring. Here they got
their first introduction to the splits that had occurred in the American Anti-Slavery Society. Although the Irish women went to Lon-

8 For a sketch of Shackleton, sometime clerk of the select meeting of Quakers in Ballitore, County Kildare, see Mary Leadbeater (ed.), *The Leadbeater Papers* (2 vols., London: n.p.,
1862), I, 393–96.

don specifically as visitors, their sympathies were aroused by the sight of Wendell Phillips pleading the right of the American female contingent to be seated as delegates. Webb's notions as to what had happened in America were understandably imprecise. But it was in London that Webb felt the first stirrings of provincial unrest at domination by the metropolitan British and Foreign Anti-Slavery Society that would explain so much of the composition and impetus of Garrisonian support in the British Isles. Webb felt that it was only because Garrison had been rebuffed by the well-heeled London Committee that he and his Irish friends had been able to make his acquaintance. Following the lead of the Scottish abolitionists, the HASS began to resent the domination by London abolitionists of the British antislavery movement. Hence, the fact that London supported the "New Organized" American and Foreign Anti-Slavery Society was one very good reason why Dublin supported Garrison and the "Old Organized" American Anti-Slavery Society. Much in the same way the inclination of some Cork abolitionists to support Frederick Douglass as opposed to Garrison in the 1850s reflected their impatience with the hegemony of Webb's HASS in Irish antislavery affairs.[9]

That summer, 1840, some ten prominent abolitionists made the crossing to Dublin. Among them, the New Organized Henry Stanton and James G. Birney were given a warm welcome: any status conferred on a small group of British reformers was more than welcome. But it was the "Old Organized" visitors, especially Garrison and Lucretia Mott, who most impressed. Webb's wife summed up the impact they had made, when she described the kind of world Garrison was working for: "A world in which there would be no slavery, no king, no beggars, no lawyers, no doctors, no soldiers, no palaces, no prisons, no creeds, no sects, no weary or grinding labor, no luxurious idleness, no peculiar sabbath or temple . . . no restraint but moral restraint, no constraining power but love. Shall we judge

---

9 These regional tensions were mirrored within the Society of Friends itself, Cork Quakers being traditionally jealous of their independence of action, and the Yearly Meeting in Ireland insisting that vis-à-vis London it acted with "some degree of subordination" but "with an independence of action not quite consistent with the position of an inferior body." Proceedings of the Yearly Meeting Committee, 1834–1853, entry for November, 1846, in Friends' Library, Dublin.

such a man because he may go a little further than we are prepared to follow? Let us first consult our consciences and our testaments." [10]

It was not that the Webbs, of course, were thinking in terms of a new leveling of society. But they were enthralled by a vision of the possibilities that might ensue if men were elevated to a new dignity. Richard Allen also sensed with some excitement this notion of moral regeneration through restoration to the first principles that he felt were at the root of Garrisonian thought. The Dublin abolitionists now defended the "Old Organizationists." Allen incurred the displeasure of many of his Irish and English brethren by likening nonresistance to basic Quaker beliefs. And Haughton sought to defuse the explosive women's rights issue by remarking that the term in itself was objectionable, since, felicitously, "in every object of a good or benevolent nature, men and women should go hand in hand." [11]

Several factors, of course, gave cause for concern. One was the vituperation of the Garrisonian attacks on abolitionists who if now "New Organized" had been long admired in Dublin. Another was the Garrisonian view that Christian nonresistance precluded political involvement. True, Webb did run off five hundred copies of a nonresistance pamphlet; but as his remark about Garrison's "peculiar government principles" had shown, [12] he privately fretted that to deny any recourse to physical force would undermine the foundations of instituted government, and lead to anarchy. And in any event the Dublin group were keen to extend the practices of the West Indian campaign by petitioning the British Parliament on such subjects as the British recognition of Texas. The picture became more clearly defined with the visit to Britain in 1841 of the Garrisonian John A. Collins, whose letter of introduction accused the rival American and Foreign Anti-Slavery Society of having for its grand object the "utter extermination" of Garrison's American Anti-

10 Hannah Webb to Sarah Poole, June, 1840, in Anti-Slavery Letters to Garrison, Boston Public Library.
11 Letter from Haughton in Belfast *Irish Friend*, XII (December, 1840), p. 99.
12 R. D. Webb to Elizabeth Pease, November 4, 1840, in Anti-Slavery Letters to Garrison, Boston Public Library.

Slavery Society. Collins went to Britain both to collect funds for the Garrisonians and to put forward the latter's views. To this mission he brought a want of tact that dismayed allies like Webb, a readiness to discuss current notions about socialism and a paid clergy that appalled his critics, and a definition of proslavery behavior that was as sweeping as the irritation of those who fell within its compass was great. Acting very much in concert with the Glasgow Emancipation Society, the HASS in 1841 broke off formal relations with the British and Foreign Anti-Slavery Society, after accusing it of conspiring to undermine both Garrison's reputation and Collins's mission. Henceforth, the antislavery movement in the British Isles was irrevocably split.

Webb was in many ways relieved that his abolitionist position was now officially clear. His preconvention misgivings about Quaker exclusiveness in antislavery work were transformed into a postconvention acceptance of the Garrisonian position that, whatever the peculiarity of a person's views on "extraneous" topics, there was no justification for refusing to join with them on the antislavery platform. Webb frequently reaffirmed his affiliation, though to his relations with his American allies he brought a quality of independence which was the more remarkable given the sincerity of his attachments and the demands the Americans made on them. His independence of mind may, in part, have come from the deflating wit that so delighted readers of Webb's letters and journalism, and which led him and Edmund Quincy to exchange a series of funny, exasperated, and irreverent comments about Garrison's adventist views, procrastination, and propensity for recommending temperance cordials containing an alcohol base. Another factor in explaining Webb's refusal to accept without question the position adopted by his Boston allies may have been what Quincy referred to disparagingly as his "truly British" curiosity: this prompted Webb, for example, to visit the 1843 convention in London though he had earlier paraded for Boston's approval the HASS's refusal to participate in any event convened by the backsliders of 1840.

But the real explanation for Webb's emergence as the most perceptive commentator on British Garrisonianism goes deeper than this. Though he frequently doubted the reformer's ability to achieve anything through an appeal to reason,[13] Webb was attracted by what he felt to be the comprehensive and uncompromising approach to reform taken by Garrisonianism. The problem as Webb saw it was that the readiness of the Garrisonians to discuss a wide and controversial range of topics merely alienated most people. He had personal experience of the social and psychological sanctions imposed on him in Dublin when he made clear where his sympathies lay. Not only was the Friends' meetinghouse denied to Collins, but Webb himself was warned as early as 1841, and regularly thereafter, of the risks he was running by associating with such men. As a naturally gregarious person, Webb felt the impact of these sanctions the more because the Quakers were a close-knit minority sect with strong family ties. True, these helped to strengthen antislavery links with Glasgow and Edinburgh. But antislavery also split families. Thus it was his cousin Maria Webb who emerged in Belfast in the 1850s as the most virulent of Garrison's British abolitionist critics. He was thus perfectly aware of the precise attractions and repulsions of Garrisonianism for British people. Nor was this all. With his experience of the presence of British troops in Ireland, he may well have been justified in suspecting that he had a better firsthand knowledge of the problems of nonresistance than those Americans such as Henry C. Wright who came across and set themselves up as pontificating mentors on the subject.

Webb, in short, was both eager to proclaim the new ideas and affiliations, and aware that to do so might prove counterproductive. Allen and Haughton even argued against the circulation of *Right and Wrong in Massachusetts*, in which Collins had outlined the Garrisonian version of the American schisms, on the grounds that this would merely alienate much potential British support.[14] When the occasion demanded, however, Webb could throw off his qualms about the effects of Garrisonian propaganda. For example, in the initial exhilaration at finding new allies in Bristol in 1851, he worked himself into a state of physical collapse, proving himself a polemi-

13 For he—like most of his class—had been gulled into an enthusiasm for the Crimean War that later appalled him.

14 Ironically, with some four hundred copies of it still in his possession, Webb arranged for its stereotyped plates to be returned to the United States by an Irish emigrant, John Armstrong, first cousin to James G. Birney.

cist of such vigor as seemed to belie his frequently, but privately expressed doubts.[15] As editor of the *Anti-Slavery Advocate* from 1852 to 1863 and regular correspondent of the *National Anti-Slavery Standard* from 1846 to 1859, his journalistic contributions alone were prodigious.

Webb's American Garrisonian correspondents, however, were often exasperated by his statements in explanation of British "New Organization." These they tended to see as unwarranted apologias, as something less than a total commitment to abolitionist Holy Writ. His position was made even more difficult, since loyalty was expected of him, not only against "New Organization," but in such internal feuds as Garrison's quarrel with Nathaniel P. Rogers. In such instances as Webb's questioning of the efficacy of Garrison's campaign against the American Union, firm rejoinders from Boston brought him pretty quickly back into line. And it was certainly the growls of discomfiture from America that finally put an end to the tentative rapprochement between the British Garrisonians and "New Organizationists" in the 1850s. Webb was extremely sensitive to likely American reactions to his opinions. He even used the unsuspecting James Haughton as a stalking horse on delicate matters. And there can be little doubt that Webb's persistent maliciousness towards Frederick Douglass stemmed partly from his irritation at the way Douglass was loath to take his advice, but also from his realization that here was something which could bring him certain plaudits from Boston.

Sensitive to his obligations to them, and aware of their greater sacrifices for abolitionism, Webb was, however, no lapdog for his Boston allies. Thus he accepted Maria Weston Chapman's decision to close the fund-raising Boston Bazaar in 1858 with manifest bad grace, since he was convinced that he knew more about British abolitionism than she did and that cash gifts to Boston could never give the donor the same sense of participation that collecting goods could. Indeed, he and Haughton (with Henry C. Wright) outraged

15 Though one less restrained than the prominent English Garrisonian, George Thompson, who branded the American "New Organizationists" a "shadow . . . sham . . . and fraud," and then requested evidence, "for I may want proof before long." See George Thompson to S. H. Gay, September 23, 1851, in Gay Papers, Columbia University.

many American "Old Organizationists" in 1847 by protesting against the acceptance of southern contributions to Irish famine relief by the Irish Friends' Central Relief Committee. And during the Civil War, relations became so acrimonious over Webb and Haughton's bitter complaints about the support the erstwhile moral force abolitionists were giving the northern cause, that in the cases of Samuel J. May and James M. McKim long-standing friendships virtually collapsed.

Webb was a shrewd, rather worldly figure and was seldom given to self-deception. For example, he often disconcerted his American allies by revealing just how financially weak, numerically few, and geographically dispersed their British support was. British Garrisonianism had no national administrative structure or central organization. True, national conventions could occasionally be held, but these, Webb felt, benefited the would-be orators in the movement and not the slave. The point was that British abolitionists operated at one remove from the American situation. They constituted a kind of moral pressure-group, but in effect they needed to work through bodies and organizations having strong transatlantic connections. By the 1850s, Webb's abolitionist tactics had essentially altered. Instead of working-class support, he was beginning to search for new sources of antislavery backing among British academics and in the type of middle-class readership he hoped to reach through the columns of the *Anti-Slavery Advocate*. But by then, slavery had become enmeshed in the intricacies of the American political structure, rendering British antislavery at even more of a loss. When Webb set up the *Advocate* with Bristol backing, he was enthusiastic about its prospects. But there was a familiar, 1840s aspect to his decision that the paper would open with a series of articles upbraiding the British churches for their mealy-mouthed position on American slavery. For their part, the Irish Garrisonians had always been further stymied by the demographic facts that they were urban-based and English-speaking. Moreover, the potato famine had caused a virtual slump in antislavery activities in Ireland because of the resulting social dislocation, and because most abolition societies there began devoting their full attention to works of local charity. And, at a time when antislavery was becoming played out in Britain in general, the Irish-Americans were providing Webb with conclusive evidence of the relative and depressing failure of the HASS activities in Ireland.

But Webb was not unaware of the irony that it was the Irish-Americans who imparted to the Dublin abolitionists an importance out of all proportion to the latter's number, strength, or impact. The central figure here was the Irish political leader Daniel O'Connell, who though not a member of the HASS had emerged as Ireland's best-known abolitionist. O'Connell had first become involved in antislavery in 1824, when he gave his backing to proposals that Ireland provide the textiles that would buy East Indian sugar, thus undercutting the West Indian sugar economy, and ending, it was argued, both West Indian slavery and Irish poverty.[16] O'Connell rapidly became a leading figure in the British agitation against colonial slavery, and his abolitionist speeches drew the attention of both critics and upholders of slavery in America.[17] From as early as 1829 he denounced slavery there. In London in 1833 he championed William Lloyd Garrison's attacks on the American Colonization Society, and in 1838 he was instrumental in persuading British abolitionists to concentrate their efforts on the situation in America. The Irish Address of 1841, whose sixty thousand signatures were largely collected by O'Connell's agents in Ireland, implored the Irish-Americans to "cling by the abolitionist." And in a series of public statements in the 1840s, most notably in the magnificent Cincinnati Address of 1843, O'Connell delivered a blistering attack on the enormities of black slavery, and advised the Irish-Americans how they could work against it.

All this was performed with a panache and rhetoric that delighted the American abolitionists, if occasionally affronting their patriotism: for example, O'Connell's comment that he could not understand the "nasal sensibility" of those northerners who complained of the smell of blacks, since he had heard that tobacco spittle was the prevailing odor in the North, was considerably better re-

---

16 These proposals were first made by the English abolitionist James Cropper, and were incorporated as resolutions of O'Connell's Society of the Friends of Ireland.

17 He was prominent in both the parliamentary and extraparliamentary antislavery agitation, and is an interesting example of the way abolitionism could appeal to Utilitarians.

ceived in British antislavery circles than in American. Problems arose, however, with the formation of O'Connell's Loyal National Repeal Association with which he hoped to effect a repeal of the Irish Union. Within the repeal association there arose a significant body of opinion, represented most clearly by the Young Irelanders, that totally rejected O'Connell's abolitionism. It was argued that by condemning American slavery, O'Connell was materially damaging Ireland's chances of securing repeal. These Young Irelanders insisted that by interfering in the question of American slavery, O'Connell would put a stop to American financial contributions to their movement. Secondly, the slavery issue was fast becoming a stumbling block to Anglo-American diplomatic relations. The Young Irelanders believed that if war broke out between those two countries, Ireland could only benefit. In short, Americans like James Russell Lowell might question how anyone could seek freedom for Ireland while doing nothing to free the slave.

But to Irishmen like John Mitchel there was no paradox involved.[18] In his view the average Irishman was in an immeasurably worse condition than the American slave; the first priority must be given to redeeming the plight of the former. And O'Connell faced pressure from yet another quarter. For Garrison believed that it was essential to persuade O'Connell that southern contributions to his Irish repeal movement were an attempt to buy both Irish-American support for the Democratic party and O'Connell's silence on slavery. This was a remarkable dilemma for the Irish leader. He attempted to solve it by refusing only those southern contributions—in effect of course, none—which made it a condition of acceptance that he desist from all further antislavery activities. Secondly, he tried to placate Irish critics of his abolitionism by dissociating himself from Garrisonian extremism. The combination of these two tactics was characteristically astute. However, it did little to silence his Irish detractors, who saw America as an ally, a haven for the Irish emigrant, and the home of Republican liberties, not of black slavery. For their part, the Garrisonians were outraged by what they saw as his

18 When he later moved to America, Mitchel became an advocate of the argument that the slave system in the South was far kinder to the slaves than the industrialism of the North was to factory operatives.

betrayal for the meanest of ends. In this situation the HASS members were well placed for both participation and observation.

For Webb, Catholicism stood as a perfectly adequate metaphor for the kind of intellectual submissiveness that he abhorred, and he believed that O'Connell's repeal movement would result in the imposition of a Catholic ascendancy in Ireland. In O'Connell's opinion, Irish Quakers tended to be both politically opposed to him and the type of middle-class reformers who combined a touching concern for the slave with a less attractive compulsion to convert Irish peasants to Protestantism. In short, the situation gave rise to the most acrimonious personal relations and public debate. When appalled by O'Connell's curt dismissal of them, the American Garrisonians would praise Webb for his perspicacious remarks about O'Connell's lack of moral rectitude. However, in general, what the American abolitionists wanted from their British counterparts was moral support: and quite simply O'Connell was their most important European champion.

In discussing O'Connell, Webb brought up the very social forces which seemed to many of his American correspondents to justify what O'Connell was doing in Ireland. Moreover, Webb's criticisms provoked a natural reaction among those such as Wendell Phillips who saw in O'Connell their great mentor in moral force agitation. Even Webb's distaste for O'Connell was balanced by the recognition that the Loyal National Repeal Association, with its grass-roots support in Ireland and extensive American contacts, provided an ideal body through which the Dublin abolitionists could seek to operate. When the repeal association slumped in 1847, the HASS was left bereft of any similar medium for its activities.[19] Hence Webb's decision to go for a new type of educated middle-class support. He had realized that it was by acting as a kind of link between O'Connell and the American Anti-Slavery Society that status accrued to the HASS. And it was a fluke of geography (if such a term does not entirely underestimate Haughton's persistence in promoting close relations with O'Connell) that secured for the Boston Garrisonians

19 The Royal Exchange meetings had been discontinued in 1846, when the building was damaged by fire.

the kudos for receiving and promoting, for example, the Irish Address.

The Americans were grateful for the role played by the HASS. O'Connell had become their greatest weapon in their efforts to win over the Irish-Americans. Despite his disavowals of them, they issued pamphlets of his speeches, and, after his death, made appeals to his memory.[20] But their relations with the Irish-Americans seemed to pose intractable problems.[21] Thus, for example, Catholic abolitionists felt insulted when Harriet Beecher Stowe put forward the exclusivist notion that abolition was the natural province of a Protestant reform community. And against this could be placed the way in which Garrison actually confronted the most entrenched orthodoxies of a Protestant community, Belfast, in 1846, and the blatantly sectarian ends to which his visit was put by most of the Dublin Catholic press. Garrison (much to Webb's dismay) had warmly supported O'Connell's repeal movement, but the Irish-Americans tended to see this as the merest opportunism, and accused the abolitionists of being anti-Catholic and anti-Irish. The HASS members they dismissed as pawns of English middle-class reformist hypocrisy. And O'Connell's abolitionism they saw as stemming from the fact that he was well-meaning but misinformed on the subject. O'Connell indeed does seem to have misjudged the temper of the Irish-Americans, and the social conditions that produced it. Thus he frequently insisted that by adhering to abolitionism the Irish-Americans would reflect credit on Ireland, and that he would recognize no man as an Irishman who countenanced slavery. Such statements were tragically in conflict with what, in their developing nationalism, most Irish-Americans took to be their civic obligations

20 In terms of propaganda, then, there was some confusion as to what O'Connell had sacrificed, or was prepared to sacrifice, for antislavery. He pointed to his readiness to alienate American support as evidence of his devotion to principle, but his detractors saw this as a foolish refusal to acknowledge that Ireland's interests must be paramount. There were considerable differences between the estimates of O'Connell's sacrifices for abolition made by the American abolitionists during his lifetime, and those made later, when they were anxious to herald him as a great and disinterested Irish abolitionist. See American Anti-Slavery Society, *Letter to Louis Kossuth* (Boston: R. F. Wallcut, 1852), 4–49.

21 G. M. Potter, *To the Golden Door* (Boston: Little, Brown, 1960), 374; O. D. Edwards, "The American Image of Ireland," *Perspectives in American History*, IV (1970), 264–68; Gilbert Osofsky, "Abolitionists, Irish Immigrants, and the Dilemmas of Romantic Nationalism," *American Historical Review*, LXXX (1975), 889–912.

as American citizens. In these circumstances, it seems hardly surprising that the main result of O'Connell's attacks on American slavery was not to convert the Irish-Americans, but to destroy the support which had been building up for Irish repeal in the American South.

Though he was well aware of their experience of status and job competition with blacks which helped to explain the Irish-Americans' position on slavery,[22] it was both as an Irishman and as an abolitionist that Webb was dismayed by the catalogue of complaints brought against his countrymen in America. He seemed to sense, however, that the Irish-Americans raised issues (such as the threat from immigration to the cities and to politics and oppression among the northern working classes) which challenged abolitionists' assumptions about ethnic plurality and social stratification in America, and hence about how they themselves perceived their function and position in American society. It was as much this as the Irish-Americans' obduracy on the slavery issue that prompted the abolitionists' fascination with them.[23] Hence the eagerness with which his American correspondents read what the loquacious Webb had to say about the roots of the problem in Ireland.[24] And a remarkable reversal of precepts became involved. For a long study of the American political system, and in particular of the Irish-American performance within that system, had come to convince Webb of the deficiencies in the structure he had once so admired. If boss-politics was all the Irish-Americans seemed to produce, then in his view it would be disastrous to introduce such "American" precepts as the extended franchise into Ireland. The United States, once held up as an example, was now pointed to as a warning. One wonders how Webb reacted during the Civil War to the irony of James Miller McKim upbraiding him for such dislike of the "people," and warning

22 *Anti-Slavery Advocate*, May, 1853; F. E. Gibson, *The Attitude of the New York Irish towards State and National Affairs, 1848–1892* (New York: Columbia University Press, 1951), 110, 151.

23 For an 1853 example of Irish impoverishment being raised as an issue against the abolitionists, see J. O. Cobden, *The White Slaves of England* (Shannon: Irish University Press, 1971), 284–369.

24 An excellent selection of Webb's letters has been published in Clare Taylor (ed.), *British and American Abolitionists: An Episode in Transatlantic Understanding* (Edinburgh: Edinburgh University Press, 1974).

him that twenty years' attentive reading of the American abolition press was hardly the best way to acquire an impartial view of American politics.[25]

By then, of course, slavery was virtually doomed. Yet Webb was dismayed to find that, for all its vaunted internationalism, so much antislavery had found a refuge in patriotism. And he was also depressed to learn that he had been rendered in the process a very minor private in the antislavery ranks. This is the paradox that makes it so difficult to determine exactly what Webb's place was in transatlantic antislavery. Much to his chagrin, he knew how liable his status was to be dwarfed by such figures as O'Connell. Yet, for all the disingenuousness he displayed towards the Irish leader, and the crass way he treated Douglass, there was about Richard Davis Webb a liveliness and verve that make most other figures on the British antislavery scene seem irredeemably drab. Unrepresentative and idiosyncratic, perhaps, but then so much of his uniqueness lay in his ability to relate his own experiences to what other people thought and did. He was able to speak for and about a host of types and individuals who composed the British reform community of the time. Therein lay his importance for his less articulate contemporaries, and for the historian.

25 J. M. McKim to R. D. Webb, December 31, 1861, in Anti-Slavery Letters to Garrison, Boston Public Library.

# HEROES, VILLAINS,
# LIBERTY, AND LICENSE
## The Abolitionist Vision
## of Wendell Phillips

*James B. Stewart*

IMMEDIATE abolitionists never gained a throng of dedicated followers. For much of the antebellum era, they referred to themselves
with pride and accuracy as a "despised minority," for they were, indeed, considered by most to be cranky fanatics. Yet no American of
that day captured the attention of northerners of all persuasions
more than the radical abolitionist Wendell Phillips. This fact alone
suggests that Phillips embodied and articulated the culture of his
section in some unusually compelling ways. No other abolitionist,
moreover, was more successful at commanding the praise of those
who despised his specific opinions. Even his most hostile listeners
admitted that while "Mr. Phillips thinks like a Billingsgate fisher-
woman or a low pothouse bully, he speaks like Cicero." [1] There was
obviously something about the way Phillips put things, as well as
the subjects he talked about, that evoked a deep response not just
among a small clique of radicals, but among an extremely broad
spectrum of more conventional northerners as well.

This essay suggests some explanations for this exceptional impact by analyzing Phillips's belief in social control and his commit-

1 Irving Bartlett, *Wendell Phillips, Brahmin Radical* (Boston: Beacon Press, 1966), 2.

ment to individual liberation, his reliance on historical precedent and his impulse to sweep away inherited restraints. This counterpoint between control and impulsiveness shaped much of Phillips's private life, his education, his marriage, his sudden embracing of abolitionism, and found its most compelling expression in powerful speeches that conveyed his contrasting visions of the heroic abolitionist. When speaking of heroes, he extolled the qualities of violent men like Elijah Lovejoy and John Brown who, according to Phillips, embodied both tradition and impulse, who were wholly disciplined and hence wholly liberated. He glimpsed in their bold actions against slavery a vigorous new order in America, a society more uniformly controlled, yet infinitely more suited to the exercise of individual freedom.

The sum of all villainy, by contrast, resided in the proslavery politician, the "northern man with southern principles," whom Phillips saw most fully exemplified in Daniel Webster. Here was a public figure who had abandoned self-discipline entirely, giving himself over completely to serving the "slavepower" in politics. As a result, according to Phillips, Webster's inward nature had been transformed, corrupted by a passion for wealth and power. He had forgotten America's most noble traditions of liberty, and thus had "artificially" set himself apart from the popular will. Debauched and enervated, Webster, in Phillips's view, possessed no autonomy whatever, no resources at all for the exercise of bold leadership. Instead, in Phillips's view, Webster had become the fawning chattel of southern overlords.

Here were matters of intense concern not only to Phillips, but to his antislavery-minded audiences as well. As several historians have recently emphasized, the North's antislavery impulse also reflected a deep preoccupation with the issues of control and liberation, concerns that went far beyond the literal position of the southern bondsman. "Slavery," for example, connoted not only an oppressive condition of ownership, but the complete breakdown of civilized restraint wherever people found themselves in positions of unchecked authority, and southerners seemed to provide the clearest example. Lacking the controls of conscience, masters and chattel alike fell prey to lascivious instinct and became "enslaved" by passion, abolitionists feared. By opposing slavery abolitionists thus reaffirmed their personal "emancipation." Seeking civilized lives of Christian control, they decried the sexual license, gambling, and drinking associated with the plantation. Yet while exalting self-control, these reformers also testified to their personal liberation, seeking to emancipate themselves from the trammels of sinful tradition so as to act on "pure" feelings toward one another and on behalf of the slaves. In abolitionism, elements of control and self-expressiveness thus became wholly intertwined and mutually supportive; self-control constituted a necessary precondition for personal liberation. Strenuous self-discipline allowed these "moral athletes" to trust their impulses, to cast off "false" conventions, and to express freely their deepest emotions. Revolutionizing society meant first revolutionizing one's self; the exercise of control insured the attainment of one's freedom.[2]

On the far more public level of mass political ideology, one can detect a somewhat analogous interplay during the pre—Civil War years. The northern voters who flocked to hear Phillips while opposing the westward expansion of slavery were hardly radical abolitionists. Yet they, too, partook of the broadly romantic character of the age, and expressed considerable concern over the effect of slavery on the interplay of control and expressiveness. As Eric Foner has shown, the Republican party's version of a "free society" was also a homogeneous one that stressed personal order. Republicans pictured a rural America peopled by sober farmers and hard-working artisans, who raised families governed by the stern dictates of the Bible and the McGuffey's *Reader*. Yet, according to this definition, this orderly regime was both the precondition and the result of a society of liberated individuals, for a free society was one that had jettisoned "artificial" restrictions for complete laissez-faire individualism. Each person, Republicans felt, must be free to follow "natural impulses," and to shape their destinies unimpeded by "unnatural" controls. David Rothman, Michael Fellman, Marvin Meyers, and sev-

2 For some recent analyses of these matters, see Ronald G. Walters, "The Erotic South: Civilization and Sexuality in American Abolitionism," *American Quarterly*, XXV (1973), 178–201, and Lewis Perry, "We Have Had Conversation With the World: The Abolitionists and Spontaneity," *Canadian Review of American Studies*, VI (1975), 3–26.

eral other scholars have discerned many of the same concerns in other aspects of American thought.[3] In short, an interplay between control and expressiveness roughly similar to the one which Phillips found so critical in ordering his own life also circulated among his abolitionist colleagues and, in very broad form, throughout the sectional culture of the North.

As he spoke of the hero-abolitionist, extolling the heroism of Elijah Lovejoy and John Brown and condemning the villainy of Daniel Webster, northerners of all antislavery persuasions sensed that Phillips's emphasis on control and liberation were all somehow bound up with their own hostility toward the slave South. They flocked to listen and often stayed to cheer. Here, one suspects, was the major source of Phillips's rhetorical mastery. As he harmonized and articulated these seemingly conflicting impulses by making order the prerequisite of freedom, he spoke to some of the deepest feelings of his age. To approach these matters, one must explore Phillips's concerns with order and impulsive expression from his student days through his sudden marriage in 1836, his abrupt entrance into abolitionism the following year, and finally to his rhetorical construct of heroes and villains. But at the outset, it is important to take note of Phillips's forensic style—the manner in which his audiences perceived him.

At once a useful impression emerges: Phillips was consistently reported as having been *both* spontaneous and controlled, simultaneously cerebral and visceral, at once restrained and uninhibited in his delivery. None doubted that his words were those of an inflammatory extremist who aimed at the passions of his audience. But by all accounts he spoke with an almost detached delivery. In contrast to Webster's sulphuric grandiloquence, Phillips seemed, as one listener put it, like "a cold but mysteriously animated statue of marble." Audiences, it was reported, could rend the air with hisses or thunder their applause, but so aloof was Phillips that nothing "could disturb a muscle in his countenance." In a period of rhetori-

3 See Eric Foner, *Free Soil, Free Labor, Free Men: The Ideology of the Republican Party Before the Civil War* (New York: Oxford University Press, 1970); David Rothman, *The Discovery of the Asylum* (New York: Prentice-Hall, 1970); Michael Fellman, *The Unbounded Frame* (Westport, Conn.: Greenwood Press, 1973); Marvin Meyers, *The Jacksonian Persuasion* (New York: Random House, 1958).

cal flamboyance, moreover, Phillips left the distinct impression of being a logician; axioms, not bombast, often seemed to dominate his paragraphs—"a succession of propositions that appeared so nearly self-evident that you were only too glad to accept them," as one listener described it.[4]

Yet along with this impression of rigorous discipline, Phillips conveyed an emphatic but easy spontaneity. In radical contrast to the prevailing practice, he never memorized his speeches. Instead, he improvised constantly. "The words came so easily," a listener once exclaimed, "it was like picking up chips." Then, of course, one must not forget the impact of Phillips's speeches themselves—the memorable sobriquets: Abraham Lincoln, "The Slave Hound from Illinois"; Daniel Webster, "a great mass of dough"—the pungent extremism of statements like the one following the raid on Harper's Ferry: "John Brown has twice as much right to hang Governor Wise (of Virginia) than Governor Wise has to hang him." There is in forensics a point at which content overtakes and begins to shape style. So it often was with Phillips's speeches. No matter how calculatedly expressed, words like these transcended the mode of delivery, bespeaking the eloquence of instinct.[5] "He had many surprises of thought and diction," one contemporary recalled, "but made most frequent use of short, terse sentences whose sense was felt the instant they struck the ear, and whose epigrammatic point made them stick (and sometimes tingle) in the memory."[6]

In light of this testimony, it is clear that Phillips hardly projected himself as being wracked by conflict between control and expressiveness. Instead, these elements seemed to harmonize in dynamic symbiosis wherein control sustained expressiveness. Feats of rhetorical mastery, not displays of ambivalence, resulted as Phillips wove these elements together, drawing his audiences wholly into the occasion. One listener summed up the effect quite well while

4 For a general consideration of Phillips's rhetoric, see Bartlett, *Phillips*, 191–99. For other reactions to Phillips's speaking style, see also Carlos Martyn, *Wendell Phillips* (New York: Charles Scribner's Sons, 1890), 489–505; Lorenzo Sears, *Wendell Phillips* (New York: Appleton-Century Crofts, 1909), 345–51; Frank P. Stearns, *Sketches From Concord and Appledore* (New York: Macmillan, 1895), 198.

5 On this point, I am grateful for the guidance of Professor Scott Nobles, Department of Speech, Macalester College.

6 Martyn, *Phillips*, 494.

displaying a clear sensitivity to the interplay: "You heard him an hour, two hours, three hours, and were unconscious of the lapse of time. . . . He had exactly the manner for an agitator, it was so entirely without agitation."[7]

Clearly, Phillips's charismatic oratory and the stylistic expectations of his audiences were significantly attuned to one another. Speaker and listeners together accepted the axiom of expressiveness as the product of restraint, and this fact alone suggests much about Phillips's unusual success in synthesizing content and style with the preferences of his audiences. Yet his high degree of congruity also bespeaks the balance of control with spontaneity that Phillips first achieved in his private life and then drew upon as an abolitionist. Indeed, these were matters he had begun to explore many years before declaring slavery a sin.

Many parts of Phillips's life remain beyond reconstruction, for materials which bear upon his preabolitionist years are practically nonexistent. Yet for some reason Phillips saved some of his schoolboy essays and orations, exercises he prepared first at the Boston Public Latin School and then at Harvard from the time he was fifteen until his baccalaureate commencement at twenty. In many of these essays Phillips revealed his deep concern over the relationships between control and emotion, and, as the years passed, he addressed various aspects of this subject with increasing complexity.

At the age of fifteen, Phillips's written opinions on these matters were predictably uncomplicated. He seems to have been satisfied to assert, as he did in 1826, that God had given man a "rational soul" which was not made to be "subject to the animal propensities . . . of that body in which it is enclosed."[8] From the first, Phillips thus made clear his conviction that man's nature was passionate, and that primal impulses had to be controlled if man was to realize his fullest potential. By June, 1831, Phillips had applied this theorem to

7 *Ibid.,* 495.
8 Wendell Phillips, "Haec olim meminisse juvabit," 1826 (MS in Wendell Phillips Papers, Harvard College Archives). It is most interesting to note that Phillips never preserved systematically any of his other correspondence or writings. Marginalia found in these essays reveal, however, that he reread these schoolboy essays in later years, and that for reasons that can only be speculated upon, he took his youthful opinions quite seriously during adulthood. The subjects to be written upon were assigned by Phillips's instructors either as essay topics or as propositions for debate.

a broad medley of topics, among them the nature of rhetorical eloquence, the relationship between individuals and societies, and the "lessons" of history. In each of these essays Phillips consistently reflected his conviction that passion alone, uninhibited by controls or traditions of any sort, was a force to be contained at all cost, for it inevitably led to personal and social destruction, the worst forms of degradation and enslavement. But if properly counterpoised, spontaneous feelings and devices of control constituted powerfully reinforcing elements, Phillips believed. In correct relationship they assured social progress and the advance of civilized liberty. In times of crisis, moreover, strong men who embodied control and tradition could come forward to exert empassioned leadership, using their bold inspiration to enforce order and strengthen liberty.

When musing at Harvard on the workings of public address, for example, Phillips made restraint the prerequisite of eloquence. An extemporaneous speaker, he wrote in 1831, must be able to "form his conclusions in an instant," while simultaneously "regulating" his thoughts, that is, controlling his line of reasoning so that he "might follow the same" in making his discourse persuasive. In another essay he analyzed the properties of eloquence as being "feelings urged forward to action, excited by intense, often personal instincts." Yet Phillips was genuinely fearful of the demagogues' "dexterous" efforts to pander to "mob passions." For this reason he emphasized that eloquence must be removed from the streetcorner and confined to the legislative chamber. Here, he explained, speech would become "*deliberative* and addressed to sensible men" who were moved by "the interests and not the passions."[9] Already recognized as an accomplished orator, Phillips thus insisted that rhetorical passion be made to serve the ends of control. Otherwise, the result would be disruption.

Young Phillips was convinced that what was true in forensics also obtained in societies the world over. He said as much in an undergraduate essay on the question of whether or not civilized man had been "sapped" of his "natural" energy by conforming to society's

9 Wendell Phillips, "Of forming habits of extemporaneous speaking," 1831, "Your idea of what makes a writing to be poetical, prose or eloquent," November, 1830 (MSS in Wendell Phillips Papers, Harvard College Archives).

traditions and customs. In his answer, an emphatic negative, Phillips saw nothing redeeming about the "noble savage," who, when left to follow natural instinct, was "self-willed, obstinate and ignorant," the antithesis of the liberated man. "The true spirit of the savage . . . is uniformly servile," he asserted, "and hence *we* see *them* always become submissive." In short, "natural" man first became debased by passion and then enslaved by his superiors. Who were these superiors? They were "civilized" men who understood that the highest feelings and truest creative power resulted not from denying, but from submitting to tradition and law, and who thereby disproved that "civilized life is tame, wanting in impetuosity and energy of character."[10] If unchecked passion led to slavery, then social control itself released man's most noble actions, enriching the character of the whole society. The dramatic contrast Phillips discerned as he wrote essays on the histories of France and England only bolstered his certainty for the "lessons of the past" on this point and seemed beyond dispute.

As he was a son of staunch Federalists, Phillips's youthful Anglophilia and Francophobia are hardly surprising. Much more significant was his consistent recourse to the categories of order and passion in his understanding of history, and his closely related emphasis on the power of aristocrats to shape their societies. Phillips, moreover, was doubtless conscious when writing these opinions of his own very privileged standing in one of Boston's wealthiest, most venerable Brahmin families. After embracing radical abolitionism he was nevertheless to exude complete aristocratic refinement, associating easily with "bluestockings" on both sides of the Atlantic. Hence as he condemned the French nobility for disruptive passions while extolling the heroic leadership of England's peers, Phillips, whether consciously or not, offered revealing comments on his own sense of self. In them, moreover, some of the outlines of his abolitionist commitment are prefigured. So are the visions of heroism and villainy that he would one day apply in the struggle to abolish slavery. In later years slaveholders and their allies were to remind Phillips strongly of the debased French aristocrats he so despised as a

---

10 Wendell Phillips, "What do we mean when we say that man is an artificial being in Society?," 1831 (MS in Wendell Phillips Papers, Harvard College Archives).

youth. Meanwhile, he transformed Lovejoy and Brown into American equivalents of England's historical giants.

Predictably enough, France's revolution was synonymous to Phillips with bloodlust, the inevitable result of giving free reign to man's base passions as "mad enthusiasts" jettisoned all vestiges of control, casting "to the wind the collective wisdom of the ages." What is arresting, however, is Phillips's emphatic condemnation of French aristocracy as the principal authors of revolutionary holocaust. The noble orders had "artificially" set themselves apart from the rest of the public, he wrote, freeing themselves from all constraints of traditions and social obligation. Hence, they encountered no difficulty in exercising the most dangerous kinds of powers. They became "a haughty set of idlers" who exploited their "odious privileges" to the "most intolerable extent." In thus degrading themselves, they naturally became "objects of popular hatred," enflamed the "licentiousness of an ungovernable populace" and initiated a self-reinforcing cycle of wantonness and revolution. In the end, the French people collapsed into that state of savagery to which Phillips had already consigned "natural man," gladly substituting enslavement by Napoleon for the terror of Robespierre.[11]

Here, indeed was a provocative meditation for one so clearly conscious of his own "aristocratic" estate. Yet Phillips's hatred of revolution did not lead him to despise change, to exalt control exclusively, or to condemn all natural inclination. Turning from French to English history, he again affirmed that submission to tradition and social control was essential for stimulating creative impulse and extending the limits of freedom. In England he discerned a "civilized" history of liberty, in sharp contrast with France's "barbarous" penchant for self-enslavement. The cause of the difference seemed obvious and again originated among the nobility. England's peers, unlike France's debauched orders, had long ago discovered that they derived their personal autonomy and political power by embracing the nation's traditions and submitting to society's obligations. Thus committed, they were perfectly equipped, in Phillips's opinion, to

11 Wendell Phillips, "Whether attachments to ancient usages be a greater evil than a fondness for innovation—a Speech," 1831 (MS in Wendell Phillips Papers, Harvard College Archives).

act on their own in behalf of the state, for England was a "natural" aristocracy, as he liked to call it. Instead of being sealed off from the body politic and immune to social responsibilities, England's peers struck Phillips as being "knit with the very vitals of the constitution," enmeshed completely in the nation's history. Their influence, he wrote, extended "down through all respectable classes," a power that was doubly secured since England's nobles owed their position to no unmerited birthright. Theirs was an aristocracy based on talent alone, always "open" to vigorous new men, "the noble spirits of every generation," as Phillips warmly described them, who boasted "personal industry and skill, military success, the influence of character." Was it not the English peerage, he rhapsodized, "those manly reformers who laid low and deep . . . without bloodshed and almost without commotion" who had thwarted the tyrant James II in 1688? England seemed about to be overrun with "atheism and anarchy" during the French Revolution. Then, Phillips wrote, Edmund Burke "arose in his might and moving among the crowd of inferior spirits, a giant among pigmies, exposed their arrogant pretensions with all the energy and fire of his mind." He "thundered," Phillips concluded, "and a tumultuous nation was stilled." [12]

Here, the young Harvard elitist decided, was an exceptional group which had submitted completely to tradition and social obligation. Consequently, they were wholly justified in taking bold, dramatic action in times of crisis to stifle man's misguided passions, to restore order and by so doing to expand the liberties of all. Here, fully developed, was also young Phillips's version of the heroic figure. He saw in Burke, Pitt, Wellington, the authors of the "Glorious Revolution," and the signers of the Magna Charta, talented men who had struck with dramatic power to enforce their passion for order. Far from promoting revolutionary change, they had acted as fervent apostles of tradition, as inspired agents of control. Consequently, liberty, the arts, literature, and science were all more advanced in England than anywhere else. "Governments may be vio-

---

12 *Ibid.;* Wendell Phillips, "Whether the present proposed parliamentary reform will endanger the monarchic and aristocratic portions of the constitution?," 1831; "A comparison of Burke and Sir Joshua Reynolds," 1831 (MSS in Wendell Phillips Papers, Harvard College Archives).

lently overturned or peaceably improved," Phillips observed. "In the
latter case . . . the peers can stand against any opponent."[13]

In 1836–1837, six years after composing most of these statements, Phillips took two bold actions of his own, making dramatic
choices about marriage and career that suddenly transformed this
Brahmin Whig conservative into an abolitionist radical. But as he
precipitously assumed lifelong commitments to a strong-minded,
chronically invalid wife, and to antebellum America's most explosive reform movement, the preoccupations of schoolboy days remained important. For forty-seven years of marriage to Ann Terry
Greene, restraint served as the key to a stable relationship. Meanwhile, as he followed his calling as an orator-radical he also insisted
that mass passion bred savagery and enslavement, that order was the
taproot of freedom, that tradition nurtured the bold spirit of human
liberation. Even from the outset, as the lynch-mob death of Elijah
Lovejoy sealed his abolitionist commitment, Phillips found himself
being shaped by these convictions. In the process, with powerful
oratory he began to extol the martyred Lovejoy for picking up the
gun. Twenty-two years later, in response to John Brown's bloody
raid, Phillips elaborated fully his image of the abolitionist-hero before huge and explosively responsive audiences.

The precise forces that shaped Phillips's volatile behavior in 1836
and 1837 can only be guessed at. Recent biographers agree that he
found himself much at loose ends as he tried between 1834 and 1837
to establish a Boston law practice. It has been suggested, moreover,
that vocational misgivings were common at about Phillips's age
among abolitionists-to-be, prompting their "conversions" to the
cause. Doubtless, some such crisis of identity lay behind his sudden
engagement to Ann Terry Greene in 1836 and his rapid migration to
abolitionism. Yet the only extended descriptions of Phillips's marriage and conversion come not from private letters or diaries, but
public statements by Phillips and his contemporaries. Such evidence hardly lends itself to precise psychological applications; it
does, however, offer dramatic documentation of Phillips's continu-

13  Phillips, "Whether the present proposed parliamentary reform. . . ."

ing concern for passion and control as he reshaped his private life and set out to purge the nation of slavery.

By all accounts, Ann Terry Greene, strong-willed and mentally aggressive, was dying in December, 1836. Phillips had been keeping company with this outspoken bluestocking abolitionist off and on for nearly a year; for the last few of those months she had experienced successive relapses and recoveries. But when informed of how ill she had now become, Phillips "fell into great distress," a friend reported, rushed into her sickroom in violation of the doctor's orders and proposed marriage as she lay on what he supposed was her deathbed. Ten months later they were married, and embarked on nearly a half-century of life together.[14] Phillips had seized the moment, and his spontaneous expression of love cemented a relationship in which mutual restraint was to become the key to emotional fulfillment.

Ann Phillips remained an invalid throughout her life, generally consigned to her bed in an upstairs room, nearly blinded by headaches, bent double by searing rheumatic pains, and usually able to travel only when carried on a litter.[15] Friends speculated about the sources of her maladies with no greater accuracy than a historian might, for none of her few surviving letters offers even veiled suggestions. But one fact appears wholly apparent: from the first, Wendell Phillips was obliged to subordinate many conventional needs to the constant demands of Ann Phillips's chronic infirmity. Great amounts of his time were given to nursing her at home, or to ferrying her on an endless circuit of homeopathic clinics and "water cure" resorts. Their home was "a perpetual leech chamber," he

14 See Bartlett, *Phillips*, 26–35; Bertram Wyatt-Brown, "Abolitionists and New Leftists: A Comparison of American Radical Styles," *Wisconsin Magazine of History*, LIV (Summer, 1971), 178–210; James Brewer Stewart, *Holy Warriors: The Abolitionists and American Slavery* (New York: Hill and Wang, 1976), Chap. II.

15 See Bartlett, *Phillips*, 77–82, for a detailed description of Ann Phillips's complaints. The historical issues posed by her illness as such have no direct bearing on this essay. It is very important, however, to note that the sublimation that her condition demanded of her husband, while exaggerated, was not unique. Judged against the norms of antebellum Yankee culture, the phenomenon was not as "aberrant" or "pathological" as it might first appear to an observer from the 1970s. For an introduction to some of these matters, see Ronald G. Walters, *Primers for Prudery: Sexual Advice to Victorian America* (Englewood Cliffs: Prentice Hall, 1974), 1–18; John S. and Robin M. Haller, *The Physician and Sexuality in Victorian America* (Champaign-Urbana: University of Illinois Press, 1974).

wrote in 1850, with "Ann, as usual . . . prostrated." Similarly, he subordinated his deeply cherished calling as an activist orator, rejecting many lecturing invitations and often refusing to leave his wife's side for months on end. Almost certainly, sexual fulfillment was impossible; considerable restraint in their physical relationship was clearly paramount at any rate, and they remained always a childless couple. Reclusive, the Phillipses never entertained, admitted no house guests, and even the look of their unfashionably located home in Boston bespoke austerity—few decorations, sparse furniture, "plain and bare, without and within," as one abolitionist recalled.[16]

At first one might sense in this setting a horrible pathology. Phillips, after all, was the picture of masculine vitality—extremely handsome, popular, a vigorous boxer and wrestler who "toned up" his skin daily with a stiff horsehair brush, a healthy young man who had written love poems and who in 1833 had become so hopelessly enamoured of the beautiful actress Fanny Kemble that he indulged an adolescent impulse of voyeurism, watching her performances for nineteen successive evenings.[17] No circumstances could seem to have a more repressive effect on such a man than the ones Phillips accepted in his long domestic life. Yet evidence exists to support a more complicated, less baleful conclusion.

Wendell Phillips displayed throughout his life an unmistakable attraction for strong-minded women. His mother, Sarah Walley Phillips, had exercised a far more formative influence in his upbringing than had his father, who died when Phillips was fourteen and whom Thomas Wentworth Higginson once described as a man of "pliant disposition." Ann and Wendell Phillips both fully recognized this fact. Ann remarked upon Sarah Phillips's death in 1846 "she was everything to him," and Wendell Phillips offered a revealing tribute of his own: "I am always best satisfied with myself when I fancy I can see anything in me which reminds me of my mother—

16 Wendell Phillips to Elizabeth Pease, February 19, 1850, in Antislavery Collection, Boston Public Library; Thomas Wentworth Higginson, *Wendell Phillips* (Boston: Higginson and Lee, 1884), viii.

17 Bartlett, *Phillips*, 20, 28–29; Wendell Phillips to Edmund Quincy, November, 1846, in Quincy Manuscripts, Massachusetts Historical Society; Wendell Phillips to Sidney Gay, July 9, 1851, in Gay Manuscripts, Columbia University.

she lived in her children."[18] For this reason, perhaps, Phillips reserved his deepest admiration for extremely powerful women like Maria Weston Chapman, Lucretia Mott, Elizabeth Cady Stanton, and Elizabeth Pease, dwelling on their intellectual and moral qualities, praising their brilliant intelligence, courage, and moral discernment. Slim evidence suggests an infatuation during his late adolescence. But never, in all of his adult writings, did he reveal the least trace of physical attraction of any sort to anyone.[19]

Here, one suspects, was the reason that Wendell Phillips found himself attracted to Ann Phillips in the first place. She was strong of mind, but physically unthreatening. Ultimately, she offered him an intellectual and spiritual presence similar to the maternal influence that Phillips valued so highly as the last of thirteen children. Meanwhile, sexual overtones were completely suppressed. As they took up a life of seclusion, their relationship became one in which Wendell Phillips submitted to self-restraint. Ann became his "Countess," as he so often referred to her, a person of regal mind and dominating soul with whom he could share his thoughts, but only after curbing his passions. She, in turn, fulfilled him, demanding that he sacrifice his needs to hers, precisely because she was completely dependent upon him for all her human contacts. Because of her helpless condition, she became the all-dominating partner. Wendell Phillips may have served as Ann's lord-consort ("my better three-quarters" she liked to call him), allowing her vicarious participation in the moral enthusiasm, high drama, and cliquish gossip of Boston abolitionism. But above all, he was preeminently her servant.[20] He read to her endlessly; they conversed for hours daily. He

18 Higginson, *Phillips*, v–vi; Wendell and Ann Phillips to Elizabeth Pease, January 31, 1846.

19 For evidence of Phillips's fascination with strong-minded women and his tendency to see them in a controlled setting, see Wendell Phillips, "Woman's Rights," in Phillips, *Speeches and Lectures*, first series (Boston: Lee and Shepherd, 1863), 13–34; Phillips, "The Boston Mob," *Speeches and Lectures* 277; Phillips, "Suffrage for Women," in Phillips, *Speeches, Lectures and Addresses*, second series (Boston: Lee and Shepherd, 1905), 110–27; Phillips, "Woman's Rights and Woman's Duties," *Speeches, Lectures and Addresses*, 128–38. Also consult his longstanding correspondence with Elizabeth Pease, conveniently reprinted in Clare Taylor (ed.), *British and American Abolitionists* (Edinburgh: University of Edingburgh Press, 1974). In his speeches Phillips often argued that since women *already* possessed such immense social power, granting them full civil rights would serve as a check on them by involving them in the responsibilities and obligations of decision-making. Bartlett, *Phillips*, 30.

20 Higginson, *Phillips*, viii; Wendell Phillips to Edmund Quincy, October, 1847, in

ferried her on endless quests for cures. Theirs was a relationship which seems to have engendered no overt expression of guilt on her part for her demands, or anger on his at being deprived. Denied physical fulfillment and a wide social circle, Wendell Phillips came to know the meaning of self-control at the most intense and personal level. Hence confronting, as he did in late 1837, the prospect that savage, enslaving passion was running amok in society, it is hardly surprising that he exploded with eloquent demands for bold action. The man whose private life was to be forever ruled by sublimation thus found a vocation where possibilities for expressiveness abounded.

For Phillips, courting Ann Greene meant only flirting with abolitionism. She was already an outspoken Garrisonian, but throughout 1836 and nearly all of 1837, he remained uncommitted and on the periphery of the movement, attending occasional meetings and giving brief speeches, one of which protested restrictions of the right to petition Congress against slavery.[21] It was the demise of Elijah Lovejoy, gunned down with a rifle in hand on November 7, 1837, by a proslavery mob—not the promptings of Ann Phillips—that finally ignited Phillips's abolitionist zeal. The familiar details of the murder need no repeating. Of significance was Phillips's spontaneous response, as next day he seized the rostrum at a protest meeting and delivered a totally unprepared address eloquently defending Lovejoy's use of guns. Impetuously, like the English nobles of his Harvard days, Phillips took bold action against disruptive passion. Emulating the expressiveness of Lovejoy himself, he came forward, speaking "from impulse" as he extolled the martyred abolitionist before a hostile audience. "The gun which was aimed at Lovejoy's breast brought me to my feet," Phillips recalled years later. "I can never forget the agony of that moment."[22]

---

Quincy Manuscripts, Massachusetts Historical Society; Edmund Quincy to Richard Webb, March 9, 1848, January 13, 1853, in Antislavery Collection, Boston Public Library; Bartlett, *Phillips*, 80–81; Martyn, *Phillips*, 87.

21 Caroline Weston to Deborah Weston, March 3, 1837, in Antislavery Collection, Boston Public Library; Wendell Phillips, "The Right of Petition," in *Speeches, Lectures and Addresses*, 1–6; Bartlett, *Phillips*, 41–46. See Phillips's "The Boston Mob," 213–19, for strong testimony that Phillips had not become "abolitionized" by mob action in earlier encounters with proslavery violence.

22 *National Antislavery Standard*, April 27, May 25, 1867. Louis Ruchames has demon-

Henceforward, Elijah Lovejoy became for Phillips an exemplar of masculine activism, the agent of civilized order in a wild, half-formed, frontier society. Here, it seemed, was a liberated figure, embodying stern discipline who "rises from the lap of artificial life, flings away softness, and startles you with the sight of a MAN."[23] In Alton mass passion encountered no restraint, the citizens lacked "fixed habits of character, molded and settled, and were not yet hardened into manhood." Vulnerable to the disruptive influence of the "slave power," the people had "forgotten the blood-tried principles of their fathers the moment they lost sight of our New England hills." Cut off from culture, tradition, and control, unalloyed passion held sway in Alton. The community, collapsing into savagery, began "staggering like a drunken man" and Lovejoy alone represented the forces of civilization as Phillips understood them. After first consulting with other "men of character" he then took heroic steps to "stun" the townsfolk "into sobriety," for Lovejoy sensed the "*necessity* of resistance," as Phillips termed it. The besieged abolitionist thus "appealed to the laws" as he picked up the gun, and in so doing "died nobler" than those who had fallen at Lexington. The essence of Lovejoy's manhood, said Phillips, had been his refusal to compromise in any way his complete devotion to freedom. This was the ultimate test of his self-discipline and the source of self-liberation.[24]

Phillips could not have stated any more clearly his vision of Lovejoy as an abolitionist hero—the man in whom control and spontaneity, tradition and bold instinct were wholly reconciled. The conservative young admirer of British aristocrats had now become the passionate devotee of the firebrand Lovejoy and an authentic

strated in his "Wendell Phillips and the Lovejoy Address," *New England Quarterly*, XLVII (Fall, 1974), 107–16, that Phillips had appeared several times before abolitionist gatherings prior to his Lovejoy address and was already developing a reputation as an orator. Ruchames also proves that Phillips was expecting to speak since he had been given an invitation to do so at the Lovejoy protest meeting. None of this information, however, detracts from the spontaneity of Phillips's actions on that occasion. For one thing, it is clear, Phillips spoke without notes while reacting with great vehemence to previous speakers who had criticized Lovejoy's "impudence" while justifying the mob's right to kill. Most important, however, are Phillips's own recollections of the event (quoted above), which reveal his strong memory of that occasion, apart from the fact that he had been invited to speak. Clearly, Phillips believed that the Lovejoy murder, the protest meeting, and the speech he delivered marked an abrupt, decisive change in his life.

23 Phillips, "The Pilgrims," *Speeches and Lectures*, 230–31.
24 Phillips, "The Murder of Lovejoy," *Speeches and Lectures*, 1–10; Wendell Phillips to the editor, April 14, 1867, in *National Anti-Slavery Standard*, April 27, 1867.

radical in his own right. Indeed, his emphatic reaffirmation of social control enhanced, not diminished, his egalitarian demand that slavery be abolished. The killing shot had "scattered a world of dreams," fundamentally violating the balance of forces upon which Phillips's view of self and society wholly rested. "Mob power," he wrote, had revealed itself to him as a fearful, "abnormal element," standing outside all constraint of law or tradition; "no check, no balance had been provided." Here was the force of savagery "growing out of southern soil . . . penetrating every altar of New England." In the Alton riot Phillips had glimpsed for the first time the same bestial passion that he felt had once reduced France to political slavery and cultural savagery. Now, as in France, an unrestrained group of slaveholding aristocrats threatened to "benumb the conscience and stifle the intellect" of all Americans, turning "politicians and statesmen into brutes."[25] A new order was desperately required in America, Phillips suddenly insisted, one which upheld the liberty of individuals and not the license of slaveowners and rioters. It must have vital new heroes to redeem it, men like Elijah Lovejoy who could transform America as Burke had once transformed England. By this process 2.5 million black slaves must be granted free and equal citizenship. "I hold that the world is wrong side up," he wrote revealingly to his Harvard classmates on the occasion of their fifteenth reunion, "and maintain the propriety of turning it upside down. . . . My surprise is that a quiet, moderate half way sort of sim-sam fellow like myself should have somehow gotten the reputation of a fanatic."[26]

In establishing Lovejoy as his hero-abolitionist, Wendell Phillips automatically discovered hosts of people who seemed to practice evil—the entire planter class, the powerful northern interests that actively supported slavery, the many citizens whose apathy and racism guaranteed the health of the peculiar institution. Yet one man, Daniel Webster, emerges from Phillips's speeches as a villain unmatched for his submission to the degrading passions of slavery. Certain things about Webster gave Phillips some particularly com-

25 *National Anti-Slavery Standard*, April 27, May 25, 1867. See also Phillips's "Louis Kossuth" in *Speeches, Lectures and Addresses*, 48.
26 Questionnaire form from Harvard Class of 1831, Antislavery Collection, Boston Public Library.

pelling motives for concern. As senator from Massachusetts, Webster may have suggested to Phillips the station that the reformer himself might have attained had not the abolitionist commitment transformed the course of his career. Phillips had greatly admired Webster during his Harvard days. Throughout his life, moreover, as the agitator himself once confessed, he remained "sorely tempted by politics." For these reasons Phillips might well have regarded Webster with a keenly felt mixture of envy and respect. But whatever the cause, Phillips did harbor a heightened sensitivity to what he believed was the senator's exceptional power to shape the nation's affairs. Indeed, for a time during the 1840s Webster did seem increasingly to be using his own oratorical power to oppose slavery while engaging in various struggles in the Whig party.[27] Hence, in 1850, when Webster abruptly abandoned "northern rights" and wholly embraced sectional compromise, his actions struck Phillips with particular force. Now Webster's forensics extolled a proslavery union, condemned abolitionists, and insisted on the return of fugitive slaves. Here were acts of grossest betrayal and apostacy, Phillips announced once, that revealed Webster as a man completely enslaved by slavery, morally emasculated and politically depraved, the archetypal villain.

"If in the lowest deep, there be a lower deep for profligate statesmen, let all former apostates stand aside and leave it vacant. 'Hell from beneath is moved for thee to meet thee at thy coming.'" It was with words such as these that Phillips greeted Webster's famous Seventh of March speech on behalf of the Compromise of 1850. The sectional crisis of that year could be met only by the exercise of bold, heroic leadership, Phillips believed, the kind that Webster himself had pretended to possess. "All the virtue the North has is aroused, and needs but a MAN as a leader to dare and do all for liberty."[28] But instead of an inspired, impassioned Lovejoy, came the timid "doughface," the man whose will for self-discipline and instinct for liberty had been dulled past the point of feeling.

27 Wendell Phillips to Elizabeth Pease, October, 1844, in Antislavery Collection, Boston Public Library. For Webster's uses of antislavery see Robert F. Dalzell, *Daniel Webster and the Trial of American Nationalism* (New York: Norton & Co., 1972), 98–156.
28 *Liberator*, March 22, 1850.

Phillips had no misgivings when identifying the sources of Webster's bankruptcy—all were somehow related to the senator's aban-
donment of self-control and his rejection of the society's restraints.
Like the nobility of the *ancien regime*, Webster had set himself
apart, Phillips believed, divorcing himself from the nation's traditions and obligations. He had mistakenly "supposed he was living
in old feudal times, when a statesman was . . . an essential power in
himself." Consequently Webster had lost touch with the true feelings of the people, following instead his own narrow impulses to
amass wealth and power by pandering to the South. "Three cheers
for Sir Pertinax McSycophant," Phillips once jeered, "who all his life
has been bowing down to the Slave Power to secure the Presidency,"
willing always to "sacrifice his manhood." Driven to satisfy these
"great temptations," Webster had "given up" completely the true
interests and honor of his state and section.[29]

Here was the reason for Webster's impotence, for his failure to
act decisively when confronting sectional crises. No figure, Phillips
asserted, had ever commanded so much autonomous power and potential mastery than Webster had seemed to in 1850. "He stood like
a Hebrew prophet between living and dead," able by simply up-
holding "the cross of common truth" to sweep away "the black dishonor of two hundred years." Instead, Webster's character melted
before the temptation of passion, leaving him incapable of the man-
liness needed for heroic action. "He gave himself up into the lap of
the Delilah of slavery, for the mere promise of a nomination and the
greatest hour of the age was thrown away." Webster, like Lucifer,
thus fell from "the very battlements of heaven" to the coldest depths
of hell, said Phillips, and ultimately he found himself incapable of
any real emotions at all. The exercise of raw passion had entirely
extinguished moral sensibility, leaving Webster to regard slavery
"with such judicial coldness, such wary and decorous impartiality
between Liberty and Despotism." Webster's conscience, numbed,
had become a "cold, tame, passionless, politic commodity." Hence
the senator remained aloof "in the director's room of the Merchants

29 Phillips, "Public Opinion," *Speeches and Lectures*, 39–40.

bank," preoccupied with his quest for meaningless power as the slave power, unchecked, continued to extend its barbarizing hegemony across the face of the nation.[30]

Thus developed, Phillips's full description of sectional villainy stressed not cerebral conspiracy, but a victimization by passion which left the individual impotent and without feeling. By casting aside restraint and tradition Webster had lost his autonomy entirely, ruining himself morally as he became the helpless abettor of slavery. In Phillips's opinion, such a figure was far more dangerous than was, for example, the forthright John C. Calhoun, "the pure, manly, uncompromising advocate of slavery; the Hector of a Troy fated to fall." Webster, he feared, was widely perceived as exemplifying national statesmanship and high-minded patriotism, a figure to be emulated and supported. "The men we honor, and the maxims we lay down in measuring our favorites, show the level and morals of the time," Phillips believed. "It is a grave thing when a state puts a man among her jewels." It therefore struck Phillips as particularly crucial to expose Webster's true nature, to reveal him as a man whose base instincts had overwhelmed him, whose "statesmanship" and "compromise" brought ever closer the prospect of a once civilized nation reduced to savagery by the slave power.[31]

Following the Compromise of 1850, radical abolitionism, like the larger sectional conflict, became increasingly studded with violent incidents. The history included rescues of recaptured slaves, Kansas border wars, the beating of Charles Sumner, and sporadic revival of antiabolitionist violence. As prescribed by the Kansas-Nebraska Act and the Dred Scott decision, slavery's sphere of westward access grew immensely, and the Phillipses became ever more receptive to violent abolitionism. Ann Phillips complained in 1856 that the foes of slavery were all "talk" and no action, while her husband led a vigilance committee in Boston and swore to defy the Fugitive Slave Law by force.[32] From the rostrum, he broadcast his

30 Phillips, "Surrender of Sims," *Speeches and Lectures*, 67, 69.
31 Phillips, "Public Opinion," 49; Phillips "Surrender of Sims," 63; *Liberator*, March 22, 1850; Phillips, "Idols," *Speeches and Lectures*, 243–62, quotations, 251, 255.
32 Bartlett, *Phillips*, 159–207.

unabashed support for slave insurrections and called on Massachusetts to crush the slave power by the same means employed at Lexington and Concord.

But as always, Phillips continued to talk, while remaining satisfied by only urging violent actions by others. The personal demands of restraint kept him from indulging his impulse for force. Instead, his relationship with violence was vicarious; he wrote, for example, in 1851 about the vigilance committee meetings that he attended. What excited him was the intrigue and the possibility of bloodshed, the "debates about secret escapes—plans to evade where we can't resist—the door watched that no spy may enter . . . intimates forbearing to ask the knowledge which it may be dangerous to have."[33] In mid-1858, when abolitionist Lysander Spooner revealed plans to send guerilla units into the South, Phillips would have none of it. Theodore Parker, Samuel Gridley Howe, and Thomas Wentworth Higginson, Phillips's closest vigilance committee associates, underwrote John Brown's armed excursion to Harper's Ferry. There is also evidence that Phillips knew at least something of Brown's plans in advance. Yet he remained uninvolved.[34] But once apprised of the news of Brown's bloody raid, Wendell Phillips burst forth with waves of rhetorical incandescence. Here was a second Lovejoy, but a figure ever so much more formidable, an abolitionist possessing superhuman qualities and awesome strength. In his extended apotheosis of John Brown, Phillips recapitulated with a vastly augmented intensity the interplay of order and impulse that had ruled his own life, creating a figure who had literally transfigured the nature of the American experience. Harper's Ferry closed an old, corrupted era in American history, Phillips believed, releasing forces which were creating a new, purer order, one that fulfilled the na-

33 Wendell Phillips to Elizabeth Pease, March 9, 1851, in Antislavery Collection, Boston Public Library. In spurning "action" for "talk," Phillips, of course, reflected a trend among abolitionists generally during the 1850s. The matter is treated in Betram Wyatt-Brown, "William Lloyd Garrison and Antislavery Unity: A Reappraisal," *Civil War History* (March, 1967), 5–24.

34 Wendell Phillips to Lysander Spooner, July 16, 1858, in Antislavery Collection, Boston Public Library; "Address to the Citizens of the Slave States," in Lysander Spooner Manuscripts, New York Public Library; Wendell Phillips to John Brown, N.C., 1859, in Antislavery Collection, Boston Public Library. The letter suggests, perhaps, Phillips's foreknowledge and his unwillingness to involve himself with Brown's plans.

tion's most noble traditions and fostered human freedom as never before. "Why, this is a decent country to live in now," he exulted.[35]

Obeying his instinct for control, Phillips adamantly refused to apply the word "insurrection" to Brown's act, and he believed it a "great mistake" to call him an insurgent. To Phillips, the events of Harper's Ferry contained the power of revolution not because they unleashed disruption, but because they put a crushing end to disorder. Brown's genius was that he acted to suppress forever the chaotic tyranny of slavery itself. Virginia, long in a state of "chronic insurrection," had contained "no basis of a government" according to Phillips, for she was peopled by a "barbarous horde who gag each other, imprison women for teaching children to read, abolish marriage, condemn half their women to prostitution and devote themselves to the breeding of human beings for sale." Into this savage anarchy marched Brown, the bringer of civilization, armed with God's warrant to enforce control: "He stood as a representative of law, of government, of right, of justice, of religion," Phillips declared. "They were a mob of murderers who gathered about him, and sought to wreak vengeance by taking his life." What Phillips had long ago perceived in Lovejoy, and in Burke even earlier, now applied with even greater force; here was a man so wholly disciplined that he could act completely from will, bringing order where once chaos had reigned. "John Brown is the impersonator of God's law, moulding a better future, and setting it for an example."[36]

Brown's irrepressible will to act derived from his primal exemplification of liberty's most ancient traditions: in three decades Phillips had not revised some of his initial opinions on history. He still located the wellsprings of liberty in the England of "two hundred years ago," when bold men had acted decisively in the name of freedom. This "impulsive, enthusiastic aspiration . . . which obeys ideas . . . with *action*" was the "Puritan Principle" that Phillips saw reflected so strongly in this "regular Cromwellian dug up from two centuries." Brown, like the opponents of Stuart tyranny, had defied the state in defense of liberty. Centuries ago "Puritanism

35 Phillips, "Harper's Ferry," *Speeches and Lectures*, 274.
36 *Ibid.*, 271–72; Phillips, "The Puritan Principle and John Brown," *Speeches, Lectures and Addresses*, 308.

went up and down England" and "tore off the semblance of law (to) reveal despotism." "John Brown has done the same for us today," not "hesitating to ask what the majority thought," but striking boldly, inspired by the "great idea" of crushing tyranny.[37]

For decades, Phillips's abolitionist commitment, his forensic mastery, even his marriage and sense of self had depended on a dynamic balance of control and expressiveness. Now, in Brown, the orator discovered a transcendent figure who united these elements totally, who had achieved a complete reconciliation of submission with liberation, restraint with passion, and tradition with revolt. "Prudence, skill, courage, thrift, knowledge of his time, knowledge of his opponents (and) undaunted daring"—these were the traits that Phillips discerned as uniting in Brown's personal character. The Brown family's wholeminded devotion to his cause, the way he was "girded about by his household" became the element which completed the picture of vital symmetry. Brown's was no "spasmodic" act of simple passion, but the "flowering of sixty years," the supreme expression which endowed his life with perfect wholeness. "Everything about him grouped itself harmoniously," Phillips exclaimed, "like the planets and the sun."[38]

Brown had achieved a level of liberation which Phillips could admire and felt he could understand. But he could never emulate it, and this was a fact that the orator realized at once: "The very easy thing (is) to say; the difficult is to do," he affirmed. Instead of talking, Brown had acted, showing the American people true "manhood," destroying savage tyranny and facing death "with two hundred thousand broken fetters in his hands." It was wholly fitting that Phillips traveled to Brown's funeral at North Elba, New York, served as a pallbearer, and delivered the eulogy for his "hero-saint." Meanwhile, as enraged planters clamored for the nationalization of slavery, uncompromising northerners also began to act, demanding an America dedicated to free soil and republican liberty. On the most fundamental level of political ideology, Yankees condemned the "barbarism of slavery" and extolled the "sober virtues" of free labor civilization. The counterpoint of order with liberation which had for

37 Phillips, "The Puritan Principle," 295, 300.
38 Ibid., 303; Phillips, "Harper's Ferry," 274.

so long enriched the words of Wendell Phillips now inspired the politics of abolition. The tyrannous, disruptive slave power must be contained and controlled, northern voters insisted. The frontier must be preserved for the free laborer and republican order must prevail in the nation's affairs.[39] In the Civil War itself, as northerners killed for freedom and southerners for independence, the issues of submission and liberation achieved a national conjoining.

In April, 1867, Wendell Phillips made a very special stop on his western speaking tour. One might even call it a pilgrimage. By this time, with the slaves freed and southern reconstruction well under way, Phillips felt the need to reflect on the previous thirty years, and there was certainly no more apt a spot to do so than Alton, Illinois. There, on a "beautiful spring day" Phillips stood on a wooded bluff and surveyed the broad valley below him. Here was where Lovejoy's gravestone should be placed, Phillips mused. It should overlook this beautiful panorama that symbolized to him so perfectly the new order and freedom which had come out of Civil War. "Grand the valley spreads," Phillips wrote, "North, East, South and West, holding great states bound together by the golden ribbon of the Mississippi." Passengers on the boats, "the millions of busy and prosperous men," ought to be able to look up as they passed by and see the monument of "him who consecrated this great valley to liberty," the man whose act of passion had begun the downfall of slavery. "What world-wide benefactors these 'imprudent' men are," Phillips thought, "the Browns, the Lovejoys, the Garrisons, the saints and the martyrs. How 'prudently' most men creep into nameless graves, while now and then one or two of them forget themselves into immortality."[40] For Phillips nearly fifteen years of egalitarian commitment still lay ahead. The career of agitation begun by Lovejoy's death was not to end until 1884. But for a few moments while in Alton, he could feel that the nation had accepted a new order and in so doing had been truly liberated.

39 Phillips, "The Burial of John Brown," *Speeches and Lectures*, 291–93; Phillips, "The Puritan Principle," 296, 302; Foner, *Free Soil*, 1–72; Major L. Wilson, *Space, Time and Freedom* (Westport, Conn.: Greenwood Press, 1974), 120–47, 178–200.

40 Wendell Phillips to the editor, April 14, 1867, *National Anti-Slavery Standard*, April 27, 1867.

# Connections

# "POVERTY IS NOT SLAVERY"
## American Abolitionists
## and the
## Competitive Labor Market

*Jonathan A. Glickstein*

AMERICAN abolitionism bore a highly complex relationship to capitalist society in the free states. On the one hand, the right for which abolitionists struggled—the slave's right to self-ownership—is the most fundamental of all rights, and its acquisition is the necessary prelude to other kinds of reform. Karl Marx could argue that abolition was fully consistent with socialist objectives on the grounds that "labor in white skin cannot emancipate itself where black skin is branded." At the same time, one of the most penetrating of recent discussions has suggested that the antislavery movement may have bolstered "the exploitative aspects of 'free' labor relations" by "glorifying northern society and by isolating slavery as an unacceptable form of labor exploitation."[1] In some respects subversive of inequalities within the northern economic order, abolitionism was in other senses evidently supportive of those inequalities; historians have only begun to clarify the nature of the contradictory tendencies.

One way of approaching the problem is through a study of the

---

1 Karl Marx to François Lafargue, November 12, 1866, trans. from the French by Saul K. Padover, in Padover (ed.), *Karl Marx on America and the Civil War* (New York: McGraw Hill, 1972), 274–75; Eric Foner, "The Causes of the American Civil War: Recent Interpretations and New Directions," *Civil War History*, XX (1974), 206.

views of abolitionists toward competition, poverty, and free labor. Abolitionist objectives and ideals may have borne only a tenuous connection to the disparate ways in which abolitionism actually affected northern society, and an examination of abolitionists' social values can therefore throw only limited light on the question of impact. But many of the contradictions that distinguished the abolition movement's relationship to northern capitalism were embodied in the values of the movement's leading participants.

Most fundamental of all were the conflicting positions assumed by abolitionists toward the idea of economic competition. The mode of emancipation in which abolitionists invested their hopes in the 1830s—the "moral suasion" and personal regeneration of every slaveholder—was grounded in highly individualistic evangelical religious tenets. But by accomplishing emancipation, individual conversion was intended by abolitionists to serve a more collectivistic religious principle: the ethic of Christian love and brotherhood among men. Some abolitionists perceived an inconsistency between that ethic and support for systems of free labor market relations that extolled the values of competition and individual self-gain. Writing for the *Liberty Bell* in 1852, American abolitionist William I. Bowditch concluded, "So long as manufacturers and traders must rely for their profits on the ability to undersell their neighbors, so long will men, women, and children be converted into wage Slaves in the factories and mines in England." No less than chattel slavery, the severe and oppressive inequalities to which "heartless, soul-destroying competition" gave rise represented a flagrant violation of the "sublime doctrine of Christianity—the brotherhood of the human family." [2]

Bowditch's attack on "wage-slavery" was significantly different from that made by more secular-minded Jacksonian Democrats, but it was hardly less radical. The Jacksonians attributed inequalities in a free labor market society to class legislation, and contended that these inequalities would greatly diminish once government-sponsored privileges were lifted and once access to property accumulation and the degree of true economic competition were substan-

2 William I. Bowditch, "Faith in Human Brotherhood," *Liberty Bell*, XII (1852), 105, 112–13.

tially increased. Bowditch was implicitly challenging this position, warning that acquisitiveness and competition would create the same disparities in America as they had in England "when our laboring population becomes equally dense." Bowditch's critique of laissez faire capitalist values was similar to that of American utopian socialists and other labor reformers, and was expressed most succinctly by the liberal Unitarian minister James Freeman Clarke: "The principle of free competition is a good one for the strong, the sagacious, for those who have talent, means, energy; but it gives no choice to the weak, the poor, the friendless."[3]

Only a few abolitionists like John A. Collins and Elizur Wright, Jr., joined Bowditch in expressing an unqualified antagonism to the competitive principle. A far greater number of abolitionists, Garrisonians and non-Garrisonians alike, remained equivocal and even receptive to that principle.[4] No less committed to the ethic of Christian love and brotherhood, they nonetheless drew back from associating individualism and self-interest with conditions of injustice and exploitation in free labor market societies. Their resistance to blanket condemnations of competition as un-Christian was typified by the claim of Gamaliel Bailey, Jr., that the "real cause" of the evils suffered by laborers in England and other nations was "to be

---

3 *Ibid.*, 104–105; J. F. C. [James Freeman Clarke], "Fourierism," *Christian Examiner and Religious Miscellany*, XXXVII (July, 1844), 70–71. Clarke was critical of some aspects of American Fourierite or Associationist doctrine, while sharing the Associationist view that the Jacksonian "let alone principle" had conservative implications.

4 John A. Collins was a close colleague of William Lloyd Garrison who adopted the tenets of Owenite socialism and shortly thereafter left the abolition movement to establish a "common property" community in Skaneatles, New York; see Collins, *A Bird's Eye View of Society As It Is, And As It Should Be* (Boston: J. P. Menderm, 1844); and various writings in *Communitist* (July 10, 1844–March 5, 1846), the community's newspaper. For the views of Elizur Wright, Jr., one of the abolition movement's leading advocates of Associationist doctrine, see the editorials "The Protection of Labor," Boston *Weekly Chronotype*, November 11, 1847, and "The Philosophy of Labor, No. 2," "Commerce and the Interests of the People, No. II," and "Laissez Faire," *Daily Chronotype*, July 20, October 27, 1846, and February 13, 1847. Wright was a member of the non-Garrisonian wing of the movement, and his case is one of those which suggest that on the issue of economic competition at least, the division between abolitionists was somewhat less systematic than that indicated by Aileen S. Kraditor in her brilliant *Means and Ends in American Abolitionism* (New York: Random House, Inc., 1967), 8–9, 102–103, 251–52. Kraditor contends that "radical" abolitionists were largely Garrisonians, and that they, unlike other abolitionists, looked to the inward moral reform of every American to effect not only slavery's eradication, but also the extinction of the competitive features of free labor capitalism in Jacksonian America. As well as underrating the radicalism of non-Garrisonians like Wright, Kraditor's typology seems to exaggerate the radicalism of virtually all the leading Garrisonians, with the possible exception of Garrison himself.

sought not in *competition*, but in the excess of labor over its actual demand."[5]

Abolitionists who minimized the inconsistency between the Christian ethic and the competitive principle were influenced by two primary beliefs, each of which merits some discussion. The first was the conviction that a truly Christian social order required not only love and brotherhood, but also the self-discipline and rationality of its members, and that economic competition was important to the development of these latter qualities. The second belief held that competition in the United States was uniquely fair and rewarding, and that here more easily than anywhere else it might encourage self-control and rationality without generating hatred and discord. It would be an oversimplification to suggest that abolitionists who shared these two beliefs attacked chattel slavery because it violated the demands of a competitive market society. But such abolitionists attached far greater value than the abolitionist minority and the utopian socialists did to the personal freedom that enabled individuals to compete in the American marketplace; they regarded that freedom as the key to both the indefinite material and intellectual improvement of the individual and the attainment of the just society.[6]

Abolitionists' acceptance of the beneficence of competition found major expression in the ambivalent attitude they displayed towards poverty. An essay by O. B. Frothingham provides a good example of this ambivalence. The principal point of contrast between poverty and slavery, Frothingham argues throughout most of the essay, is not that poverty constitutes a lesser evil than chattel servitude, but that it is a relatively intractable problem, the responsibility for which is far more diffuse. Unlike slavery, other evils

5 Gamaliel Bailey, Jr., review of Chancellor Harper's *A Memoir of Slavery*, in Cincinnati *Philanthropist*, December 11, 1838.

6 The view presented here owes a good deal to the work of Foner, "Causes of Civil War," 201–14; George M. Frederickson, *The Black Image in the White Mind* (New York: Harper and Row, 1971), 27–38; and William Appleman Williams, *The Contours of American History* (Cleveland: World Publishing Co., 1964), 253–55. All these works suggest that American antislavery ideology was one expression of the bourgeois competitive individualism that distinguished the climate of antebellum northern society. Although such an interpretation qualifies in many respects as a "Marxist" one, it is perhaps more helpful to consider it an extension of the "entrepreneurial" interpretation of Jacksonian Democracy advanced by Richard Hofstadter, Joseph Dorfman, and other historians in the 1940s and the 1950s.

. . . are providential . . . they grow out of the inevitable condition of things: nobody in particular causes them, or is answerable for them. . . . Pauperism, in all its dismal shapes, with all its terrible sorrows, is an old fact resulting from man's ignorance, error, and general imperfection, and will be outgrown as man becomes more wise and powerful. . . . The process must be long and painful. . . . Slavery, on the other hand, is an institution which the conscious will of man has built up, and which the same will, faithfully exerted, might . . . abolish in a year, a month, a week, a day. . . . Pauperism, from its nature involves no direct Guilt. Slavery is essential Guilt.

When colonizationists had denied that slavery was an act of willful perversity, and had insisted that it was a "social problem" not amenable to rapid amelioration, abolitionists had accused them of wishing to perpetuate the peculiar institution. Frothingham's defense of a gradualist approach to the eradication of poverty may not have reflected a similar covert approval of great economic disparities. But he did proceed to add to his comparison the argument that poverty served a useful social function, that it was not the unmitigated evil that slavery was, after all: "The irreligion of Slavery consists in the very absence and banishment of the soul itself. . . . The exigencies of Poverty stimulate the mind if they do not elevate it."[7]

Other abolitionists shared Frothingham's sense of the salutary features of poverty. Wendell Phillips observed that "Poverty, wholesome poverty, is no unmixed evil; it is the spur that often wins the race; it is the trial that calls out, like fire, all the deep great qualities of a man's nature." Similarly, Theodore Parker, after acknowledging that poverty often demoralized and enfeebled its victims rather than spurring them on, nonetheless insisted that "Want is the only schoolmaster to teach" the idle and the lazy "industry and thrift."[8]

The recognition accorded the "utility of poverty" by American abolitionists bore a certain similarity to the views of eighteenth-century English mercantilists who had repeatedly extolled "Nature's penalty" for sloth and indolence. But the premises of the abolitionists were in fact fundamentally different. The mercantilists had assumed that the laboring poor were necessarily irrational and

7 O. B. Frothingham, "Pauperism and Slavery," *Liberty Bell*, XIII (1853), 167–70.
8 Wendell Phillips, "A Metropolitan Police," in *Speeches, Lectures, and Letters*, first series (Boston: Lothrop, Lee and Shepard Co., 1891), 503; Theodore Parker, "A Sermon of Poverty," *Daily Chronotype*, January 26, 1849.

brutish creatures, incapable of foresight and ambition. The disciplining power of hunger constituted the only effective labor incentive because workers would labor only to satisfy their immediate physical needs. Abolitionists, in contrast, valued the fear of hunger as a stimulus to rationality, not as a substitute for it. When the antislavery newspaper *Philanthropist* argued that the free worker "labors from *motives*, peculiar to an intelligent being," it included among those motives the desire to obtain a mere subsistence. The labor induced by the slaveholder's lash was an expression of degrading "physical force," but the labor induced by economic compulsion was one expression of the worker's moral and rational pursuit of self-interest.[9]

The influence of Scripture, specifically the injunction "By the sweat of your face you shall eat bread," may partially explain why abolitionists emphasized the moral character of labor induced by hunger. But abolitionists' confidence that poverty might stimulate and discipline rather than demoralize and sink the poor was largely born of the optimism of evangelical Protestantism. Evangelicalism was not only egalitarian and romantic in its conviction that salvation was attainable by all, it was also middle class in its tendency to associate salvation with values like sobriety and self-control and in its corresponding hostility to all practices and forms of vice—such as slaveholding and intemperance—that led to the "extinction of reason" and to the primacy of the individual's appetites and "lower nature." Lewis Tappan and other abolitionists participated in an array of temperance, Bible, and other evangelically based benevolent societies whose leading object was the reformation of the lifestyles of the urban poor. Inculcated with middle-class values, laborers

9 For the views of mercantilists, which showed more variety than space permits me to indicate here, see Edgar J. Furniss, *The Position of the Laborer in a System of Nationalism: A Study in the Labor Theories of the Later English Mercantilists* (New York: Kelley and Millman, Inc., 1957); and A. W. Coates, "Changing Attitudes to Labour in the Mid-Eighteenth Century," *Economic History Review*, second series, I (1958), 38–50. "The Advocates of Association and Slavery—Horace Greeley," *Philanthropist*, June 18, 1845; for similar views, see "'Wages and Chattel Slavery'—The Elevation of the Working Classes," Washington, D.C. *National Era*, March 25, 1847; see also William Ellery Channing, "Slavery," in *The Works of William E. Channing, D.D.* (Boston: American Unitarian Association, 1896), 720–27. While not an abolitionist, Channing shared the abolitionist critique of slavery, and he made an extensive contrast between the degrading coercion of the lash and the "kindly" stimulus of poverty.

would respond meaningfully and not destructively to their poverty.[10]

But a meaningful response to poverty required that its victims strive to escape it; the material improvement of the poor would presumably follow upon their spiritual uplift. If abolitionists went beyond the mercantilists in stressing the moral character of economic compulsion, their attitude towards poverty nonetheless remained more ambivalent, and the role they assigned it was a far more limited one. The mercantilists had maintained that the laboring population inevitably squandered any excess recompense in drink and other debauchery, and that it was as pointless as it was destructive to the economic needs of the state for employers to pay their workers anything above subsistence wage levels. While abolitionists agreed that hunger exerted a continuous external pressure, and remained the ultimate labor incentive, they insisted that all men possessed the capacity to internalize discipline and utilize a generous recompense to raise their living standard and expand their moral and intellectual horizons. William Goodell revealed his ideological distance from the mercantilists as well as from American proslavery apologists when he explained why even those slaves who obtained sufficient food and clothing could not aspire to the condition of free laborers: "Wages, to be 'just and equal,' must be sufficient to the support of the laborer, not as a mere animal, but as an intelligent and moral being. Something which he can earn without consuming all his time, so as to leave no adequate space for rational improvement and social enjoyment."[11]

If American abolitionist views of poverty were ambivalent, and bore only limited similarities to mercantilist doctrines, they did have important roots in the transformation undergone by British

10 W. E. Channing, "Address on Temperance," in *Works of William E. Channing*, 100. Tappan was probably the closest counterpart among American abolitionists to William Wilberforce as an epitome of that kind of paternalism which sought to make the poor disciplined and self-directing; see Bertram Wyatt-Brown, *Lewis Tappan and the Evangelical War Against Slavery* (Cleveland: Case Western Reserve University Press, 1969), 20–21, 46–56, 257–59; and Wyatt-Brown, "God and Dunn & Bradstreet, 1841–1851," *Business Historical Review*, XL (1966), 433, where Tappan's efforts to train the employees of his New York mercantile house in sobriety, frugality, and industry are described.

11 William Goodell, "Slavery Tested By Its Own Code," *Quarterly Anti-Slavery Magazine*, I (October, 1835), 29.

economic thought in the late eighteenth and the early nineteenth centuries. On the one hand, Thomas Malthus and other architects of the "dismal science" of classical economy shared the opinion of the mercantilists that the fear of hunger must continue to play an important role in keeping the laboring population disciplined and orderly. The tradition of opposition in Britain to compulsory poor relief reflected the belief that securing laboring men from the threat of starvation, without penalizing them as a consequence, stifled their ambition; they would lose all incentive to seek work that offered more than a mere subsistence remuneration if they did not, indeed, relinquish all desire to perform any labor at all. Nassau Senior developed this argument to its extreme conclusion, contending that chattel slavery and the "aid-in-wages" relief system were equivalent evils because both imposed paternalism on workers ideally subject only to competitive market forces: "The instant wages cease to be a bargain—the instant the labourer is paid, not according to his *value*, but his *wants*, he ceases to be a free man. He acquires the indolence, the improvidence, the rapacity, and the malignity, but not the subordination of a slave."[12]

Yet as several historians have shown, both classical economic thought and the rise of antislavery agitation in Britain at the end of the eighteenth century were manifestations of a basic change in middle-class attitudes toward the laboring poor, or what might be termed a transition in bourgeois economic thought from the mercantilist to a more industrial phase. The conviction of British abolitionists that the lash employed by West Indian slaveowners was an ineffective, inhumane, and obsolete means of inducing labor reflected the movement away from the notion that negative labor incentives generally—the "lash of hunger" or "necessity" which drove the free worker as well as the whip that motivated the chattel slave—were the most effective and desirable incentives. The new view stressed the free worker's internalization of controls and restraints as more appropriate to the discipline and coordination required by factory work and other emerging forms of labor.[13] But in

12 Nassau Senior, *Three Lectures on the Rate of Wages* (New York: Augustus M. Kelley, 1966), ix–x.

13 J. H. Plumb, "Slavery, Race, and the Poor," *New York Review of Books*, XII (March 13, 1969), 3–5; David Brion Davis, *The Problem of Slavery in the Age of Revolution, 1770–1823*

part because many of these new forms appeared so unsatisfying and even debasing in their influence upon the worker, the middle-class injunction that he internalize the "work ethic" and acquire an appreciation of the intrinsic value of his labor was rarely absolute; it was never far removed from appeals to the worker's ambition and from an emphasis on the money-making value of work for laborers who had moral and intellectual wants deserving of encouragement. Adam Smith's *The Wealth of Nations* incorporated if it did not introduce many of the elements of the new view, coupling the argument that the happiest and most industrious workers were the best-paid ones with the warning that they must be educated if their mental faculties were not to suffer serious impairment from the division of labor. Developing modes of production that called for the unprecedented subordination of the worker's individuality thus also encouraged the view that he receive new recognition as a rational being.

It was this complex of British middle-class notions about the laboring poor that entered the American "public domain" of ideas and contributed to American abolitionists' own equivocal attitudes towards work motivation, specifically their sense that the fear of want provided a disciplining and even ennobling labor incentive yet one that was still less effective and exalted than man's hope of actually raising his condition. The uniqueness of the American context, its relative freedom from class stratification and pressing social problems like pauperism, naturally encouraged the emphasis of special themes. Many abolitionists shared the conviction of Daniel Webster and other Whigs that the openness of competition in America legitimated existing economic disparities, and that those disparities were not a proper object of resentment and discord since they did not result from exploitation and oppression. A number of historians have been drawn to the very first issue of the *Liberator*, in which William Lloyd Garrison's famous manifesto that he would "BE HEARD" in defense of the oppressed slave was accompanied by a less well-known editorial taking to task northern workingmen's parties for their misguided attempts "to enflame the minds of our

(Ithaca: Cornell University Press, 1975), 82, 264–66, 458–62; E. P. Thompson, "Time, Work-Discipline, and Industrial Capitalism," *Past and Present*, XXXVIII (December, 1967), 56–91.

working class against the more opulent, and to persuade men that they are contemned and oppressed by a wealthy aristocracy." In a follow-up editorial Garrison noted that "a republican government . . . where the avenues to wealth, distinction and supremacy are open to all . . . must, in the nature of things, be full of inequalities." His denunciation of the "pernicious doctrines" that presumed to challenge the legitimacy of these inequalities was seconded years later by Wendell Phillips, when he maintained that the "elevation and improvement" of laborers in the free states were impeded only by their own failure to acquire "economy, self-denial, temperance, education, and moral and religious character."[14]

If abolitionists' emphasis upon the opportunities and openness of American society at times prompted harsh and unsympathetic reactions to the grievances of northern workers, it also relieved them from following British economists and dwelling on the value of punitive labor incentives. When Frothingham, Phillips, and Parker cited the beneficial features of poverty, their remarks were atypical in the sense that they rendered explicit what abolitionists usually left implicit in their thinking on the subject. Widespread belief that the American worker could secure a generous price for his labor without the need of government's interference in fact encouraged abolitionists to underplay the role of economic compulsion in both their critique of southern slave labor and in their defense of northern free labor. Senior had suggested that chattel slaves were lazy and inefficient because they enjoyed a guaranteed subsistence; abolitionists found the root evil in the fact that slave labor was "uncompensated," carrying no hope of reward or improvement. Reformers fearful of growing pauperism in the northern urban centers maintained that the industriousness and "dignity" of American workers depended on their fear of poverty and on continued efforts to resist adoption of Britain's corrupting and debilitating poor relief practices. Abolitionists stressed that workers in the free states were "voluntarily" stimulated by the expectation of property accumulation, upward mobility, and moral and intellectual development; northern

---

14 "Working Men" and "The Working Classes," Boston *Liberator*, January 1, 29, 1831; W. P. [Wendell Phillips], "The Question of Labor," *Liberator*, July 9, 1847.

free laborers who were industrious would inevitably accumulate property and not merely subsist.[15]

But the confidence which abolitionists shared with other Americans in the predominance of positive labor incentives in the free states also generated enthusiasm for the competitive labor market generally; and that enthusiasm could actually strengthen support for any punitive labor incentives upon which that market might also rely. The northern free labor system was superior to southern slavery because it embodied the principles of independence and self-interest, and the fear of want and the expectation of economic improvement were equally subsumed by these principles. One of the most comprehensive statements of this view appeared in Henry Ward Beecher's lecture "Northern and Southern Theories of Man and Society," delivered before the New York Anti-Slavery Society in 1855. Although a relative late-comer to the antislavery crusade, and never a true abolitionist, Beecher had in the space of a few years become one of the foremost defenders of the northern social system. To his rather routine contrasts between the universality, intelligence, and dignity of labor in the free states and the idleness and degraded labor prevalent in the aristocratic South, Beecher added a few revealing remarks on the motivation of free labor in the North:

We ordain that a man shall have the fullest chance, and then he shall have the results of his activity. He shall take all he can make, or he shall take the whole result of *indolence*. It is a double education. It inspires labour by hope of fruition, and intensifies it by the fear of non-fruition.... The northern system intends to punish those who will not work. It is not a system calculated for slaves nor for lazy men ... nowhere else in the world is the penalty of indolence, and even of shiftlessness, so terrible as in the North, as

---

15 For a recent study claiming that American slaves did in fact enjoy positive labor incentives, see Robert William Fogel and Stanley L. Engerman, *Time on the Cross: The Economics of American Negro Slavery* (2 vols.; Boston: Little, Brown and Co., 1974). The assumptions that the lash was an ineffective incentive and that slave labor was less productive than free labor went largely unquestioned in antislavery circles; for an exception see "Slavery at the South-West," *New York Evangelist*, quoted in New York *Emancipator, and Journal of Public Morals*, February 3, 1835. For the apprehensions of American poor law critics, many of which were aroused by the Irish immigrant, and for claims comparable to Senior's that compulsory relief was "slavery," see *Joseph Tuckerman on the Elevation of the Poor* (Boston: Roberts Brothers, 1874), 98, 103–105, 140–50, 166–69; and Isaac Southern Hartley (ed.), *Memorial of Robert Milhan Hartley* (Utica: Press of Curtiss and Childs, 1882), 311–16.

nowhere else is the remuneration of a virtuous industry so ample and so widely diffused.[16]

Most abolitionists were neither so zealous nor so explicit as Beecher in their assertion of the competitive ethic; certainly few of them were as emphatic that the rewards of industry and the penalties of indolence comprised equally integral mainsprings of the northern free labor system. But the very concept of freedom which abolitionists articulated and defended often served to legitimate both the competitive principle and emerging inequalities under northern capitalism. That concept of freedom must be examined in the context of changes within the northern economy and within northern systems of work.

The United States was in 1860 still a predominantly "preindustrial" nation. The mill towns of New England were scarcely more typical of the country's manufacturing activity than New York City was representative of American cities; and only a minority of the small proportion of the country's work force which was employed in manufacturing was engaged in factory production. But like New York's contribution to urban imagery, the mill towns, particularly Lowell, Massachusetts, exercised a far more important impact on antebellum industrial consciousness than their economic representativeness alone would have justified. To a nation rapidly growing in wealth and complexity and shedding the more primitive features of its economy, the factories were important symbols of the direction in which developments were moving.

One can find many instances of abolitionists who deplored as inadequate the wages of factory workers and who took the operatives' part in strikes against capital; a few like Nathaniel P. Rogers even embraced the position that the factory system and "labor-saving" machinery were systematically exploitative.[17] While a de-

16 Henry Ward Beecher, "Northern and Southern Theories of Man and Society," New York National Anti-Slavery Standard, January 27, 1855. The "terrible . . . penalty of indolence" may have been as much a reference to the public disgrace that befell the idle who sought poor relief as a reference to the possibility that such men actually starved. Beecher proceeded to go further than most abolitionists, singling out the care of old and disabled slaves by their masters as one of the ways in which slavery violated the demands of a competitive market society; see also Channing, "Slavery," 710–20.

17 "Strikes," Philanthropist, July 1, 1836; "The Maryland Mining Company and the Miners," National Era, May 15, 1851; Thomas Franklin Currier, "Whittier and the Amesbury-Salisbury Strike," New England Quarterly, VIII (1935), 105–12. For Rogers's views, see his

termination to defend the dignity of all labor moved abolitionists in one direction, however, their terminology pulled them in another. The abolitionist definition of freedom conformed closely to what C. B. Macpherson has described as one of the basic assumptions of the theory of "possessive individualism": "that man is free and human by virtue of his sole proprietorship of his own person." [18] As a basic characteristic of an industrial wage-earning class is its economic dependence and consequent vulnerability to exploitation, abolitionist terminology tended to minimize inequities in free labor societies by equating freedom with self-ownership and by slighting the significance of economic independence. In contrast to George Henry Evans and the National Reformers, for whom land ownership remained an indispensable criterion of freedom, abolitionists retained only a qualified commitment to traditional republican ideals that extolled a society of farmers and self-employed craftsmen. Their insistence that "even the name of Liberty is much" dovetailed with their perception of poverty as a limited evil; both reflected a certain receptivity to conditions of early industrialization, in which increasing numbers of free workers whose only resource was their labor power could be expected to bargain and compete on the labor market. [19]

Like the factory proprietors and the Whig partisans of the factory system, abolitionists often maintained that the relationship between capitalists and wage-earners in the free states was one of mutual dependence and benefit between equal parties, and that the "freedom of contract" which the factory worker exercised in his individual capacity was a meaningful one. This argument did in fact draw some support from conditions in Lowell and other mill towns organized under the "Waltham system"; the native New England farm girls who comprised most of the system's labor force generally earned higher wages than did women in other occupations of the time, and they could, in some cases at least, avert a disadvantageous

"Letter from the Editor," "The Factory System," and "Letter from N. P. Rogers," Concord (N.H.) *Herald of Freedom*, April 11, 1845, January 26, 1844, and August 21, 1846.

18 C. B. Macpherson, *The Political Theory of Possessive Individualism: Hobbes to Locke* (London: Oxford University Press, 1962), 270.

19 Sidney Howard Gay, "Progress is the Law of Humanity" (MS in Sidney Howard Gay Papers, Columbia University); see also Foner, "Causes of Civil War," 209; and Davis, *Problem of Slavery*, 268.

dependence upon the mills for work by returning to the homes of their parents. To abolitionists and others who maintained that even the comparatively desperate proletariat and "pauper labor" of the Old World was "free," the notion that New England factory workers were entrapped in "wage slavery" seemed especially ludicrous.[20]

Abolitionists' opposition to the factory system was limited not only by their concept of freedom and by their perception of actual conditions in the mill towns; it was also limited by abolitionists' favorable view of factory labor itself, their sense that it stimulated discipline and mental acuteness. If, as some historians have suggested, the work habits which Lewis Tappan and other antebellum reformers sought to inculcate in the laboring population were habits conducive to industrialization,[21] it also seems that abolitionists believed that factory labor itself might develop these qualities. Hostile attitudes toward southern slavery and favorable ones toward factory labor likely fed upon each other here. The common assumptions that slave labor was unintelligent labor and that slavery had retarded industrialization in the South appear to have prompted many abolitionists to infer that factory labor required intelligence, just as they also commonly held that continued efforts to industrialize slave labor would stimulate the intelligence of slaves and thereby subvert slavery. "A manufacturing people must be intelligent, and an intelligent people cannot be slaves," the *National Anti-Slavery Standard* observed. "If there were no other differences in the conditions of the poor freeman of Manchester and the poor bondsmen of the Carolinas, than that which the discipline of machinery creates, that alone is a difference as wide as the gulf between Slavery and Free-

20 Q [Edmund Quincy], "Chattel Slavery and Wages Slavery," *Liberator*, October 1, 1847; John Greenleaf Whittier, *The Stranger in Lowell* (Boston: Waite, Peirce and Company, 1845), 20–22, 118–19. The actual well-being and mobility, both social and geographic, of the New England mill girls continues to be the subject of much research. Scholars have generally concluded, however, that working conditions and wage scales in the Waltham system were by the mid-1840s losing their superiority over those in other employments open to women, and that the great influx of Irish immigrants after this date accelerated the system's decline. Moreover, many mills in the northern states had always been organized under the contrasting "family system," where conditions such as the relatively heavy use of child labor more closely approximated those in Britain's "satanic" mills; see Garrison's criticism of factory conditions in Providence, Rhode Island, the stronghold of the family system, in Walter M. Merrill (ed.), *The Letters of William Lloyd Garrison: "I Will Be Heard," 1822–1835* (Cambridge: Harvard University Press, 1971), 166–72, Vol. I of Walter M. Merrill and Louis Ruchames (eds.), *The Letters of William Lloyd Garrison* (5 vols. projected; Cambridge: Harvard University Press, 1971– ).

21 Foner, "Causes of Civil War," 205–209, is but one example.

dom." To support its position, the *Standard* quoted an article in an English periodical that extolled the dangerous character of factory machinery for requiring the operatives to develop their powers of alertness and mental discipline. There could hardly have been a more dramatic convergence of uncompromising hostility to chattel slavery with unabashed enthusiasm for the coming of industrialization.[22]

Such a convergence may well have been atypical in its extremity; certainly abolitionists' attitudes toward social change were no less complicated and ambivalent than those of many other antebellum Americans. If most abolitionists looked favorably upon industrialization, they did so largely because they approached it with "preindustrial" expectations. Just as they chiefly valued poverty for stimulating the poor to escape it, so abolitionists suggested that the work habits and character virtues which operatives either brought to or developed through factory labor in the North would in time enable them to leave their wage-earning status behind them.[23] When Orestes Brownson maintained in his famous essay "The Laboring Classes" that the situation was changing, that diligent and disciplined wage-earners in the free states were increasingly unable to accumulate the resources to rise from their condition, the antislavery *Emancipator* was quick to refute his pessimism:

The theory which is here developed is utterly false and pernicious, because the fact on which it is founded is no fact at all. It is not true that the body of laborers in this country are obliged to remain such during their lives, in consequence of the inadequacy of their wages. Of the young men who began life with ourselves, we know of no one who has remained a mere day laborer, with nothing but his hands, unless there is a manifest and special reason in his case, while the great body of them were long ago raised by their wages to the class of freeholders and accumulators. . . . To assume the existence of a distinction between employers and paid workmen, as a permanent state, is either to dream or to deceive.[24]

22 "Manufactures at the South," *National Anti-Slavery Standard*, August 5, 1847, quoting from Hepworth Dixon, "Manchester: Its Mental and Social Physiognomies Considered," London *People's Journal*, III (June 26, 1847), 356–59.

23 Foner, "Causes of Civil War, 209, 213. Yet it should be noted that the factory proprietors and other propagandists for industrialization invoked the same "preindustrial" values, citing as a signal virtue of New England factory labor its escapability through the operative's upward mobility.

24 "Prospects and Projects of the Democracy," New York *Emancipator*, December 31, 1840.

To the extent that the *Emancipator* and other antislavery voices associated the elevation of laborers with individual mobility out of the wage-earning class rather than with improvement in the conditions of the class as a whole, they could hardly be said to have displayed a truly industrial mentality, one that sought an accommodation with hardening class divisions under industrial capitalism. Brownson and other labor reformers with whom abolitionists engaged in a series of acrimonious disputes in the 1840s were in a sense no different. Owenite and Associationist socialists, National Reformers, and radical Democrats like Brownson showed a similar unwillingness to accept the inevitability of a permanent industrial wage-earning class; all of their various schemes were designed to forestall the development of such a class, either by establishing wage-earners as members of socialist communities or by converting them into independent freeholders or self-employed laborers. Where the labor reformers primarily differed from the abolitionists was in their explanation for developing inequalities under northern capitalism, as well as in their tendency to regard those inequalities as more objectionable. A comparison between abolitionists and labor reformers will underscore these differences.

As suggested earlier, the labor reformers and the abolitionist minority which joined them held a strong antipathy to the competitive ethic; slavery was but a special form or symptom of the antagonism prevailing between capital and labor everywhere, an antagonism that inevitably worked to the disadvantage of the weaker party. From this perspective, the degradation of labor in the free states was attributable to the "Europeanization" of America—to the impact of industrialization, urbanization, and increasing population density upon a society that had retained the same defective property and labor relations as Old World nations.[25]

Abolitionists could not generally accept this perspective; and when they did express criticism of northern inequalities, their criticism was rarely such as to contradict their basic belief that the

25 I have no wish to exaggerate the radicalism of the disparate critics of northern labor conditions whom I have designated "labor reformers." With the exception of the Owenites, their attacks on the competitive principle did not lead to a repudiation of private property itself or the desirability of acquiring wealth as an incentive for workers. Associationists, for example, repeatedly charged that the "common property" communities of the Owenites would prove "the graveyard of individual liberty."

northern free labor system was inherently sound. Slavery was more than just a "branch" of the "great question of the age"—the elevation and protection of all labor. Contrary to the labor reformers, it was the root cause of any degradation experienced by northern labor, its corrupting presence giving rise to pernicious social attitudes that glorified idleness and scorned honest industry. William Goodell's explanation was characteristic: "Labor is despised at the south, and therefore is becoming to be despised at the north. The idlers of the south, live upon the unrequited toil of the laborer, and the idlers of the north are forward to emulate, as far as possible, their example."[26]

The viewpoint that black slavery caused northern free labor to be held in contempt led to exaggerations and inconsistencies. It occasioned, for one thing, abolitionist claims that northern capitalists hoped to go so far as to formally enslave free labor—even though abolitionists typically insisted that slaveholders should join northern capitalists in realizing that free labor was more productive and profitable than slave labor. A more basic weakness was the parochialism, specifically the apparent inattention to labor conditions in the Old World, which distinguished the viewpoint that the degradation of free labor in America must have a strictly indigenous cause. The Associationist author of an address to the Labor Reform League of New England criticized the abolitionists for their preoccupation with the peculiar institution, noting, "There is no chattel slavery in England, France, Germany. Is the condition of the laborers there better than yours?"[27]

In some cases, abolitionists' failure to accept the relevance of European labor conditions was intentional, reflecting the belief in American uniqueness. Thus Wendell Phillips warned "of the errors [of] . . . looking at American questions through European spectacles, and transplanting the eloquent complaints against capital and monopoly, which are well-grounded and well-applied there, to a state of society here, where they have little meaning or application."[28] Yet

26 "The Protection of Labor," *Weekly Chronotype*, November 11, 1847; William Goodell, "Lecture VII," Utica *Antislavery Lecturer*, July, 1839; see also "Mr. Greeley's Lecture," *National Anti-Slavery Standard*, January 27, 1855.
27 *The Condition of Labor: An Address to the Members of the Labor Reform League of New England, By One of the Members* (Boston: privately published, 1847), 15.
28 W. P. [Wendell Phillips], "The Question of Labor," *Liberator*, July 9, 1847.

many developments in the North—the struggle of New England factory operatives for a ten-hour day, the appeal of Pennsylvania miners and their advocates for safety regulations, the plight of the Philadelphia handloom weavers and the New York seamstresses—were manifestations of urban and industrial changes common to the Western world. All had instructive counterparts in Europe and especially England, and suggested that European spectacles were not so blinding as Phillips claimed.

A similar preoccupation with slavery distinguished other abolitionists in their treatment of particular social problems in the free states. It was characteristic of abolitionists, "A Southern Man" wrote in a contribution to the *Emancipator*, to attribute the commercial prostitution and other evils of New York City to the "influence and example of slaveholding visitants and dictators." In suggesting that abolitionists ignored the dozens of Old World cities which contained identical problems and which therefore indicated that such conditions were somehow endemic to urban life everywhere, "A Southern Man" may have somewhat exaggerated the myopic tendency of abolitionist agitation; but his analysis still held a substantial element of truth. Edmund Quincy, for example, could oversimplify a complex and widespread social phenomenon, the migration from farm to city, by contending that the contempt in which southern slavery placed honest and healthy manual labor explained why New England farmers now preferred "the thick atmosphere and at best dubious pressures of the city."[29]

The insistence that abolition was vital to the well-being of northern workers did not require this kind of oversimplification; and monistic explanations of the degradation of northern labor in fact became less characteristic of abolitionists who developed through their crusade an increased sensitivity to other kinds of exploitation. By the mid 1840s Garrison was no longer the narrow opponent of labor movement activity that he had been in 1831; and political abolitionists especially, such as Goodell and Gerrit Smith, had actively taken up the cause of land reform. Like Marx, aboli-

29 "A Southern Man," "Dialogue on Free and Slave Labor," and "Dialogue on Free and Slave Labor—No. 2," *Emancipator*, October 10, December 26, 1839; Edmund Quincy, "Ancient and Modern Reform," in Edmund Quincy Papers, Massachusetts Historical Society.

tionists could support antislavery as the first reform, not the only reform; and their denunciation of northern labor reformers might be based less on the latter's substantive criticisms of northern labor conditions than on their refusal to acknowledge abolition's primacy. As the *Liberator* observed, the National Reformers' attacks on land monopoly were well-directed, but "what possibility is there, that, in a nation where it is reputable to steal men, the right of every man to a just portion of the soil will be conceded and enjoyed?"[30]

The change of perspective which some abolitionists experienced indicated one of two developments: either some loss of confidence in the fairness of competition in America, or limited movement towards the position that competition itself was intrinsically unfair and productive of injustice and oppression. The first development signified greater agreement with the Jacksonian advocates of liberal capitalism; the second development indicated stronger affinity with the radical labor reformers themselves, including the small group of extreme abolitionists who had moved altogether into the latter's camp. In either case, however, it must be emphasized that the change undergone by most abolitionists was not substantial enough to significantly reduce their differences with the severest critics of northern labor conditions. The disputes over reform priorities and the role of slavery in the degradation of northern labor were secondary to the larger issue upon which abolitionists and labor reformers could never reach agreement: whether that degradation was comparable to slavery itself.

Reflecting the traditions of utopian and Ricardian socialism rather than the classical economic and evangelical religious tra-

---

30 "Straining At A Gnat," *Liberator*, March 19, 1847; see also "The Associationists and the Abolitionists," *National Anti-Slavery Standard*, October 14, 1847. For Goodell, see his address at the National Nominating Convention of the Liberty League, assembled June 8–10, 1847, where he repudiated Garrisonian "one-ideaism" and defended the league's platform of free homesteads, free trade, and other measures, in Gerrit Smith Miller Collection, Syracuse University. The change in Gerrit Smith's perspective is particularly evident. In 1844 Smith had rebuked George Henry Evans for believing that "the horrors and essence of slavery were to be found in any, even the most unfavorable, condition of a freeman." But by 1849 Smith was writing Lewis Tappan that "poverty, especially that which is extreme and abject, does . . . so crowd and debase the mind with its low cares and low objects, as almost irresistibly to shut out the refining and elevating influences of Christianity." Such developments as the great Irish famine had clearly led Smith to temper the optimism of evangelically based moral reform with environmentalist considerations: see "Second Letter from Gerrit Smith," New York *Young America*, August 10, 1844, and "Gerrit Smith's Letter to Lewis Tappan," *Daily Chronotype* January 24, 1849.

ditions that influenced the abolitionists, labor reformers were un-
equivocally hostile to poverty, and equated the enslavement and
total degradation of labor with the predominance of any kind of
negative labor incentives. They agreed that the "lash of necessity"
which drove most wage-earners was a more effective incentive than
the lash wielded by slaveholders, but they often held that it was
even more illegitimate and immoral precisely because the wage-
earner produced more than the chattel but enjoyed a smaller proportion of what he produced. To the extent that the southern slave
might fall back upon a guaranteed subsistence in sickness and old
age, he possessed a crucial advantage over the nominally free laborer, who was not the property and hence not the responsibility of
any capitalist. Abolitionists intent only upon "freeing" the chattel
were consequently promoting ineffectual or "technical" abolition
that would merely subject the chattel to the crueler "slavery of poverty" and economic compulsion. Finally, labor reformers frequently
argued, every evil and injustice that abolitionists condemned in
southern slavery—licentiousness, ignorance and illiteracy, the separation of families—were hardly less inevitable among poor, exploited free workers.[31]

Abolitionists advanced two major responses to the arguments of
the labor reformers. To those who confined themselves to criticizing
the material deprivation of free laborers, and who maintained that
slaves were more fortunately situated because they were better fed
and clothed, abolitionists replied that such a comparison reflected
the grossest kind of sensualism; for it discounted the moral and
spiritual evils that were the heart of slavery. To those who stressed
the consequences of poverty, the vulnerability of destitute free
workers to these very same moral and spiritual evils, abolitionists
insisted that even the most unfavorable circumstances did not impose degradation on the free worker, and that he retained the power

31 For samples of these views, see two letters of William West to Garrison, both entitled
"Wages Slavery and Chattel Slavery," *Liberator*, April 2, 23, 1847; "Freedom of the Public
Lands," *Northampton Democrat*, January 26, 1847; J. M. B., "Chattel Slavery Vs. Poverty Slavery," *Communitist*, February 26, 1845; Albert Brisbane, "The Question of Slavery," Boston
*Harbinger*, June 21, 1845. Of course, there were significant differences of emphasis in the views
of the various labor reform groups; and in the case of radical Democrats like Mike Walsh,
racism and southern ties figured especially prominently in the tendency to minimize chattel
slavery's evils.

to resist the evils inevitably suffered by slaves. By any criterion, the "wage-slavery" concept was a "vicious phraseology" that ignored the fact that "Poverty is not Slavery, and bears no resemblance to Slavery."[32]

The important ideological differences between abolitionists and labor reformers were often obscured by exaggerated accusations and the impugnment of motives. The Associationist journal *The Phalanx* observed in 1843 that "the Abolition party . . . seems to think that nothing else is false in our social organization" but slavery. Labor reformers frequently joined with proslavery apologists to charge that abolitionists were guilty of selective compassion, hypocritically indulging in a cheap and painless philanthropy "at a distance" as a pretext for ignoring the more pressing demands of "charity at home." On rarer occasions, there were cruder accusations that abolitionists themselves were wealthy capitalists whose crusade was motivated merely by economic self-interest.[33]

Abolitionists' mistrust was in turn aroused by the frequently outrageous character of the parallels drawn by labor reformers between the indignities suffered by southern slaves and those experienced by northern workers. When one notes that the recruitment of New England farm girls for the factories was sometimes likened to the capture of African blacks for enslavement in America, one can more fully understand why irate abolitionists would concede little to their opponents and why they would accuse them of seeking to protect slavery under the guise of promoting reform in northern labor conditions.[34]

Yet had abolitionists and labor reformers credited one another with the best of intentions, they would have been no closer to agreement. On one level, abolitionists argued that labor reformers

32 "Slavery Better Than Poverty!," *Liberator*, December 24, 1841; "A Convert to Slavery" and "Land and Liberty," *National Era*, August 23, 1849, March 2, 1848; "From the Lowell Journal—Black Slavery and White Slavery," *National Anti-Slavery Standard*, August 5, 1847; see also Garrison's strictures upon Robert Owen's "doctrine of circumstances" for denying free will and individual responsibility, in Walter Merrill (ed.), *The Letters of William Lloyd Garrison: "No Union With Slaveholders," 1841–1849* (1973), 240–41, Vol. III of Merrill and Ruchames (eds.), *Garrison Letters*.

33 "Dangers Which Threaten the Future," New York *Charles Fourier's The Phalanx*, November 4, 1843. At the very least, labor reformers charged the abolitionists with misguided zeal.

34 "Factory Mode of Obtaining Operatives," *Cabotville Chronicle*, quoted in Fitchburg and later Lowell (Mass.) *Voice of Industry*, January 2, 1846.

both exaggerated the extent and mistook the causes of the decline of positive labor incentives in the North. On another level, abolitionists seemed to suggest that this debate was irrelevant; labor reformers to the contrary, the superiority of "free society" was not at bottom dependent on the laborer's economic improvement. As Garrison indicated in his exchange with the Chartist Charles M'Ewan, oppressed British workers threatened with starvation were no more slaves than were prosperous American laborers: "They may go dressed in rags, it is true; but their bodies and souls belong to them, and not to another." And the *Emancipator*, after denying Brownson's claim that northern wage-earners were fixed in their position, suggested that the legitimacy of a competitive labor system did not in any case require that workers acquire property and achieve upward mobility: "Unless Mr. Brownson can devise a 'social system' that will make one and one equal to two and two, it will always take place that of the laborers for wages, a part will receive enough to accumulate, and a part only enough to subsist, on the simple principle that each receives what he earns."[35]

Abolitionists did in general identify the laborer's right to compete as a "free agent" with the likelihood of his improving his material well-being: free laborers would prove receptive to middle-class values, and the acquisition of those values insured economic independence if not more substantial success in America's open if competitive system. Against this optimism must be set the pessimistic determinism of the labor reformers, their sense that increasingly in America as in other societies the economic success of one individual was built on the oppression of another, and that individual freedom entailed membership in one of two classes, the class of the exploiters or the class of the exploited.

Abolitionists correctly perceived how easily the labor reform emphasis on the helplessness and insecurity of free workers might lead to an endorsement of proslavery doctrines. They were less ca-

---

35 "The Late Anti-Slavery Meeting," *Liberator*, December 18, 1840; "Prospects and Projects of the Democracy," *Emancipator*, December 31, 1840. While Republican party leaders took over many of the abolitionist themes, one way they may have departed from abolitionists was in a greater tendency to equate freedom with positive labor incentives; Republicans, as well as other Americans, were less likely than abolitionists to regard the "pauper labor" of the Old World as invariably better off than southern slaves.

pable of perceiving how their own belief in the resilience and moral power of the individual might contribute to conditions of exploitation in free society. In 1852 Samuel Gridley Howe could align himself with Massachusetts factory proprietors and oppose a ten-hour law for factory workers principally on the grounds that it "emasculates people to be protected in this way. Let them be used to protecting themselves."[36]

Howe's position may well have been more extreme than that of most abolitionists. It seems clear that the convergence of abolitionist principles with opposition to humane paternalism and with support for the capitalist *status quo* proceeded much further in England than it did in the United States. One would be hard pressed to find among leading American abolitionists a real equivalent to the antislavery Englishwoman Harriet Martineau, with her use of vulgarized laissez faire tenets to defend the interests of manufacturing proprietors and deny the right of the laboring poor to compulsory relief. There are a number of possible reasons for the contrast. The ethic of Christian love and responsibility for the poor and downtrodden that animated American abolitionists—including Howe himself in his many capacities as a social reformer—imposed some limits on their adherence to the competitive principle. Abolitionists' understanding of their crusade as a labor movement—by destroying servile slave labor abolition would advance the cause of free labor—imposed additional limits on the degree to which they would deliberately use the competitive principle to protect the interests of capital. Finally, American abolitionists were simply not confronted either with England's crisis of the laboring poor, or with its entrenched tradition of aristocratic paternalism and privilege, circumstances that contributed significantly to the extreme positions taken by Martineau and others in defense of a competitive market economy.[37]

---

36 Samuel Gridley Howe to Horace Mann, October 21, 1852, in Laura E. Richards (ed.), *Letters and Journal of Samuel Gridley Howe* (2 vols.; Boston: Dana Estes and Company, 1906), II, 343.

37 For Martineau's views, see *The Factory Controversy: A Warning Against Meddling Legislation* (Manchester: A. Ireland and Co., 1855); *Illustrations of Political Economy* (London: C. Fox, 1834); and *Poor Laws and Paupers Illustrated* (London: C. Fox, 1833–34). I am indebted to David Brion Davis for some of the thoughts expressed here.

American abolitionists' values, their exultation of the free individual's self-improvement and self-direction, bore a subtle and complex relationship to exploitative conditions under free labor capitalism. That relationship had important roots in the ambiguous character of evangelical religion. If abolitionists and other reformers of the period did not expect individual regeneration to ultimately erase all social distinctions along with slavery, they did expect it to render these distinctions irrelevant by eliminating selfishness and injustice and by suffusing society with Christian love and brotherhood. Yet many of the same reformers also looked to moral reform and the competitive process to actually reduce inequalities by disciplining the laboring poor and by inculcating them with the acquisitive drive of the middle class. There were elements in the abolitionists' evangelical faith that could easily become a spur to the very selfishness and injustice which that faith rebuked. The dilemma was probably unresolvable, but abolitionists generally underrated it, nonetheless.[38]

38  As I have indicated, abolitionists shared this dilemma with other Americans whose reform impulse was grounded in evangelical religion. Charles Loring Brace, the first president of the New York Children's Aid Society, attributed the disorderly and criminal behavior of elements of the urban poor to the fact that "society hurried on selfishly for its wealth, and left this vast class in its misery and temptation. . . . The worldliness of the rich, the indifference of all classes to the poor, will always be avenged." Yet Brace's prescription for the street children who came under his charge was "to awaken in them the instinct of property" and encourage them to pursue occupations that promised advancement and substantial material reward; see the *Fourth Annual Report* of the Children's Aid Society, in Emma Brace (ed.), *The Life of Charles Loring Brace: Chiefly Told in His Own Letters* (New York: Charles Scribner's Sons Inc., 1894), 217; C. L. Brace, *Sketch of the Formation of the Newsboys' Lodging House* (n.p., 1867), 5; and Brace, *Short Sermons to News Boys, With a History of the Formation of the News Boys' Lodging-House* (New York: Charles Scribner and Co., 1866), 129. My emphasis on the tension between economic rationality and acquisitiveness and other, less worldly and materialistic values promoted by evangelical religion owes much to Max Weber's *The Protestant Ethic and the Spirit of Capitalism*, tr. Talcott Parsons (New York: Charles Scribner's Sons, 1930).

# LATIMER
## Lawyers, Abolitionists, and the Problem of Unjust Laws

*William M. Wiecek*

AMERICAN attitudes toward the philosophical problem of obligation —must one obey an unjust law?—have always been ambivalent. On one hand, a part of our cultural heritage, extending back from English common-law commentators through St. Thomas Aquinas to Aristotle and Sophocles, affirms that a human law contravening divine law is void and must not be obeyed. This tradition was obliquely affirmed during the American Revolution, and crept into the constitutive documents of that era. On the other hand, since the Revolution, legal commentators, political leaders, and many theologians have inculcated a positivist attitude about obligation: validly enacted laws bind the individual. The legal order cannot recognize a legally enforceable right of conscientious disobedience, much less resistance, lest the state slide into "anarchy." Positivist respect for laws—the preference, if you will, for legality over justice when the two conflict—has dominated the American tradition since the 1790s. Conscientious disobedience has appeared only occasionally and briefly, quickly snuffed by a peculiarly American insistence on respect for law based on republican ideology.

Positivism was first challenged in a series of confrontations between abolitionists and blacks on one hand, and persons enforcing the federal Fugitive Slave Act of 1793 on the other. Beginning around 1840 and extending to the Civil War, these encounters between conscience and law produced a countertradition of conscientious disobedience. One of the earliest of these incidents, George Latimer's brush with the Fugitive Slave Law in Boston during the autumn of 1842, stimulated the most thorough professional, ministerial, and popular debate over the duty of resistance heard in America before the Vietnam years.

When William Blackstone, greatest of the common-law English legal commentators, asserted the primacy of divine over positive law, he helped acclimate a religious and philosophical principle to a working legal tradition. In his magisterial *Commentaries on the Laws of England* (first edition, 1765), Blackstone wrote that the "law of nature, being coeval with mankind, and dictated by God himself, is of course superior in obligation to any other. It is binding all over the globe, in all countries, and at all times: no human laws are of any validity, if contrary to this." He illustrated this by reference to homicide: "If any human law should allow or enjoin us to commit [murder], we are bound to transgress that human law. . . . But with regard to matters that are themselves indifferent, and are not commanded or forbidden by [natural] laws, here the inferior legislature has scope and opportunity to . . . make that action unlawful which before was not so." A human law bound men's consciences only when it inherently wrong—or where disobedience to law would involve "public mischief or private injury."[1]

An influential American divine, the Reverend Jonathan Mayhew of Boston, anticipated Blackstone in his noted 1750 sermon on "Nonresistance to Higher Powers." Mayhew insisted that "all commands running counter to the declared will of the supreme legislator of heaven and earth, are null and void: And therefore disobedience to them is a duty, not a crime."[2] The events of the American Revolution ratified Mayhew's views. The Declaration of Independence justified disobedience to unjust metropolitan law. The new republi-

1 William Blackstone, *Commentaries on the Laws of England* (Oxford: Clarendon Press, 1765–1769), I, 41, 43, 57–58.
2 Jonathan Mayhew, *A Discourse Concerning Unlimited Submission and Non-Resistance to Higher Powers. . . .* (Boston: D. Fowle, 1750), 38.

can constitutions were studded with rationales for disobedience. Even before Thomas Jefferson drafted the declaration, George Mason proclaimed in the Virginia Bill of Rights (Article III) that "when any government shall be found inadequate or contrary to these purposes," a majority has a right "to reform, alter or abolish it." The Preamble to the Massachusetts Constitution of 1780 declared that "whenever these great objects [of government] are not obtained, the people have a right to alter the government, and to take measures necessary for their safety, prosperity and happiness." The New Hampshire Constitution of 1784 (Part I, Article X) went so far as to guarantee a right of revolution against unjust laws: "when the ends of government are perverted, and public liberty manifestly endangered, the people may, and of right ought to reform the old, or establish a new government. The doctrine of nonresistance against arbitrary power, and oppression, is absurd, slavish, and destructive of the good and happiness of mankind." These constitutional precepts, however, were addressed to the people *en masse*, not to the individual conscience. The moral justification for a whole people rising against oppression might be different from, and perhaps inapplicable to, the dilemmas of an individual forced to comply with an unjust law. Their counsel was directed, not to Antigone, but to the Long Parliament.

The Revolutionary tradition is once again in vogue today because of the civil rights struggles, Vietnam, and Watergate, all of which made the legitimacy of government in America questionable. Martin Luther King's modern classic, the "Letter from the Birmingham Jail" (1963), reasserted the tradition of Aristotle and Blackstone: "An unjust law is a human law that is not rooted in eternal and natural law. An individual who breaks a law that conscience tells him is unjust, and willingly accepts the penalty by staying in jail to arouse the conscience of the community over its injustice, is in reality expressing the very highest respect for law." Ronald Dworkin, an Anglo-American legal scholar, suggested in 1968 that widespread doubt about the morality of a statute made the statute itself constitutionally suspect.[3]

3 Martin Luther King, "Letter from the Birmingham Jail," in Stuaghton Lynd (ed.), *Nonviolence in America: A Documentary History* (Indianapolis: Bobbs-Merrill, 1966), 468–69;

Ironically, the sources of the Revolutionary era justifications for resistance forced American legal theorists to repudiate a literal acceptance of Blackstone's divine-law principles. John Adams's well-known encounter with a former client who hoped for an end to all laws is instructive. The man hoped that courts had been permanently abolished in Massachusetts; Adams assumed his motive was to avoid payment of his debts. If political power should pass to such people, Adams mused in a gloomy mood, "to what purpose have We sacrificed our Time, health and every Thing else? Surely We must guard against this Spirit and these Principles or We shall repent of all our Conduct." In 1786, even James Madison complained vigorously of the mutability, multifariousness, and injustice of state stattutes.[4] Shays's Rebellion in Massachusetts (1786–1787) demonstrated that a high priority for American lawyers would be to stabilize legal development, in order to encourage popular respect for laws, to suppress any incipient disrespect loosed by the Revolution, and to restrain the legislative exuberance of republican lawmakers.

American jurists willingly turned to the task promoting respect for law by appeals to republican ideology.[5] Judge Nathaniel Chipman of the United States District Court for the District of Vermont was able to deny the obligation of laws violating "moral duty" only because he assumed that the laws of the new republics would always conform to natural law. Jesse Root, judge of the Connecticut Superior Court, similarly identified his state's common law with Blackstonian natural law, concluding that inconsistent "positive laws" were void. Zephaniah Swift, an influential Connecticut treatise-writer, stated that "no laws may contravene the principles

Ronald Dworkin, "On Not Prosecuting Civil Disobedience," New York Review of Books, June 6, 1968, p. 14.

4 L. H. Butterfield (ed.), Diary and Autobiography of John Adams (Cambridge: Harvard University Press, 1962), III, 326 (Autobiography, August, 1775); James Madison, "Vices of the Political System of the United States," in William T. Hutchinson, et al. (eds.), The Papers of James Madison (Chicago: University of Chicago Press, 1961– ), IX, 348–57.

5 Gordon Wood, The Creation of the American Republic, 1776–1787 (Chapel Hill: University of North Carolina Press, 1969), 612–13; Pauline Maier, "Popular Uprisings and Civil Authority in Eighteenth-Century America," William and Mary Quarterly, XXVII (1970), 33–34.

of morality," but insisted that no one was free to disobey a law enacted by a republican legislature because the people were "virtually present by their representatives" at the enactment. "The laws therefore operate with the force of command, and obedience becomes the duty of the citizens."[6]

If the authority of these New England legalists was insufficient, George Washington's "Farewell Address" (1796) redefined the problem of obligation definitively. With the painful memory of the Whiskey Rebellion (Pennsylvania, 1794) still fresh, Washington urged his countrymen to have "respect for [the federal government's] authority, compliance with its laws, acquiescence in its measures." Conceding that the people have a right to change the government, Washington cautioned that "the constitution which at any time exists till changed by an explicit and authentic act of the whole people is sacredly obligatory upon all. The very idea of the power and the right of the people to establish government presupposes the duty of every individual to obey the established government."[7] Thus, by conceptual legerdemain, Washington transformed the liberating notion of popular sovereignty into the confining limits of positivism and obedience.

Legal conflicts during the next half-century eroded the easy confidence of the early republic that American laws would always square with justice. The Blackstonian concept crumbled and gave way to a positivist respect for all human laws. This new positivism was avowed by Judge John Gilchrist of the New Hampshire Superior Court of Judicature two years after the Latimer incident. Gilchrist rejected Blackstone's distinction between *malum in se* and *malum prohibitum*. An individual could not exempt himself on conscientious grounds from the obligation to obey a law because "subtle casuistry," "obtuseness," and "self-interest" often confused the

6 Nathaniel Chipman, *Sketches of the Principles of Government* (Rutland: J. Lyon, 1793), 220; Jesse Root, "Introduction" to *Reports of . . . the Superior Court and the Supreme Court of Errors [of Connecticut]* (Hartford: Hudson and Goodwin, 1798), ix; Zephaniah Swift, *A System of the Laws of the State of Connecticut* (Windham: John Byrne, 1795), I, 38.

7 George Washington, "Farewell Address" (1796), in James D. Richardson (comp.), *Messages and Papers of the Presidents* (Washington, D.C.: Bureau of National Literature, 1), I, 209.

moral judgment. "If obedience to the law should depend entirely on the conscience of the individual," Gilchrist warned, "all legal restraints would soon be abolished."[8]

Protestant moral theology provided little more encouragement to conscientious disobedience. Two theologians dominated American thinking on the subject in the 1840s: an eighteenth-century English divine, William Paley, and a nineteenth-century American, Francis Wayland. Paley based his Whiggish teachings on the principle he called "public expediency": an individual must determine for himself whether or not he would obey a law he saw as unjust, weighing on one side the danger of disobedience and the extent of oppression, and on the other the cost of resistance and probability that his act of disobedience will succeed. From an abolitionist viewpoint, Paley provided a partial resolution of this weighing problem by his sharp condemnation of slavery and his call for gradual emancipation.[9]

In the United States, Francis Wayland, sometime president of Brown University, attacked the problem of obligation in *The Elements of Moral Science*, a book that enjoyed unprecedented sales before the Civil War, both in its unabridged 1837 edition and in a school edition.[10] In it, he taught that people must obey all laws. If the state enacts an exceptionally unjust or harsh law, Wayland called on individuals to choose martyrdom—he called it "suffering in the cause of right"—rather than passive obedience or resistance. But Wayland repudiated even this weak advice in response to the challenge of abolition and the suffragist cause in the Dorr Rebellion of Rhode Island, which occurred in the same year as the Latimer incident. In his antiabolitionist tract *The Limitations of Human Responsibility* (1838), he argued that abolitionists or other reformers confronted with legally sanctioned evil had no obligation to act against it, and fulfilled their moral duty by merely preaching against

---

8 Lewis v. Welch, 14 New Hampshire Reports 296 (1844).

9 William Paley, *The Principles of Moral and Political Philosophy* (School ed.; New York: Harper, 1860), 201–209; the condemnation of slavery is at pp. 97–99.

10 On the influence of Wayland, see Wilson Smith, *Professors & Public Ethics: Studies of Northern Moral Philosophers Before the Civil War* (Ithaca: Cornell University Press, 1956), 196, and Joseph L. Blau's introduction to Francis Wayland's *Elements of Moral Science*, reprinted in the John Harvard Library (Cambridge: Harvard University Press, 1963), ix–xlix. References to the *Elements* that follow are from pp. 318–21 and 334–38 of this edition.

it to sinners. Going beyond this call to quietism, Wayland reacted to the Dorr Rebellion by demanding obedience to all extant law and calling on the established government of Rhode Island to crush all resistance to its laws by force.[11]

The political, legal, and theological insistence on obedience to law was so influential that no serious formal opposition to the Fugitive Slave Act of 1793 surfaced in American courts before 1835. On the few occasions when a bold lawyer did question the statute, eminent jurists shrugged off the challenge. Chief Justice Isaac Parker of the Massachusetts Supreme Judicial Court, Chief Justice William Tilghman of the Pennsylvania Supreme Court, and Justice Joseph Story of the United States Supreme Court all upheld the constitutionality of the 1793 fugitive act.[12] Chief Justice John Marshall of the United States Supreme Court in 1825 disapproved of an effort by Story three years earlier on circuit to claim intrinsic powers for American courts to delegitimate the international slave trade. Marshall held that the trade had been established by the positive laws or customs of the maritime nations and hence was not open to attack via natural law principles.[13] Thenceforth natural law was not normative for American jurists, who, in slavery cases, were guided by positive law and not by their consciences, as later abolitionist lawyers discovered.

Thus by 1842 abolitionists and lawyers found little in America's post-Revolutionary legal and religious thought that endorsed individual noncompliance with or opposition to an unjust law. Moreover, having recently been themselves victimized by mobbings, lynchings, and other breakdowns of law and order, abolitionists had a keen sense of the value of law for the protection of person and property. Self-interest combined with general inclination to produce respect for law and disapproval of conscientious lawbreaking. This

11 Francis Wayland, *The Limitations of Human Responsibility* (Boston: Gould, Kendall & Lincoln, 1838), 167–96; Francis Wayland, *The Affairs of Rhode Island* (Rev. ed., Providence: B. Cranston and H. H. Brown, 1842).

12 Commonwealth v. Griffin, 2 Pickering (Massachusetts Reports) 11 (1823); Wright v. Deacon, 5 Sergeant and Rawle (Pennsylvania Reports) 62 (1819); Joseph Story, *Commentaries on the Constitution of the United States* (Boston: Hilliard, Gray, 1833), sec. 1812; Justice Joseph Story in Prigg v. Pennsylvania, 16 Peters (41 United States Reports) 608 (1842).

13 The Antelope, 10 Wheaton (23 United States Reports) 66 (1825); Story's effort was United States v. La Jeune Eugenie, 26 Federal Cases 832 (number 15551) (Circuit Court for the District of Massachusetts, 1822).

was revealed in 1836, when the Massachusetts Anti-Slavery Society and William Lloyd Garrison both condemned the mob rescue of two black women, allegedly fugitives, from a hearing on a writ of habeas corpus before Chief Justice Lemuel Shaw of the Massachusetts Supreme Judicial Court.[14]

Then suddenly on October 9, 1842, abolitionists in Boston found themselves unexpectedly confronting the problem of obligation incarnate when a Boston constable arrested George Latimer and detained him as the fugitive slave of a Norfolk merchant, James Gray. Abolitionists immediately began legal proceedings to rescue Latimer. First, Samuel E. Sewall, a young abolitionist Boston lawyer, secured a writ of habeas corpus on Latimer's behalf from Chief Justice Shaw, seeking his release on the grounds that the constable's act was illegal.[15] Shaw disappointed Sewall by holding that Latimer's detention was legal under the Fugitive Slave Act.[16] The slaveowner-claimant Gray began the next legal maneuver by requesting a certificate of rendition under the 1793 act from Justice Joseph Story, then in Boston in his circuit-riding capacity as presiding judge of United States Circuit Court. Story gave Gray two weeks to obtain proof of title from Virginia.

While the hearing in the federal court was pending, Sewall tried again, producing the third confrontation between abolitionists and the law, when he sought a writ of personal replevin from Shaw.[17] When the jailer refused to honor the writ, Sewall secured a second writ of habeas corpus and thus got another hearing before Shaw.

14 *Liberator*, August 6, 1836.
15 The *Latimer Journal*, bound together with many other primary sources in the Henry I. Bowditch Papers of the Massachusetts Historical Society, Boston, constitutes the fullest trove of materials on the incident. Henry I. Bowditch edited a useful collection of published primary sources on Latimer: *Proceedings of the Citizens of the Borough of Norfolk, on the Boston Outrage, in the Case of the Runaway Slave George Latimer* (Norfolk: T. G. Broughton, 1843). The writ of habeas corpus, the single most important procedural guarantor of individual liberty in the Anglo-American legal tradition, is a means of inquiring into the legality of a person's detention. The best modern account of the Latimer affair, with a heavy emphasis on legal matters, is Leonard W. Levy, *The Law of the Commonwealth and Chief Justice Shaw: The Evolution of American Law, 1830–1860* (Rev. ed.; New York: Harper & Row, 1967), 78–85.
16 *Liberator*, October 28, 1842. Shaw's actions and opinions were not officially reported.
17 The writ of personal replevin, technically known as the writ *de homine replegiando*, was an old procedural device used to regain custody of one person from another. Sewall here relied on a Massachusetts statute (Act of 19 April 1837, ch. 221, *Laws of . . . Massachusetts . . . 1837 and 1838*), which restored the writ of *homine replegiando* as a means of protecting personal liberty.

Shaw again discharged the writ on the grounds that the Massachusetts statute restoring the writ of personal replevin was subordinate to the 1793 federal act.[18] Shaw now relied on the recent decision in *Prigg* v. *Pennsylvania* (1842), in which the United States Supreme Court had held unconstitutional a Pennsylvania statute interfering with the fugitive rendition process under the federal law. Shortly afterwards, however, the Latimer incident aborted when Boston abolitionists persuaded Gray to sell his claim to Latimer for $400. George Latimer thereupon passed into historical obscurity, but the questions of conscience his case raised intensified.

Throughout the Latimer hearings, the participants donned what John T. Noonan has called "masks of the law": that is, they adopted (or repudiated) ways of concealing their personal moral responsibility for the consequences of applying the law to a human being.[19] Masks of the law are of two sorts. The first kind is like the blindfold or hood put on someone about to be executed: it covers the humanity of the law's victim. The other kind is the mask that the agent of the law puts on himself, like ceremonial vestments, enabling him to deny his personal agency in applying the law.

The judge and lawyers enforcing or supporting the Fugitive Slave Act had to adopt masks. They were all Bostonians, all claimed to be hostile to slavery in the abstract, none had any reason to want spontaneously to condemn George Latimer to slavery. But their professional obligations and their commissioning oath required them to support the United States Constitution, and that, in turn, as they understood their obligation, meant that they had to support enforcement of the fugitive statute as the supreme law of the land. After William Lloyd Garrison pilloried Chief Justice Shaw in *The Liberator*, an anonymous lawyer contributed a defense of Shaw's conduct, which Garrison promptly published. The lawyer figuratively clove Shaw into two persons: "Lemuel Shaw, in his private capacity," and "Lemuel Shaw, as Chief Justice of Massachusetts." A moral appeal based on the injustice of a law can reach only the former; it cannot affect the latter, who as a condition of exercising

18 *Liberator*, November 4, 1842.
19 John T. Noonan, *Persons and Masks of the Law: Cardozo, Holmes, Jefferson, and Wythe as Makers of the Masks* (New York: Farrar, Straus and Giroux, 1976).

his power, can do so only within the limits of that power prescribed by statute. What is morally wrong is not legally enforceable. For that reason, enforcing a morally repugnant law is not morally wrongful.[20]

Shaw himself relied on his oath of office. He paid his devoirs to morality, claiming that "he probably felt as much sympathy for the person in custody as others." But the United States Constitution and the act of 1793 obliged Shaw to remand fugitives, and he, Shaw, had sworn to uphold that Constitution and that law. Shaw here voiced what was overwhelmingly the judicial opinion of the time. Robert Cover has compiled numerous instances of judges like Shaw who had at least nominal antislavery sympathies and who responded in fugitive slave cases just as he did.[21] One of them, Justice Levi Woodbury of the United States Supreme Court (like Shaw, a native New Englander), bluntly asserted the superiority of oath over morality in another case arising under the Fugitive Slave Act: "Whatever may be the theoretical opinions of any as to the expediency of some of these [proslavery] compromises, or of the right of property in persons which they recognize, this court has no alternative, while they exist, but to stand by the Constitution and the laws with fidelity to their duties and their oaths." An Ohio judge three years later explicitly defended republican positivism: "the question is not, what conforms to the great principles of natural right and universal freedom— but what do the positive laws and institutions which we as members of the government under which we live, are bound to recognize and obey, command."[22]

These judges did have one rationalization for their action: the troublesome cases came to them, and they could not morally or legally evade them. This excuse was not available to Elbridge Gerry Austin, the young member of the Boston bar who took Gray's case. Austin might have declined to represent the slaveowner and sidestepped the moral issue. But he did not, and thereby laid himself

20 *Liberator*, November 18, 1842.
21 *Ibid.*, November 4, 1842; Robert M. Cover, *Justice Accused: Antislavery and the Judicial Process* (New Haven: Yale University Press, 1975).
22 Jones v. Van Zandt, 5 Howard (46 U.S.) 215 (1847) at 231. Woodbury's predecessor on the Court and fellow New Englander, Justice Story, agreed with this oath rationale; see William W. Story (ed.), *Life and Letters of Joseph Story* (Boston: Little, Brown, 1851), II, 392; State v. Hoppess (Ohio Supreme Court, 1845), printed in *Ohio Decisions Reprints* (Norwalk, Ohio: Laning, 1896), I, 105–18.

open to abolitionists' imputation that he was a legal whore, selling himself and the honor of Massachusetts for a slave-catching fee. Austin naturally resented this and felt obliged to defend himself in a public letter. He emphasized that his client "has conducted all his proceedings strictly according to law." Then he launched into a personal apologia:

I cannot close this statement without a single remark on my own behalf. I have acted in this matter throughout in my professional capacity. I have no more favorable view of the institution of slavery, than the most [illegible] of those who seek its immediate abolishment—but I have yet to learn that the counselling and advising of a stranger, in the exercise of his constitutional privileges, is a crime. I have no feeling at all in the matter . . . and no feeling of regret that Latimer is a free man. I would have wished, however, that his emancipation had been effected in a different manner. I am one of those who think that the dismemberment of the Union would not accomplish the end proposed, or favorably affect any portion of the country—and that as long as we are a united people, the citizens of the South, whenever they seek to enforce their rights, are entitled to the services of those persons, who, by education, are qualified to advise them how to observe the provisions of the Constitution and laws of their country.[23]

Where Shaw donned the judicial mask, Austin adopted the lawyer's mask, expressing sentiments about the lawyer's role in administering a morally questionable system that, *mutatis mutandis*, would be familiar to any lawyer in practice today.

Perhaps the extreme form of the oath rationale was expressed by a conservative member of the Boston bar, Peleg Chandler, the editor of the *Law Reporter*, who demanded unquestioning obedience to all laws and who argued that moral scruples were irrelevant. "A judge has nothing to do with the moral character of laws which society chooses to make," Chandler argued. Their oath binds judges "*not* to judge according to their opinion of the moral character of the law." Mortimer and Sanford Kadish refer to this judicial rationale as the "rule-of-law model" for official behavior, and point out that it has its counterpart, the "law-and-order model," which requires ordinary citizens to obey all laws.[24] George Washington's exhortation to citi-

23 *Liberator*, November 25, 1842.
24 [Peleg W. Chandler], "The Latimer Case," *Law Reporter* (1843), 493–95 (italics in original); Mortimer R. Kadish and Sanford H. Kadish, *Discretion to Disobey: A Study of Lawful Departures from Legal Rules* (Stanford: Stanford University Press, 1973), 96–97.

zen obedience, read as an essay in civil morality, quickly found theological support when law was challenged by the abolitionist conscience. An orthodox New Hampshire minister, Reverend Nathaniel Bouton, found a convenient surrogate for the individual citizen's conscience when he insisted that people must obey all laws, whatever their perceived inconsistency with higher law. The duty of reconciling statutes with morality, Bouton argued, was the job of legislators. "No citizen is at liberty to treat [Massachusetts statutes] as contrary to natural or divine law, while he is a citizen," wrote Theodore R. Sullivan, another New England antiabolitionist.[25]

The oath controversy was so significant, so much a focus of the Latimer arguments, because it represented the juncture of law and morality. The oath was a solemn, almost sacred, act; at the same time, it was a statutory requirement for the commissioning of judges and attorneys. It was thus a perfect vehicle for debates over obligation. Abolitionists seized on it readily. An antislavery Unitarian minister, Reverend John Pierpont, provoked intense debate when he dismissed the oath rationale espoused by judges like Shaw and Woodbury on the grounds that an oath to do an immoral act was void. In addition to scriptural authorities, Pierpont cited the passages from Blackstone quoted at the beginning of this paper to support his void-oath theory. This raised a variant of the larger question of Latimer: does the oath of itself alter the moral position of a lawyer or judge vis-à-vis an unjust law? Most judges responded that it did: it intensified their obligation to enforce laws despite moral reservations. Others, a tiny minority, saw it differently. Francis Jackson, a wealthy Boston merchant and a Garrisonian abolitionist, held a minor judicial commission, that of a justice of the peace. In 1844, he surrendered his commission, arguing in a public letter that he could no longer comply with his oath to defend the United States Constitution because the Constitution protected slavery and made it a national institution.[26]

25 Nathaniel Bouton, *The Good Land in Which We Live: A Discourse Preached at Concord* . . . (Concord: McFarland & Jenks, 1850); T. R. Sullivan, *Letters Against the Immediate Abolition of Slavery, Addressed to the Free Blacks of the Non-slaveholding States* . . . (Boston: Hilliard, Gray, 1835), 30.
26 *Massachusetts Revised Statutes, 1835*, ch. 88, sec. 21; John Pierpont, *A Discourse on*

Jackson was a Garrisonian, so such a conclusion was not surprising. The dilemma of a non-Garrisonian abolitionist judge could be exquisite, though. William Jay, a judge of a Westchester, New York, county court, wrestled with it inconclusively for years. Jay was one of the most fascinating of the abolitionists. The son of Chief Justice John Jay, he was a conservative by all criteria: in politics, he described himself as being "of the old Washington [Federalist] school"; in religion, he was an orthodox (though evangelical) Episcopal layman; socially, he was a well-born, independently wealthy elitist. Yet he was a strong abolitionist, tireless in writing for the cause, whose opinions became steadily more radical until, from a non-Garrisonian position, he adopted disunion in revulsion at America's aggression against Mexico.

As a judge, Jay was acutely conscious that the Fugitive Slave Act might someday oblige him to give a certificate of rendition for an alleged fugitive.[27] At the same time, he was repelled by the anti-statist arguments of the Garrisonians, who, he assumed, rejected the legitimacy of all human government. He had himself taken the oath; did this mean he would some day have to send a black man or woman back to slavery? No, he reasoned, unpersuasively. His oath was "*not* a promise to obey any and every law or order of the govt. made in pursuance of the Constitution. We must obey god rather than man." But, being candid and scrupulously honest by nature, Jay recognized that he had just evaded the issue, and he rephrased the issue to attack it again: "Can a public officer sworn to support the Constitution ... refuse to *enforce* a law strictly constitutional merely because *he* esteems it immoral?" He conceded the constitutionality of the slave-rendition statute, and so with much difficulty and reluctance "came to the determination, whenever called to take jurisdiction of a slave case, to tear up my commission and leave the bench."[28] (It never came to that, however.) Other abolitionists,

---

*the Covenant With Judas* ... (Boston: Little and Brown, 1842); Francis Jackson to George N. Briggs, July 4, 1844, reprinted in [Wendell Phillips], *The Constitution a Pro-Slavery Compact* ... (New York: American Anti-Slavery Society, 1856), 171–81.

27 Act of Feb. 12, 1793, ch. 7, sec. 3, in *United States Statutes at Large*, I, 302.

28 Jay's conscientious struggle may be followed in William Jay to "Dear Sir" [Ellis Gray Loring?], September 13, 1843, William Lloyd Garrison MSS., Boston Public Library (autograph copy signed; italics in original); nearly verbatim copy, endorsed "Judge Jay's argument on ye

though they lacked the immediacy of Jay's position, reached conclusions similar to his and Pierpont's.[29]

Abolitionist lawyers responded to the Latimer challenge in different ways. One group, typified by Latimer's counsel, Samuel Sewall, professed their allegiance to what might be called "the legality of process." Their antislavery moral impulse was refracted through their respect for law, leading them to try to use law for abolitionist ends, just as their colleague Austin was using it in the service of slavery. Sewall had been tirelessly active in antislavery affairs since the early thirties, organizing petition campaigns, creating antislavery societies, defending fugitives, and putting his legal expertise at the service of lay abolitionists. He continued this activism into the turbulent fifties, always insistent that the law was morally neutral and might be turned to just ends. Ellis Gray Loring, another young member of the Boston bar, pursued a similar avocation.

The devotion to process as an approach to justice was exemplified by yet another young lawyer who made possible some of the legal skirmishing of the Latimer case, and whose premature death after his election to Congress in 1840 deprived him of the pleasure of seeing his legal handiwork put to use. James C. Alvord enjoyed a high reputation among contemporaries for combining legal ability with moral rectitude. Wendell Phillips, a good judge of both traits, said in a eulogy of Alvord that "the practice of the law is said to . . . prison conscience in the statute book," but that Alvord rose above such positivism. It was Alvord who, as a member of the General Court (legislature) in 1837, restored to the Massachusetts statutes the procedural remedy of human replevin that Sewall used in the second hearing before Shaw. He also popularized it among the bar as a device available to abolitionist lawyers.[30] His colleague Charles Francis Adams was responsible for passage of the 1843 Massachusetts Personal Liberty Law, a direct consequence of the Latimer in-

---

constitution, published by me in the Williamsburg Gazette July 29/46," Jay to Amos A. Phelps, July 3, 1846, both in Lewis Tappan MSS., Library of Congress.

29 *Latimer Journal*, May 10, 1843; Lysander Spooner, *The Unconstitutionality of Slavery* (Rev. ed; Boston: Bela Marsh, 1860), 152.

30 [Wendell Phillips], "James C. Alvord" (autograph note signed) (1840), in Weston Papers Antislavery MSS. collection, Boston Public Library; James C. Alvord, "Trial by Jury, in Questions of Personal Freedom," *American Jurist and Law Magazine*, XVII (1837), 94–113.

cident, which prohibited Massachusetts state and local officials from participating in proceedings under the federal act, from making arrests under the federal law, and from using state facilities to imprison fugitives pending rendition. Sewall, Loring, Alvord, and Adams were willing to work within an imperfect system, minimizing or excising moral deformities and improving on opportunities provided by morally acceptable components of the law. Their posture was endorsed by the prominent Unitarian theologian William Ellergy Channing, who in a contemporary tract conceded that justice might tolerate the rendition of a fugitive, but only if all procedural impediments were scrupulously respected.[31]

Wendell Phillips had little patience with this respect for process. "Men are too much accustomed to think law synonymous with justice—and to bind up the statute book as an appendix with the gospel," he wrote in 1844. By 1842, Phillips had been an active abolitionist for five years. Of Brahmin background, he was a lawyer who relinquished a languid practice shortly after the start of his career in preference for antislavery activism. He was acknowledged by all to be the premier orator of the movement, and was a Garrisonian. In his famous Faneuil Hall speech on the night of October 30, 1842, Phillips insisted that George Latimer was not the impersonal abstraction referred to in the constitutional euphemism "Person held to Service or Labour" (Article IV, section 2), but rather "a son and a husband . . . an innocent man." He flayed all those who helped enforce the unjust law: "[the] poor officer, who, for a dollar obeys his writ . . . needy attorneys, who would sell the fee simple of their souls for an attendance fee of thirty-three cents a day . . . ambitious lawyers, panting to see their names blazoned in southern papers as counsel for slave-catchers." And finally the public before him: "*You* are the guilty ones . . . the white slaves of the North."[32]

Phillips reserved his harshest treatment for the mask of law that Chief Justice Shaw had put on himself. Phillips held this portrait of Shaw up to the readers of Garrison's *Liberator*:

---

31 "An Act to Protect Personal Liberty," ch. 69, in *Acts and Resolves . . . of Massachusetts . . . 1843*; William Ellery Channing, *The Duty of the Free States: Remarks Suggested by the Case of the Creole* (Boston: William Crosby, 1842).
32 *Liberator*, July 26, 1844; November 11, 1842.

. . . when the overbearing insolence of the Slave Power had thrown down, in the usurped name of the Constitution, all the bulwarks of individual freedom, [Shaw] betrayed, without an effort, against law, the honor of Massachusetts. From the battlefields of liberty in every age—from martyrs at the stake and on the scaffold—from the graves of the Puritans, there came a voice which besought him to be faithful to the high trust reposed in his hands. Yielding to bad law and worse morals, he was recreant to all.[33]

The last words on Latimer as a crisis of law and morality came not from lawyers or theologians, but from Henry David Thoreau and Herman Melville. In his *Essay on Civil Disobedience* (1849), Thoreau scanned the options presented seven years earlier: "Unjust laws exist: shall we be content to obey them, or shall we endeavor to amend them, and obey them until we have succeeded, or shall we transgress them at once?" Thoreau rejected Paley's criterion of expediency, and urged instead: "If the injustice [of a law] . . . is of such a nature that it requires you to be the agent of injustice to another, then, I say, break the law. Let your life be a counter friction to stop the machine."[34]

Subsequent fugitive slave recaptures in the 1850s, together with the behavior of Chief Justice Shaw and his associates in abetting them, forced Thoreau into a harsher condemnation of those who put on the masks of the law. Adding his opinion tardily to the debate a decade earlier as to whether a judge must resign his commission, Thoreau observed that "the law will never make men free; it is men who have got to make the law free. They are the lovers of law and order who observe the law when the government breaks it." The spectacle of Chief Justice Shaw stooping under chains to get into his own court during the excitement over the Thomas Sims rendition in 1851 rankled Thoreau as much as it did abolitionists. Perhaps with that degrading picture in his mind, he continued:

I doubt if there is a judge in Massachusetts who is prepared to resign his office, and get his living innocently, whenever it is required of him to pass sentence under a law which is merely contrary to the law of God. [Judges]

    33 *Ibid.*, November 18, 1842.
    34 Henry David Thoreau, "Civil Disobedience" in Thoreau, *Miscellanies*, Vol. X of *The Writings of Henry David Thoreau* (Boston: Houghton Mifflin, 1893), 138, 144, 146.

put themselves, or rather are by character, in this respect, exactly on a level with the marine who discharges his musket in any direction he is ordered to. They are just as much tools, and as little men. . . . their master enslaves their understandings and consciences, instead of their bodies.

To the basic position of the legal positivists, that a constitutional law must be obeyed, Thoreau responded that "in important moral and vital questions, like this, it is just as impertinent to ask whether it is profitable or not." As for Shaw's ratiocinations in the Latimer hearings, Thoreau wrote that "the judge still sits grinding at his organ, but it yields no music, and we hear only the sound of the handle. He believes that all the music resides in the handle, and the crowd toss him their coppers the same as before."[35]

The nineteenth century's final response to the challenge posed by the Latimer case came in that rich and complex parable, Melville's *Billy Budd* (written 1886–1891). Robert Cover has reminded us of the remarkable fact that Melville's father-in-law was none other than Lemuel Shaw,[36] and it is inviting to see in Captain Vere the Shaw of the Latimer case, justifying distasteful duty by a stern allegiance to law and oath.

This, however, only begins to describe the subtlety of Vere's character and the attitudes he personifies. Another dimension of the austere captain is revealed by considering him the embodiment of American jurisprudents bidding a final good-bye to the innocent early years of American law, when jurists like Judge Chipman could assume that positive law in the new republics would always be consonant with natural law. Vere did not avow a positivist legal outlook, but rather a view of the judge's role best articulated by Shaw's contemporary fellow judges, Chief Justice Roger B. Taney and Associate Justice Levi Woodbury, in their response to the Rhode Island Dorr Rebellion (which occurred just a few months before the Latimer incident). Taney and Woodbury both emphasized that the proper role of the judge is not to make law (as they assumed he would if he paid heed to his moral beliefs or political ideology), but rather to

35 Henry David Thoreau, "Slavery in Massachusetts", in Thoreau, *Miscellanies*, 181, 187–88, 191.
36 Cover, *Justice Accused*, 4.

enforce impartially the law given them by others.[37] Law, to such judges, had to be divorced from spontaneous impulses to justice, lest, as an artificial creation, it become deranged when diverted from its creators' purposes, no matter how human the motive for the diversion.

We can see further into Melville's thought on law and justice by forgetting, for once, that Billy is a Christ figure and seeing him as just who the author himself tells us he was: Orpheus, captivating the animals and stones in the forests—the wild spirit of impulse, abandon, feeling. Vere explicitly saw him this way, and deliberately adopted the opposite qualities: reason, deliberateness, order. This Dionysian-Apollonian dichotomy has an obvious parallel in the contrast between justice (expressed in the humane reservations of the marine captain) and law (the Articles of War—or any positive law). Billy: Rousseau's natural man: justice: Orpheus: Dionysus—to suppress these, Vere insisted that "forms, measured forms, are everything."[38]

But why? Why, if Vere was the voice of American law in its maturity, in all its formalism, did he so unflinchingly repudiate the impulse toward justice? Vere uttered those words (or at least had those thoughts) after Billy's hanging, as he stood on the afterdeck above his sailors, drummed and piped to their battle stations, standing in formation under armed marines and officers with sabers. Melville looked back not only on American law in its innocence one hundred years earlier, but also on the French Revolution. What was this revolution if not the demand for justice, smashing the forms of society (i.e., law)? Whatever Melville's own political views in 1890, it is clear that Vere opposed the disturbance of society's order, not because it threatened the privileged class of which he was a member, but because the Revolutionary impulse, justice, was "at war with the peace of the world and the true welfare of mankind."[39] George

37 Luther v. Borden, 7 Howard (48 United States reports) 1 (1849); see Chief Justice Taney's majority opinion, at 39–47, and Justice Levi Woodbury's concurrence/dissent, at 51–55.
38 Herman Melville, Billy Budd, Sailor, ed. Harrison Hayford and Merton M. Sealts (Chicago: University of Chicago Press, 1962), 128.
39 Ibid., 63.

Washington found here an unlikely echo a century after his Farewell Address, as American law embraced the ideal of obedience in the teeth of moral obligation. Hanged from a yardarm in the sunrise, by a man who acted in obedience to positive law, Billy was an image of justice in the American republics.

# WOMEN'S RIGHTS
# AND ABOLITION
## The Nature of the Connection

*Ellen DuBois*

IT IS a common error among historians of American feminism to attribute American women's consciousness about the oppression of their sex to the impact of the antislavery movement, particularly to its ultraist Garrisonian element. This argument suggests that, reasoning by analogy, female abolitionists perceived the similarities between their status before the law and that of the chattel slave.[1] Certainly the rhetoric of the prewar women's rights movement abounded in the use of the slave metaphor to describe women's oppression. "Slaves are we, politically and legally," wrote J. Elizabeth Jones in an 1848 address to the women of Ohio.[2] Yet other historical studies have contradicted this hypothesis of a direct connection between antislavery partisanship and awareness of women's oppression by demonstrating the incipient feminism in a wide range of other early nineteenth-century female activities. Since it is undeniably true that antislavery women provided the political leadership for the prewar women's rights movement, we must therefore look

---

1 See for example Andrew Sinclair, *The Better Half* (New York: Harper & Row, 1965), 37.

2 Elizabeth Cady Stanton, Susan B. Anthony, and Matilda Joslyn Gage (eds.), *History of Woman Suffrage* (6 vols.; Rochester: Susan B. Anthony, 1889), I, 108.

for other explanations for the connection between their abolitionism and their historic contribution to American feminism.

Starting in the 1820s and 1830s, American women began to express what might be called caste consciousness in a wide range of contexts. They evidenced a critical awareness of the importance of their
femaleness in determining their experiences, began to think of themselves as united by the fact of their sex, and most important, exhibited considerable discontent with their womanly lot. Scholars have
discovered such "prepolitical" elements in church-affiliated benevolent societies, the domestic novels written and read by women,
pioneers of women's education, and the prewar popular health
movement.[3] Caste consciousness and a sense of discontent among
women, what we might call protofeminism, seems to have been a
phenomenon carried widely through the social fabric and culture of
early nineteenth-century America. Many antislavery women experienced it prior to or independent of their abolitionist activity.
Lucretia Mott, the matriarch of female abolitionists, was an active
member of a female moral reform society in Philadelphia, and
Paulina Wright Davis began her public career as an itinerant lecturer
on women's physiology. Elizabeth Stanton was a student of Emma
Willard, Angelina Grimké considered becoming a pupil of Catherine
Beecher, and Lucy Stone, for a short period, studied with Mary Lyon.
Willard, Beecher, and Lyon were the early nineteenth-century tri-
umvirate of women's education. As a self-supporting woman, Susan
B. Anthony had defended women's right to speak publicly in New
York state teacher's conventions well before her first contact with
abolitionists.[4]

3 See for instance Keith Melder, "Ladies Bountiful: Organized Women's Benevolence in
Early Nineteenth Century America," *New York History*, XLVIII (1967), 231–54; Helen Waite
Papashvily, *All the Happy Endings* (New York: Harper & Brothers, 1956); and Kathryn Kish
Sklar, *Catherine Beecher: A Study in Domesticity* (New Haven: Yale University Press, 1973).
See E. J. Hobsbawm, *Primitive Rebels: Studies in Archaic Forms of Social Movement in the
Nineteenth and Twentieth Centuries* (New York: W. W. Norton and Co., 1965) for a full exposi-
tion of the concept of "prepolitical" activity.

4 Carroll Smith Rosenberg, "Beauty, the Beast and the Militant Woman: A Case Study in
Sex Roles and Social Stress in Jacksonian America," *American Quarterly*, XXIII (1971), 580;
Alice Felt Tyler, "Paulina Kellogg Wright Davis," in Edward T. James, Janet Wilson James, and
Paul S. Boyer (eds.), *Notable American Women*, (3 vols; Cambridge, Mass.: Harvard University
Press, 1971), I, 444–45; Alma Lutz, "Elizabeth Cady Stanton," *Notable American Women*, III,
342–47; Betty L. Fladeland, "Sarah Moore and Angelina Emily Grimké, *Notable American*

In some of these contexts, women were beginning to move from a generalized caste consciousness and sense of discontent to a specific program for altering woman's situation, that is, to activism. A more detailed examination of one such attempt, the moral reform societies of the 1830s and 1840s, can suggest the problems women were meeting in translating their protofeminist consciousness into a genuine feminist movement. Contrasting moral reformers with women abolitionists suggests why the latter were able to execute this transformation successfully and therefore to build the women's rights movement.

In her analysis of the feminism of the New York Female Moral Reform Society, Carroll Smith Rosenberg portrays the society as one manifestation of "a growing self-awareness among middle class American women . . . [and] an ordinarily repressed desire for an expansion of their role." In turn she attributes this widespread female restlessness to the contradiction between the passive, constricted, and static role prescribed for women and a general belief in the possibilities for and desirability of social change in Jacksonian America. Smith Rosenberg finds many aspects of the society's pursuit of moral purity that seem to have gone beyond contemporary notions of female propriety. On the grounds of their traditionally pietistic prerogatives, female moral reformers developed a militant stance on issues explicitly prohibited to women, such as prostitution, the double standard, and male sexual behavior. They resisted male efforts to supersede their work and, in Smith Rosenberg's phrase, claimed moral reform as a "self consciously female" endeavor. They projected a nationwide union of women dedicated to purifying American sexual morals. The activities they undertook in pursuit of their goals went well beyond those permitted in woman's sphere to include visiting brothels, managing the society's finances, editing their own journal, and even lobbying for ten years in the New York legislature in behalf of an antiseduction statute.[5]

Women," II, 97–99; Louis Filler, "Lucy Stone," Notable American Women, III, 387–90; Alma Lutz, "Susan Brownell Anthony," Notable American Women, I, 51–57.

5 Carroll Smith Rosenberg, Religion and the Rise of the American City: The New York City Mission Movement 1812–1870 (Ithaca: Cornell University Press, 1971), 118; Smith Rosenberg, "Beauty, the Beast and the Militant Woman," 562–84.

Yet the Female Moral Reform Society did not continue to develop a feminist program, and evolved instead in the direction of a charity organization. Most of the protofeminist militance which so impresses Smith Rosenberg had disappeared by 1840. The reasons for this are complex, but an episode early in the society's history permits the identification of two of the major obstacles to the development of feminism within the reform society. In 1838, the society's journal printed an article by Sarah Grimké, then at the height of her notoriety as the first woman in the abolitionist movement to become a public lecturer and agitator. While Smith Rosenberg interprets this episode as evidence of the moral reform society's sympathy with women's rights, it also indicates important differences between the protofeminism of moral reformers and that of female abolitionists. The journal's readership found Grimké far too radical for their tastes. They seem to have objected, first to her disregard for woman's proper sphere, and second to her anticlericalism. Moral reformers castigated men for usurping women's power, but limited their attack to "male tyranny in the HOME department."[6] Grimké's call for women to reject the limitations of home and family and pursue their rights and duties outside the domestic sphere greatly disturbed them. Moreover, they objected to her explicit attack on "priestcraft." Like her, their sense of religious vocation had carried them out of passivity and into new realms of thought and action, but unlike her, they could not distinguish between religion and religious institutions, between their own vocation and the authority of ministers and the church. Grimké's identification of the priesthood as a source of moral corruption and her charge to women to reinterpret the Bible for themselves was her most specific affront to moral reformers' sensibilities.

By contrast with the moral reform movement, Garrisonian abolitionism provided women with a political framework that assisted the development of a feminist movement. As Garrisonians, women learned a way to view the world and a theory and practice of social change that they found most useful in elaborating their pro-

---

6 Smith Rosenberg, *Religion and the Rise of the American City,* 116 and *passim;* Smith Rosenberg, "Beauty, the Beast and the Militant Woman," 580–84.

tofeminist insights. In addition, the antislavery movement provided them with a constituency and a political alliance on which they were able to rely until the Civil War. Thus, American feminism developed within the context of abolitionism less because abolitionists taught women that they were oppressed than because abolitionists taught women what to do with that perception, how to develop it into a social movement.

Two aspects of the way that Garrisonians approached social reality were particularly important to the development of nineteenth-century American feminism: the ability to perceive and analyze entire institutions; and the assumption of absolute human equality as a first principle of morality and politics. Both habits of mind, though seemingly abstract, were derived from the concrete task facing abolitionists, to make slavery a burning issue for northern whites. The women who built the women's rights movement borrowed these approaches and found them eminently useful in overcoming obstacles that had stopped other protofeminists. The habit of institutional analysis permitted Garrisonian women to escape the control of the clergy and move beyond pietistic activism. The principle of absolute human equality freed them from the necessity of justifying all their duties in terms of woman's sphere.

Stanley Elkins has argued that the "anti-institutionalism" of Garrisonians was their basic political weakness. While it is true that Garrisonians refused to act through institutions, it is certainly not true that they were blind to them. On the contrary, Garrisonians broke new ground for the antislavery movement by analyzing and moving to attack at least two basic institutions—organized religion and the institution of slavery itself. Unlike many other antislavery people, Garrisonians' indictment of slavery did not rest on specific incidents of cruel treatment, and therefore could not be refuted by evidence that many masters were kind and generous to their slaves. Instead, Garrisonians located evil in the institutional arrangements of chattel slavery, which permitted even one case of brutality. Garrisonians criticized the institution of slavery, not the behavior of individuals within it. Similarly, Garrisonians grasped the fact that the churches were human institutions, therefore subject to human criticism.[7] Their ability to comprehend religious institutions and to distinguish them from their own profoundly religious impulses was an impressive achievement for evangelicals in an evangelical age.

The abolitionist women who built the women's rights movement profited from this ability to criticize entire institutions, most specifically from the militant anticlericalism of Garrisonians. This can best be seen in the 1837 conflict between the Grimké sisters and the Congregational clergy of Massachusetts. Like women in moral reform and other pious activisms, the Grimkés had been led by their religious vocation to step outside woman's sphere. At that point, like other benevolent women, they were confronted by clerical authority and ordered to return to more womanly pursuits. Yet the fact that they were Garrisonians enabled them to hold fast to their religious convictions, ignore clerical criticism, and instead indict the churches themselves for being institutional bulwarks of slavery and women's oppression.[8] In the face of the clerical authority that had long restrained women's impulses for a larger life, the Grimkés continued to pursue their feminist inclinations and to lay the groundwork for the women's rights movement a decade later. The Grimkés' successors also relied on the anticlericalism that they had learned as abolitionists. Elizabeth Stanton had wrestled with religious dogma throughout her adolescence and early adulthood, but credited Garrison with her ultimate spiritual liberation.

In the darkness and gloom of a false theology, I was slowly sawing off the chains of my spiritual bondage, when, for the first time, I met Garrison in London. A few bold strokes from the hammer of his truth, I was free! Only those who have lived all their lives under the dark clouds of vague, undefined fears can appreciate the joy of a doubting soul suddenly born into the kingdom of reason and free thought. Is the bondage of the priest-ridden less galling than that of the slave, because we do not see the chains, the

---

7 Stanley Elkins, *Slavery* (Chicago: University of Chicago Press, 1959); Aileen S. Kraditor, *Means and Ends in American Abolitionism: Garrison and His Critics on Strategy and Tactics* (New York: Pantheon Books, 1967), 20, Chap. IV.

8 "Pastoral Letter of the Massachusetts Congregational Clergy," in Aileen S. Kraditor (ed.), *Up From the Pedestal: Selected Writings in the History of American Feminism* (Chicago: Quadrangle Books, 1968), 50–52; see Sarah Grimké's response to the Pastoral Letter in *Letters on the Equality of the Sexes and the Condition of Woman: Addressed to Mary S. Parker* (Boston: Isaac Knapp, 1837), 16–17.

indelible scars, the festering wounds, the deep degradation of all the powers of the God-like mind?[9]

Almost until the Civil War, conflict with clerical authority was the most important issue in the women's rights movement. The 1854 National Women's Rights Convention resolved: "We feel it a duty to declare in regard to the sacred cause which has brought us together, that the most determined opposition it encounters is from the clergy generally, whose teachings of the Bible are intensely inimical to the equality of woman with man." With increasing defensiveness, representatives of the clergy pursued their fleeting authority onto the very platform of the women's rights movement. However, Garrisonian women had learned the techniques of biblical exegesis and absolute faith in their own interpretations in numerous debates over the biblical basis of slavery. They met the clergy on their own ground, skillfully refuting them quote for quote. "[T]he pulpit has been prostituted, the Bible has been ill-used," Lucretia Mott said during an argument with the Reverend Henry Grew at the 1854 National Women's Rights Convention. "It has been turned over and over in every reform. The temperance people have had to feel its supposed denunciations. Then the anti-slavery, and now this reform has met, and still continues to meet, passage after passage of the Bible, never intended to be so used."[10] When ministers with national reputations started to offer their support to the women's rights movement in the late 1850s, the issue of clerical authority began to recede in importance. It was not a major aspect of postwar feminism, both because of changes in the movement and changes in the clergy.

The principle of absolute human equality was the other basic philosophical premise that American feminism borrowed from Garrisonian abolitionism. Because the abolitionists' target was northern racial prejudice and their goal the development of white empathy for the suffering of the slave, the core of their argument was the essential unity of whites with blacks. Although many Garrisonians be-

---

9 Elizabeth Cady Stanton, "Speech to the 1860 Anniversary of the American Anti-Slavery Society," in Elizabeth Cady Stanton Papers, Manuscript Division, Library of Congress.
10 Stanton, Anthony, and Gage (eds.), *History of Woman Suffrage*, I, 380, 383.

lieved in biological differences between the races, their politics ignored physical, cultural, and historical characteristics that might
distinguish blacks from whites. They stressed instead the common
humanity and the moral identity of the races. They expressed this
approach as a moral abstraction, a first principle, but its basis was
the very concrete demands of the agitational task they faced.[11]

Garrisonian feminists appropriated this belief and applied it
to women. The philosophical tenet that women were essentially
human and only incidentally female liberated them from the sexual
ideology that had constrained their predecessors in other reform
movements, who had felt it necessary to justify their actions as appropriate to woman's sphere. Abolitionist women did not. Although
they continued to believe in the existence of such a sphere, its demands were secondary to those of the common humanity that
united women and men, blacks and whites.

As with the issue of clerical authority, this lack of concern for
woman's sphere characterized the first episode in abolitionist feminism, the Grimkés' 1837 answer to the pastoral letter. In response
to the Congregational clergy's demand that she return to "the appropriate duties and influence of women," Sarah Grimké wrote:

The Lord Jesus defines the duties of his followers in his Sermon on the
Mount. He lays down grand principles by which they should be governed,
without any reference to sex or condition. . . . I follow him through all his
precepts and find him giving the same direction to women as to man, never
even referring to the distinction now so strenuously insisted upon between
masculine and feminine virtues. . . . Men and women are CREATED EQUAL!
They are both moral and accountable beings, and whatever is *right* for man
to do, is *right* for woman.[12]

The prewar women's rights movement continued to be distinguished from other movements for the improvement of women's
status by its refusal to be sidetracked into the consideration of what
was appropriate to woman's sphere. At the fifth national convention, Lucy Stone rejected the notion that the women's rights movement was a matter "of sphere." "Too much has already been said and
written about woman's sphere," she contended. "Trace all the doc-

11 Kraditor, *Means and Ends, passim,* especially p. 59.
12 Grimké, *Letters on the Equality of the Sexes,* 16.

trines to their source and they will be found to have no basis except in the usages and prejudices of the age. . . . Leave woman, then, to find her own sphere." Similarly, the 1851 convention resolved that "we deny the right of any portion of the species to define for another portion . . . what is and what is not their 'proper sphere'; that the proper sphere for all human beings is the largest and highest to which they are able to attain." The approach of Garrisonian women to the ideology of sexual spheres appears all the more remarkable in light of the facts that the three decades before the Civil War were precisely the years in which that ideology was being elaborated, and that benevolent women played an important part in its elaboration.[13]

As Aileen Kraditor has demonstrated, the Garrisonians' focus on "empathy" had important political limitations, both tactical and analytical. By stressing the moral identity and human equality of blacks and whites, Garrisonians were unable to explain why blacks were regarded and treated so differently from whites. Similarly, the women's rights belief in the moral irrelevance of sexual spheres ignored the reality of women's domestic confinement, which distinguished them from men, structured their relative powerlessness, and gave credence to the doctrine of spheres. Indeed, Garrisonian women ignored the question of woman's sphere while simultaneously believing in its existence. They accepted the particular suitability of women to domestic activities and did not project a reorganization of the division of labor within the home. Like women outside the antislavery movement, they believed that domestic activities were as "naturally" female as childbearing, and as little subject to deliberate social manipulation. This contradiction between the belief in woman's sphere and in its moral irrelevance remained unexamined in the prewar women's rights movement. A convention in Ohio in 1852 simultaneously resolved that "since every human being has an individual sphere, and that is the largest he or she can fill, no one has the right to determine the proper sphere of another," and that "in demanding for women equality of rights with their

13 Stanton, Anthony, and Gage (eds.), *History of Woman Suffrage*, I, 165, 826; Barbara Welter, "The Cult of True Womanhood: 1820–1860," *American Quarterly*, XVIII (1966), 151–74.

fathers, husbands, brothers and sons, we neither deny that distinctive character, nor wish them to avoid any duty, or to lay aside that feminine delicacy which legitimately belongs to them as mothers, wives, sisters and daughters." [14] During this early period in the development of an American feminism, the Garrisonian emphasis on the ultimate moral identity of women with men helped the women's rights movement to establish sexual equality as the definition of women's emancipation. The work of examining sexual *in*equality, its origins and the mechanisms that preserved it, remained for the future.

In addition to this philosophical basis, Garrisonianism provided the women's rights movement with a theory of social change, a strategy that gave coherence and direction to efforts for the emancipation of women. Garrisonians began from the premise that fundamental social change required a change in people's ideas as well as in legal and institutional arrangements. "Great political changes may be forced by the pressure of external circumstances, without a corresponding change in the moral sentiment of a nation," Lydia Maria Child wrote in 1842, "but in all such cases, the change is worse than useless; the evil reappears, and usually in a more exaggerated form." In *Means and Ends in American Abolitionism,* Kraditor has reconstructed the way that Garrisonians simultaneously worked for institutional and ideological change. Their demand for immediate, unconditional abolition was both a concrete reform program and the means to launch an ideological attack on white racism. The Garrisonian scenario called for a long-term educational program, in which the constant exposition of the demand for abolition by a well-trained cadre would bring public opinion up to the high principle of racial equality. Thus, the ultimate achievement of abolition would bring, not only a formal adjustment in the legal status of blacks, but a revolution in the racial consciousness of whites as well. While not providing for the political mechanisms by which abolition could be achieved, this strategy was well suited to the early years of the antislavery movement, when its primary problem

14 Kraditor, *Means and Ends,* 243–44; Stanton, Anthony, and Gage (eds.), *History of Woman Suffrage,* I, 817.

was overcoming political and public indifference.[15] It proved useful for feminists when they faced the same task.

None of the early women's rights leaders held to the Garrisonian program for change more firmly than Elizabeth Stanton. Throughout her long political career, she frequently took the position that anything that focused public attention on women's oppression, anything that *agitated* the issue, was desirable. She wrote in her diary in 1888, "If I were to draw up a set of rules for the guidance of reformers ... I should put at the head of the list: Do all you can, *no matter what*, to get people to think on your reform, and then, if the reform is good, it will come about in due season." Stanton made no distinction between agitation that generated public sympathy and agitation that generated public antipathy. Either was preferable to the apathy that particularly characterized popular opinion on the woman question in the 1840s and 1850s. Only by heightening the level of intellectual attention to women's oppression, and therefore only by ideological attack, was enduring reform in women's position possible. Stanton understood that other reformers must be ready to translate agitation into concrete reform, but she did not believe that this was her function, nor perhaps the function of the women's rights movement. "I am a leader in thought," she wrote late in her life, when her methods were alien to young feminists, "rather than numbers."[16]

Just as antislavery agitators used the demand for immediate abolition to stimulate change in the racial beliefs of northern whites, Garrisonians in the women's rights movement used the demand for women's suffrage to launch their own ideological campaign. The demand for suffrage served two functions; it was a concrete reform in women's legal status and a way to educate public opinion in the principle of the equal humanity of the sexes. This was possible because, like unconditional abolition, women's suffrage was regarded as an extreme demand, far beyond the willingness of legislators to

15 Lydia Maria Child, "Dissolution of the Union," *Liberator*, May 20, 1842, as quoted in Kraditor, *Means and Ends*, 23; Kraditor, *Means and Ends*, Chap. II.

16 Theodore Stanton and Harriot Stanton Blatch (eds.), *Elizabeth Cady Stanton as Revealed in Her Letters, Diary and Reminiscences* (New York: Harper, 1920), 252; Elizabeth Stanton to Olympia Brown, May 8, 1888, in Olympia Brown Willis Collection, Schlesinger Library, Radcliffe College.

enact. While many politicians, journalists, social commentators, and influential women outside the movement supported demands for equal property and wage-earning rights and rejected women's suffrage, no one supported women's suffrage and not other equal rights. Women's suffrage was regarded, inside and outside the women's rights movement, as the ultimate legislative demand.

The theory of social change borrowed from Garrisonian antislavery affected the organizational shape of the women's rights movement in the prewar period. Activists saw their primary task as agitating public sentiment on the woman question. Ernestine Rose described it as "breaking up the ground and sowing the seed." Thus, they were not particularly concerned with the deliberate recruitment of new women, with differing levels of commitment to women's rights, into the work. Instead the movement relied on a small group of highly skilled and deeply committed women, willing to shoulder the opprobrium of "strong-mindedness." Nor did those activists feel the need for much coordination of their own agitational efforts. They spread the women's rights faith largely as individuals who undertook canvassing or lecture tours on their own hook. Petition and lobbying campaigns were highly individualistic matters, dependent upon uncoordinated bursts of personal initiative.[17]

The organizational requirements for this kind of political work were minimal. As Kraditor has described it, the Garrisonian concept of a reform organization was a limited one, primarily directed towards providing resources for propagandizing and agitation. Before the Civil War, the women's rights movement had no national or state bodies to guide it. Instead, an informal and constantly changing coordinating committee planned the annual conventions. This process was so spontaneous that in the second half of the 1850s, when several national leaders were simultaneously incapacitated by childbarg, the annual convention was barely arranged in time, and, in 1857, bypassed altogether. These yearly women's rights meetings were oriented to the needs of activists. They concentrated on exchanging information, sharpening rhetorical tools, and revitalizing

---

17 Stanton, Anthony, and Gage (eds.), *History of Woman Suffrage*, I, 693; see for example Clarina Nichols's lobbying activities, *ibid.*, 172–74.

dedication. The 1852 national convention discussed and rejected a proposal for tighter coordination and the formation of a national women's rights society. Only Clarina Nichols spoke in support of the motion. Angelina Grimké Weld, Elizabeth Oakes Smith, Harriot Hunt, Ernestine Rose, Paulina Wright Davis, and Lucy Stone opposed it, agreeing that formal societies "fetter and distort the expanding mind." All looked with suspicion on any arrangement that placed limits on the individual's prerogatives and activity. Lucy Stone "had had enough of thumb-screws and soul screws ever to wish to be placed under them again." "The present duty is agitation," she concluded.[18]

Formal organization was further impeded by the existence of the American Anti-Slavery Society and its ability to bestow political coherence on the women's rights movement. Articles were printed in antislavery newspapers and tracts were published with antislavery funds. Several of the most effective agitators were paid antislavery agents and spread the women's rights faith as they traveled and lectured on behalf of immediate abolition.[19] Perhaps most important, the women's rights movement relied on the antislavery community for its constituency. The First National Women's Rights Convention was called by antislavery women at an antislavery meeting.[20] Activists expected and got a favorable hearing from Garrisonian abolitionists. The majority of women who joined the women's rights ranks were abolitionists. They had already received a political education. Moreover, their antislavery activity put them outside the pale of respectable womanhood.[21] Already branded as abolitionist extremists, they were not frightened by public hostility or press indictments of long-haired men and short-haired women. They provided the women's rights movement with an audience

18 Kraditor, Means and Ends, 165; Eleanor Flexner, Century of Struggle: The Woman's Rights Movement in the United States (Cambridge, Mass: Harvard University Press, 1959), 82; Ida Husted Harper, The Life and Work of Susan B. Anthony (2 vols.; Indianapolis and Kansas City: The Bowen-Merrill Company, 1898), I, 171; Stanton, Anthony and Gage (eds.), History of Woman Suffrage, I, 540–42.

19 Both Lucy Stone and Susan B. Anthony were paid agents of the Anti-Slavery Society in the 1850s.

20 Stanton, Anthony, and Gage (eds.), History of Woman Suffrage, I, 216.

21 Perhaps the best example of this was Lydia Maria Child, whose abolitionist activities led her to abandon a successful career as a genteel authoress. See Louis Filler, "Lydia Maria Child," in James, James, and Boyer (eds.), Notable American Women, I, 330–33.

well-suited to the conflict and controversy which its politics invited.

Although primarily a source of strength, the relationship of the women's rights movement to antislavery was also a potential liability. Because of the many resources which abolitionism provided them, women's rights leaders were very dependent on the willingness of the antislavery movement to support and encourage their efforts. Moreover, the partnership between the two reforms was an unequal one, and occasionally women's rights suffered because of its subordinate status. Finally, the availability of a ready-made constituency of antislavery women kept women's rights leaders from learning how to reach the many women who were not active reformers. The fearlessness of female abolitionists protected the women's rights movement from a confrontation with the very real fears of family opposition and public disapproval that lay between it and the majority of women.

The basic precepts, strategic methods, and organizational forms of Garrisonian abolitionism sustained the women's rights movement through its first dozen years. On this basis, women's rights leaders were able to transform insights into the oppression of women which they shared with many of their female contemporaries into a social movement strong enough to have a future. Their self-definition as ultraists helped them to endure and overcome hostility and ridicule. By 1860, they had succeeded in commanding a modicum of political respect, establishing the woman question as a serious political issue, and winning important legislative victories. These achievements, due in large measure to their Garrisonian inheritance, created the conditions for the women's rights movement to assume a new set of political tasks, and therefore to move beyond Garrisonianism to a politics of their own making.

# "AM I NOT A WOMAN AND A SISTER?"
## Abolitionist Beginnings of Nineteenth-Century Feminism[1]

*Blanche Glassman Hersh*

NINETEENTH-CENTURY feminists talked of "the slavery of sex" in describing married women's legal subservience to their husbands and, in a broader sense, the imprisonment of all women within the traditional concept of woman's proper sphere. This phrase had a double connotation: it suggested not only the parallel position of woman and slave, a principal theme of nineteenth-century feminist rhetoric, but also the close historical link between abolitionism and feminism. All the women who were the first to speak out and to organize for woman's rights were abolitionists, as were the men who supported them. Feminism grew naturally out of antislavery because the abolitionists' argument for human rights transcended both sex and color, and because the obstacles that women faced made their efforts to work against slavery a feminist consciousness-raising experience.

The actions of the early antislavery women in defending their right to speak out against slavery became the bridge between abolitionism and feminism. Motivated by the same moral indignation as

1 This essay is adapted from Blanche Glassman Hersh, *The Slavery of Sex: Feminists-Abolitionists in America* (Urbana: University of Illinois Press, 1978).

men, they found themselves outside of woman's traditional sphere and faced with cries of "unsexed women." Though their primary commitment was to abolish slavery, they moved surely and inevitably to the realization that the enslavement of human beings took many forms. As deeply religious people, they felt that it was divine will that placed them in a position to fight for the emancipation of women as well as slaves, and they responded to what they considered a sacred obligation. The controversy which resulted from this stand divided the antislavery movement and produced the first public discussion of woman's rights. Their efforts to gain support from other antislavery women was essentially a "pre-movement" which led directly to the first attempts to organize women in defense of their rights in the 1840s and 1850s. The arguments they used to defend their unpopular position as public antislavery agents became the basis for a feminist ideology.

The early abolitionist women were also prototypes for the first generation of feminists. Like the feminist-abolitionists who became leaders of the woman's movement—Susan B. Anthony, Elizabeth Cady Stanton, Lucy Stone, and others—they were united by similar cultural origins, a common world view, and parallel life patterns. These shared characteristics define them as a special group and help to explain why feminism developed as it did and why certain women became feminists. All were products of a New England heritage that shaped their consciousness of class and sense of self; their world view embraced both a Puritan conception of duty and sense of life as a battle with evil, and a nationalistic pride in their Yankee roots blended with a strong belief in the ideals of the Christian Republic. Their sense of heritage gave them an aura of righteousness and superiority but also contributed to feelings of security and self-confidence which enabled them to survive in the face of hostility and disapproval.

Growing up as gifted and strong-willed young women in a period of great optimism and social change, they faced both frustration and opportunity. The Puritan belief that men and women are born into the world for a purpose had special meaning for this new class of urban, middle-class women who were becoming increasingly freed by industrialization from many of women's former burdens but

faced also with a loss of usefulness. The religious impulse was an
important part of their lives from an early age and impelled them
into reform work—eventually reform would become their religion.
Caught up in the religious fervor of the period, they retained the
evangelical zeal of Calvinism but rejected orthodox dogma which
they saw as intolerably narrow and binding on the spirits of all
people, but especially women. They developed an eclectic, nondoc-
trinal faith strongly influenced by Quakerism as well as the liberal,
rationalist religions of the day. They were driven by a romantic perfectionism which aimed at no less than the emancipation of the entire human family and the regeneration of the world. Unlike other
radical reformers who shared these goals, they brought to each
crusade a feminist perception of woman's peculiar obstacles as well
as her special needs and her equal moral obligations.

By venturing into the male domain of antislavery work, the
feminist-abolitionist women also became the cutting edge for the
creation of new social roles for women. In defending woman's
domestic role but demanding that she have equal access to a broader
sphere, they foreshadowed the basic tone of nineteenth-century
feminism. By expanding their own spheres to include the dual roles
of wife-mother and reformer, they provided models for other women
eager to free themselves from old patterns in order to exert an
influence on the world about them. By marrying men who were also
feminist-abolitionists and willing to apply the doctrine of human
rights to their own unions, they became partners in relatively egalitarian marriages that afforded them the freedom to pursue their
goals. Though not completely resolving the female dilemma of balancing family and work outside the home, they suggested important
patterns and possibilities for the future. By modifying their society's
definition of woman's sphere in important ways, they set the example for a new type of woman who was both a private and a public
person.

II

Though the "woman question" did not burst into public view until
William Lloyd Garrison launched his radical crusade for immediate
emancipation in the 1830s, there were intimations of the issue in an

earlier period. They appeared in the writings of Elizabeth Chandler, a little-known reformer whose extraordinary career was cut short by her early death. A serious and scholarly writer, she was raised in Philadelphia by her Quaker grandmother and began her antislavery work in 1826 at nineteen by sending contributions to Benjamin Lundy's weekly, *The Genius of Universal Emancipation.* Lundy was so impressed with her ability that he placed her in charge of the "Ladies Repository" section of the paper when she was only twenty-two.[2]

Though Chandler migrated with a Quaker group to Michigan territory in 1830, she continued her work with Lundy and also contributed to Garrison's newly founded *Liberator.* After her death in 1834 she was hailed as the foremost female worker for the cause, and revered as a saint by abolitionists who made pilgrimages to her grave. Her poems were sung as hymns at meetings of female antislavery societies and quoted by antislavery lecturers, especially this stanza:

> Shall we behold, unheeding
> Life's holiest feelings crushed;
> When woman's heart is bleeding
> Shall woman's voice be hushed?[3]

Elizabeth Chandler was taking on a daring role for a woman, but her Quaker upbringing had provided her with a special kind of preparation, as it would for many women reformers. Quakers were accustomed to seeing women preach in meeting and play an active role in the home; they were taught that, spiritually at least, women were the equals of men. They were also spared the need to rebel, as so many women would, against a fundamentalist interpretation of the Scriptures which would be used to oppose abolitionism as well as feminism. The Quaker concept of "inner light," making the individual the center of moral authority rather than the church, would

2 See *The Poetical Works of Elizabeth Margaret Chandler, with a Memoir of Her Life and Character by Benjamin Lundy* (Philadelphia: L. Howell, 1836), hereinafter cited as Chandler, *Poetical Works;* see also passages of Lawrence J. Friedman, *Inventors of the Promised Land* (New York: Alfred A. Knopf, 1975).

3 Chandler, *Poetical Works,* 64; for treatment by abolitionists, see *Liberator,* February 13, 1852, and John W. Chadwick (ed.), *A Life for Liberty: Antislavery and Other Letters of Sallie Holley* (New York: G. P. Putnam's Sons, 1899), 93.

enable the feminist-abolitionists to "come out" of the church and
rely on the force of their individual consciences. Finally, the Quaker
meetinghouse was an important training ground for abolitionists
and feminists because it gave its members the experience from an
early age of being part of an unpopular minority. All of these elements probably made it easier for Chandler to pursue her unconven-
tional course of action.

Chandler saw her main function as agitator, her goal to arouse
the women of the country to their special moral duty, as women, to
oppose slavery. Though not consciously a feminist, she suggested in
her writings many of the themes that would appear regularly in
the rhetoric of the antebellum woman's movement. She especially
stressed that women, as the more sensitive and sympathetic sex,
were the natural foes of slavery; as women they had a special obligation because members of their own sex were in bondage. Her emphasis on the plight of slave women was a useful rhetorical device,
but it also reflected the belief of all the abolitionists that women
were especially victimized by slavery because of their delicate nature and their vulnerability to sexual abuse.

Chandler became the first of the antislavery women called upon
to defend her right as a woman to speak out against slavery. Shortly
after she became an editor for the *Genius*, she was rebuked by a New
England woman who questioned the propriety of females becoming
public advocates of emancipation, a "man's work." Chandler denied
that she was acting improperly: "To plead for the miserable . . . can
never be unfeminine or unbefitting the delicacy of woman." She was
not advocating emancipation for political (*i.e.*, "male") reasons, she
explained, but because slavery was "an outrage against *humanity*
and *morality* and *religion* . . . and because a great number of *her own
sex* are among its victims." Woman, she continued, was not seeking
to share a political role with man, but only pleading that he "lift the
iron foot of despotism from the neck of her sisterhood." This, she
argued, was "not only quite within the sphere of her privileges, but
also of her positive duties."[4]

4 Chandler, *Poetical Works*, 22–23.

In this defense, she also related the cause of slave women to that of all women: "It is a restitution of *our own* rights for which we ask:—their cause is our cause—they are one with us in sex and nature."[5] Here she came very close to an idea that would be expressed a few years later and become a mainstay of feminist-abolitionist rhetoric: women, like slaves, were in bondage. Even in this earliest antislavery argument there was the unspoken, and perhaps unconscious assumption that slaveholding was a male institution; southern white women were seen as victims, not perpetrators, of the system. Later abolitionist women would make more specific this argument that Chandler only hinted at: both slave and nonslave women suffered from the oppression of dominant males.

Elizabeth Chandler's female critic assailed her with that classic tenet of antifeminism: women are privileged by having their duties confined to the domestic sphere, and ought to be properly grateful. To this Chandler replied: "It is because we highly prize ... the domestic privileges of our sex, that we would have them extended to those who are less fortunate than ourselves." Like all the feminist-abolitionists, Chandler shared the nineteenth-century belief in woman's special moral and domestic attributes and used these very distinctions to justify expanding woman's sphere: antislavery was a natural activity for woman, calling on her tenderness, pity, and devotion to philanthropic causes. At the same time that she defended women's domestic and philanthropic work, Chandler expressed a feminist objection to limiting them to these activities. Woman, she argued, should be free to share equally with man the world of the mind: "She with him shall knowledge's pages scan/ And be the partner not the toy of man."

Unlike the women who followed her, Chandler's vision never extended to men and women sharing power: "It is not hers to guide the storm of war, to rule the state, or thunder at the bar ... these things are not for her."[6] Her voice was nevertheless prophetic, a harbinger of feminist awareness to come.

5 *Ibid.*, 23.
6 *Ibid.*, 24, 177; see also Chandler's essay, "Female Character," in her *Essays, Philanthropic and Moral* (Reprint ed.; Philadelphia: T. E. Chapman, 1845), 50–51.

III

The controversy over the "woman question," only hinted at in Chandler's experience, came to a head in the late 1830s. Although these events have been detailed in antislavery studies, they need to be reexamined here from a new perspective. For abolitionism, the internal dispute over women's role in the movement was a serious, divisive blow. This same controversy, however, sparked an increased feminist consciousness and the beginnings of an important and continuing debate over woman's rights, and also led to an expanded role for women in the radical wing of the movement.

In the early 1830s, women were still content to play a subordinate role in antislavery, but their activities were given new impetus with Garrison's arrival on the scene. One of his goals was to arouse American women to indignation and sympathy for the cause, much as Chandler was trying to do. The early issues of his *Liberator* contained a "Ladies Department" headed by a picture of a kneeling slave woman in chains and the entreaty "Am I Not A Woman And A Sister?" In the text he implored his female readers to take note of the one million enslaved women "exposed to all the violence of lust and passion—and treated with more indelicacy and cruelty than cattle," and urged them to work for immediate emancipation.[7]

Garrison's appeal struck a responsive note in at least a few New England women who became his staunch supporters. The abolitionist cause would change their lives drastically and move them from positions of status and respectability to places among the social outcasts and martyrs of their society. They in turn would, in the next decade, transform the traditional auxiliary role of women in antislavery into a more active, independent force.

Maria Weston Chapman, who became known as "Garrison's chief lieutenant," was a member of Boston's aristocracy. In 1832, she and three of her sisters organized the Boston Female Anti-Slavery Society as an auxiliary to Garrison's newly formed New England Anti-Slavery Society, an all-male group. They were supported in their work by Maria's husband Henry Chapman, a wealthy merchant, and the entire Weston and Chapman families. As the moving

7 *Liberator*, January 7, 1832.

force of the female society, Maria Chapman concentrated initially on fund-raising, which would be the main task of all the women's groups. She organized yearly antislavery fairs, which became models for fairs in other cities, and edited the *Liberty Bell*, a gift book containing articles and poems by well-known abolitionists.

From this relatively conventional start, Maria Chapman moved later to the more "male" role of propagandist and agitator, initiating petition campaigns and publishing the annual report of the society as a propaganda vehicle. Increasingly she took on more of Garrison's job, editing the *Liberator*, for example, when he was busy elsewhere. When the American Anti-Slavery Society was formed in 1833 as a national parent organization, Chapman became, in effect, its general manager. In the next decade she would apply her enormous talent and energy to a wider circle of activities and become an organizer and spokeswoman for many of the radical causes of the day.

Lydia Maria Child in the 1820s was a popular author of romantic novels, editor of the first periodical for children, *Juvenile Miscellany*, and a member of Boston's intellectual and literary circles. Following her marriage to a Garrison disciple, David Lee Child, she became in the 1830s an important propagandist for antislavery. She would recall how Garrison had gotten hold of the strings of her conscience and pulled her into reform: "It is of no use to imagine what might have been if I had never met him. Old dreams vanished, old associates departed, and all things became new." He inspired her to write in 1833 *An Appeal on Behalf of That Class of Americans Called Africans*, the first antislavery work to be published in book form in America, and an influential tract that had a strong impact on such distinguished Boston citizens as Charles Sumner, Wendell Phillips, and William Ellery Channing. Basically a call for immediate emancipation, Child's work was also notable for its condemnation of racial prejudice in the North, an important Garrisonian theme.[8]

The *Appeal* was a turning point in Child's career, antagonizing

---

8 *Letters of Lydia Maria Child, with Biographical Introduction by John G. Whittier and Appendix by Wendell Phillips* (Boston: Houghton, Mifflin & Co., 1883), 255, hereinafter cited as *Child Letters*; for the influence of her *Appeal*, see Bernice G. Lamberton, "A Biography of Lydia Maria Child" (Ph.D. dissertation, University of Maryland, 1953).

Boston's literary circles with its controversial and unwelcome subject, and bringing a sharp halt to her popularity with the general
public. Anticipating this reaction, she had explained in the text that
duty and conscience compelled her to write it, at the risk of displeasing all classes. Her courage in taking this step is especially
noteworthy since, more than any of her contemporaries, Child disliked controversy. She had been warned when she published her first
novel in 1824 that female writers were considered "unsexed," but
chose then not to take issue with her critics. Now, too, she preferred
to stay in the background and let her words speak for her. In spite of
herself, she became a symbol of independent, defiant womanhood.[9]

Though individual women in the early 1830s were challenging
the traditional female role, the issue of woman's rights was still far
from the minds even of abolitionists. The events of the first national
convention in 1833 confirmed this. Male antislavery workers from
New England and New York joined their coworkers in Philadelphia
in December of that year for a three-day meeting at which the
American Anti-Slavery Society was organized. On the second day,
apparently as an afterthought, an invitation was sent to the Philadelphia antislavery women. Lucretia Mott, accompanied by her
mother, her daughter, and two sisters, joined the group of about sixty
men.[10] Mrs. Mott, tiny but with a commanding presence, was a
Quaker minister who, with her husband James Mott, had been involved with antislavery since the 1820s. The other women who attended this first convention left no record, but Lucretia Mott's contribution, at least, was more than nominal. When the crucial first
session of the day was delayed because two prominent men failed to
appear, causing doubt and confusion, Mrs. Mott rallied the group by
reminding them that "right principles are stronger than great
names." She was helpful also in lesser ways. When a "Declaration of
Sentiments and Purposes" was drafted, she suggested it would sound
better if its key sentences were transposed. Later she recalled "one of

9 The warning is described in Child's article "Concerning Women," undated, in Lydia
Maria Child Scrapbook, Child Papers, Cornell University.
10 The invitation to the women is described in Martha Coffin Wright to David Wright,
December 5, 1833, in Wright Family Letters, Sophia Smith Collection, Smith College.

the younger members turning to see what woman there was there who knew what the word 'transpose' meant."[11]

Though Lucretia Mott helped to draft this historic document, it did not occur to her, or to any member of the convention, that the women present should also sign it. Instead they were rewarded with a resolution of thanks "to our female friends, for the deep interest they have manifested in the cause of antislavery." The fact that the women present were not invited to add their signatures, and evidently did not expect to be, reveals the state of feminist consciousness in 1833 even among the more independent and outspoken women. Samuel J. May, Unitarian minister and beloved elder statesman of the feminist-abolitionist group, wrote many years later that his pride in recalling this convention "will be forever associated [with] the mortifying fact, that we *men* were then so blind, so obtuse, that we did not recognize those women as members of our Convention."[12]

Following this convention, the women organized a meeting of female abolitionists, consisting mostly of Friends and both blacks and whites like the parent body, and formed the Philadelphia Female Anti-Slavery Society. Even an experienced speaker like Lucretia Mott hesitated to take on the "male" role of chairing this meeting, and a black male friend was called upon for the job.[13]

Lucretia Coffin Mott was the pivotal person among antislavery women in Philadelphia as Maria Weston Chapman was in Boston, but her role in the development of a woman's movement was even greater. Her stature among the feminist-abolitionists would be unparalleled. An important part of her enormous influence was in moving them from orthodox religious dogma to her special brand of intellectual liberalism, which was built upon Quaker beliefs but extended beyond them.[14] She prided herself on placing fidelity to con-

---

11 From an account by abolitionist J. Miller McKim in Anna Davis Hallowell (ed.), *James and Lucretia Mott: Life and Letters* (Boston: Houghton, Mifflin & Co., 1884), 115.

12 Both quotations are from *The History of Woman Suffrage* (6 vols.; New York: Fowler & Wells, 1881–1922; first 3 vols. ed. Elizabeth Cady Stanton, Susan B. Anthony, and Matilda Joslyn Gage), I, 324.

13 Mott's account is in a talk she gave in 1853, quoted in Otelia Cromwell, *Lucretia Mott* (Cambridge: Harvard University Press, 1958), 131.

14 For her influence on Garrison, see Hallowell, *Mott*, 470, 296–97.

science above external strictures and relied on her favorite motto in speeches and sermons: "truth for authority, not authority for truth." Like Chapman and Child who were Unitarians, she was attracted to the emphasis placed by the liberal religions on human rationality and free will, and preached that intellectual light was a guide to spiritual truth. Like all the feminist-abolitionists, she believed that God revealed himself through natural laws, and it was through knowledge of these rational forces governing the universe that women and men could perfect themselves and their society and do God's will. This optimistic belief in self-improvement through knowledge and reason was especially attractive to women trying to emancipate themselves from orthodox views of woman's sphere.

This was the kind of leadership—women who rejected traditional social roles as well as orthodox religious beliefs—that inspired the small abolitionist circle of women first to organize in their separate groups and later to think about challenging the accepted pattern of segregated societies and male dominance. In the years following the 1833 national meeting, the women busied themselves with circulating petitions, raising funds, and organizing new groups. The movement was expanding in an exciting manner—in 1838, the Massachusetts society alone recorded 183 local chapters including both female and juvenile auxiliaries, the membership of each ranging from less than twenty to more than three hundred.[15] Though abolitionists were still a tiny minority, their success in this period undoubtedly raised the sights of some of the women in the direction of greater participation.

By 1837, there were intimations that abolitionist women were feeling hampered in the auxiliary role assigned to them. Their first attempt at national organization, the Anti-Slavery Convention of American Women, met in May of that year with about one hundred delegates from ten states attending the three-day meeting. Lucretia Mott, in recalling the mood of the group, noted that one of their first resolutions proclaimed that it was time for "woman to act in the sphere which Providence had assigned her, and no longer to rest satisfied with the circumscribed limits in which corrupt custom and

15 *Annual Report of the Massachusetts Anti-Slavery Society, 1838* (Reprint ed.; Westport, Conn.: Negro Universities Press, 1970), VI, Appendix, xxxix.

a perverted application of the Scriptures had encircled her." Mary S. Parker of Boston, president of the convention and sister of Unitarian minister and reformer Theodore Parker, was authorized to send a circular to all female antislavery societies of the country. In it she urged action on current petitions and gave the women some feminist advice. They should follow their own consciences, she said, not the will of their husbands—women could be "very obstinate concerning a gay party, a projected journey, or a new service of china, but when great *principles* were at stake, they very promptly sacrificed them to earn the reputation of meek and submissive wives." [16]

The question of woman's proper role in the antislavery movement was finally raised publicly later in 1837. The woman's rights issue was never quiescent thereafter. The central figures in the first stage of the controversy were Angelina and Sarah Grimké. Reared in an aristocratic, slaveholding South Carolina family (they would remain anomalies in the New England-dominated movement), they had moved to Philadelphia in the 1820s. Looking for something that would give their lives meaning, they found this sense of purpose first in Quakerism and, more lastingly, in antislavery work.

Like all abolitionists, the Grimkés felt they were doing God's work in battling slavery. This sense of divine mission would enable them to endure the public censure and private criticism heaped on them. Angelina especially exhibited a self-assurance that came from feeling "called" to the work of reform. Responding only to the demands of an inner voice, she seemed naturally endowed with the kind of protective shield that other reformers worked hard to acquire. She had displayed an awesome sense of duty at an early age—a sister recalled her single-minded "devotion to an idea" as a girl. As a young woman of twenty-three, preparing to leave South Carolina, she wrote in her diary: "I feel that I am called with a high and heavy calling, and that I ought to be peculiar, and cannot be too zealous." [17]

16 Lucretia Mott to Nathaniel Barney, October 8, 1842, in Hallowell, *Mott*, 233; Circular to the Societies of Anti-Slavery Women in the United States from the Anti-Slavery Convention of American Women, 1837, in Weston Papers, Antislavery Collection, Boston Public Library.

17 The sisters' recollection is in *Woman's Journal*, August 7, 1880; the 1828 diary entry is in Gerda Lerner, *The Grimké Sisters from South Carolina* (New York: Schocken Books, 1971), 74.

In 1836, Angelina Grimké came to public attention by writing *An Appeal to the Christian Women of the South* in which she urged her southern sisters to use their influence with husbands and brothers to act against slavery. In explaining her bold action she wrote: "God has shown me what I can do ... to speak to them in such tones that they *must* hear me, and through me, the voice of justice and humanity." [18] She followed this *Appeal* with an eloquent address to the convention of antislavery women in 1837, challenging the "Women of the Nominally Free States" to break their own bonds to aid those of their sex in slavery. Published as a pamphlet by the convention, it served to enhance the reputation of both sisters among the abolitionists. Following this convention, they were invited to address the Boston Female Anti-Slavery Society. They were especially desirable as speakers because of their unique experience with slavery. They went on from there to speak to other women's groups in the area. Prim and plain in their Quaker bonnets, they impressed their audiences with their intense devotion to their cause. In addition, Angelina was becoming known as an eloquent orator. For all of these reasons, they attracted large numbers of men as well as women to their lectures. Churches and meeting halls were filled to overflowing. They found themselves addressing mixed audiences, a situation which even abolitionist women had not faced before. Even staunch antislavery people had doubts about the wisdom of defying convention to this extreme.[19]

The Grimkés' speaking tour, which lasted about six months and included over sixty New England towns, was successful in gaining attention for the cause. It also brought down upon them the wrath of the orthodox clergy of Massachusetts. The General Association of Congregationalist Ministers issued an edict to all its member churches, in effect condemning the Grimkés—without specifically mentioning them—for the unfeminine act of addressing "promiscuous" or mixed audiences.

18 Catherine H. Birney, *The Grimké Sisters, Sarah and Angelina Grimké* (Reprint ed.; Westport, Conn.: Greenwood Press, 1969), 138.
19 See Samuel J. May, *Some Recollections of Our Antislavery Conflict* (Boston: Fields, Osgood, & Co., 1869), 234–35.

The pastoral letter attacking the Grimkés triggered the first extended public controversy over woman's rights because it spoke directly to the question of her proper sphere, an issue that would dominate the nineteenth-century movement. Its language clearly revealed the boundaries of acceptable female behavior in 1837. Citing the New Testament as its authority, the letter emphasized that woman's power lay in her dependence. Likening her to a vine "whose strength and beauty is to lean upon the trellis-work," it warned that the vine which "thinks to assume the independence and the over-shadowing nature of the elm" would not only cease to bear fruit, but "fall in shame and dishonor into the dust." The character of the woman who "assumes the place and tone of man as a public reformer . . . becomes unnatural."[20]

This was a harsh public attack on the Grimkés and a warning to other women who might dare to venture outside their prescribed sphere. Against this the sisters could rely on their own piety, an important weapon in the battle as well as a source of strength for them personally. Frances Wright, Scottish radical reformer, had lectured on woman's rights in 1828–1829 but, as a "notorious" advocate of free love, she was not taken seriously. The Grimkés were so obviously pious and respectable that their defiance of social custom forced many people to rethink the question of woman's proper sphere.

Their own state of mind is revealed in the large correspondence the Grimkés carried on during the ensuing controversy, each letter closing with "Thy sister in the bonds of woman and the slave." To Henry C. Wright, their most loyal supporter, Sarah wrote that Angelina was troubled about the clerical uproar, "but the Lord knows that we did not come to forward our own interests but in simple obedience to his commands." In another letter she reiterated their determination to resist intimidation: "If in calling us thus publicly to advocate the cause of the downtrodden slave, God has unexpectedly placed us in the forefront of the battle which is to be

20 Maria Weston Chapman, *Right and Wrong in Boston* (Boston: Annual Report of Boston Female Anti-Slavery Society, 1837), 46–47; *History of Woman Suffrage*, I, 81–82.

waged against the rights and duties and responsibilities of woman, it would ill become us to shrink from such a contest."[21]

Though it was their critics who initiated the controversy, the abolitionist women were not entirely unprepared for it. At the start of their New England tour the Grimkés had spent a social evening at the Chapman home and discussed their situation with "the brethren." Angelina's comments on this meeting are significant: "I had a long talk with the brethren on the rights of women, and found a very general sentiment prevailing that it is time our fetters were broken. L. M. Child and Maria Chapman strongly supported this view; indeed, very many seem to think a new order of things is very desirable in this respect. . . . I feel it is not only the cause of the slave we plead but the cause of woman as a moral, responsible being."[22] The most immediate issue for the women was the right to continue their public antislavery work. The question of women's equal participation with men in the work of the American Anti-Slavery Society was not made explicit at this point but would emerge naturally from the initial debate. Other basic grievances were also brought to mind by the controversy: the denial of legal rights to married women, the lack of opportunity for higher education and dignified employment, and a host of other inequalities and indignities that burdened women. The cause of the slave would open a Pandora's box of grievances and demands.

Many of the abolitionist women were not ready for the Grimkés' "new order of things." They felt comfortable in their separate female auxiliaries and useful in their work of gathering petitions and holding fund-raising affairs. Sharing the prevalent view of woman's sphere, they were content to allow their men to represent them in public and make the decisions for the national organization. Although radical in their defense of the slave, they had not made the connection, as the Grimkés had, between the rights of the slave and the rights of woman. The controversy over the sisters' public speaking forced them to become involved in this "woman question."

Anne Warren Weston, sister of Maria Weston Chapman, was one

21 Sarah Grimké to H. C. Wright, August 27, 1837, in Garrison Papers; Sarah Grimké to Amos A. Phelps, August 3, 1837, in Phelps Papers, Boston Public Library.
22 Birney, *Grimké Sisters*, 178.

of those who attempted to gain support for the Grimkés' right to speak. Addressing the Boston Female Anti-Slavery Society, she used many of the principal arguments of the feminist-abolitionist cause. The very theologians who had used the Scriptures to justify slavery, she reminded her audience, were now "perverting the same sainted oracles" to sanction woman's inferiority and subordination. "Will you," she demanded, "allow those men who have been for years unmindful of their own most solemn duties to prescribe you yours?" Those who considered women as goods and chattels, she continued, were not fit judges of the sphere woman should occupy; they had not objected that the slave woman in the rice fields was "out of her sphere," nor the southern woman who held her fellow creature as property. It was the Grimkés working for the slave, she concluded, who were "in the very sphere to which God has appointed every Christian."[23]

The Grimkés stood firm in their defense, claiming the same moral right and duty as men to oppose slavery. They were clearly sensitive to the broader implications of the controversy and made a conscious decision to speak for all women, calling on the broad doctrine of human rights, rather than merely claiming rights for themselves. At stake was not merely the right of women to an equal role in antislavery but to an equal position in all areas of society. They were defending not only their right to speak publicly but the right of all women to be as free as men to develop their talents and to enjoy lives of usefulness, respect, and independence. The arguments they had used to defend slave women would merge easily and logically with their own defense to become an ideology espousing equality for all women.

This high degree of feminist consciousness was revealed in their correspondence in this period. "The whole land seems aroused to discussion on the province of woman," Angelina noted defiantly in 1837, "and I am glad of it. We are willing to bear the brunt of the storm, if we can only be the means of making a break in that wall of public opinion which lies right in the way of woman's rights, true

23 Anne Warren Weston Address to Boston Female Anti-Slavery Society, August 21, 1837, in Weston Papers.

dignity, honor and usefulness." She had a strong sense of the importance of their role and understood that the question, once raised, could not be suppressed. To Anne Warren Weston she confided, "It is causing deep searchings of heart and revealing the secrets of the soul." She also displayed a keen insight into the basic nature of the opposition. In a letter written during her speaking tour, she admitted to scolding "most terribly" while lecturing on slavery, and noted that many of the men in the audience "look at me in utter amazement." "I am not at all surprized," she wrote, "they are afraid lest such a woman should usurp authority over the men." Sarah would later reveal a similarly sophisticated understanding of the power struggle between the sexes.[24]

Because Angelina was more in demand as a speaker, Sarah Grimké took on the job of publicly defending their position in a series of "Letters on the Province of Woman" which ran in the *New England Spectator* beginning in July, 1837. They were published the following year as *Letters on the Equality of the Sexes and the Condition of Woman* and became the first serious discussion of woman's rights by an American woman, preceding Margaret Fuller's *Woman in the Nineteenth Century* by seven years.

The publication of these letters caused the sisters difficulty with friends who had not opposed their speaking but feared that a public defense would stir unnecessary controversy and injure the antislavery cause. John Greenleaf Whittier, poet and abolitionist, asked whether their aggressiveness was really necessary: "Is it not forgetting the great and dreadful wrongs of the slave in a selfish crusade against some paltry grievance of our own?" Theodore Weld, their close coworker who was to become Angelina's husband, took their cause more seriously and, in fact, was a solid "woman's rights man." But even he, for purely tactical reasons, opposed "agitating the question" and advised them to go on with their lecturing "without making any ado about 'attacks' and 'invasions' and 'oppositions' ";

---

24 Lerner, *Grimké Sisters*, 183; Angelina Grimké Weld to Anne Warren Weston, July 15, 1838, in Weston Papers; Gilbert H. Barnes and Dwight L. Dumond (eds.), *Letters of Theodore Dwight Weld, Angelina Grimké Weld and Sarah Grimké, 1822–1844* (2 vols.; New York: D. Appleton-Century Co. for the American Historical Association, 1934), I, 417, hereinafter cited as *Weld-Grimké Letters*.

their example alone would be the most convincing argument for woman's rights and duties.[25]

To the sisters, woman's rights was not "a paltry grievance." As Angelina explained in a letter to Whittier and Weld, *"We must establish this right* for if we do not, it will be impossible for *us* to go *on with the work of Emancipation."* She pleaded with them: "Can you not see that woman *could* do, and *would* do a hundred times more for the slave if she were not fettered?" To the charge that the time was not right, she wrote to Weld: "I think this must be the Lord's time and therefore the *best* time, for it seems to have been brought about by a concatenation of circumstances over which we had no control." After much debate, a compromise was effected: Sarah's letters were continued in the press but the subject was not discussed in their talks and Angelina gave up her idea of a series of lectures on woman's rights.[26]

In her *Letters*, Sarah Grimké made an important contribution to the development of a nineteenth-century feminist ideology by basing her defense of woman on the Sciptures, thus challenging her critics on their own ground. Starting from her belief that the Bible had been falsely translated by men, she developed her thesis that men and women had been created in perfect equality, subject only to God; as human beings, they had the same responsibilities and the same rights. Adam and Eve fell from innocence, she insisted, *but not from equality*, since their guilt was shared. This argument would be at the heart of much of the debate over women in the next decades.[27]

The controversy that followed the pastoral letter served to heighten the awareness of all the abolitionist women of the obstacles they faced because they were women. It also intensified the feminist sensitivities of some not yet in the movement. Lucy Stone, who became in the 1840s the first abolitionist to lecture solely on woman's rights, heard the pastoral letter read in the Congregationalist Church in North Brookfield where she was teaching. Only

---

25 *Weld-Grimké Letters*, I, 424, 433.
26 *Ibid.*, I, 429, 415.
27 Sarah Grimké, *Letters on the Equality of the Sexes, and the Condition of Woman* (Boston: Isaac Knapp, 1838; reprint ed., New York: Source Book Press, 1970).

nineteen, she was already sensitized to her inferior position as a woman by the refusal of her church to permit her to vote or join in its discussions, and by the adamant objections of her father to her plea to follow her brothers to college. The low pay she received as a teacher, compared with male salaries, undoubtedly added to her mortification. All these resentments were intensified as she heard the condemnation of the Grimkés. She later described her feeling of rebelliousness: "If I had felt bound to silence before by interpretation of Scriptures, or believed that equal rights did not belong to woman, that 'pastoral letter' broke my bonds."[28] The orthodox church became anathema to Lucy Stone, as to most feminist-abolitionists, because of its proslavery stance as well as its antifeminism.

More significant even than the pastoral letter was the condemnation of these "women out of their sphere" by clergymen *within* the antislavery movement. What began in 1837 as a confrontation with forces which were antiabolitionist as well as antifeminist, became an internecine conflict that lasted from 1838 to 1840 and eventually contributed to the division of the entire abolitionist movement.

The focal point of this controversy was the right of women to vote and participate in the business of the "male" antislavery societies. The final division in the movement came in 1840 when Abby Kelley was appointed to a committee of the American Anti-Slavery Society—Whittier called her "the bomb-shell that *exploded* the society."[29] Garrison and his supporters defended her, while their opponents in the organization demanded her resignation. Kelley refused to resign and, like the Grimkés, defended her position on the ground that men and women had the same moral rights and duties. The impasse over her appointment split the national society. The group of New York abolitionists who opposed her—the Garrisonians called them "New Organization Men"—seceded to form a second organization.

Abby Kelley was the appropriate person to stand firmly at the center of the explosion over the woman question. An intense young Quaker whose attractive features were set against a severe hairdo

28 An address by Lucy Stone, "Workers for the Cause," *circa* 1888, in Blackwell Papers, Library of Congress.

29 John B. Pickard, "John Greenleaf Whittier and the Abolitionist Schism of 1840," *New England Quarterly*, XXXVII (June, 1964), 250–54; quotation on p. 253.

and plain dress, she was among the most radical and uncompromising of the Garrisonians. While the Grimkés' role in the limelight was brief, Abby Kelley's public stand in 1840 was only the beginning of a long and arduous service in the defense of the rights of slaves and women. When the sisters retired to the sidelines after Angelina's marriage to Theodore Weld in 1838, the role they had created as female antislavery lecturers was taken over by the younger Kelley.

Like the Grimkés, Abby Kelley was driven by a desire to rid the world of evil, a religious perfectionism that was shared by all the Garrisonians. As a young teacher in Massachusetts, she had circulated petitions and solicited funds for her local antislavery society. She saw her father's death in 1836 as a sign of God's will and threw herself even further into reform work, contributing her small inheritance to the cause and selling some of her clothing to obtain additional funds. A family letter written the following year reveals her ingenuous optimism: " 'Tis a great joy to see the world grow better in anything—Indeed I think endeavors to improve mankind is the only object worth living for."[30]

Abby Kelley gave her first public speech at the second Anti-Slavery Convention of American Women in May, 1838, a meeting which coincided with the Grimké-Weld wedding. This convention was a traumatic one for all concerned, and a dramatic beginning to Kelley's career. The abolitionists were attacked by a stone-throwing mob on the first day and saw their newly built Pennsylvania Hall burned to the ground on the second. Maria Weston Chapman became so distraught that she suffered a temporary mental breakdown.[31]

In spite of the threatening crowd outside, Abby Kelley's speech had been so eloquent that Theodore Weld assured her that God meant her to take up the antislavery mission: "Abby, if you don't, God will smite you." She spent the next year in intense soul-searching, confessing in a letter to the Weld-Grimké family that she

---

30 Abby Kelley to Olive and Newbury Darling, December 10, 1837, in Kelley-Foster Papers, Worcester (Mass.) Historical Society.

31 Garrison described Chapman's illness in Louis Ruchames (ed.), *Letters of William Lloyd Garrison; Vol. 2, 1836–1840* (Cambridge: Belknap Press of Harvard University Press, 1971), 366.

was praying most earnestly "that this cup might pass from me."
They responded that the Lord was trying her faith and advised her to
"wait for *him* to make a way where there seems now to be no way."
In 1839 she decided to go ahead, after seeing divine confirmation for
her "call" in this scriptural passage: "But God hath chosen the
foolish things of the world to confound the wise." She gave up her
teaching job to become an antislavery agent. A year later she was
at the center of the culminating controversy over women in the
movement.[32]

The "woman question" was the more explosive of the two issues
that divided the abolitionists in 1840. The other conflict, more tactical and less ideological, was over the value of political action. The
radical Boston group associated with Garrison, which defended
women's equal participation, chose to remain with the use of moral
suasion as their chief antislavery tactic. The New York group favored
broadening the base of the movement by political activity and coalition tactics. They accused the Garrisonians of dragging in "extraneous
questions" like the woman's rights issue which they feared would
antagonize possible supporters and hurt the antislavery cause. They
sensed that woman's rights was an even more controversial issue than
the abolition of slavery.[33]

While some "New Organization" men wished to suppress the
woman's rights issue purely for tactical reasons, their leaders included
a core of evangelical clergymen who, like their proslavery counterparts, saw the woman question as a social threat. One of this group
expressed "grief and astonishment" that this issue was forced upon the
antislavery cause. The woman's rights principles, if carried out, he said,
"would strike a death blow at the purest and *loveliest* social condition
of man" and tear up the "foundations of human virtue and *happiness*."[34]

32 Weld's admonition is in W. P. and F. J. Garrison, *William Lloyd Garrison 1805–1879,
The Story of His Life Told by His Children* (4 vols.; Boston: Houghton, Mifflin & Co., 1894), II,
216; *Weld-Grimké Letters*, II, 747; Angelina and Theodore Weld to Abby Kelley, February 24,
1839, in Kelley-Foster Papers, Abby Kelley Foster's Reminiscences, Worcester Historical Society.

33 See Aileen S. Kraditor, *Means and Ends in American Abolitionism* (New York: Pantheon Books, 1969).

34 Rev. Rufus A. Putnam to Rev. Amos A. Phelps and Rev. Orange Scott, March 27, 1839,
in Phelps Papers.

The Garrisonians accused their opponents of sectarianism and argued that woman's rights, like antislavery, was only one aspect of the broad struggle for human rights. James Mott commented in a letter to Anne Weston: "Verily some of our northern gentlemen are as jealous of any interference in rights they have long considered as belonging to them exclusively as the southern slave-holder is in the right of holding his slaves—both are to be broken up, *human* rights alone recognized." Maria Weston Chapman viewed the woman's rights controversy as an inevitable development of the antislavery struggle. She summed it up tersely: "Freedom begets freedom." Lydia Maria Child accused the New Organization men of harboring the "pro-slavery spirit in new disguise," although she acknowledged that many were sincere abolitionists who were "frightened at new and bold views." Summing up the Garrisonian philosophy, she wrote to Lucretia Mott: "It requires great faith to trust truth to take care of itself in all encounters."[35] Though the Garrisonians exhibited the righteousness of true believers by claiming a monopoly on the truth, in practice their philosophy often meant that they were open to new ideas and supported a variety of reforms, like woman's rights, believing "all good causes help one another."

The women received some support from political abolitionists who were not antifeminists. Joseph C. Hathaway, antislavery agent in western New York, wrote to an associate that he could not remain silent while the rights of women were "rudely trampled upon by a corrupt clergy" who thought that "woman was made for the slave of man, instead of a *helpmeet* for him." "What earthly objection can there be to her standing on the same platform with us," he asked. "Are we afraid that the overflowing exuberance of her sympathising heart will eclipse *us?*"[36]

Virtually all of the antislavery women who were feminists, regardless of their stand on political action, remained with the Gar-

35 James Mott to Anne Warren Weston, June 7, 1838, in Weston Papers; Chapman made the judgment later while looking back on this period of turmoil, in *National Anti-Slavery Standard*, March 20, 1845; Lydia Maria Child to Louisa Loring, June 28, 1840, in Loring Papers, Schlesinger Library, Radcliffe College; Lydia Maria Child to Lucretia Mott, March 5, 1839, in Hallowell, *Mott*, 137.

36 J. C. Hathaway to James C. Jackson, August 12, 1839, in Garrison Papers, Boston Public Library.

risonians because it was only there that they were accepted on an equal basis with men. Many were not sympathetic to the feminist cause, however, and chose to continue in their traditional role in the male-dominated organizations. One of Maria Chapman's associates wrote her of a New Organization meeting in which the women present dutifully left when the men got down to business. She deeply regretted, she wrote, "that they can find any 'sisters' who will allow themselves to be dismissed for I feel that if Woman would not consent to her own degradation her Emancipation would be sure."[37]

Maria Weston Chapman and her sisters themselves resisted an attempt by anti-Garrisonian women to dissolve the Boston Female Anti-Slavery Society. Chapman was a fierce protagonist in the controversy, condemning her opponents as traitors and tools of the clergy and citing their "hypocrisy as abolitionists" and "want of integrity as women." When her opponents withdrew from the organization to form the Massachusetts Female Emancipation Society, Chapman wrote a friend that the group would continue without the defectors and with "more vigour than ever."[38] This unwillingness of many women to be "emancipated" would remain, of course, one of the major obstacles in the woman's movement.

Following the right over the woman question in the United States, the Garrisonians shortly faced a similar challenge at the World's Anti-Slavery Convention in London in 1840. This meeting became another direct link in the bond between abolitionism and feminism. The controversy at home had been so traumatic and so destructive of antislavery unity that even the most dedicated of the feminist-abolitionists felt ambivalence about further harming the movement. Sarah Grimké wrote to a friend that she hoped women would not present themselves as delegates in London because it would "divert the attention of the meeting from the great subject of human liberty," ironically using the same argument that had been used against her in 1837.[39]

Lucretia Mott and the other women delegates from the United

37  Charlotte Austin to Maria Weston Chapman, October, 1839, in Weston Papers.
38  Maria Weston Chapman to Elizabeth Pease, April 20, 1840, in Garrison Papers.
39  Sarah Grimké to Elizabeth Pease, May, 1840, in Garrison Papers.

States did, however, stand on principle and demand to be seated in spite of intense opposition. (Though the Motts' liberal Quaker views were also anathema to the Orthodox Friends who organized the convention, it was Mrs. Mott's sex that was crucial; James Mott had no difficulty being seated.[40]) In a heated debate reminiscent of the exchange between the Grimkés and the Massachusetts clergy, members of the English clergy cited the Scriptures as the authority for relegating women to their "God-ordained" sphere. To give the vote to females, they argued, was to act in opposition to the word of God. They also called upon the powerful force of custom which, they insisted, prevented them from subjecting the "shrinking nature of woman" to the indelicacies involved in a discussion of slavery.[41] The decision was ultimately made to adhere to custom and the women were relegated to a screened-off area.

The rejection of the women delegates was an important feminist experience for Elizabeth Cady Stanton, then a young bride who had chosen to accompany her husband to this meeting as a honeymoon trip. Her long talks with Lucretia Mott made an even more lasting impression on her. Hearing Mrs. Mott deliver a sermon in a Unitarian church in London was to her "like the realization of an oft-repeated, happy dream." Out of the meeting of these two women came the idea to organize women to take action in their own defense. The Seneca Falls meeting would be the logical fruition of the "woman question" controversy.[42]

In the period following the split in the movement and the London meeting, the Garrisonian women merged their societies with the male groups remaining in the American Anti-Slavery Society. They were now able to work with greater freedom and expand their activities. Child, Chapman, and Mott served on the executive committee of the national society; Child became editor of their newspaper, the *National Anti-Slavery Standard*; Abby Kelley lectured and

40 See Frederick B. Tolles (ed.), *Slavery and "The Woman Question," Lucretia Mott's Diary of Her Visit to Great Britain to Attend the World's Antislavery Convention of 1840* (Haverford, Pa.: Friends Historical Assoc., 1952); Cromwell and other historians have attributed Lucretia Mott's rejection as much to religion as sex.

41 *History of Woman Suffrage*, I, 58–59, 60.

42 Stanton is quoted in Hallowell, *Mott*, 187.

organized in the West. Maria Chapman insisted that they were stronger for the defection because women "who were not easily discouraged" were more valuable to the cause than men "whose dignity forbade them to be fellow-laborers with women."[43] This rhetoric notwithstanding, the movement as a whole was weakened by the division and never again achieved the strength and unity of the 1830s. The New Organization abolitionists moved into the broader stream of political antislavery while the Garrisonians continued their "no-government" moral crusade. The decade had been, however, a productive one for radical reform. Not only had the question of the immediate emancipation of the slaves been raised, but also the possibility of the future emancipation of women.

## IV

The Garrisonian women—the Grimkés, Mott, Chapman, Child, Kelley, and their supporters—all were actually playing two kinds of roles on two separate but overlapping stages. In the foreground, the more visible drama revolved about their part in antislavery. On the larger stage, a more subtle kind of action was occurring: a new dialogue for women was being shaped, and new images created that would endure long after the antislavery action was ended. Although the women were propelled into this dual action by circumstances they had not controlled, they were aware of the implications for the future.

Angelina Grimké, capping her brief public career in a spectacular way by appearing before a committee of the Massachusetts legislature in 1838, typified this new image and this feminist awareness. Accompanied by Chapman, Child, and other friends, she presented antislavery petitions on behalf of 20,000 women. Arguing for the right of women to have an equal voice in political decisions, and clearly anticipating the later demand for the suffrage, Grimké declared: "Are we aliens, because we are women? Are we bereft of citizenship because we are mothers, wives and daughters of a

---

43 Maria Weston Chapman, *Right and Wrong in Massachusetts* (Reprint ed., New York: Negro Universities Press, 1969), 12.

mighty people?" Excited by her triumph she wrote to a friend: "We Abolition Women are turning the world upside down."[44]

While "turning the world upside down" was more hyperbole than fact, Grimké and others were setting important precedents for future leaders. By challenging their society's view of woman's proper sphere and expanding their own roles to include public work as well as private duties, they became role models for a new type of woman. With the support of their feminist-abolitionist husbands, they became antislavery agents, lecturers, editors, agitators—blasphemous violations of their society's code of behavior for well-bred ladies.

This expansion of woman's role was done consciously and justified by modifying their society's doctrine of separate spheres in a significant way. They shared the popular view that woman's primary duty was to the home and man's to his work outside the home, but they saw these spheres as overlapping rather than distinct. Both women and men, they believed, shared responsibility to the community as well as to the home. There was an apparent contradiction between their demand for equality and their belief in woman's special moral and domestic obligations, but they dealt with this by distinguishing between women as human beings and women in their more narrow function as wives and mothers. The Grimkés, for example, defended their public speaking by arguing that the spheres and duties of women as citizens and as spiritual beings were identical with those of men; it was only in their social roles that their responsibilities were different. These special roles were seen as derived from inherent sex differences: women were physically weaker, exhibited different intellectual strengths, and were endowed with superior moral and spiritual qualities. "Equality" meant that women would be free to develop their physical and intellectual abilities like men, and men would be free to act in their highest moral capacities like women. Elizabeth Cady Stanton and others would rely heavily on this concept of equality and special social roles to reconcile woman's domestic obligations with the demand for an equal public role.[45]

44 *Child Letters*, 259; *Weld-Grimké Letters*, II, 574.
45 See Sarah Grimké, *Letters on the Equality of the Sexes*, and Angelina Grimké to Amos A. Phelps, September 2, 1837, in Phelps Papers; cf. Elizabeth Cady Stanton speech "The Solitude of Self," in Stanton Papers, Library of Congress.

This concept of overlapping spheres was translated into practice by an impressive number of married feminist-abolitionists, creating significant models of a radically new kind of marriage based on shared responsibility and shared public work. In this early group, only Angelina Grimké and Theodore Weld failed because of practical obstacles to achieve this goal. They continued to be among the few exceptions to the rule. In their case, family needs impeded Weld's public work as well as his wife's, so that theirs was not solely a female dilemma.[46]

The more typical feminist-abolitionist marriages proved to be most unusual. In an age of rigidly defined sex roles, Stephen Foster often stayed home to care for their daughter while Abby Kelley Foster traveled on extended lecture tours. David Lee Child also accepted his wife's equal and autonomous role and the fact that it was often necessary for her to be the breadwinner and to live apart so that both could perform their antislavery tasks. Both men were exceptional in considering their wives' work at least as important as their own. Neither appeared threatened by the loss of man's traditional and exclusive authority in the home.

As always, it was Lucretia Mott who came closest to the feminist-abolitionist ideal. More than any other woman, she was idolized by younger feminists as both consummate reformer and perfect wife and mother. Her marriage to James Mott, in which she retained her independence and received his wholehearted support, was regarded as a model union. It would convince important feminists like Lucy Stone and Antoinette Brown to risk marriage themselves. Because she married early and completed much of the raising of her five children before she began her reform work, they could also look to her for one type of practical life plan. Most important, however, was the Motts' enlightened view of woman's sphere, which contrasted dramatically with the constricted legal and social role assigned to nineteenth-century women.

Equality in marriage proved to be not only a belief but a liberat-

---

46 See Blanche Glassman Hersh, "'The Slavery of Sex': Feminist-Abolitionists in Nineteenth-Century America" (Ph.D. dissertation, University of Illinois, 1975), chap. 8, especially pp. 414–17.

ing force for the women. It was the closest they came to a practical solution to the dilemma of balancing home and work, and virtually the only solution available to them given the cultural milieu within which they functioned. They never questioned the importance of the family as the central institution of society and indeed attempted to elevate it to an even higher position. They rejected the few radicals who advocated free love and often birth control, and kept them at a safe distance from the woman's movement. Their goal was to broaden woman's sphere to include both family and whatever else she was capable of doing. Their husbands' commitment to woman's equality enabled most of them to achieve this goal in their own lives.

In the process of expanding and reshaping female roles, the abolitionist women also set precedents for different styles of feminist leadership. Maria Weston Chapman and Abby Kelley were boldly aggressive, willing to take on "male" roles and choosing agitation and direct confrontation as their tactics. They were archetypal leaders of the radical, uncompromising genre whose positions move the mainstream into action, albeit reluctantly, and force public discussion of issues which other more moderate types can then negotiate and attempt to resolve.

Lydia Maria Child preferred a softer, more private way, using her pen rather than her voice and putting a high value on setting an example for others to follow. When criticized for not being more zealous in defense of the Grimkés, she explained her position in the *Liberator*: "It is best not to *talk* about our rights, but simply go forward and *do* whatsoever we deem a duty. In toiling for the freedom of others, we shall find our own."[47] It was through her writings that she exerted the greatest influence in the woman's movement, especially her *History of the Condition of Women*, written in 1835 as a pioneer effort to uncover the origins of woman's inequality. It was an important source for Sarah Grimké's *Letters* as well as for later feminists.

Again, the most effective style of leadership was displayed by

47 *Liberator*, September 6, 1839.

Lucretia Mott. Her practical brand of idealism enabled her to work with, and be accepted by, all the factions in abolitionism and feminism, and to act as a bridge between the two movements. While Kelley and others were rigid and uncompromising in their perfectionism, Mott was able to combine her radical vision of the future with a realistic assessment of what was possible in the here and now. Though she appreciated the importance of a few women leading the way, for example, she understood that centuries of custom and indoctrination could not be overturned overnight. During the storm over women speaking to mixed audiences, she encouraged those who wished to take this step to "act in accordance with the light they have." Meanwhile, she suggested, other women might go on meeting by themselves "without compromise of the principle of equality" until they were ready for "more public and general exercise of their rights."[48] Like Child, she put a high value on the creation of models and new female roles, but was also unwilling to force women into them until they were ready.

The double heresy of acting both as abolitionist and as public woman was committed by all the women at the cost of immense personal sacrifice. They suffered a total loss of social prestige and were subjected to insults and harassment. They had important strengths, however, to deal with abuse and censure. As a group, they were brighter and better-educated than average; they were also "strong-minded," with a sturdy consciousness of self and a keen sensitivity to all infringements on personal liberty. Even more significant was the strength of their religious beliefs. Though they rejected the orthodox tenets and formal trappings of Protestantism, their personal perfectionism and sense of moral duty and "calling" sustained them through difficult trials. They also received invaluable support for their feminism from the radical wing of the antislavery movement. As husbands, the Garrisonian men made it possible for their wives to pursue unorthodox careers. As coworkers, they acted as a "reference group," providing the social approval and reinforce-

---

48 Lucretia Mott to Abby Kelley, March 18, 1839, in Kelley-Foster Papers, American Antiquarian Society, Worcester, Mass.

ment of values that made it easier for the women to defy social mores.

Another important link was formed in this period between abolitionism and feminism. Forced to justify their "unfeminine" behavior, the women drew naturally on the ideology of radical antislavery to articulate the first coherent arguments for woman's rights. Their language reflected the sources of abolitionist rhetoric: the Enlightenment ideology of human rights and the republican ideals of the Revolution; the Quaker interpretation of the Scriptures, especially the belief that all people are one in Christ Jesus (and therefore what is morally right for a man to do is morally right for a woman); the Puritan concept of duty, work, and suffering as the means of serving God; the romantic, perfectionist goal of elevating and emancipating the whole human race.[49]

At least partly because of this common origin, the parallel between woman and slave became an integral element of feminist rhetoric. Abby Kelley, for example, dwelled constantly on the similarity between the subservience of the slave to his master and the dependence of the wife upon her husband. Both, she argued, were subject to sexual and personal domination and prevented from developing into independent human beings; both, while privately lamenting their degraded and helpless position, were forced to appear contented because of fear of displeasing their lords and masters.[50] As a corollary to this theme, the feminist-abolitionist women stressed the importance of using their own names rather than their husbands'—Abby Kelley Foster, never Mrs. Stephen Foster—as a symbolic gesture comparable to the frequent shedding of masters' names by slaves on gaining freedom.[51] The influence of abolitionism on feminist ideology and rhetoric would continue to be a striking characteristic of the antebellum woman's movement and would carry over into the postwar suffrage movement.

49 See Sarah Grimké, *Letters on the Equality of the Sexes*, and Chapman, *Right and Wrong in Massachusetts*, 13.
50 See *Liberator*, September 6, 1839.
51 See *History of Woman Suffrage*, I, 528; this also reflected Quaker custom which stressed simplicity as well as equality.

V

In the 1830s there was as yet no woman's rights "movement"—this would begin in the next decade with lecturers, newspapers, political campaigns, and the first conventions. Significant beginnings had been made during these early years, however, and the important bond between abolitionism and feminism had been forged. The two movements were linked in crucial ways: by the antislavery events and controversies which proved to be feminist consciousness-raising experiences, by the feminist-abolitionist people whose leadership spanned both movements, and by the belief in human rights which provided the ideological underpinning for both causes.

The controversy over woman's role in antislavery had been the important catalyst in moving a few independent-minded abolitionist women to take action in defense of woman's rights. Stirred to a realization of their own enslavement in "woman's sphere," feminism became for them a necessary adjunct to abolitionism. Abby Kelley expressed this best when she noted in 1838 that women had good cause to be grateful to the slave "for the benefit we have received to *ourselves* in working for *him*." "In striving to strike his irons off," she continued, "we found most surely that *we* were manacled *ourselves*." In order to free the slaves, they were forced to move to free themselves.[52]

Abolitionism also bequeathed to feminism the basic philosophy which sustained all radical reform, the idea that all good causes are linked together. Maria Weston Chapman expressed it clearly in one of her reports: "Truth is like a strong cable." The belief in fundamental principles, she wrote, would lead inevitably to the emancipation of *all* people from bondage, not only slaves but "women from the subjugation of men" and people oppressed by poverty, religion, and government—in short, emancipation "of the whole earth from sin and suffering."[53] It was with this belief that the women who began

51 Abby Kelley's entry in the 1838 album of the Western Anti-Slavery Society, in Western Anti-Slavery Society Papers, Library of Congress.
53 Maria Weston Chapman, *Ten Years of Experience; Ninth Annual Report of Boston Female Anti-Slavery Society* (Boston: Oliver Johnson, 1842), 15.

their antislavery work with the plea "Am I not a woman and a sister?" went on to speak in the name of a sisterhood which included not only slave women but all women.

# Collisions

# REHEARSAL FOR
# THE CIVIL WAR
## Antislavery and Proslavery at the Fighting Point in Kansas, 1854–1856

*Michael Fellman*

To all men like him and many less incisive, it all seemed starkly plain in black-and-white. Issues have to seem so at the fighting-points of history. It was only later, looking back, that one saw the assumptions we had made, the ignorant hopes we had indulged, the acts of faith that looked strange in the light of what was actually to come.

C. P. SNOW [1]

EVEN AS her riverboat went down the Mississippi to St. Louis in the spring of 1855, Julia Louisa Lovejoy confirmed her preconceptions of the slave states. The very scenery, was, "as we supposed, low and monotonous"; all the planters' dwelling places "dilapidated"; everywhere in Missouri she felt "the blighting mildew of slavery." How unlike this place was her native Vermont, with its "thrifty looking villages [and] stately mansions." If only her "energetic Yankee" brethren would leave the "sterile unproductive soil" of New England, and "for a few years occupy these rich lands, how greatly would the face of things be changed!"

---

1 C. P. Snow, *The Light and the Dark* (New York: Charles Scribner's Sons, 1947), 281.

At Jefferson City, Missouri, on her trek to the open West of Kansas, Lovejoy was appalled by the appearance of the capitol building erected by the western slavestaters. "One thing seemed to us like *neglect* or *indolence*, the *rusty* appearance of the unpainted cupola of the structure, that by heavy rains had soiled the exterior of the walls the entire heighth." In the very shadow of this contaminated statehouse, she was shocked to see a mule cart "being relieved from its contents of manure" by a colored woman, while her white male overseer supervised her "with an air of content . . . whilst he moved not a finger to assist the poor creature in her masculine task." Indignantly, she concluded, slavery was an accursed "unsexing demon."

Further west, in Kansas City, on the border of Kansas Territory, she, a minister's wife, found only one church, "and this unpainted, uncarpeted, and *filthy*" from the spit of tobacco chewers. In all of slaveholding Missouri "the inhabitants and the morals are of an *undescribably repulsive* and undesirable character."

In contrast to blighted Missouri, Lovejoy arrived in Kansas to find a spring garden. Untilled bottom land, rolling prairies "undulating like the waves of the sea" awaited human cultivation for good or for ill. The Lovejoy cabin along the Big Blue was in the middle of a town site, "literally in the centre of a garden of flowers of varied form and hue, surrounded with acres of rose bushes, which, when in blossom must perfume the air for miles around."[2] In 1855 Kansas was the West, the future.

The passage of the Kansas-Nebraska Act in 1854 had not only destroyed the Whig party, but through its popular sovereignty provision—actual settlers rather than Congress would determine the legal existence of slavery when the territory became a state—had guaranteed a sectional race to establish political hegemony in Kansas itself. From 1854 until 1858 Kansas became both the central symbol and actual battleground of the fundamental American conflict between North and South. That conflict was most intense when protagonists fought openly from December, 1855, until Sep-

---

2 Julia Louisa Lovejoy to the Concord (N.H.) *Independent Democrat*, March 13, April 13, and May 22, 1855, in "Julia Louisa Lovejoy, Letters from Kansas," *Kansas Historical Quarterly*, XI (1942), 31–34, 37. Also see Michael Fellman, "Julia Louisa Lovejoy Goes West," *Western Humanities Review*, XXXII (Summer, 1977), 227–42.

tember, 1856, when the national government imposed a fragile peace.[3]

Most of the settlers who came to Kansas were westerners who may not have had strongly developed proslavery or antislavery sentiments; nearly all shared a basic negrophobia.[4] But general preconceptions, day-to-day friction, and battle turned vague feelings into strident sectional identities. In northern terms, Kansas brought antislavery up to the fighting point. By comparison, the abolitionism of the 1830s and 1840s, which has been studied far more intensively by historians, had a much narrower, if more intellectually resonant base and appeal. In the 1850s, a new generation of antislavery leaders responded to a broader northern antislavery public with a harsher and more vengeful ideology.[5] In this response, the new abo-

3 The best account of events in Kansas, set in the context of national politics, remains Allan Nevins, *Ordeal of the Union: A House Dividing, 1852–1857* (New York: Charles Scribner's Sons, 1947); *The Emergence of Lincoln: Douglas, Buchanan and Party Chaos, 1857–1859* (New York: Charles Scribner's Sons, 1950). Alice Nichols, *Bleeding Kansas* (New York: Oxford University Press, 1954), is a useful, if uncritical, recapitulation of contemporary accounts of the events in Kansas. James A. Rawley, *Race and Politics: "Bleeding Kansas" and the Coming of the Civil War* (Philadelphia: J. B. Lippincott, 1969), concentrates on national politics. James C. Malin, *John Brown and the Legend of Fifty-Six* (2 vols., Rev. ed.; New York: Haskell House, 1971), provides a mine of information. Don W. Wilson, *Governor Charles Robinson of Kansas* (Lawrence: University of Kansas Press, 1975), is a useful biography of a central antislavery leader. The New England Aid Company has been perhaps overemphasized. Two solid accounts are Samuel A. Johnson, *The Battle Cry of Freedom: The New England Aid Company in the Kansas Crusade* (Lawrence: University of Kansas Press, 1954); and Ralph V. Harlow, "The Rise and Fall of the Kansas Aid Movement," *American Historical Review*, XLI (1935), 1–25. Paul W. Gates, *Fifty Million Acres: Conflicts over Kansas Land Policy, 1854–1890* (Ithaca: Cornell University Press, 1954), is an elegant and brilliant study. Two essays concentrate on Kansas journalism as unnecessary, irrational, but effective propaganda: Bernard A. Weisberger, "The Newspaper Reporter and the Kansas Imbroglio," *Mississippi Valley Historical Review*, XXXVI (1950), 633–56; David Potter, *The Impending Crisis, 1848–1861* (New York: Harper and Row, 1976), 199–224. The reader might wish to relate this episode to a larger American tradition of violence, such as those patterns depicted in Richard Maxwell Brown, *Strain of Violence: Studies of American Violence and Vigilantism* (New York: Oxford, 1975), and Richard Slotkin, *Regeneration Through Violence: The Mythology of the American Frontier, 1600–1860* (Middletown, Conn.: Wesleyan University Press, 1973).

4 Malin, *John Brown* II, 515, uses the 1855 voter census to suggest that only 6.4 percent of the settlers at that point were New Englanders; 1.6 percent from the Lower South; 19.6 percent Northern Border states; 7.7 percent Southern Border states; and 47.6 percent from Missouri. In the 1860 census, Malin finds 16 percent from New England and the northern tier of states; 13.5 percent from the Lower South; 35.3 percent from Northern Border states; 13.5 percent from Southern Border states; 10.6 percent from Missouri; and 11.8 percent foreign born. Of course a mountain Tennessean may have been antislavery back home, and a southern Indianan of Virginia origins proslavery, but the northern and western slant of the population increase from 1855–1860 is unmistakable.

5 On abolitionist reattunement in the 1850s see Eric Foner, *Free Soil, Free Labor, Free Men: The Ideology of the Republican Party Before the Civil War* (New York: Oxford University

litionists were riding the tiger born from the aspirations and resentments of a vast public of small farmers and artisans. Popular
antislavery ideology was not created by abolitionist pens, although
many abolitionists did amplify and focus this ideology. A deep and
growing suspicion of the South, a traditional and endemic fear of
competition from black slave labor, prepared northern settlers for
conflict with southern settlers in the West. Given this background,
the direct experience of physical contact and competition elicited an
antislavery passion in the masses of ordinary northern settlers in
Kansas. However, the anger and ensuing bloodshed cannot be explained fully as part of a cultural tradition. Engagement in the field
opened a dark cavern of expression and action that took ordinary
men and women into a new realm of self-definition and cultural
justification.

     This essay then is concerned with the popular ideological developments which led up to and lent meaning to the guerrilla
struggle. Letters, journals, diaries, and especially journalism written
from the field of battle comprise most of the materials analyzed
here. Such writing, frequently purple with anger, was composed to
call others to action. It was not balanced, dispassionate, and "rational." Yet as such passion distorted, it also purposefully plumbed
and expressed emotional reactions in readers not touched by more
polite literature. Writing intended to pick open and flay inner
wounds should not be dismissed as propaganda: exhortative writing
such as this also reveals, in an only partly intentional manner, fundamental cultural tensions, fears, and aspirations.

     Open conflict in Kansas was finally welcomed as a necessary cleansing event, as a means to purge the vulnerable land and populace
of those evil, presumably external, forces that threatened it.
Furthermore, blood sacrifice could apparently purge one's own
people of the tendency to backslide into a degenerate moral state,
and could lead to self-regeneration. Thus among both publicists and
ordinary folk, in the cauldron of the Kansas struggle, the northern
denunciation of an evil slaveholding southern race was heightened,

---

Press, 1970), and Michael Fellman, "Theodore Parker and the Abolitionist Role in the 1850s,"
*Journal of American History*, LXI (1974), 666–84.

and juxtaposed to the assertion of a heroic northern free people. These opposite images led to open conflict during the establishment of Kansas, which, most Americans fervently believed, would determine the entire future of the trans-Mississippi West, and hence the nation. Southern settlers in Kansas also established their own opposing images of the people of God and those of the devil. Brotherhood was thus rendered into fratricide, settlement into sectional struggle.

For northern settlers, the enemy was neither the plantation owner nor his slaves, but his by-products and minions, poor southern white trash—"Border Ruffians" as they referred to themselves; "Pukes" as northerners came to call them. These southern frontiersmen, who came primarily from Missouri and the southern border states, were especially threatening because they represented to northerners the degraded material and moral condition into which the slave system forced the independent white of modest means—people, in other words, of their own social position. But for the grace of free institutions, northern whites could be compelled back towards an impoverished, regressive barbarism, as had been the Pukes, back into an infantile ooze, and away from the increasingly mature prosperity and moral tidiness by which northern freemen justified their individual moral existence and the purpose of their society. Perhaps at some unacknowledged level there was something enticing about a wilder, unstructured life; the guilt induced by this possibility, projected upon the Pukes, made all the more intense the necessity to conquer the southern foe.

Consciously to northerners, it was clear that the Pukes were indeed savages who threatened, beasts who had to be expunged if free white civilization were to be implanted. Frequently the Pukes were defined as children of an earlier stage of civilization, or as atavistic throwbacks, "men who cannot stand the control which civilization imposes upon every citizen," the *Christian Inquirer* asserted, "and who revel with delight in the license which frontier life holds out to all lawless tendencies."[6] The *New York Tribune* reporter comically

6 New York *Christian Enquirer*, July 6, 1854. Unless otherwise noted, copies of all non-

described the average, repulsive Puke for his broad northern readership:

Imagine a fellow, tall, slim, but athletic, with yellow complexion, hairy faced, with a dirty flannel shirt, red or blue, or green, a pair of commonplace, but dark-colored pants, tucked into an uncertain altitude by a leather belt, in which a dirty-handled bowieknife is stuck, rather ostentatiously, an eye slightly whiskey-red, and teeth the color of a walnut. Such is your border ruffian of the lowest type. His body might be a compound of gutta percha, Johnny-cake, and badly-smoked bacon, his spirit, the *refined* part, old bourbon, double-rectified.[7]

Although absurd in this satire, Pukes were feared by their northern neighbors as dirt-wallowing, elemental brutes, suspended in a worthlessly comatose state between bouts of primitive violence. They had never really left childhood, many northern settlers believed; hence their proclivity for, in Julia Lovejoy's words, "sucking whiskey," for a self-degrading, regressive orality.[8] Similarly, another northern settler believed that when Pukes were not fighting, they were "either whimpering with a desire to see their mothers, or complaining for the want of whiskey."[9] Childish and drunken, the Pukes loafed and blindly fought their way through life rather than structuring, through hard and persistent work, a stable family and home.[10]

Pukes were often described as being essentially subhuman. One midwestern journalist asserted, "They are a queer-looking set, slightly resembling human beings, but more closely allied to wild

---

Kansas journalism quoted can be found in the *Webb Scrapbooks*, Kansas State Historical Society. A broad and representative sampling of newspaper opinion is in Malin, *John Brown* I, 31–245. The similarities of "Gooks" to "Pukes" are more than verbal. For an analysis of "Gooks" which illuminates the study of "Pukes" as well, see Robert Jay Lifton, *Home From the War: Vietnam Veterans, Neither Victims nor Executioners* (New York: Simon and Schuster, 1973), 189–216.

7 William Phillips, *The Conquest of Kansas by Missouri and Her Allies* (Boston: Phillips, Sampson and Company, 1856), 29.

8 Lovejoy to the Concord (N.H.) *Independent Democrat*, September 5, 1856, in "Letters of Julia Louisa Lovejoy, 1856–64," *Kansas Historical Quarterly*, XV (1947), 131.

9 Charles B. Lines to the New Haven *Daily Palladium*, May 30, 1856, in "The Connecticut Kansas Colony: Letters of Charles B. Lines to the New Haven *Daily Palladium*," *Kansas Historical Quarterly*, XXII (1956), 144.

10 See especially the Lawrence (Kan.) *Herald of Freedom*, February 16, December 20, 1856.

beasts."[11] The British journalist Richard J. Hinton wrote in his diary of a Border Ruffian leader whose face appeared "carbuncled and his nose 'rum-blossom' of the deepest hue. Small piggish eyes looked out from his mass of gross fat."[12] Uncivilized, unclean, drunken, and incontinent (as in Lovejoy's image of the stained copper cupola of the Jefferson City capitol), Pukes were freed to act bestially.[13] Filthy language, tortures, stabbings, shootings in the back followed in northern depictions of southern behavior, as did the most dreaded rape. "Think of this, my sisters in New Hampshire," Lovejoy wrote, "pure-minded, intelligent ladies fleeing from fiends in human form whose brutal lust is infinitely more to be dreaded than death itself."[14] Similar to the savage black rapist of the post–Civil War South, this beastly Puke attacked every civilized value.

The beast must die. Even Charles B. Stearns, perhaps the only pacifist Garrisonian in the whole territory, could come to justify killing Pukes as subhumans sunk in a pit below the realm of humanity. To Stearns these were "drunken ourang-outans," "wild beasts," and thus it was his "duty to aid in killing them off. When I deal with men made in God's image, I will never shoot them; but these pro-slavery Missourians are demons from the bottomless pit and may be shot with impunity."[15] Contact with such a monster race could turn even pacifist abolitionists into outraged racist warriors.

Perhaps inevitably in this competitive arena, Missourians confirmed northern preconceptions, but they may also have been no good measured by the general American standards of the 1850s.

11 Chicago *Tribune*, April 20, 1857.

12 Journal of Richard J. Hinton (MS in the Kansas State Historical Society), September 9, 1856. In a similar vein, see New York *Tribune*, March 21, 1856.

13 In his "Crime Against Kansas" speech of May 21, 1856, Charles Sumner vilified Senator Andrew P. Butler of South Carolina, for, among other things, his verbal incontinence, with innuendo of a wider loss of control by slaveholders. Cf. David Donald, *Charles Sumner and the Coming of the Civil War* (New York: Alfred A. Knopf, 1960), 286.

14 Lovejoy to the Concord (N.H.) *Independent Democrat*, September 19, 1856, in "Letters of Julia Louisa Lovejoy, 1856–64," 134.

15 Boston *Liberator*, January 4, 1856; Milford (Mass.) *Practical Christian*, January 26, 1856. These passages are quoted and Stearns analyzed in Lewis C. Perry, *Radical Abolitionism: Anarchy and the Government of God in Antislavery Thought* (Ithaca: Cornell University Press, 1973), 240–46.

They may well have drunk more whiskey, deserted more families, bragged more and worked less than most of their contemporaries. The undoubtedly different mores of frontiersmen and farmers fed an intraclass agrarian conflict every bit as real and brutal as interclass warfare in an industrialized society. Missourians, who were damned primitives in the eyes of northern settlers, may well have been adjudged atavistic by the general American populace in the context of the almost universal belief that American culture was progressing to "higher," more civilized forms. But experience is always received and refracted through the hard glass of self-justification and fear of threatening outside forces, and so in this sense we can learn of the Pukes only through the evaluations made of them by northern settlers. Received tradition and experience were intermingled and inseparable; conflicts of cultural styles were meshed with material struggles in the attempt to establish social hegemony.

In defensive contrast to the threatening Pukes, northerners in Kansas were therefore compelled to create a heightened image of themselves. Reinforcing themselves with their lineage from their tribal Old Testament War God, evoking their heritage as Puritans, Yankees, and American Revolutionaries, they sought, in combat with the servants of evil, to regenerate themselves morally, to reconstruct their class of freeholders, to save Kansas, and to serve as exemplars of freedom to the nation.

William Phillips, the *Tribune* man, satirized the Pukes as restless, whiskey-soaked illiterates who were passing frontier hunter types. "Deer-hunting was with them a science, coon-hunting a purely business affair." He felt that they were being forced further south and west, to be replaced by the solid, enrooting northern farmers. Of this succeeding class, "You can tell by the fences, and look of the houses, and by a thousand other things, that an industrious and calculating people are here." [16] Fencing in land would follow and improve upon its use for deer-hunting; industry would replace drift. In a similar vein, one Connecticut settler going west noted

16 Phillips, *Conquest of Kansas*, 64–65. The reporter for the New York *Herald*, who was not antislavery, came to similar conclusions: George Douglas Brewerton, *The War in Kansas* (New York: Derby and Jackson, 1856), 381–84.

with abhorrence the violence done to baggage by Missourian rail-road teamsters, and wished that "some enterprising Yankee" could gain control of the Missouri line: "extraordinary carefulness" in baggage handling and a railroad timetable such as "to make arrivals and departures with a good deal of regularity" would inevitably fol-low.[17] Once settled on his homestead, this new Kansas citizen painfully felt the absence of "female society," the protection of the cultural and legal institutions he had known back home, and feared the "new temptations . . . new physical, mental and moral influ-ences" of the unstructured, dangerous West. Almost immediately he and his friends set up a debating institute, where the first two sub-jects wcrc, "Resolved: That a good wife contributes more to the happiness of a man than a fortune," and "Resolved: That life in Kan-sas is preferable to that in Connecticut."[18] Here, the appropriate re-sponse to threats to freeholder values was to dig in one's heels and to attempt to recreate the secure underpinnings of civilization one had known in the East. Regression to a frontier stage of civilization would mean accepting Puke-like values; one had always to fight against any appearances of such degeneracy.

Yet, implicitly, industry and calculation, though good and re-ward-bringing, provided insufficient defenses against the effects of the environment and the enemy. Greed for land and pursuit of purely material gain could lead to worship of Mammon, as northern settlers were well aware. To be morally sound, taking up the land and pushing off the Pukes (and Indians) had to be tied to a higher set of moral purposes, to serve God and to establish progressive civiliza-tion. This moral purpose was not merely a "rationalization" for "real" material interests and motives: truly serving the higher good would alone ennoble self-improvement, and thus make regenerative the struggle against the Philistines in the land of Canaan. As the War God aided the Hebrews, so would he keep his covenant with his chosen people once more. "Jehovah will triumph and the people will

17 Charles B. Lines to the New Haven (Conn.) *Daily Palladium*, April 5, 1856, in Lines, "The Connecticut Kansas Colony," 4–5.
18 Charles B. Lines to the New Haven (Conn.) *Daily Palladium*, July 31, 1856, in Lines, "The Connecticut Kansas Colony," 171.

be free," wrote one settler. Echoed another, "Jehovah is on the side of the oppressed, and He will yet arise in His strength, and His enemies will be scattered."[19]

The ethnic origins of the northern settlers gave clear evidence that they were a chosen people, the leading Kansas antislavery newspaper editorialized. "We know no State where the pure Anglo-Saxon Native American so thoroughly occupies the ground, as in this. So far as settlements are made, they are purely American. A few of the better class of foreigners are scattered here and there; but not enough to be objectionable."[20] The growing, polyglot eastern and midwestern cities were cluttered with seemingly unassimilable Irish and German Catholics and could not lead national reformation; in Kansas the homogeneous Anglo-Saxon American type could be recreated. Here, through such stock, would "Yankee enterprise" be "actuated by hallowed principle," a New Hampshire newspaper insisted. The Puritan spirit, which had "long since uprooted the upas tree of slavery" from northern soil, would, rekindled in "beautiful and fertile" Kansas, destroy the "dark plottings of the oppressor," represented by the slave forces.[21] That ideal which had impelled the Puritans to flee to "their Western wilderness . . . a desire to plant the institutions of a pure Gospel on this virgil soil," a Massachusetts newspaper insisted, was now being repeated by the heirs of the same stock in Kansas.[22]

For this replication of the Puritan experience, the necessity of struggle and suffering was also central. Discipline and duty could not arise from the cushioned life which had come to too many northerners as a result of their prosperity. Character could come alone from seeking the harsh bedrock experience of original covenanters.[23] Rewards that had come to industrious northern

19 Charles B. Lines to the New Haven (Conn.) *Daily Palladium*, May 23, 1856, in Lines, "The Connecticut Kansas Colony," 141; Julia Louisa Lovejoy to the Concord (N.H.) *Independent Democrat*, August 1, 1855, in "Letters from Kansas," 43.

20 Lawrence (Kan.) *Herald of Freedom*, April 12, 1856.

21 Dover (N.H.) *Morning Star*, November 24, 1854.

22 Worcester (Mass.) *Daily Spy*, May 22, 1854.

23 Such was the interpretation by the founder of the New England Emigrant Aid Company, Eli Thayer, in his speech "Suicide of Slavery," given in the House of Representatives, March 25, 1858, and reprinted in Eli Thayer, *A History of the Kansas Crusade: Its Friends and Foes* (New York: Harper and Brothers, 1889), 253–71.

people had thus also signaled, over the long run, their moral slippage. This double-edged meaning of work and resultant accumulation created a tension and a moral complexity that could best be sublimated by heroic action. Struggling to serve Him would lead to those rewards due His true servants, to goods without guilt.

The Puritan hero could indeed be reborn in Kansas. "Splendid faces" characterized the antislavery men of Lawrence, Hinton recorded in his journal. One was "a puritan brought back from the days of Cromwell or a vision of the old Revolutionary times, to show the world that all the fearless energy and strong integrity that characterized those epochs, has not yet faded out."[24] If the blood of these heroes would flow, it would be the sanctified blood of martyrs.[25] For William Phillips, Old John Brown was the very archetype of the Puritan hero: "He is one of those Christians who have not quite passed from the face of the earth." Brown, the Cromwellian patriarch writ superhuman, both thrilled and frightened the unqualifiedly antislavery man Phillips. "He is a strange, resolute, repulsive, iron-willed, inexorable old man. He stands like a solitary rock in a more mobile society, a fiery nature, and a cold temper, and a cool head,—a volcano beneath a covering of snow."[26] Brown's otherwise socially dangerous nature, in its rightful time and setting, had become both heroic and necessary.

Eighty years before, many of those antislavery people engaged in the Kansas struggle believed, the American Revolution had called forth similar heroic qualities in the true American people. One October Sunday in 1856, Thomas Wentworth Higginson, the fiery young abolitionist, preached in Lawrence, the free-state center, taking as his text "Be ye not afraid of them," the same text, Higginson wrote to the *New York Tribune*, which "John Martin used in preaching to the patriots after the Battle of Bunker Hill." Ever since the humiliating rendition of the fugitive slave Anthony Burns from Boston in 1854, Higginson declared, aligning himself to the Kansas milieu, "I have been looking for men. I have found them in Kan-

24 Journal of Richard J. Hinton, September 3, 1856.
25 For example see the letter of Amos A. Lawrence to Mrs. Charles Barber, January 8, 1856, in the Amos A. Lawrence Letterbook, New England Aid Company Papers, Kansas State Historical Society.
26 Phillips, *Conquest of Kansas*, 327.

sas."[27] The freedom-loving moral manhood achieved in the American Revolution, subsequently gone flabby as unchallenged slave-hounds desecrated that true national spirit, could now be regained in Kansas. As evocations of the American Revolution inspired antislavery forces in Kansas, so, through immediate action, could they now fire the first shot in the ever-deepening civil conflict and build a new Bunker Hill monument for their descendants. "As the people of Kansas have been encouraged by the memory of their fathers' heroic struggle for right, so will the struggle in the future be strengthened by the remembrance of the Kansas contest," a Lawrence paper editorialized.[28] Again, as in the American Revolution, women too served the glorious banner of freedom, tilling the fields and bringing in the crops as the men took to arms.[29] Rendered in the gloss of this vision, the American Revolution had been a people's war, engaging all the efforts of every member of the community. To whatever degree this actually may have been the case in 1776 or in 1856, such a unity in struggle as that attributed to the Hebrews, Puritans, and Revolutionaries was the very marrow of the antislavery self-image in Kansas. The moral ambiguities involved in the settlement of this frontier, the fundamental divisions within the antislavery forces were masked by engagement in the sanctified struggle for the good. The guilt over the lax lives they had led and into which they might again backslide served as a powerful prod to be up and at the Lord's work. Such a vision counterposed to such an enemy, and in such a setting, engaged vast numbers of northern settlers in Kansas, and masses of northerners elsewhere by sympathy, in an antislavery struggle they had previously ignored or even condemned.

Thus were northern preconceptions—ideal types of self and the southern other—confirmed and fortified in Kansas. This process occurred in an engagement, not a rhetorical or social vacuum, and slave state settlers had corresponding preconceptions and reactions.

27 New York *Tribune*, October 7, 1856. On July 10, 1856, Gerrit Smith told a Buffalo convention called to aid Kansas that they should be "looking to bayonets" not to ballots, that "if all manhood has not departed from us" plentiful arms had to be shipped forthwith to Kansas. Quoted in Harlow, "The Rise and Fall of the Kansas Aid Movement," 15.

28 Lawrence (Kan.) *Herald of Freedom*, December 27, 1856.

29 Phillips, *Conquest of Kansas*, 359. The incorporation of women in this male set of nineteenth-century ideals demonstrated the totalist nature of the struggle.

They naturally resented the dehumanizing Puke image imposed on them and fought against it, and for the true morality which they felt they represented and northerners violated. They too knew of the forces of the devil and of the Lord, and reversed the identities of the combatant forces.[30]

Proslavery settlers defined themselves as defenders of the status quo and of law and order. Coming by the wagonload over from Missouri in 1855, proslavery voters had first organized the territory with a slave constitution. Some historians have also suggested that there was a tacit understanding in Congress in 1854 that, popular sovereignty notwithstanding, the northern half of the territory, Nebraska, would be organized as a free state and the southern half, Kansas, as a slave state. Thus proslavery soldiers could construe their role as upholders of duly constituted authority against the northern rebel. "The crisis has arrived," a proslavery newspaper proclaimed late in 1855, "when it behooves every Law and Order man to aid in enforcing the laws. Resistance by force cannot be countenanced. . . . we [must] aid in quelling the rebellion now existing." Not feeling any compulsive need for regeneration as did northern settlers, they stood for home, church, private property, and male authority; they were the conservative party, guarding tradition from anarchic northern radicals. Wrote a Leavenworth editor, "Every man must place a guard around his house to protect his distressed wife and sleeping babes, and dare not pass beyond the rounds of that guard or [he will] be shot down in cold blood."[31]

To proslavery Kansans, northerners were "the foreign foe," committed to "the one idea of crushing us of the South as a people." The abolitionist ideas they imputed to all northerners were bad enough; what was worse than false principles in themselves was

---

30 For accounts of the proslavery position in Kansas see James C. Malin, "The Proslavery Background of the Kansas Struggle," *Mississippi Valley Historical Review*, X (1923), 285–305; William E. Parrish, *David Rice Atchison of Missouri: Border Politician* (Columbia, Mo.: University of Missouri Press, 1961); Elmer L. Craik, "Southern Interest in Territorial Kansas, 1854–1858," in *Collections* of the Kansas State Historical Society, XV (1919–1922), 334–450; Walter L. Fleming, "The Buford Expedition to Kansas," *American Historical Review*, VI (1900), 38–48.

31 Leavenworth (Kan.) *Weekly Herald*, December 1, 1855, May 24, 1856. The ideal of southern patriarchy is developed in Bertram Wyatt-Brown, "The Ideal Typology and Ante-Bellum Southern History: A Testing of a New Approach," *Societas*, V (1975), 1–29.

that such ideals masked underlying moral corruption. Asserting freedom and their own moral superiority, northerners were really a pack of evil hypocrites . . . "Oh! those long-faced, sanctimonious Yankees!" one proslavery newspaper moaned.[32] Assertions of the Higher Law served as an excuse and a cover for the destruction of positive law. "Who else would call Sharpes rifles *moral* weapons to be used in place of the *Bible*?" Lawbreakers who chanted to Higher Law—peace-lovers who emigrated armed to the teeth—Christians who read southerners out of the human race—"Surely none but the Yankee abolitionists could go to such heights and depths of duplicity, falsehood and hypocracy [*sic*]. But these are the cardinal virtues in Abolitionism together with stealing."[33]

"Nigger-stealing" became the central symbol of all that was base in these northern invaders: not only would slave-stealing serve northern purpose by purloining southern property—a vital element plucked from southern manhood—it would reverse the natural, good order of society in general. To southern settlers, northerners were not devoted to "the welfare of the country," but "alone to the one idea, sickly sycophantic love for the nigger," which compelled stealing him and setting him free. Underlying this purpose of destroying private property in slaves raged northern white lust to couple with filthy black women. Northerners came to Kansas not to increase the area of freedom but "for the express purpose of stealing, running off and hiding runaway negroes from Missouri [and] taking to their own bed and their own arms, a stinking negro wench."[34] That combination of aversion and desire which southerners felt towards their black slaves they projected onto their northern enemy. In this vision, northerners wished to regress towards bestiality; desiring to have congress with creatures of the dirt, they themselves became, in southern eyes, subhuman beasts of the earth, who claimed infuriatingly that they were saints.

In sum, northerners sought to reverse the entire moral and social order, to enshrine the low and debase the high. If the nigger-stealers gained power, a proslavery newspaper insisted, "Our white men

32 Leavenworth (Kan.) *Weekly Herald*, August 30, September 13, 1856.
33 *Ibid.*, March 29, 1856, December 8, 1855.
34 *Ibid.*, March 29, 1856, March 30, 1855.

would be cowards, our black men idols, our women amazons."
Those northern whites who were sent to conquer Kansas were thus,
in a second southern image of the northerner set beside that of the
Yankee abolitionist, the worthless minions of the northern bosses,
the impoverished northern urban slum-dwellers, "the filth, scum
and off-scourings of the East and Europe [sent] to pollute our fair
land."[35] Such scum, a preindustrial subproletariat, were the counterpart of the antislavery creation, the Puke. Here in southern eyes
was the independent white degenerated to the level of worthless
subhumanity. In the summer of 1856, an Illinois newspaper reported
that "seventy-five drunken rowdies from the 'sands' of Chicago
passed through our town, accompanied with a quota of *nymph du
pave* on their way to Kansas."[36] Proslavery settlers thus believed
that they were the repository of the independent yeoman ideal and
that northern urban society, not slavery, had produced the threatening underclass of beastly and socially corrosive whites.

The appropriate analogue for the nigger-stealing abolitionists and
their dirty troops was hence not the American Revolution, which
the antislavery press had so freely appropriated, but the nihilistic
French Revolution which had destroyed the entire social fabric, and
even then "the French Revolution itself affords no adequate picture
of the startling scenes and horrors [the Kansas invasion] unfolds."
On the contrary, southerners felt that *they* represented the true
spirit of the American Revolution: "Let us arise, buckle on the
armor of our patriotic sires."[37] By the time that they sacked the antislavery bastion of Lawrence in May, 1856, the proslavery forces
were certain that they embodied American legal, moral, and social
order against lawless, revolutionary northern invaders. Destruction
of the nigger-stealing, filth-wallowing beast was a sanctioned act.
"We simply executed to the letter of what the law decreed," wrote
John H. Stringfellow, the leading proslavery ideologue, "and left as

35 *Ibid.*, July 19, 1856; William Walker to David R. Atchison, July 11, 1854, in Atchison Papers, Western Historical Manuscripts Collection, Columbia, Missouri.
36 Springfield (Ill.) *Register*, reprinted in Leavenworth (Kan.) *Weekly Herald*, July 5, 1856. At other times, employing the reverse side of the nativist coin, proslavery forces sought im-migrant, especially Irish, support on the grounds that Anglo-Saxon Yankees were the real op-pressors of the Celts, in northern cities as well as in the Motherland. C.f. Atchison (Kan.) *Squatter Sovereign*, August 28, September 18, 1855.
37 Leavenworth (Kan.) *Weekly Herald*, August 30, 1856.

though we had been to church—by the way, there is *no church* in Lawrence, but several *free love associations*."[38]

The roiling anger present in these contradictory conceptions of the other was released into action by the friction of social contact. Free-soil and proslavery settlers would cluster together with their own kind on farms and in towns, but formed antagonistic communities cheek-by-jowl throughout much of the territory. The inevitable arguments, endemic in the West, over defining valid claims for the best land, quarrels over rights of way and access to water and transportation, were politicized along sectional lines in Kansas. When the competitor could be collectively targeted as a moral and social pariah, the explosions of violence against him were less sporadic and disorganized. Thus pushing and shoving in taverns, gang fights in the streets, and finally murder took on a sectional color. The weak forces of the law were also controlled by one side or the other, and so justice was not expected within the system and two vigilante organizations emerged, as did dual legislatures, governors, and constitutions.

When actual bloodshed began with the premeditated murder of an antislavery settler in December, 1855, aggression was usually justified on the surface as defensive response to the systematic attacks of the beastly others. Northerners had instituted "a system of highway robbery, and midnight plunder, worse than has ever been known in this country, and equalled only by the Bedouin tribes of the desert," wrote a southern defender of his New Jerusalem, while an antislavery defender of *his* chosen land wrote that "human patience cannot long endure this system of terrorism and persecution." Defense of a sacred cause blended into and justified a crushing response to evil, encouraged, even demanded obliteration of the other. "Our people propose acting *only on the defensive* . . . but when the issue shall be forced upon them . . . take care. A volcano is under your feet, and lightnings are overhead. Omnipotence is watching your every movement, and 'Those who take the sword shall perish by the sword.'"[39] In defending truth the sanctified people would come rightly to embody wrathful omnipotence.

38 Atchison (Kan.) *Squatter Sovereign*, May 27, 1856.
39 Leavenworth (Kan.) *Weekly Herald*, September 20, 1856; Lawrence (Kan.) *Herald of Freedom*, May 10, 1856, June 16, 1855.

When it came, war was welcome. In the absence of any agreed-upon over-arching authority and after months of unbearable resentment and tension, a just war would free morally sanctioned passion to render the issue into an open and conclusive test of force. "We are glad that the issue is thus finally reduced to one single, starting point, annihilation," an antislavery newspaper wrote. "We are ready."[40] At long last, cleansing conflict would prove the masculine worth of antislavery. Thomas Wentworth Higginson declared, "War only educates men to itself, disciplines them, teaches them to bear its fatigues, anxiety and danger, and actually to enjoy them."[41]

Each act by the other side demanded revenge. A small force of federal dragoons rendered impossible most open engagements of large proslavery and antislavery troops, but wide-ranging, vicious guerrilla actions of small groups were frequent. All means to intimidate the other side into capitulating or leaving the territory were used: crop and house burnings, theft of livestock and draft animals, tarring and feathering, torture, murder and disfigurement of the slain. Reports of torture of captives and mutilation of corpses led to like responses. At Pottawatomie Creek, on May 24, 1856, for example, John Brown cut off the hands of his five captives (in perhaps acting out the Old Testament judgment on the theft of slave lives), stabbed them in the side, and then bludgeoned them to death with his broadsword. Vengeance demanded that all violence be unleashed. "Blood for Blood! But for each drop spilled we shall require one hundred fold! . . . Every man shall be a law unto himself, adopting as his guiding star the 'golden rule.'"[42] In this eye-for-an-eye version of the golden rule, each side attempted the blood purge of the other and those evils which the other embodied.

Under these conditions no one could remain disengaged. Hundreds of northern and southern settlers were compelled, whatever their prior position on slavery, to become openly proslavery or antislavery, and to use violence, as the guerrilla war polarized the community. The diary of Samuel Reeder, a young French-Canadian,

40 Topeka (Kan.) *Tribune*, August 25, 1856.
41 New York *Tribune*, October 23, 1856.
42 Atchison (Kan.) *Squatter Sovereign*, May 8, 1856; Lawrence (Kan.) *Herald of Freedom*, February 2, 1856.

records his being goaded into identifying himself as an abolitionist by mocking southern neighbors. In the summer of 1856 he joined a northern guerrilla band, and marched around without seeing action. He was frightened and repelled by the Pukes. After a day of farm labor, Reeder went to bed with a "kinky back," and that night "dreamed of getting a ball in the back by the Missourians of Topeka."[43] To give another example, Charles Lines, a Connecticut pacifist, who settled thirty miles from Lawrence, hoped as late as May, 1856, that "prudent councils" would lead his neighbors to refrain from "unnecessarily involving themselves in trouble." However, in June, the war came to them. Lines himself was particularly activated by the testimony of a "naturally very mild" man, much like himself, who had been tortured by the Pukes, and left, tied up, to die. "Blood *must* end in the triumph of the right," Lines responded, and in anger took to arms.[44]

In September, 1856, the national government imposed peace through the clever device of nationalizing both the antislavery and proslavery militias. This de-escalated open conflict as a mixed militia would fire on neither side, nor be fired upon. Defused at the more organized level, the worst of the guerrilla warfare slowed as well. The northerners won their struggle essentially by standing their ground against the proslavery forces. More important, the immigration of 1856 and the years that followed was overwhelmingly from the North. Southern political attempts in Congress to impose a slave state admission of Kansas through the Lecompton Constitution, the last device proposed by a proslavery Kansas legislative rump, would continue, unsuccessfully, until 1858, breaking the Democratic party in two in the process, but by the end of 1856 prosouthern military forces in Kansas had packed their tents and left the territory.

One aftermath of the struggle of 1854–1856 was the terrible guerrilla conflict in Missouri and Kansas during the Civil War. In this second round, as each side was licensed and armed by a different

43 Diary of Samuel J. Reader (MS in the Kansas State Historical Society), September 30, 1855, February 19–20, June 20–21, July 4, August 9, September 3, 1856.
44 Charles B. Lines to the New Haven (Conn.) *Daily Palladium*, May 2, June 13, 16, 17, 1856, in Lines, "The Connecticut Kansas Colony," 35, 151, 155, 160.

government, the level of violence increased. The climax of this warfare came on August 21, 1863, when William C. Quantrill, a former proslavery Kansas settler, brought his troop of Pukes-turned-Confederates to Lawrence, that symbolic capital of the antislavery Kansans, burned the city, and systematically killed 183 unarmed civilian men and boys.[45] Yet this was a raid, based on old scores to be settled, which in no fundamental way challenged northern control of Kansas.

After the Kansas struggle concluded, however, came the irony of the Great Barbeque. As Paul W. Gates has so sumptuously described it in *Fifty Million Acres: Conflicts over Kansas Land Policy, 1854–1890,* this feast was consumed down to the last bone in Kansas. With railroads, towns, and so much fertile land at stake, when the worst of the guerrilla war ended in 1856 and free-soil was clearly established, those lambs who chose to remain within the new order lay down with the lions in mutual self-interest. A proslavery Missouri newspaper reported, quite accurately, in 1857 that in the railroad terminus of Atchison, several prominent proslavery and antislavery chieftains who had been shooting at each other less than a year before were now "lying down together, hale fellows well met and partners in taste; growing fat in their purses and persons by speculations in town sites; eating roasted turkeys and drinking champagne with the very money sent from Missouri and elsewhere to make Kansas a *slave state.*"[46] Betrayal of the Holy Cause came quickly on the heels of victory. Gates argues, in effect, that the original ideological struggle was an ephemeral and insincere tissue of rationalizations, and that undiluted land greed was the sole real interest of Kansas settlers from both sections from the onset. While his position contains a pleasing and clarifying cynicism, it tends to argue back too loosely from the undoubtedly corrupt nature of the hegemony of the northern-dominated freeholder society to presumptively corrupt origins. *Plus ça change, plus c'est la même chose,* as an argument

45 Nichols, *Bleeding Kansas,* 256–59.
46 St. Joseph (Mo.) *Journal,* August 7, 1857. Also see Wendell H. Stephenson, *The Political Career of General James H. Lane* (Topeka: Kansas State Printing Plant, 1930), 85. On the Civil War in Kansas, see William E. Parrish, *A History of Missouri,* Volume III, 1865–1875 (Columbia, University of Missouri Press), and books and articles by Richard S. Brownlee, Jay Monaghan, Albert Castel, and others cited in Parrish's bibliography.

tends to dismiss or at least undervalue the moral effort which goes into intentional efforts for cultural change at the beginning. Results constitute a perhaps unfortunately separate series of problems.

Kansans did join the rest of the nation in the postwar spate of construction and corruption. Without continued engagement in moral struggle, the much-feared backsliding ensued; or perhaps the commitment was too difficult to sustain and a release from duty into self-service was needed. Eras of declension tend to follow from periods of engagement, just as they serve to spur on a feeling for the need for reengagement. Recollection of the Puritan and American Revolutionary experiences had served Kansans as measures and guides to communal moral effort; the Kansas struggle did bring people together in deep and mutual struggle, in an attempt to reach once more the heights presumably scaled in those earlier efforts. However, once burning necessity—which had been to a great extent imposed on the people by the people—was removed, backsliding did follow.

The moral energy created in Kansas in 1854–1856 and in the North as a whole in the Civil War, for which Kansas was a rehearsal, was spent in the war. The society that followed, despite the efforts of the few valiant reformers who remained in the field, was generally understood to be characterized by that moral declension which the war effort had been meant to overcome. The moral vision exemplified by the Kansas efforts extended only to defining the uses of the land, the form of labor, and the proper type of freeholder. Settling these issues was moral as well as material, but once free white individuals could possess the land, the purpose of the battle had been attained. Collective antislavery effort went only up to this point. With equal men at the free starting line, the race to accumulate could begin. As antislavery, free labor ideology in Kansas contained neither analysis of the social and economic inequalities and power imbalances in northern capitalist society, nor belief in a positive state to secure equality, it could serve only to clear the field. Thus a frightening, intense, and sincere general effort ironically, if unintentionally, opened the new land to the work of greedy interests who knew how to exploit free soil when they saw it.

In 1856, the northern industrialist Amos A. Lawrence had provided letters of introduction for Samuel C. Pomeroy, a Kansas agent to Washington. He "comes of pure New England stock, through Bunker Hill, and therefore cannot have any love for those who have oppressed" free men.[47] Seventeen years later, Pomeroy, grown fat and rich with boodle, was driven from the United States Senate after being caught in an unforgivably blatant effort to buy his reelection. Pomeroy had become Dilworthy, openly ridiculed in *The Gilded Age* by Mark Twain, as a temperance and Sunday school advocate who debased every real moral value. Pomeroy-Dilworthy was Twain's archetypal hypocrite for a corrupt age. In 1856, Twain might have added in all fairness, Pomeroy had indeed well served a free people in an earnest struggle. The moral collapse following the victory should not be read back into an easy condemnation of the purposes of the battle for the covenant, nor of the motives of the warriors, even if those purposes and motives had been more complex and troubling than those some historians admire and others debunk.

47 Amos A. Lawrence to S. G. Haven, July 20, 1856, in Amos A. Lawrence Letterbook.

# PROSLAVERY AND ANTISLAVERY INTELLECTUALS
## Class Concepts and Polemical Struggle

*Bertram Wyatt-Brown*

IN 1845 Lewis Tappan, a prominent abolitionist, businessman, and active churchman, engaged in an unusual exchange of letters. His correspondent was James Henry Hammond, a wealthy slaveholder, southern polemicist, and recent governor of South Carolina. Their purpose was not to strike up one of those intimate friendships of which Victorian men and women were so fond.[1] In fact, two individuals could hardly have presented a greater contrast. Hammond, for instance, had closed his days as governor with scandal of a sexual nature snapping at his heels. The whispers never reached northern ears, but they forced him into exile at "Silver Bluff," his plantation not far from Augusta.[2] If Lewis Tappan had ever fallen from grace, no

1 See Drew G. Faust, "Men and Women in Nineteenth-Century America: Groups, Values and Social Change," paper presented at the 2nd Berkshire History Conference, Radcliffe College, October, 1974; Noel G. Annan, "The Intellectual Aristocracy," in John H. Plumb (ed.), *Studies in Social History: A Tribute to G. M. Trevelyan* (London: Longsmans, Green & Co., 1955), 243–87; Carroll Smith Rosenberg, "The Female World of Love and Ritual: Relations Between Women in Nineteenth-Century America," *Signs: Journal of Women in Culture and Society*, I (1975), 1–29. Financial assistance and office facilities, gratefully acknowledged, were provided for the preparation of this essay by the John Simon Guggenheim Foundation, the Woodrow Wilson International Center for Scholars, and the Shelby Cullom Davis Center for Historical Studies.

2 Clement Eaton, *The Mind of the Old South* (Rev. ed.; Baton Rouge: Louisiana State University Press, 1967), 44–68; James Henry Hammond Secret Diary, "Thoughts. . . ." (au-

hint ever came from his lips or those of anyone near to him. Being an abolitionist was his sole badge of notoriety, one of diminishing strength, at least in northern circles.

Business, not pleasure, prompted the exchange. A controversy had arisen over the way Governor Hammond and Judge John Belton O'Neall had handled the case of a young man who had helped his slave mistress escape from her master. Joseph Sturge, Thomas Clarkson, and other British emancipationists joined Lewis Tappan and his associates in public and private protests against the harsh sentence imposed and the illustration of southern licentiousness the affair allegedly offered. "Having abundant leisure," Hammond published a defense of slavery and southern morals in the form of letters to Thomas Clarkson. Seeking further information, the author asked Lewis Tappan about antislavery publications so that, as Tappan rephrased it, he could "fortify" himself "against the doctrines & measures" of northern and English adversaries.[3]

Tappan did not merely fulfill the request. Instead, he welcomed the nullifier to the polemical contest. Tappan had traded insults with Judge O'Neall, a fellow evangelical, in their private communications. The exchanges with Hammond, however, were not based upon churchly infighting, but upon a sense of common membership in a secular world. There was a subtle, tacit, and mutual acceptance on both sides, as if the protagonists were emissaries of belligerent states assigned to a neutral court. For all their differences they understood one another. After all, both were gentlemen of property and standing.

The connection rested upon another basis as well. Tappan and Hammond relished the life of the mind and the tough, hard-headed

---

tobiography), February 24, 1852, Hammond to Marcellus Hammond, January 28, 1844, both in James Henry Hammond Papers, South Caroliniana Library, University of South Carolina. On Tappan's career, see Bertram Wyatt-Brown, *Lewis Tappan and the Evangelical War against Slavery* (Cleveland: Press of Case Western Reserve University, 1969).

3 James H. Hammond, *Gov. Hammond's Letters on Southern Slavery: Addressed to Thomas Clarkson, the English Abolitionist* (Charleston: Walker V. Burke, 1845), 3; Lewis Tappan to James Henry Hammond, June 6, 1845, in James Henry Hammond Papers, Library of Congress. On this episode, see also Tappan to John B. O'Neall, April 29, July 19, September 28, 1844, Tappan to Thomas Clarkson, May 6, 1844, Tappan to Joseph Sturge, April 30, 1844, letterbook, all in Lewis Tappan Papers, Library of Congress; Betty Fladeland, *Men and Brothers: Anglo-American Antislavery Cooperation* (Urbana: University of Illinois Press, 1972), 292–96.

struggles required to translate ideas into public action. Like other intellectuals of the age, they believed in the feasibility of remaking society so that their separate visions of godliness, order, reason, and virtue would prevail. The prospect of a new utopia, one embracing slavery and the other crushing all distinctions of color, animated them both, convinced as they were that the intellectual's role would determine the outcome. But they also knew of a grimmer side. Almost by definition, the antebellum thinker was a self-annointed spokesman for one kind of righteousness or another. He had to create his own following, no easy task in the workaday world of popular suspicion, indifference, or outright truculence. Unhappy with things as they were, the ideologue was bound to estrange the average citizen, eager for flattery and sensitive to rebuke. Making matters still worse, he was often a snob by reputation if not also in fact. In the sectional contest, the southern man of letters stressed the cultural superiority of the leisure and gentility that slavery provided the class to which he gave allegiance. Likewise, the abolitionist claimed for himself and colleagues a moral and spiritual insight into divine purposes. Arrogance, whatever the form it took, did not win much public favor for either side.

Although neither Tappan nor Hammond were conscious of temperamental similarities along these lines, they shared a common problem: how to reach a national public that really would rather have preferred silence on the subject of slavery.[4] In comparison with the southern group, abolitionists had the very worst of it by far. But even the proslavery enthusiast had to face the anti-intellectuality of his region and the complacency and ridicule of the free-state audience. Up North the social theorizing of slaveholders seemed the work of some "very curious maggots," who had managed to stir "the torpid stagnation" of a few "planter brains," though leaving everybody else stiff with boredom.[5] Rather naturally, proslavery writers,

---

4 George M. Fredrickson, *The Black Image in the White Mind: The Debate on Afro-American Character and Destiny, 1817–1914* (New York: Harper & Row, 1971), is the only recent study to treat proslavery and antislavery ideas in the same context and framework. For a penetrating study of the proslavery intelligentsia, see Drew G. Faust, *A Sacred Circle: The Dilemma of the Intellectual in the Old South, 1840–1860* (Baltimore: Johns Hopkins University Press, 1977).

5 New York *Tribune*, June 5, 1855.

like the northern reformers, felt alienated. Their mutual dissatisfaction did not arise from the absence of proper institutional channels for resolving social issues, as Stanley Elkins once asserted. Instead, the problem lay in two spheres, the first being the intellectual's sense of transcendence above the ordinary ways of the world, a legacy from the Romantic intellectual ferment abroad. The second source of discontent and aggression arose from the ambiguity of the intellectual's relation to the social classes, to which he had to refer his case for approval or rejection. Proslavery and antislavery writers scarcely lacked self-confidence, but they all had to recognize the shifting and difficult nature of the battle terrain. The American social system was fluid and diverse, so much so that both parties argued mostly within social spheres they knew best. Common social preconceptions, as shall appear, shaped their views of themselves as moralists, underscored the significance of church controversy over slavery, set the boundaries of arguments used, and determined which social ranks would be fought over and which would be excluded from much involvement in literary debate.

For both sets of ideologues the public stage was exceedingly small. It was on the whole confined to what northerners and southerners vaguely identified as "the respectability," that is, to those who acknowledged religious and civic interest, owned some property or aspired to decent status, and met the conventional standards of personal conduct. One is tempted to call this audience "the middle class." The term, however, is inappropriate. It excludes the upper tier of society, an important reference point in the polemical warfare, and it fails to reveal the peculiar relationship between the intellectual and professional class and the local elites whom abolitionists and proslavery writers sought to recruit. Besides, "middle class" does not describe the strategy by which antebellum polemicists defined their audience. It was a much narrower and more genteel group than so inclusive a word as middle class can convey. As we shall later see, great numbers of Yankees did not share the moral assumptions of the American Victorians, so to speak, yet their economic status identified them as bourgeois.

Rather than conceive of society as divided among the modern schemes of lower, middle, and upper classes, abolitionists, like other polemicists of the day, preferred moral designations, such as "the respectability." In addition, the "workingman" or "humble toiler" was allegedly the very "sinew" of national strength upon which the reformers claimed to rely. Actually, they did not have in mind Irish navvies or unskilled laborers and domestics, but rather anyone of decent aspect who supported himself, feared the Protestant God, and contributed to community well-being, as the evangelical mind conceived it. Left out were the various ethnic groups that displayed hostility to questions of public evangelical plans for social uplift. Likewise, "aristocracy" did not refer to bloodlines or old wealth, but to those that supported or were indifferent about slavery, whatever their economic level. Thus, the abolitionist William Jay, himself to the manor born, unself-consciously growled that "the liberty of speech, of the press, and of conscience" were the targets of "the political and commercial aristocracy" in the free states. Lydia Maria Child, of respectable lineage, exclaimed, "Withdraw the aristocratic influence," meaning newsmen, clergymen, and shopkeepers with southern ties, individuals not necessarily wealthy or well-born, "and I should be perfectly easy to trust to the good feelings of the people." The populace in question, as *Human Rights* explained, were those "who support themselves in the good old-fashioned republican way of honest and honorable industry," as contrasted with dissolute slaveholders.[6]

One might perceive a spirit of democracy and classlessness in these rhetorical flourishes from antislavery pens. Certainly the reformers liked to stress "aristocratic" or upper-class opposition to their aims. "God and Truth," not endorsements from "distinguished men," ought to be the boasts of antislavery reform, Tappan complained upon observing some antislavery backsliding in the New York *Independent*, a Protestant newspaper he helped to found. To be sure, some abolitionists entertained sweeping notions of Christian egalitarianism and complained of blue-nosed prejudices within and outside antislavery circles.[7] Yet the bulk of abolitionist opinion

6 William Jay quoted in Bayard Tuckerman, *William Jay and the Constitutional Movement for the Abolition of Slavery* (New York: Dodd, Mead & Co., 1883), 80; Lydia Maria Child to Convers Francis, December 19, 1835, in *Letters of Lydia Maria Child* (Boston: Houghton Mifflin & Co., 1883), 18; (New York) *Human Rights*, July, 1835.

7 Quoted in Wyatt-Brown, *Lewis Tappan*, 319.

found no fault with the social hierarchy except as it affected southern bondage. With the exception of the perfectionist fringe of the movement, most abolitionists were hostile toward the possessing classes out of disappointment, not because of fixed ideological conviction. Eagerly the reform spokesmen sought the patronage of the wealthy, only to be rebuffed or, still worse, ignored. Therefore, crusaders like William Lloyd Garrison used the phrase "gentlemen of property and standing" in a sardonic way, both denying and affirming its applicability to their foes. True gentlemen and ladies would share their antislavery convictions. Others merely mocked the banner they uprighteously assumed.

What rejoicing there was when penetration of the social wall did occur. The acquisition of Wendell Phillips, James Russell Lowell, Gerrit Smith, William Jay, and others from high-toned families heartened the soul of the most doctrinaire reformer. In 1843, for instance, Theodore Weld boasted, "There is now every prospect that progress will be made on the question of Colored Citizenship in Congress. Abott Lawrence, S. T. Armstrong, Henry Lee, Franklin Dexter, the rich Perkins, and 150 others of high 'respectability' in B[oston]" had signed the petition. In 1849 William Lloyd Garrison, Elizur Wright, Theodore Parker, and other prominent abolitionists were invited to help form a literary supper club which Samuel Ward and other Boston Brahmins had initiated. After gaining reassurances that gentlemen of color would not be automatically excluded, they joined without the slightest twinge of a democratic conscience.[8]

The point is not to register the antislavery elect in an antebellum blue-book. Abolitionists were seldom given to social climbing anyhow. Practicing plain speaking and plain living, they were confident in meeting the social criteria of respectability—moral repute, decent family connections, sometimes education at college, seminary, or professional school or else a promising apprenticeship, and occa-

8 Theodore Dwight Weld to Lewis Tappan, January 6, 1843, in Gilbert H. Barnes and Dwight L. Dumond (eds.), *The Letters of Theodore Dwight Weld, Angelina Grimké Weld, and Sarah Grimké, 1822–1844* (2 vols.; Gloucester, Mass.: Peter Smith, 1965), II, 958; Stow Persons, *The Decline of American Gentility* (New York: Columbia University Press, 1973), 105–107; Julia Ward Howe, *Reminiscences 1819–1899* (Boston: Houghton, Mifflin & Co., 1900), 152–64. See also, Raimund Goerler, "Family, Self, and Antislavery: Sydney Howard Gay and the Abolitionist Commitment" (Ph.D. dissertation, Case Western Reserve University, 1974), a sensitive study of class and family problems in an aspiring abolitionist.

sionally inherited or personally acquired property. They belonged to the ranks of the professional class—schoolteachers, ministers, and writers. As members of the intelligentsia, they moved within that small band of neighborhood citizens who started lyceums, campaigned for common schools, organized temperance chapters, raised funds for colleges, libraries, and asylums, welcomed professors, clergymen, and foreign missionaries to their homes, humble or grand as the case might be. Upon this foundation, a reformer like Tappan felt himself as worthy of respect as James Hammond or any other luminary. Angry or pleased according to upper-class receptiveness at the moment, the abolitionist was intent upon fulfilling his role as he saw it: the persuasion of individuals who could strengthen the cause. Anyone was welcome, but obviously those with power and prestige, particularly in the Anglo-Saxon, Protestant milieu, took precedence. Personal worries about status had little effect upon a reformer's motives.

Therefore, it would be a mistake to categorize economic standings as a way to distinguish those who were abolitionists and those who opposed the crusade. Community elites, especially in the smaller northern towns, welcomed more than just those within the highest decile of income. Take for example the influential group of Hudson, Ohio, a flourishing settlement on the Western Reserve. Wealthy residents naturally led the various benevolent, civic, and church organizations in the 1830s. (On the other hand, some with equal incomes took no interest at all in such matters.) Founder of the community and its largest landholder, David Hudson established the local Congregational church, Western Reserve College, a temperance society, and a colonization chapter. Owen Brown, the father of John Brown, was just as active as Hudson, though he had begun his career at the very bottom of the economic ladder. By 1830 Owen Brown had gained wealth and repute. Associated with David Hudson, Owen Brown, and other substantial figures were Elizur Wright, Jr. and Sr., both teachers, Charles Storrs, college president, and Beriah Green, clergyman and professor. On an economic scale, however, they were poor—the usual status of the American intellectual. In 1832 the Hudson leadership divided on the question of slavery. One pious faction, including Owen Brown, adopted Garrisonian policy, whereas David Hudson rallied the conservative friends of Liberia. Eventually he purged the college, seat of "radicalism." Obviously the fight involved religious and ideological, not economic, differences.

The point is further shown in the fact that another Hudson leader named Benjamin Whedon formed a third faction. A Jacksonian of humble beginnings but recent wealth, Whedon had ousted David Hudson as village postmaster, denounced teetotalism, left the Congregational church to start a rival Methodist group, and fulminated against the abolitionists. In terms of property-holding, Whedon *belonged*. Yet, he did not meet the standards of "respectability" in the eyes of Adamsonian and Congregational neighbors.[9] This kind of factionalism in a local elite suggests that any interpretation of antislavery based upon rigid class and economic categories is very doubtful. Moreover, the illustration reveals the social ambiguities in which the abolitionist was involved. He needed patrons like David Hudson; they sometimes failed him. Still more frustrating was the lack of cohesion in the local upper ranks, so that even if the Congregational element under David Hudson had championed Garrisonian ideals, Benjamin Whedon provided an alternative counterforce, one that could draw upon the Democratic and Methodist opponents of the Whiggish, puritan elite.

Thus, within the orbit of local power and religious engagement, there were individuals like Whedon and Hudson who opposed abolitionism from somewhat different perspectives. Whedon represented in a small town the kind of hostility that unrefined, anti-intellectual storekeepers, commercial agents, and other entrepreneurs of the larger cities sometimes displayed. On the other hand, David Hudson, with distinctly evangelical sensibilities, typified the response of these who supported the array of good causes then in motion, but could not stomach abolitionist "fanaticism." In more influential

---

9 Michael A. McManis, "Range Ten, Town Four: A Social History of Hudson, Ohio, 1799–1840" (Ph.D. dissertation, Case Western Reserve University, 1976), 134–38. See also James H. Stuckey, "The Formation of Leadership Groups in a Midwest Frontier Town, Canton, Ohio, 1805–1855" (Ph.D. dissertation, Case Western Reserve University, 1975), which corroborates the same findings in a more ethnically diverse community. See also David French, "Puritan Conservatism and the Frontier: The Elizur Wright Family on the Connecticut Western Reserve," *The Old Northwest*, I (1975), 85–95.

centers than Hudson, Ohio—such places as Andover, Massachusetts, or Princeton, New Jersey, Rittenhouse Square or Beacon
Hill—clergymen, pious merchants, schoolteachers, and others of orthodox religious and social principles sympathized with colonization but feared the effects of "immediate emancipation" upon the
stability and prosperity of the Union. Just as abolitionists themselves ran a gamut along ideological lines, so too did antiabolitionists in the North span a number of positions. The abolitionist tactic
was to recruit among the more moderate and pious wing of the opposition, especially in the early years.

It would be almost impossible to compute the relative strengths
of the "Hudson" and "Whedon" groups across the thousands of
communities in the free states. Yet, something more specific can be
mentioned in regard to the vociferous "Whedon" wing. These
antiabolitionists not only objected to antislavery reform but also
disapproved all the major tenets of evangelical rule and Victorian
morality, attitudes which they associated with Protestant "priestcraft" and aristocratic pretensions of effete gentility. The antievangelicals, if the term is permissible, repudiated the temperance pledge,
frequented beer halls and crossroads taverns, and went fishing or rolled
over for another snooze on Sunday morning—all violations of a
so-called "middle-class morality." It is not an easy group to single
out because it often surfaced in negative responses, and its adherents,
like Benjamin Whedon himself, could be found in the various Protestant denominations, too. Temperament, not theology, determined
the hard-mindedness of this class of citizens. Although seldom identified before as a distinct factor in the polemical war over slavery,
abolitionists knew the type very well, often at the receiving end of a
brickbat.

These men were not confined to one economic class, least of all to
"gentlemen of property and standing." Some were upwardly mobile
parvenus unsure of their position. Yet the rationale that the antievangelicals espoused attracted the less well-to-do, less educated
portion of the populace. It sanctioned their most cherished prejudices and flattered their self-image. Socially (though not economically) reactionary, these Yankees adhered to traditional and as-

criptive values: the dominance of males; the subjection of women; the purity of race; the authority of parenthood; the prestige of physical prowess, and even the violent expression of courage. To such people, abolitionists represented forces of general subversion—the elevation of blacks, women, and prim intellectuals. Indeed, abolitionists were proclaiming the irrelevance of old standards of merit based on gender, color, and bloodlines. And they sought to replace them with universal moral codes of individual achievement and ethical integrity as the sole measurements of personal worth. For the traditionalist, the social order would soon collapse in anarchy, amalgamation, and tyranny if the "fanatics" triumphed.

Under these circumstances, the abolitionists were even more estranged from the ranks below them than from those above, not because of economic differences but educational and cultural discrepancies. They had very little in common with artisans, clerks, draymen, or with non-churchgoing entrepreneurs rising from obscurity to new prominence. An antislavery reformer was not likely to buy a lottery ticket, attend a cockfight, speculate in risky business affairs, or sit about a country store on a lazy afternoon. In fact, his opinions turned him in a different direction at times. In recalling the 1834 mob in New York City, Lewis Tappan observed how reformers and men of wealth found common cause against the ruffians who had stormed his house. Though at first pleased at his household losses in a street bonfire, "the 'respectable portion' of the community," Tappan remarked, brought public pressure to bear against further rioting as soon as rumors floated that Wall Street banks were the upcoming target for looters.[10] Likewise, the demonstrators who disrupted a Garrisonian assembly in New York in 1850 were totally unrelated to the city's social elite, customarily horrified rather than pleased by street violence whatever the cause might be. In this instance, Captain Isaiah Rynders, boss of the Sixth Ward, had mustered butcher-boys and journeymen from the old Dead Rabbit, Shirt

---

10 Lewis Tappan, *The Life of Arthur Tappan* (New York: Hurd & Houghton, 1870), 212. Cf. Leonard L. Richards, *"Gentlemen of Property and Standing:" Anti-Abolition Mobs in Jacksonian America* (New York: Oxford University Press, 1970), 150, and Theodore M. Hammett, "Two Mobs of Jacksonian Boston: Ideology and Interest," *Journal of American History*, LXII (1976), 845–68.

Tail, and Roach Guard gangs—"the purlieus of Park Row," screamed
Wendell Phillips over the hubbub.

To explain how it happened that undereducated commoners
could be so hostile to the egalitarian cause, the reformers resorted
to a familiar argument. The lords of lash, loom, and countinghouse
had misled them from their true interests. Thus, the abolitionist
Stephen S. Foster shouted from the podium during the Rynders affair
that the swaggering youngsters were cap-doffing slaves of New York
merchants. Actually, the b'hoys had their own grudges to bear.
Rynders and company resented the pieties and pretensions of those
claiming to be their social betters. The appearance of abolitionists
provided the excuse for violent and noisy demonstrations which
could express a class protest without in any way questioning the
social order itself. The working classes had powerful if not genteel
allies, particularly amongst ward politicians and journalists. James
Gordon Benett, editor of the New York *Herald*, for instance, for
years had spoken up for those who blamed their various miseries
upon prissy clergymen, "white-coated philosophers," friends of the
"nigger," greedy lawyers, girls from finishing schools, overpaid and
underworked Columbia professors, mannish women from the country, Wall Street brokers, and the indolent rich and roguish poor who
deceived foolish judges and chiseled the simple-hearted workingman—the whole gaggle of stereotypes that contemporary "hard-
hats" identified with the fads and practices of the established
ranks.[11] One did not have to be a bricklayer to follow Bennett's reasoning. Yet, more bricklayers than gentlemen of means and education probably did so.

The feelings of antipathy and contempt were mutual. Abolitionists were men and women of refined and literate sensibilities, intense religious concerns, and self-restrictive moral tastes. They
lived in a world quite apart from drummers, tavern-owners, and

11 Bertram Wyatt-Brown, "The Abolitionist Controversy: Men of Blood, Men of God:
James Gordon Bennett, William Lloyd Garrison and John Brown," in Howard H. Quint and
Milton Cantor (eds.), *Men, Women, and Issues in American History* (2 vols.; Homewood, Ill.:
Dorsey Press, 1975), I, 216–23, 226–30; Herbert Asbury, *The Gangs of New York* (New York:
Alfred A. Knopf, 1928), 5, 43, 44, 77–79; New York *Herald*, May 8, 9, 17, 1850, April 28, May
10, 1860; Boston *Liberator*, May 10, 17, 1850; Oliver Carlson, *The Man Who Made the News*
(New York: Duell, Sloan & Pearce, 1942), 127.

readers as well as writers of penny sheets. As a result, the anti-slavery host was socially more comfortable in the presence of "gentlemen of property and standing," even slaveholders like Hammond, than with those in the lower educational strata. Yet, the situation did not lead to an identification of mutual class interests. As intellectuals and reformers, the antislavery leaders preserved their special identity, though, of course, divided into ideological factions themselves. Nonetheless, their education, background, manners, aspirations, and religious interests bound them to the established ranks of culture and power. This affinity by no means led to compromising deference to the rich, but it promoted distrust of most antislavery leaders among the working and nonevangelical ranks of northern society. In addition, it permeated the reformer's view of himself as a dispenser of good deeds, as a Christian steward.

Hammond's literary colleagues were scarcely less socially self-aware than their northern counterparts. They, too, knew their place in the pecking order, but they suffered, perhaps more acutely than the abolitionists, because of their dull, restrictive surroundings. Far from being the bitter victims of family misfortune that David Donald once described, they were simply ambitious but intellectually fastidious men. These southern cultural leaders—Edmund Ruffin, William L. Grayson, Hammond, to mention a few—were restless and sometimes alienated not because, as a brilliant young scholar has observed, "they or their ancestors had possessed a social standing which was becoming meaningless, but because changing social *values* had denied their undisputed talents the deference they might well have earned in an earlier, more rigidly hierarchical world." The creation of a social philosophy, they found, paid off in recognition, so often craved, so frequently disappointed in other lines of work. Edmund Ruffin, the agricultural reformer, for instance, remarked in 1859, "I have had more notice taken . . . of my late pamphlet" on a proslavery theme "than of anything I ever wrote before." It was even "showing effect in Congress." [12] Even so, the

12 William K. Scarborough (ed.), *The Diary of Edmund Ruffin: Toward Independence October, 1856–April, 1861* (Baton Rouge: Louisiana State University Press, 1972), January 28, 29, 1859, p. 276; Avery O. Craven, *Edmund Ruffin, Southerner: A Study in Secession* (Baton Rouge: Louisiana State University Press, 1966), 78, 81; Harvey Wish, *George Fitzhugh, Propagandist of the Old South* (Gloucester, Mass.: Peter Smith, 1962), 113, 126.

publication of a piece of literary proslavery propaganda seldom created much of a stir, except among the author's closest friends and political allies.

To rescue sagging morale, letters of commiseration and praise flowed back and forth among the southern intelligentsia, each member mired down in some quiet hamlet and surrounded by planting neighbors whose intellectual repertoire was often no more than a grunt about predestination or a curse upon "niggerologists" up North. For James Henry Hammond, the richest and most self-obsessed among the group, even wealth provided dim consolation. Beset on every hand, he thought, by "Tea Table Goddesses," "degenerate" old families, political conspirators, and "low-Irish" in-laws, Hammond gloried in the thought that "I beat them in their own line—furniture, balls, & dinner parties." But mostly, the proslavery writers, including Hammond at other times, sought not the embrace of a "brainless" gentry, but regional, even national deference to the ideals of southern high culture and to its leaders. Whereas abolitionists asserted moral superiority over the worldly-wise, whether rich or poor, the proslavery authors stressed an intellectual transcendence.[13] Neither the abolitionist nor the proslavery author abandoned claims to gentility, but the aims of these ideologues lay in the realm of moral and intellectual power, not in the world of democratic politics and commerce.

During the Jacksonian era church allegiance was often a means to identify class standing, and religion helped enormously to shape pro- and antislavery polemics. Even in the South, slower to join the evangelical awakening than was the North, participation in church affairs was becoming a prerequisite for the socially ambitious. By 1830, Thomas R. Dew of William and Mary College and author of an early defense of bondage, was accurate in declaring that among the southern gentlefolk, "he who obtrudes on the social circle his infidel notions, manifests the arrogance of a literary coxcomb, or that want

13 Hammond Secret Diary, December 9, 1846, September 2, 1848, June 7, 1852; see also, George Fitzhugh to George F. Holmes, March 27, 1855, in George F. Holmes copybook, Duke University Library. Henry Hughes Diary (typed transcript), October 24, 1852, Mississippi Department of Archives and History, Jackson.

of refinement which distinguishes the polished gentleman."[14] Although the pace was rather leisurely, voluntary associations, church buildings, seminaries, and other charitable and religious institutions were springing up to service the spiritual and social needs of the antebellum slaveholding class.

Upon the foundations of this religious activity the proslavery writers made their case for the positive benefactions of the "home system." Judge John Belton O'Neall, for instance, prided himself on his application of evangelical principle to the cases reaching his bench. His antipathy to sexual and liquor offenders would have warmed the heart of the most puritanical Yankee justice. In the same light, O'Neall had expanded the legal rights of the criminal slave. For him, as for other professed Christians among the southern gentry, "the goals of Christian trusteeship," to borrow David B. Davis's phrase, were implicit in the proslavery argument.[15] Stewardship in the South involved the establishment of high Christian standards for masters, the suppression of vice among all the social groups, but especially the unlettered and unwashed, and the legal and moral elevation of slaves with due regard to their supposed limitations.

Given these religious and class identifications, the pro- and antislavery polemicists tried to instruct fellow Christians, fellow gentlemen. Welcome though antiabolition street protests and formal rallies in northern cities were, the southern propagandists made no attempt to reach the likes of Captain Rynders, the petitbourgeoisie, and the Yankee working classes. It would hardly have been fitting to rouse northern "wage slaves" to rise up against the very class upon which the southern intellectuals depended for outside support. Nor could the proslavery apologist launch full-scale attack on the whole gaggle of benevolent enterprises out of which

14 T. R. Dew quoted by Clement Eaton, *The Freedom-of-Thought Struggle in the Old South* (Rev. ed.; New York: Harper & Row, 1964), 300.

15 Tappan to O'Neall, September 26, 1844, letterbook, in Tappan Papers; Eugene D. Genovese, *Roll, Jordan, Roll; The World The Slaves Made* (New York: Pantheon Books, 1974), 34, 40, 559, 600; A. E. Keir Nash, "Fairness and Formalism in the Trials of Blacks in the State Supreme Courts of the Old South," *Virginia Law Review,* LVI (1970), 64–100; David B. Davis, *The Problem of Slavery in the Age of Revolution, 1770–1823* (Ithaca: Cornell University Press, 1975), 212.

abolitionism had emerged. Bible societies, temperance chapters, and other forms of religious activity caused much grumbling in some circles of both sections, but they enjoyed the support of the better elements. In any case, proslavery writers did not seek recruits among antievangelicals.

Likewise, the abolitionists ignored the southern lower orders, concentrating instead upon the literate and pious "respectability" in both sections. As early as October, 1833, Ralph R. Gurley, agent of the rival Liberian effort, complained that the abolitionists "send their publications" free "to all the Clergy, & to a large portion of all respectable men in the Union." Even after Thomas R. Dew, the professor at Williamsburg, and William Lloyd Garrison had turned opinion against the African colonizationist scheme, the battle for dominion over the Christian, genteel public continued. The antislavery postal effort of 1835 was exclusively devoted to bringing the message of black freedom to *"inquiring, candid, reading* men" in all sections of the Union.[16] Lesser folk, white or black, appeared on the mailing lists only by inadvertance if at all. The objective was to reach the locally and nationally powerful alone.

Later, antislavery policy changed. The advent of political abolitionism in the 1840s required a broader approach. Nonetheless, much abolitionist literature continued to reflect the early preference. Excluding free southern blacks, slaves, and poor and middling yeoman was not simply a practical recognition of the slave-state *cordon sanitaire*. Racial prejudice within reform circles probably contributed to the decision for omitting even upstanding southern free blacks from the 1835 postal effort, but chiefly the problem was an underlying assumption about responsible class leadership. Indiscriminate broadcasting about slaveholding sinfulness raised the uncongenial specter of race and class rebellion, cast doubt on abolitionist good sense, and stirred misunderstanding about antislavery goals among people who counted. Throughout the prewar period, most abolitionists, with only a few notable exceptions, believed that slaves and southern poor whites ought not to be encouraged to vio-

16 Ralph R. Gurley to Philip R. Fendall, October 1, 1833, American Colonization Society Papers, Library of Congress; Elizur Wright to Weld, June 10, 1835, in Dumond and Barnes (eds.), *Weld Letters*, I, 225.

lence. Initiatives for emancipation should instead emerge from reliable, influential, and, above all, Christian sources.

In a similar vein, southern vindicators took little notice of the South's white underclasses. Propertyless whites simply did not impinge much upon the minds of the closet philosophers of slavery. They wrote for quarterlies, like *De Bow's Review*, church periodicals, and agricultural journals appealing to "book farmers," not to hard-handed yeomen. Being nineteenth-century intellectuals, they naturally supported the kinds of improvements that abolitionists usually encouraged in their communities: educational advance; civic improvements; the cause of Christian evangelism; and sometimes even temperance work. Moreover, they envisioned for the South diversified cropping and even industrial progress (within limits). These aims would elevate the populace out of mere "gorging in fat stupidity," Beverley Tucker, the Virginia zealot, proclaimed. Progressive trends, men like William L. Grayson believed, would enhance respect for cultural pursuits among all southern whites, high or low. Yet, direct appeals to the cabin-dweller could neither be framed in the language of the intelligentsia nor appear in its journals. The less well-to-do were consigned to popularizers and politicians, the latter a breed which southern proslavery writers and intellectuals despised for demagoguery and corruption. Besides, one must recall, as late as 1860 over 15 percent of all adult white southerners were unable to read and write. An equal proportion was seldom called upon to do so. It hardly made sense for an ambitious author to focus on that market.[17] Finally, proslavery writers did not wish to demean their erudition by translating ideas into common parlance. Instead, they sought confirmation of their views among intellectual and social peers, North and South.

Both by excluding the lower educational and social ranks from the polemical arena and by embracing the Christian and substan-

---

17 Tucker quoted by Faust, *Sacred Circle*, 72; James E. B. De Bow (ed.), *The Seventh Census of the United States, 1850* (Washington: Government Printing Office, 1853), lxvii–lxxix; Eaton, *Freedom-of-Thought Struggle*, 64–88. Cf. William B. Hesseltine, "Some New Aspects of the Proslavery Argument," in Richard N. Current (ed.), *Sections and Politics: Selected Essays of William B. Hesseltine* (Madison: State Historical Society of Wisconsin, 1968), 70–84; Kenneth M. Stampp, "An Analysis of T. R. Dew's 'Review of the Debates in the Virginia Legislature,'" *Journal of Negro History*, XXVII (1942), 380–87.

tial public in the nation, the ideologues confined themselves to
a struggle over the "respectability," local, sectional, and crosssec-
tional. The abolitionists thus sought to win the same southern audience to which their proslavery opponents belonged. The effort
was futile, but these slaveholders, reputable merchants, and professionals were supposed to be reachable as professing Christians and
"thinking" men. Their example and reputation, abolitionists believed, set the tone of society and swayed thousands who deferred to
upper-class opinion. Lewis Tappan, for instance, was prompted to
tell James H. Hammond in 1845, "I sometimes wish I could go
among your people—not to spirit away slaves or excite revolt—but
to reason with the best part of your population. Would they hang
me? I trow not if you were in the Executive chair."[18] Gentlemen, he
implied, behaved in a Christian manner, even under provocation.
Moreover, they were so well regarded that the disreputable and vulgar would not dare to act violently on their own.

To be sure, Tappan did not reflect the most advanced ideas in the
antislavery movement, owing to his seniority, religious preoccupation, and rather stubborn temperament. Yet, younger and newer
converts also combined reform with unexceptional social attitudes
about class and deference. As late as 1855, for instance, Samuel
Gridley Howe and other Boston leaders invited Henry W. Hilliard of
Alabama, Dr. William A. Smith, John Mason, and Henry Wise of
Virginia, and Pierce Butler of South Carolina to address a large
gathering. After all, the reasoning went, should there not be exchanges of views among the movers of society, among the better
class? To his credit, William Lloyd Garrison would have none of it.
The invitation, he fumed, had gone out to "slave-holders, whose
souls are steeped in pollution, whose hands and garments are drip-
ping with the blood of enslaved millions." Yet, even Garrison occasionally took pleasure in the enlistment of some new dignitary for
the antislavery cause.[19]

---

18 Tappan to Hammond, June 6, 1845, in Hammond Papers, Library of Congress.
19 Louis Ruchames (ed.), *The Letters of William Lloyd Garrison: From Disunion to the
Brink of War, 1850–1860* (7 vols. projected; Cambridge: Belknap Press of Harvard University
Press, 1975), IV, 361, contains Garrison to Dr. Samuel G. Howe and others, Committee,
November 12, 1855, in which he repudiates slaveholders but venerates the Honorable Samuel
Hoar. See also, Aileen S. Kraditor, *Means and Ends in American Abolitionism: Garrison and*

Having in mind a national constituency of "wise and good" Christians, proslavery writers likewise hoped to make inroads in the heart of enemy country. Far from relinquishing the northern religious and social elites to the abolitionists, as Donald claims, they sought to influence the Yankee respectability, just as the abolitionists yearned to do the same in the South. In *De Bow's Review*, George Fitzhugh presented the policy for his colleagues to carry out: "We must meet agitation by counter-agitation. . . . We must establish and support presses, deliver lectures, and write books and essays, to sustain the cause of government against anarchy, of religion against infidelity, of private property against agrarianism, and of female virtue and christian marriage against free love."[20]

Although the means to execute the plan was not sufficient to the task, the proslavery authors knew exactly why they were writing and to whom the message ought to be directed. Following his own advice, Fitzhugh in 1855 brought the southern case to the northern intelligentsia. At New Haven he spoke before "a large and attentive audience." The listeners, he boasted, were compelled "to thinking and talking. . . . Professor Silliman [of Yale] and many of the leading citizens paid me great attention after my lecture was delivered," he told George F. Holmes. The case that the Virginia thinker presented was the necessity for the union of all moral and social conservatives, with slavery being only one of other venerable systems of hierarchy and social control to be strengthened. Fitzhugh's position departed from the more narrowly focused proslavery argument in his denial of nearly all forms of social progress. Yet, he, too, wished to insure that "conservatives of the South" were not cut off from their natural "alliance with conservatives of the North," a strategy which underlay all southern literature directed northward.[21]

No less than the abolitionists, the proslavery authors wanted to make their gospel as intellectually and socially respectable as pos-

---

*His Critics on Strategy and Tactics, 1834–1850* (New York: Pantheon Books, 1969), 257–60. See also, on the close affiliation of the Garrisonians to the Unitarian elite, Douglas C. Strange, *Patterns of Antislavery Among the Unitarians, 1831–1860* (Cranbury, N.J.: Fairleigh Dickinson University Press, 1977).

20 George Fitzhugh, "The Conservative Principle; Or, Social Evils and their Remedies," *De Bow's Review*, XXII (1857), 427.

21 *Ibid.*, 423; Fitzhugh to Holmes, March 27, 1855, in Holmes copybook.

sible. The aim encompassed appeals and challenges to three influential groups: the celebrated minds of the English-speaking world; the leadership of the Protestant churches in the North; and the upper and high middle class bulwarks of Yankee society. Briefly, in regard to the first, Hammond, for instance, had penned his remarks in reply to Thomas Clarkson. Lewis Tappan, aware of the significance of English intellectuality to which Americans often deferred, had even offered the governor some assistance. In a sly display of his own intimacy with British leaders, he informed Hammond that Clarkson was much too old to respond. But, the abolitionist volunteered, "How would you like to have [Thomas Babington] Macaulay reply to you on Clarkson's behalf?"[22]

Like the abolitionist, the proslavery author was quite aware of the power and social prestige which the evangelical aims of the major churches enjoyed. With an eye upon this audience, southern apologists stressed the rapid missionary gains that pious masters and clergymen were harvesting in the fields and patches. David Christy, a northern proslaveryite, was only one of many to observe that in spite of all the foreign mission labors to which the age was addicted, the results were negligible compared with the gospel work among southern slaves. Nehemiah Adams, an antislavery defector won over to the "South-Side," personally testified to the Christian submission, orderliness, and contented character of black bondsmen. If only, he sighed, the "underswells" of Boston were equally tranquil and deferential to their social superiors.[23] These and other points were substantive, up-to-date, and class-oriented arguments. The presumption was that northern members of the gentility would be as convinced by them as any well-read planter in the South. Besides, much proslavery literature actually was penned by northern divines and conservatives, thereby indicating the level of northern support that southern advocates could expect.

22 Tappan to Hammond, July 23, 1845 in Hammond Papers, Library of Congress; Fitzhugh to Holmes, undated, April 11, 1855, February 14, 1857, in George F. Holmes Papers, Library of Congress. Southern proslavery writers were acutely sensitive to English disapproval. See, for example, James W. Walker to Hammond, June 11, 1845, in Hammond Papers, Library of Congress.

23 David Christy, *Pulpit Politics; Or, Ecclesiastical Legislation on Slavery, in its Disturbing Influences on the American Union* (Rev. ed.; New York: Negro Universities Press, 1969), 108–254; Nehemiah Adams, *A South-Side View of Slavery: Three Months at the South, in 1854* (Rev. ed.; Port Washington, N.Y.: Kennikat Press, 1969), 25, 44.

Because of the high importance attached to religious regularity as a sign of social as well as intellectual integrity, the proslavery propagandists devoted much of their energies to the Bible argument. Stale though these "wearisome exertions" might seem to the modern scholar, they were at the very heart of the controversy.[24] No polemicist, North or South, could ignore the pertinence of Holy Scripture, touchstone of the cultivated as well as the ordinary churchgoer. In church councils where clerics and influential laymen quarreled over the rights and wrongs of slavery, these heavy signs of scholarship were useful stageprops to point to, as a courtoom lawyer might employ a stack of leather-bounds or grandly wave about the *Commentaries*. (One suspects that the lengthier ones were seldom read carefully; weightiness alone offered intellectual verification.) John Fletcher's Bible defense was 637 pages, under the quaintly fetching title *Studies on Slavery, In Easy Lessons*. Though ostensibly aimed at northerners and southerners without regard to their political "sects," the work was studded with Greek, Latin, Arabic, and Hebrew citations. Obviously Fletcher had in mind a theological, northern reception. Laymen, too, claimed Fletcher, ought to beware "the bitter waters of error" poisoning the works of Wayland, Paley, Channing, Barnes, and other Yankee moral philosophers of high reputation. Quite reasonably, Fletcher anticipated a learned readership and critical acclaim, however pointless his labors might seem in retrospect. After all, moral philosophy did excite attention among well-read gentlemen of the age. The serious-minded layman, as well as the seminary scholar, placed solemn treatises and tracts on the reading-stand. In 1845, Tappan forwarded Theodore Weld's mercifully short *Bible against Slavery* to Governor Hammond. Dutifully, he read it but politely characterized the gift as "erudite & able, but not *precisely to the point*."[25]

In searching out a northern constituency, the proslavery enthusiast was scarcely limited to the religiously orthodox but looked

24 David Donald, "The Proslavery Argument Reconsidered," *Journal of Southern History,* XXXVII (1971), 4.

25 John Fletcher, *Studies on Slavery, In Easy Lessons, Compiled into Eight Studies, and Subdivided into Short Lessons for the Convenience of The Readers* (Natchez: Jackson Warner, 1852), ix; Hammond to Tappan, June 17, 1845 in Claude W. Unger Collection, Pennsylvania Historical Society. See also, Caroline L. Shanks, "The Biblical Anti-Slavery Argument of the Decade 1830–1840," *Journal of Negro History,* XVI (1931), 132–57.

also for approval from the conservative ranks of society. Proslavery authors read the common literature and criticized the common failings of their times in consort with critics elsewhere. In England, for instance, Matthew Arnold reproached the vulgarity and acquisitiveness of the businessman who "thinks it nothing that the trains carry him from an illiberal, dismal life at Islington to an illiberal, dismal life at Camberwell." The complaint reeked of the social and intellectual hauteur so prevalent in the Anglo-American world of *belles-lettres*. Southern spokesmen felt quite comfortable in echoing these sentiments. James Henry Hammond, for instance, denounced "the modern *artificial money power system*, in which man—his thews and sinews, his hopes and affectons, his very being, are all subjected to the dominion of *capital*—a monster without a heart." The charge of gross materialism that Hammond and other proslavery authors leveled against the industrial world was based not upon some backward, mindless rurality nor upon Marxian insights but upon the moral, class, and intellectual perceptions of conservative and intellectual Victorians, here and abroad.[26]

Southern authors tried to build upon conservative worries regarding the future of the social order, but in doing so, they knew better than to reject the principles of moral and economic uplift which even the most reactionary northern men of wealth cherished. It would not do to boast of southern racing and cockfight gambling, prowess with gun and dogs, bloodlettings, and other examples of masculinity in which southerners at home took pride. Instead, William Harper, Beverley Tucker, and William Gilmore Simms in their polemical writings, the Reverends Thornton Stringfellow, James Smylie, James Thornwell, and others depicted a southern Christendom with the best attributes of rural modernity coupled with old-fashioned values still honored in the absence of failings currently prevalent elsewhere. Only George Fitzhugh adopted a curious, antimodern approach which in its way was no less roman-

26 Matthew Arnold, quoted in Walter E. Houghton, *The Victorian Frame of Mind, 1830–1870* (New Haven: Yale University Press, 1957), 184; Hammond, "Letters on Slavery," in *The Pro-Slavery Argument: As Maintained by the Most Distinguished Writers of the Southern States . . .* (Rev. ed.; New York: Negro Universities Press, 1968), 163; Neal C. Gillespie, *The Collapse of Orthodoxy: The Intellectual Ordeal of George Frederick Holmes* (Charlottesville: University Press of Virginia, 1972).

tic and abstract than the Fourieristic communitarianism of Stephen Pearl Andrews, his Yankee friend. In adopting this position, he may well have been following the technique of Thomas Carlyle (a southern favorite) who in *Past & Present* glorified the medieval Abbot Samson of St. Edmundsbury as a literary comment on machine age vulgarity and artificiality.[27]

In keeping with this appeal for upper-class northern support against radical, democratic experimentations, proslavery writers celebrated slave attachments to white families and the reciprocations they elicited from the owners themselves. Nothing could appeal more to the intellectual moralist of the upper social ranks of the North than the vision of orderly domesticity controlled by sound Christian stewards. William Gilmore Simms, for instance, could accurately observe that New York City, according to Arthur Tappan's own investigations, and London had more "brothels" and "stews," "alleys" and "sinks" than ever the South could supply the lower orders. When Clarkson complained of southern licentiousness, Hammond quickly rejoined that in the slaveholding states "there are fewer cases of divorce, separation, crim[inal] con[duct], seduction, rape and bastardy, than among any other five millions of people on the civilized earth."[28] Hammond was hardly a living illustration of southern sexual rectitude. The argument itself was hopelessly specious, but the domestic relations of whites and blacks was a subject of immediate interest to the literary, Christian, and "respectable" audience for which it was designed.

Southern spokesmen also invested their energies in uplifting

27 William S. Jenkins, *Pro-Slavery Thought in the Old South* (Chapel Hill: University of North Carolina Press, 1935), 200–41; Drew G. Faust, "Evangelicalism and the Meaning of the Pro-Slavery Argument: Reverend Thornton Stringfellow [1788–1869]," *Virginia Magazine: History and Biography*, LXXXV (1977), 3–17; Albert G. Seal (ed.), "Notes and Documents: Letters from the South, A Mississippian's Defense of Slavery," *Journal of Mississippi History*, II (1940), 212–31; Thomas Carlyle, *Past & Present*, ed. Edwin Mims (New York: Charles Scribner's Sons, 1918), 75–157. Cf. George Fitzhugh, *Cannibals All! Or, Slaves without Masters*, ed. C. Vann Woodward (Cambridge, Mass.: Belknap Press of Harvard University Press, 1960), vii–xxxix; Gillespie, *Collapse of Orthodoxy*, 197–98; Robert Brugger, *Beverly Tucker: Heart over Head in the Old South* (Baltimore: Johns Hopkins University Press, 1978), 159–61.

28 Simms, *Pro-Slavery Argument*, 210–11; Hammond, *Pro-Slavery Argument*, 118–19; see also, Ronald G. Walters, "The Erotic South: Civilization and Sexuality in American Abolitionism," *American Quarterly*, XXV (1973), 177–201, as well as his book *The Antislavery Appeal: American Abolition after 1830* (Baltimore: Johns Hopkins University Press, 1976).

home morale, a goal which the appeals to the northern constituencies helped to realize. They did not rally a disgruntled yeomanry but instead hoped to overcome a sense of intellectual inferiority among the churchgoing, slaveholding respectability. The region had few presses and colleges, in fact little that might be called a literary infrastructure. As a result, when confronted with a display of liberal pyrotechnics from foreign parts, the southern planter sometimes felt bludgeoned to inarticulateness or to moody acquiescence about the wrongfulness of bondage. Early in the controversy, William Harper of South Carolina remarked that "some individuals among ourselves, instead of attending to what passes before their eyes . . . are content to take up their opinions, ready made, from the haphazard and vehement invectives of these . . . distant instructors." The uninformed heart could be made to feel guilty—or at least discomfitted. The South was "cut off, in some degree," he later said, "from the communion and sympathies of the world."[29]

The problem was not exactly worry that slaveholders would be touched with antislavery enthusiasms, though that possibility might lie further down the road. The issue was much more immediate: to inculcate a regional ideology, one that could cheer the southern gentry as well as gain respect for southern culture abroad. Home instruction included attention to the youth. Henry Hughes, the proslavery laureate of Mississippi, argued, "The young men must be taught to reason the matter. They must learn why our home system is *not* wrong; why it is right: and be able to give the reasons for it."[30] Thus, Hughes and others considered their productions a means to educate the future leaders of the region, who would in turn impress the general southern population with the benefactions of slavery. Yet, this call to duty appeared in an obscure Port Gibson paper; Hughes's other writings also had pathetic circulation. Like Fitzhugh's peculiar notions, Hughes's ideas were too abstract and philosophical for a truly popular southern reception. Political

29 William Harper, quoted in William W. Freehling, *Prelude to Civil War: The Nullification Controversy in South Carolina, 1816–1836* (New York: Harper & Row, 1965), 79; second Harper quotation in E. N. Elliott (ed.), *Cotton Is King, and Pro-Slavery Arguments . . .* (Augusta, Ga.: Pritchard, Abbott & Loomis, 1860), 550.

30 Henry Hughes, "New Duties of the South," in Port Gibson (Miss.) *Southern Reveille*, November 18, 1854, clipping in Henry Hughes scrapbook.

drum-beatings—the cadences of William L. Yancey—not learned disquisitions like Hughes's *Treatise on Sociology*, stirred the masses for secession. The situation caused some consternation among the slave apologists, jealous of rivals but unable to make the necessary adaptation to the southern marketplace.

Although the more exotic and scholarly defenses of slavery probably fell on deaf ears in the South, the southern intellectuals, assisted by the clergy whose sermons spread the welcome news, tried to link their ideas to the day-to-day needs of the slaveholding class. With some success they made use of the same evangelical preoccupations that drew abolitionists and the "respectability" into common, Christian causes. Just as the antislavery reformer labored for the moral improvement of northern Christendom, so, too, did the southern intelligentsia hope to build an enlightened, forward-looking class of slaveowning patriarchs. The authors portrayed the generality of masters as uniformly kind and pious. Yet the stereotype was in a sense the setting of an ideal for all to reach for as well as being a claim for universal magnanimity, outrageous though it was. Prospering small farmers, Yankee and Scottish immigrants were entering the gentry, slaveholding ranks. Many of them, conceded writers like Hammond, were out of tune with contemporary humanitarian and Christian goals, but the future would witness improvement, they believed, in general slave management.

The most common form of address was advice literature. It had become practically an industry in northern publishing circles. Clergymen, women, professors, and physicians prescribed nostrums to assure business success for young men, happy marriages for women, obedient, self-disciplined children for parents, and sound morality and physical well-being for all. In the South a similar phenomenon was taking place. Produced for regional consumption, the advice literature pointed to local moral problems to be remedied, sometimes with more rigor than the propaganda for outside recipients could have afforded. In the cautionary mode, Mrs. Cary of Virginia, for instance, grieved in *Letters on Female Character*: "I know cruelty to slaves is not now as common as it has been. The progress of civilization, and, above all, of gospel light, has taught many people their duty. . . . But alas! I am forced to acknowledge" from personal obser-

vation, that "this abuse is still tolerated in society." Young ladies
should not act like hussies, chasing servants about with a stick. Parents, she warned, were much too unobservant or indulgent in allowing their youngsters to learn tyranny over dependents. Clergymen and pious planters like Charles C. Jones of Georgia and Edward
Pringle of South Carolina, educators like Calvin H. Wiley of North
Carolina, and journalists like James De Bow explained in some detail how the wise master ought to behave and why it paid off hand-
somely in the toting of accounts before both creditors and God. Calvin H. Wiley's manuscript was the most elaborate. This mammoth
compendium (never published) of practical advice resembled the
still popular works of Richard Baxter, the seventeenth-century
evangelical divine.[31]

Just how successful the religious and intellectual forces in the
South were in transforming slavery from a primitive to a civilized
system is open to serious doubt. Certainly the proslavery authorities
made insupportable claims, but the effort itself provided further
justifications for the plea to outsiders to let the South alone, allowing the region to advance morally at its own pace. For instance, the
aristocratic Edward Pringle of South Carolina explained that he
wrote not just "to answer the objections of opponents of slavery,"
but also to "prove for the slaveholder that his dependent laborer is
capable of better things than the world would have him believe, and
especially to remind" owners that their rationales "in favor of the
slave's position" were "of necessity so many pledges for the faithful
discharge" of their own obligations. Pringle was a proslavery moderate, but his efforts were designed to counter abolitionist strategy by
appealing to the civic-minded, possessing classes of both sections,
urging northerners to permit southern benevolent experimentation
in peace and arousing southerners to make Christian stewardship
the reality that current trends were promising.[32]

31 Mrs. Virginia Cary, *Letters on Female Character Addressed to a Young Lady on the
Death of Her Mother* (Richmond: Ariel Works, 1830), 203–204; Charles C. Jones, *The Religious
Instruction of the Negroes in the United States* (Rev. ed.; New York: Negro Universities Press,
1969); Calvin H. Wiley, "Christian Duty of Masters," in Calvin H. Wiley Papers, Southern
Historical Collections, University of North Carolina Library.
32 Edward J. Pringle, *Slavery in the Southern States* (Cambridge, Mass.: J. Bartlett, 1853),
43, 47–49.

The mutual social and intellectual assumptions of the two parties and their shared public arena, small, intimate, and rather exclusive though it was, suggest that much of what has been written about them has not done justice to the social dynamics of controversy. Had both sides spoken only to the broad ranges of their respective and regional classes, they could have ignored the counterthrusts of distant opponents. As it was, however, proslavery and antislavery writers wrote for a common, generally well-read, and civically engaged public, North *and* South. As a result it was impossible to ignore outside criticisms or to mutter incoherently. To remain silent risked contempt abroad and intellectual perplexity at home. To treat the causes as if their spokesmen had only discrete, local constituencies in mind would miss the major point of sectional, literary controversy.

In view of the mutual and interacting desire to convert the church-going, decent, and literary audience of all sections, one could hardly expect much internal consistency in the arguments of either camp. For instance, abolitionist writers seemed to entertain antithetical views of slave character. As George Fredrickson has wisely observed, they sometimes asserted an alleged natural Christian demeanor for the African race—submissive, long-suffering, and accepting, almost to a fault. On the other hand, they also claimed that in southern denials of the ordinary privileges of holy matrimony, Bible study, and moral instruction of a voluntary kind, the slaves' family attachments were stunted, superstitions augmented, and self-indulgent traits given free play. As Albert T. Bledsoe, a proslavery intellectual of Virginia, pointed out, the reformer could "make the slave a brute or a saint just as it may happen to suit the exigency of his argument."[33] The purposes of the debate itself often determined the writer's characterization. To counteract the concept of a southern, Christian trusteeship, he had to portray the black as morally depraved; to assert the right of Christian interference in the face of southern barbarity, he had to reveal the slave's resilience against evils imposed upon him.

Likewise, much might be made of discrepancies in proslavery

33 Bledsoe, in Elliott (ed.), *Cotton Is King*, 416.

logic, as if southerners were too backward and self-absorbed to recognize legitimate criticism from abroad. How could, for instance,
southern defenders claim that slaves were inferior members of the
human family, as Josiah Nott and other ethnologists asserted, and
yet maintain the Adamic unity of the species under biblical doctrine? In the infancy of biological science and in the conservative
reluctance to abdicate scriptural authority, there was indeed ample
room for vexation. But southern intellectuals were hardly alone in
perceiving such difficulties. Like other well-educated gentlemen of
the day, they desperately hoped for the time when religion and science would join hands once more. A benevolent deity could not
leave such organic unities in perpetual disarray. The problem was
especially worrisome because the man of letters was already an object of southern suspicion simply because his interests could not be
widely shared, his tastes and temperament could not conform to
community pleasures. To challenge openly the legitimacy of the
Bible, even in the cause of slavery, was to separate the intellectual
from his social peers still further.

In the long run, the antislavery forces won the polemical field,
but only by reaching for mass opinion through a coarsening of their
writing. With greater sophistication in the arts of propaganda than
their southern literary foes displayed, they learned by the 1850s to
build effectively upon the visceral feelings of Yankees against things
southern, no longer restricting themselves to the conversion of an
evangelical gentility. Sectional mistrust ran much deeper than historians, preoccupied with national sources of persistent racism,
have been aware. The process involved a secularizing of the message
as the revival impulse of the Second Awakening declined in the last
two decades before the war. To a degree Christian imperatives gave
way to humanistic rationales as well as economic and political ones.
The result was a broadening of the antislavery base, so that rich man
or poor found reason for alarm in a slave regime forever expanding,
forever inhibiting free-state interests.

Nourished by the same social and intellectual forces toward
modernity and secular self-interest, the proslavery intelligentsia
also sprouted some secular foliage. George Fitzhugh and Henry
Hughes, the prime examples, adopted the language of "sociology,"

and all but left out biblical injunctions. James De Bow in 1860 published a tract outlining the advantages of black subordination that even nonslaveholders should appreciate. He too stressed matters of self-interest, not Christian benignity. Nevertheless, "Bible slavery," with its genteel connotations, continued to be the bedrock of southern justifications just as "Bible antislavery" was the centerpiece of tractarian abolitionism.

By observing the class concepts as they affected the opposing causes, one can readily see that neither movement was exclusively modern and democratic nor hopelessly retrogressive. Traditional patterns of thought and social attitudes changed only gradually but inexorably. The concept of the Christian gentleman as the source of power in America affected abolitionist and proslavery writer alike. "I do not despair," Lewis Tappan wrote Hammond in 1845, "of your becoming one of us ere long! What a noble spectacle it would be to see S.C. taking the lead among the slave States on the subject of Universal emancipation."[34] The sentiment was above reproach. Yet the assumption underlying Tappan's words, even if he doubted them as he filled the page, was that the fate of African bondage rested not upon the initiative of slaves but upon the good feelings of those with talent, position, and sensibility.

Though unable to win over the southern "respectability," the northern crusaders did make considerable progress by 1860 with the northern half of that amorphous but significant designation. Even among the "disreputable," as the Yankee nonchurchgoing bourgeoisie and working class were thought to be, there was less hostility toward the antislavery advocate, no longer quite so easily identified as merely a priest-ridden eccentric. But most important, the skillful polemicists had persisted until their southern adversaries withdrew from the churches, the national political parties, and finally from the nation itself. The retreat into southern nationhood was the only recourse left for injured pride. It meant that the battle for the northern "respectability" had been lost, a circumstance that caused much pain among some members of the proslavery intelligentsia. Not all

---

34 Tappan to Hammond, June 6, 1845, in Hammond Papers, Library of Congress; Eaton, *Mind of the Old South*, 53.

of them shared the joy of Edmund Ruffin and Henry Hughes at the prospect of social as well as political dismemberment.

In 1858, James H. Hammond had left the banks of the Savannah to represent Carolina in the Senate. Always torn between the pleasures of political power and the discipline of study, Hammond in 1860 relinquished the seat to satisfy his countrymen, but not himself. The situation reminded him "of the Japanese who when insulted rip open their bowels."[35] The description was more accurate of southern destiny than he knew, but it reflected his fear that Carolina risked isolation from both the centers of power and of intellect. The southern thinker was always a man apart, covering his vulnerability by glorifying the "home institution." Aloof, he had to make the best of "the contracting influence of a very small circle, in which the standards are necessarily humble," wrote William Gilmore Simms. "But why is it," Hammond once cried out, "that I have no one in 50 miles of me more sensible & companionable than my driver Tom?" The Confederacy was an unlikely means to remedy matters. Godliness, order, reason, and virtue, the ideals that Hammond and his colleagues thought bound to a flourishing slave system might well be casualties of thoughtless, impulsive demagogues in their midst. Disillusioned, Hammond confided to Simms that "solid men" would soon be "victims" not only of "the black & savage negro" but also of "the brutal San Culotte" as well.[36] The ties of class and Christian intellectuality that once had permitted the curious exchange with Lewis Tappan had been broken forever.

35 Hammond, quoted in Albert D. Kirwan (ed.), *The Civilization of the Old South: Writings of Clement Eaton* (Lexington: University of Kentucky Press, 1968), 239.

36 Simms and Hammond, quoted in Drew G. Faust, "Sacred Circle: The Social Role of the Intellectual in the Old South, 1840–1860" (PhD. Dissertation, University of Pennsylvania, 1975) 14, 20; Hammond to Simms, November 13, 1860, in Hammond Papers, South Caroliniana Library.

# CONTRIBUTORS

ELLEN DUBOIS is associate professor of history and American studies at the State University of New York, Buffalo. She is author of *Feminism and Suffrage: Emergence of an Independent Women's Movement in America, 1848–1869* (1978), and editor of *The Stanton-Anthony Reader* (1979). She is currently writing a study of changing sexual ideology in the United States, 1890–1920.

MICHAEL FELLMAN is associate professor of history at Simon Fraser University. He has written *The Unbounded Frame: Freedom and Community in Nineteenth-Century American Utopianism* (1973), and with Anita Clair Fellman, is completing a study of late nineteenth-century American advice literature.

CAROL V. R. GEORGE is associate professor of history and Third World studies at Hobart and William Smith Colleges. She is author of *Segregated Sabbaths: Richard Allen and the Rise of Independent Black Churches, 1790–1850* (1973), and editor of *"Remember the Ladies": New Perspectives on Women in American History* (1975). She is now engaged in a study of Harriet Beecher Stowe and the reformist mentality.

JOHNATHAN A. GLICKSTEIN is a graduate student at Yale University. His Ph.D. dissertation is entitled "Concepts of 'Free Labor' in Antebellum America."

337

BLANCHE GLASSMAN HERSH is coordinator of the Women's Studies Program at Northeastern Illinois University. She is author of *The Slavery of Sex: Feminist-Abolitionists in America* (1978).

ALLEN M. KRAUT is associate professor of history at the American University. He is author of *The New Immigrants, 1880–1921* (1980) and is working on a study of the Liberty party in New York State.

LEWIS PERRY is professor of history at Indiana University. He is editor, with Leonard I. Krimerman, of *Patterns of Anarchy: A Collection of Writings on the Anarchist Tradition* (1966), and author of *Radical Abolitionism: Anarchy and the Government of God in Antislavery Thought* (1973), and of a forthcoming book on Henry C. Wright.

DOUGLAS RIACH studied history at the University of Edinburgh, and has taught at the University of Jyvaskyla, Finland.

C. DUNCAN RICE, who is associate professor of history at Yale University, is author of *The Rise and Fall of Black Slavery* (1975). He has recently completed a study of the Scots abolitionists.

LEONARD L. RICHARDS is associate professor of history at the University of Massachusetts—Amherst. He has written *"Gentlemen of Property and Standing": Anti-Abolition Mobs in Jacksonian Democracy* (1970) and *The Advent of American Democracy* (1977). He is now working on a book concerning John Quincy Adams' congressional years, 1831–1848.

DONALD M. SCOTT is associate professor of history at North Carolina State University. He has written *From Office to Profession: The New England Ministry, 1750–1850* (1978) and is currently working on a study of the professions and the formation of public culture in nineteenth-century America.

JAMES BREWER STEWART is professor of history in Macalester University. He is author of *Joshua Giddings and the Tactics of Radical Politics* (1970) and *Holy Warriors: The Abolitionists and American Slavery* (1976). He is currently working on a study of Wendell Phillips.

RONALD G. WALTERS is associate professor of history at the Johns Hopkins University. He is editor of *Primers for Prudery: Sexual Advice to Victorian America* (1974), and author of *The Antislavery Appeal: American Abolitionism After 1830* (1976), and *American Reformers: 1815–1860* (1978). He is now writing a study of the evolution of professional popular entertainment in America, 1800–1913.

WILLIAM M. WIECEK is professor of history in the University of Missouri—Columbia. He has written *The Guarantee Clause of the U.S. Constitution*

(1972) and *The Sources of Antislavery Constitutionalism in America, 1760–1848* (1977).

BERTRAM WYATT-BROWN is professor of history in Case-Western Reserve University. He is author of *Lewis Tappan and the Evangelical War Against Slavery* (1969) and editor of *The American People in the Evangelical South* (1974). Currently he is completing a book entitled *Yankee Saints and Southern Sinners*.

# INDEX

341